L.A. STREET SHOTS

A PHOTOGRAPHIC EXPLORATION

SCOTT SHAW

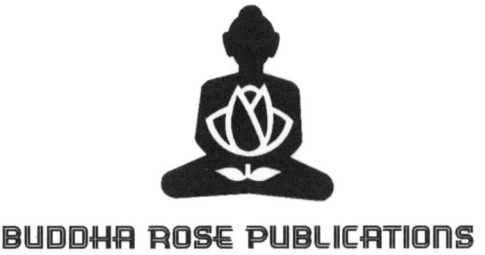

BUDDHA ROSE PUBLICATIONS

L.A. Street Shots: A Photographic Exploration
Copyright © 2015 by Scott Shaw
www.scottshaw.com
All Rights Reserved
No part of this book or any of these photographs may be reproduced
in any manner without the expressed written permission of
Scott Shaw or the publishing company.

First Edition 2015

ISBN 10: 1-877792-84-5
ISBN 13: 978-1-877792-84-7

10 9 8 7 6 5 4 3 2 1

L.A. STREET SHOTS

The photographs presented in the book where taken in
Los Angeles, California and surrounding Southern California.

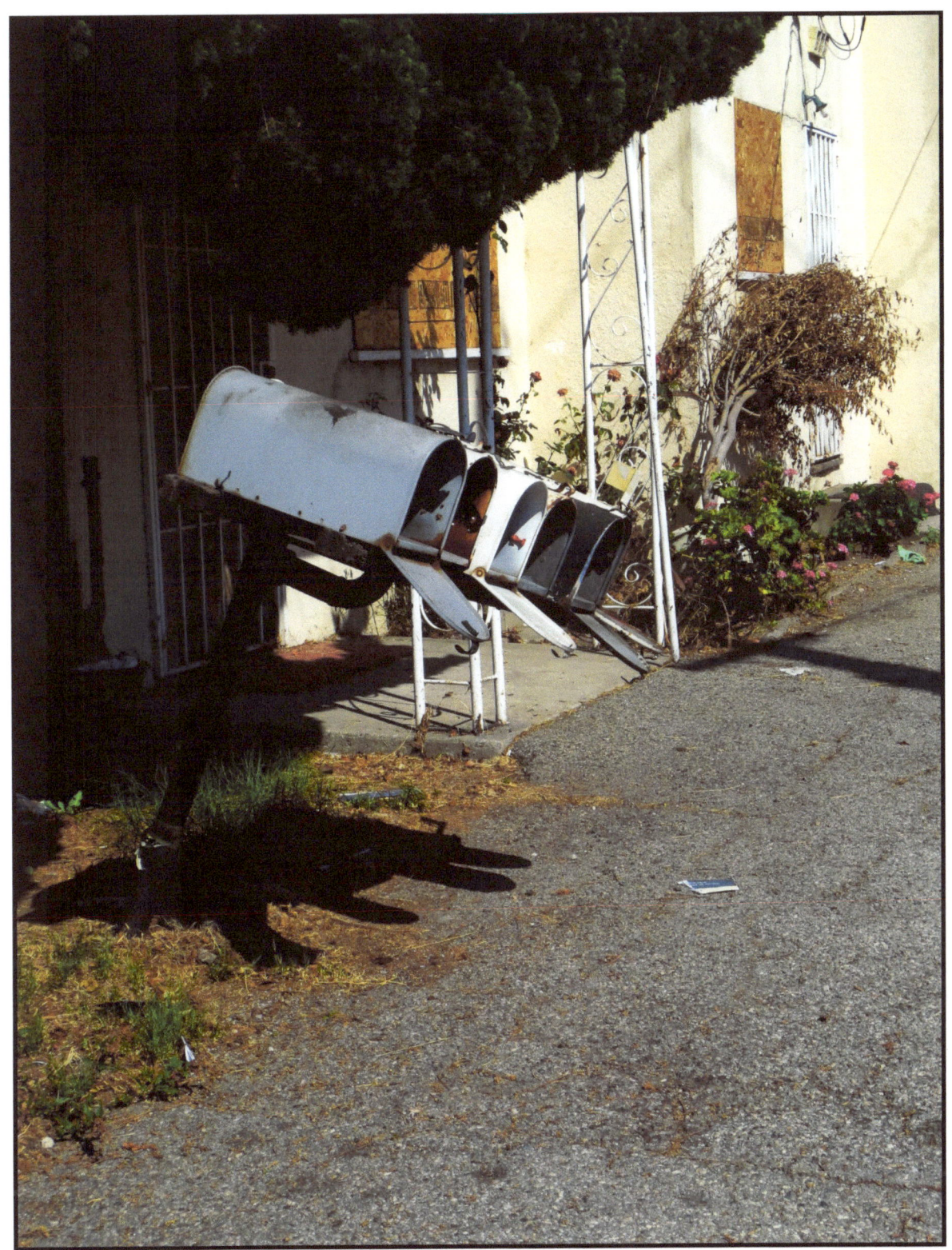

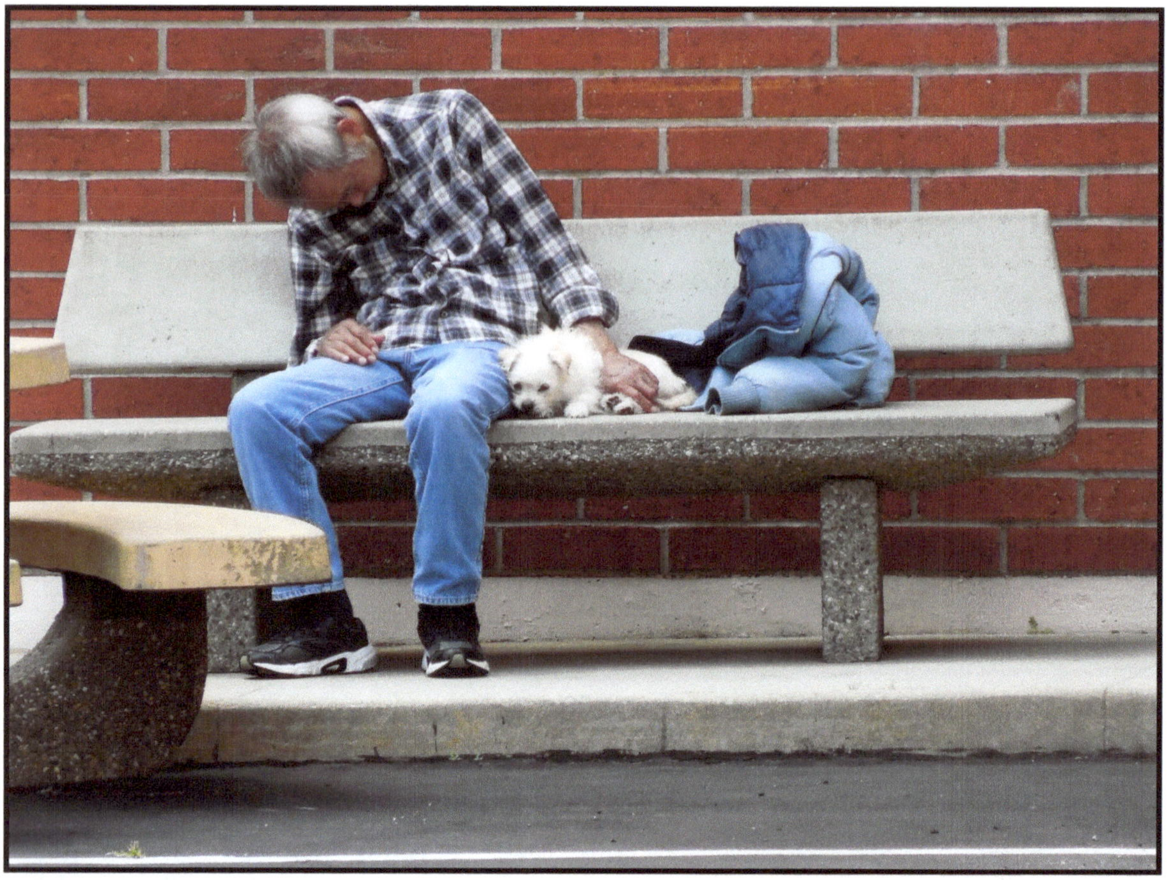

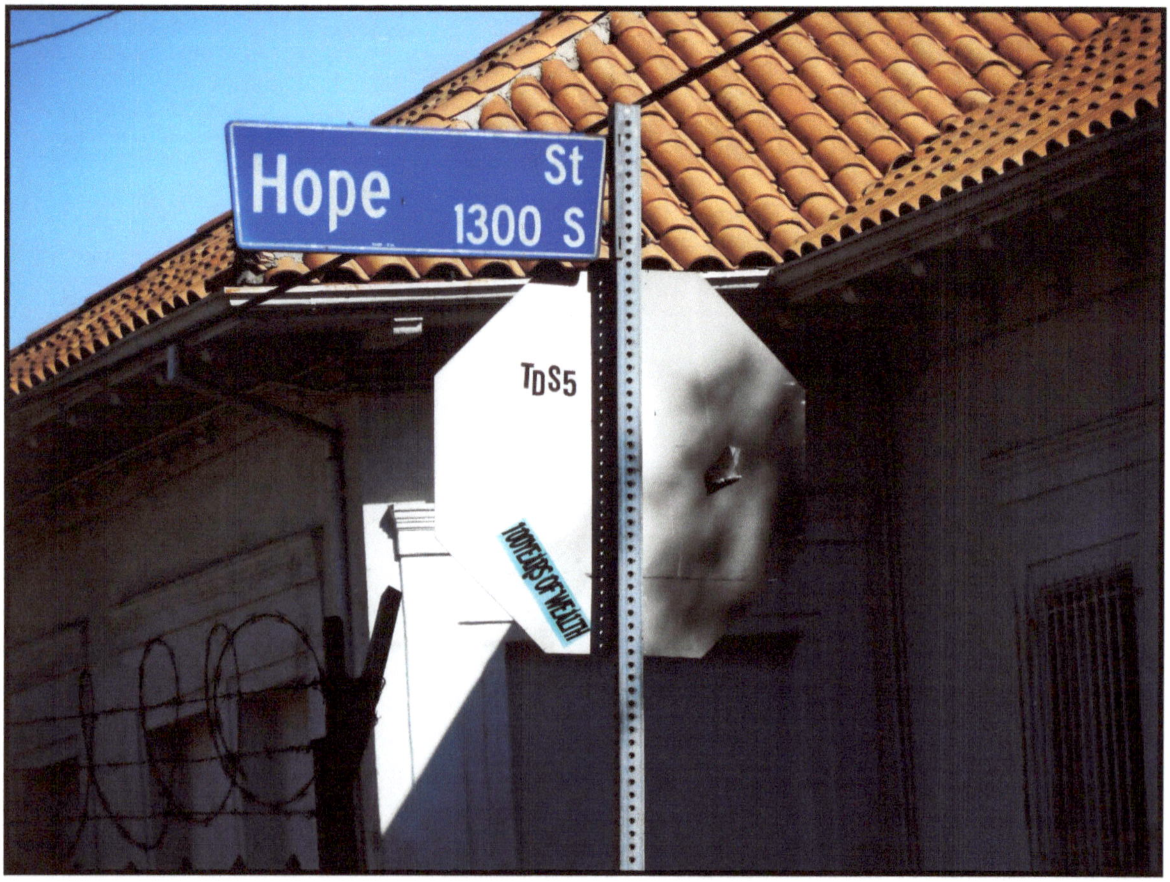

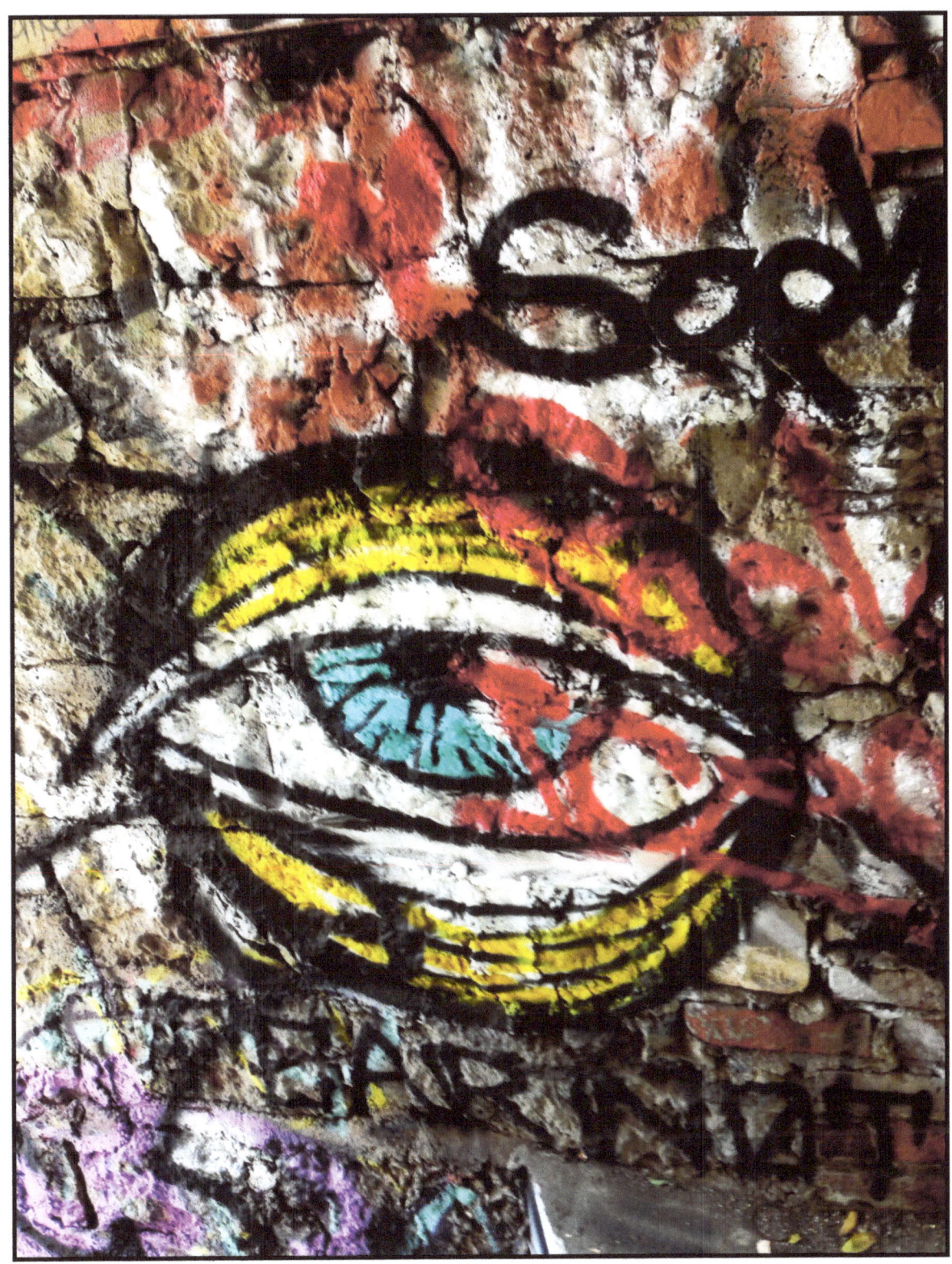

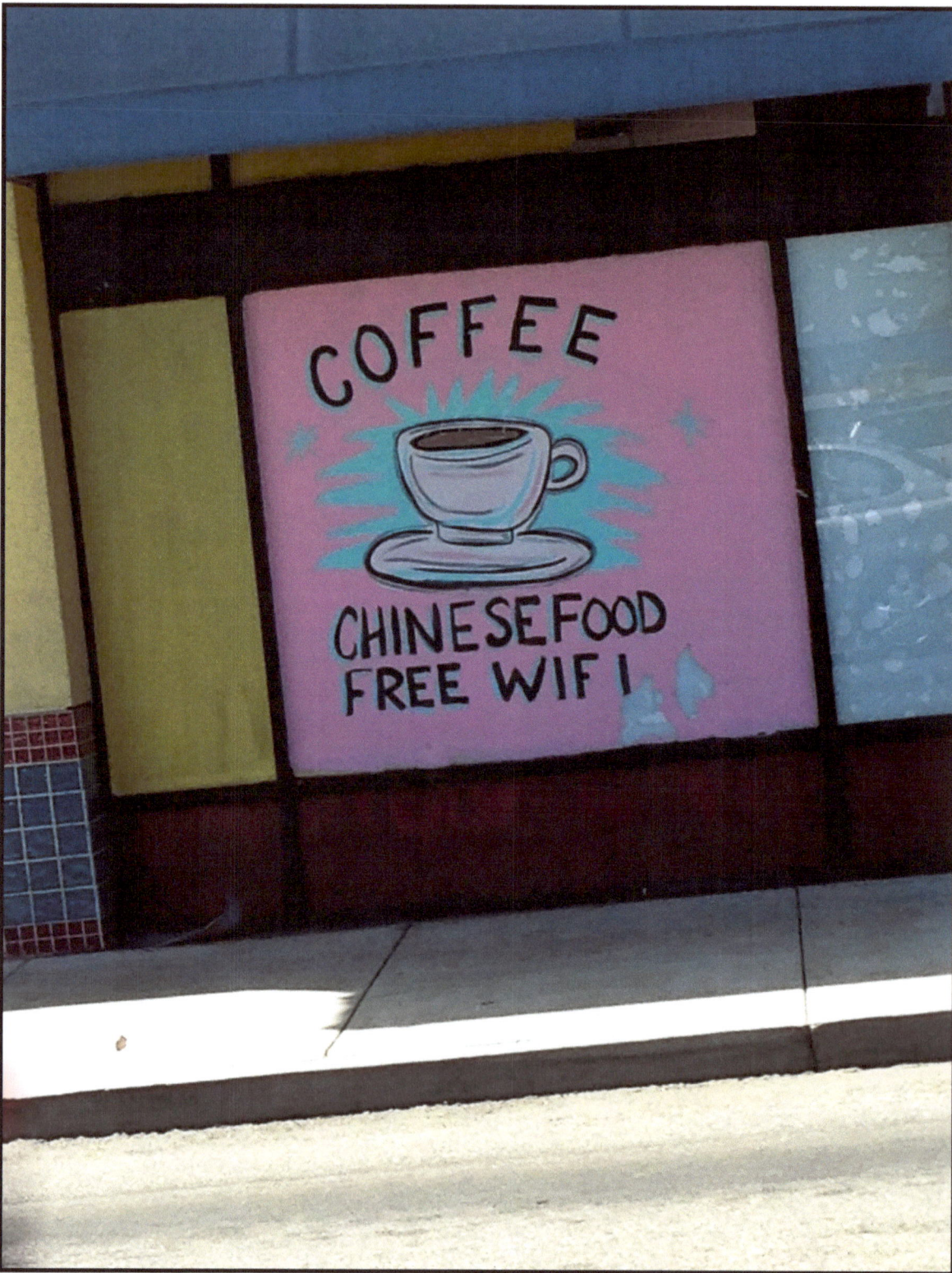

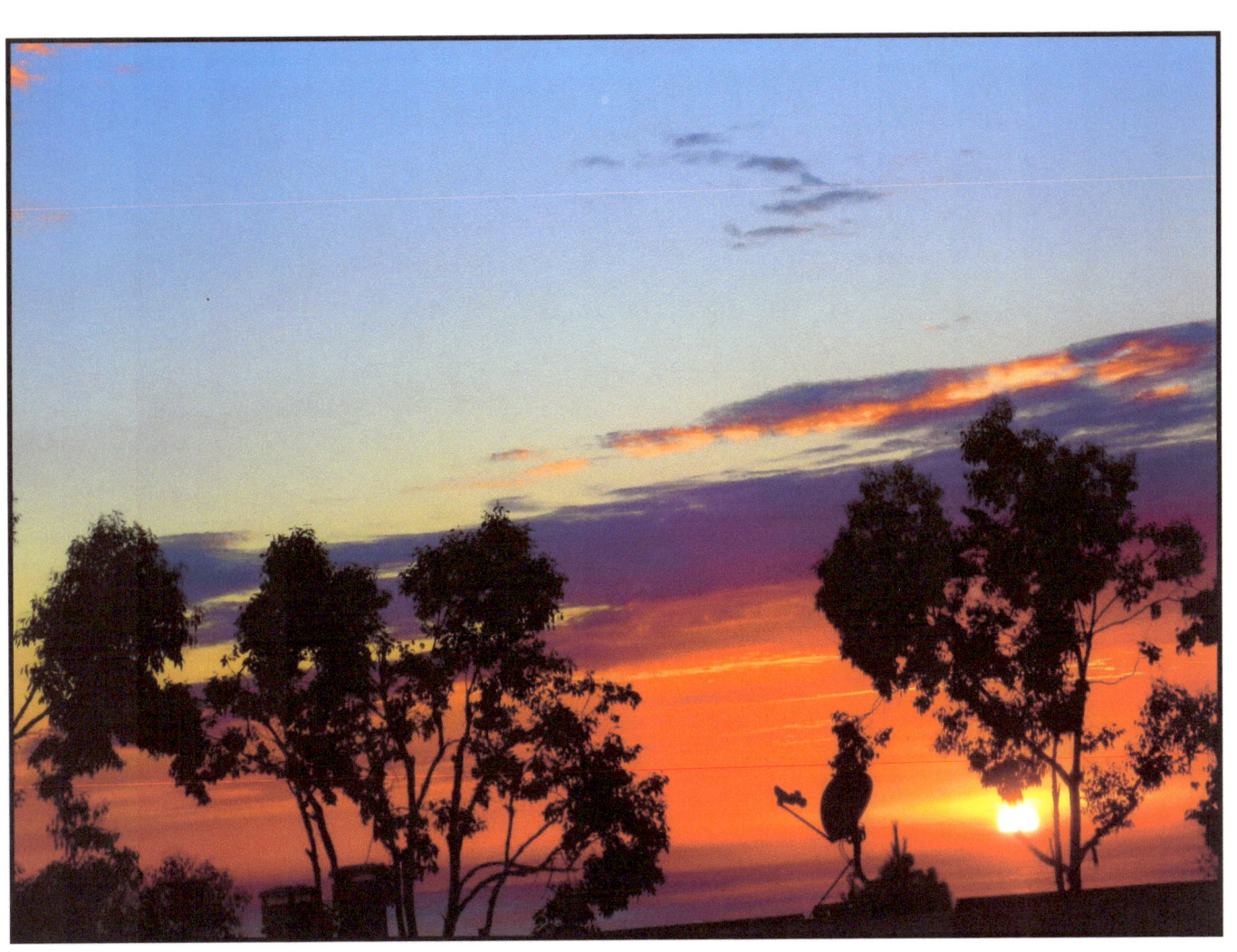

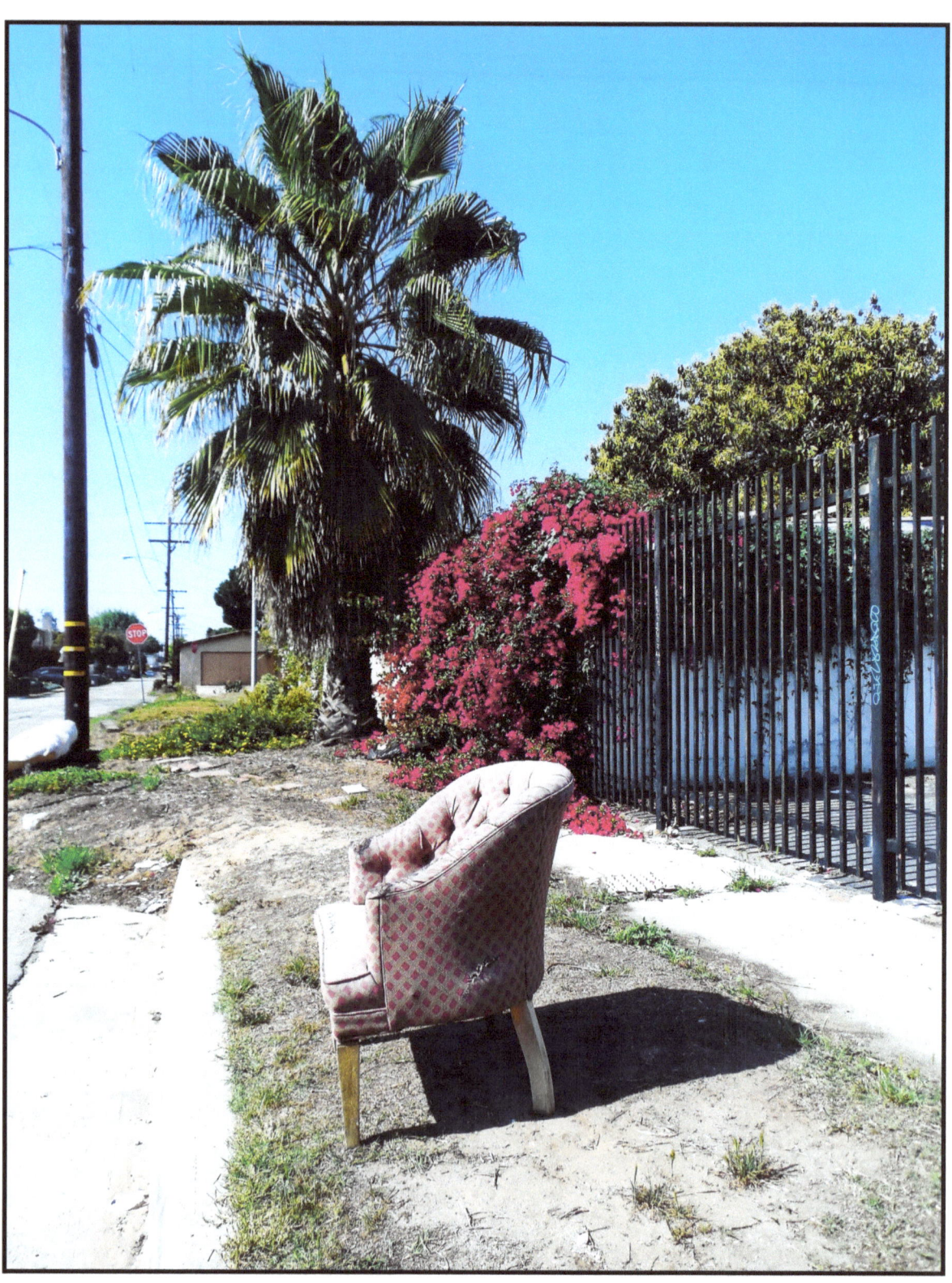

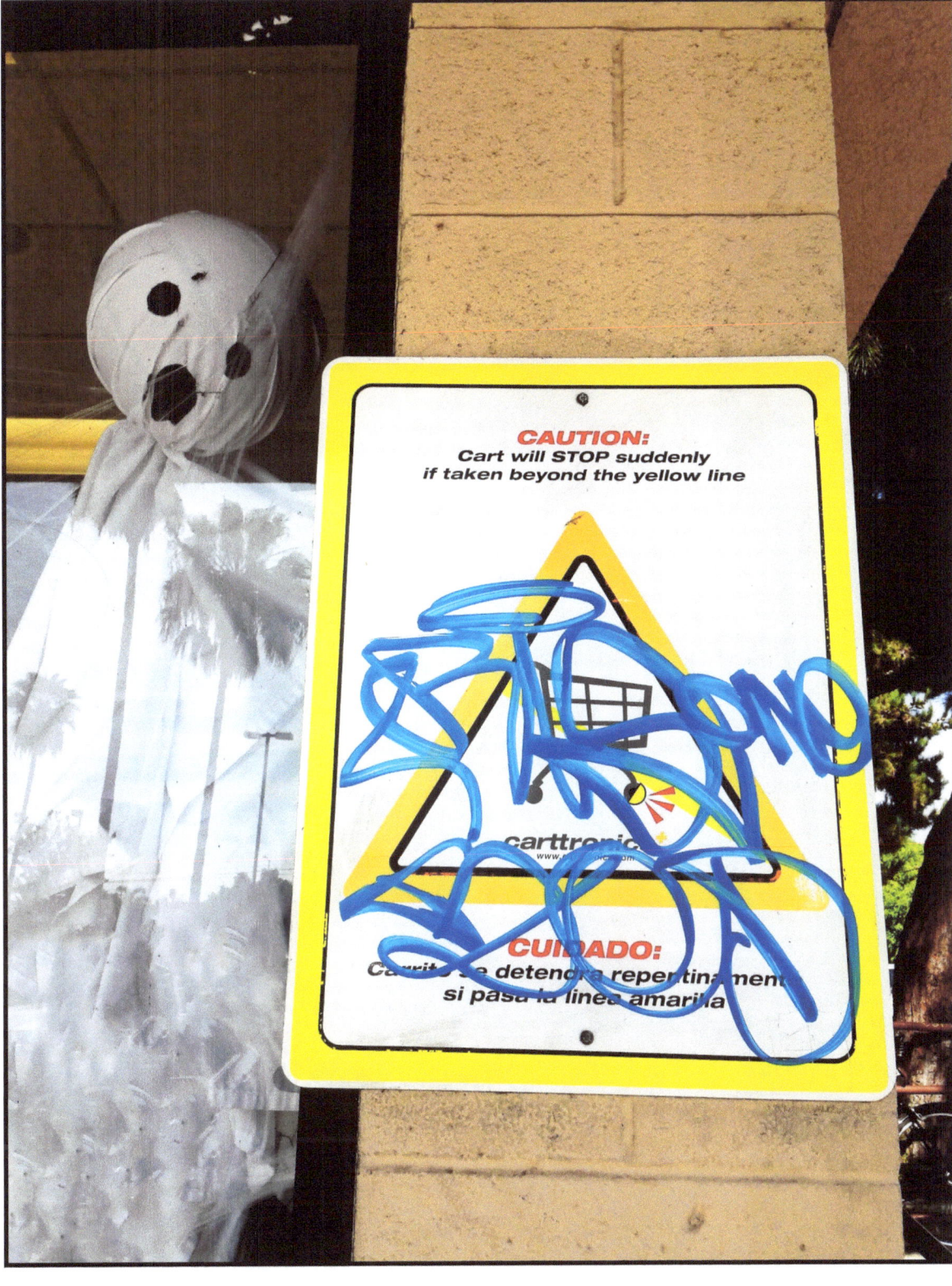

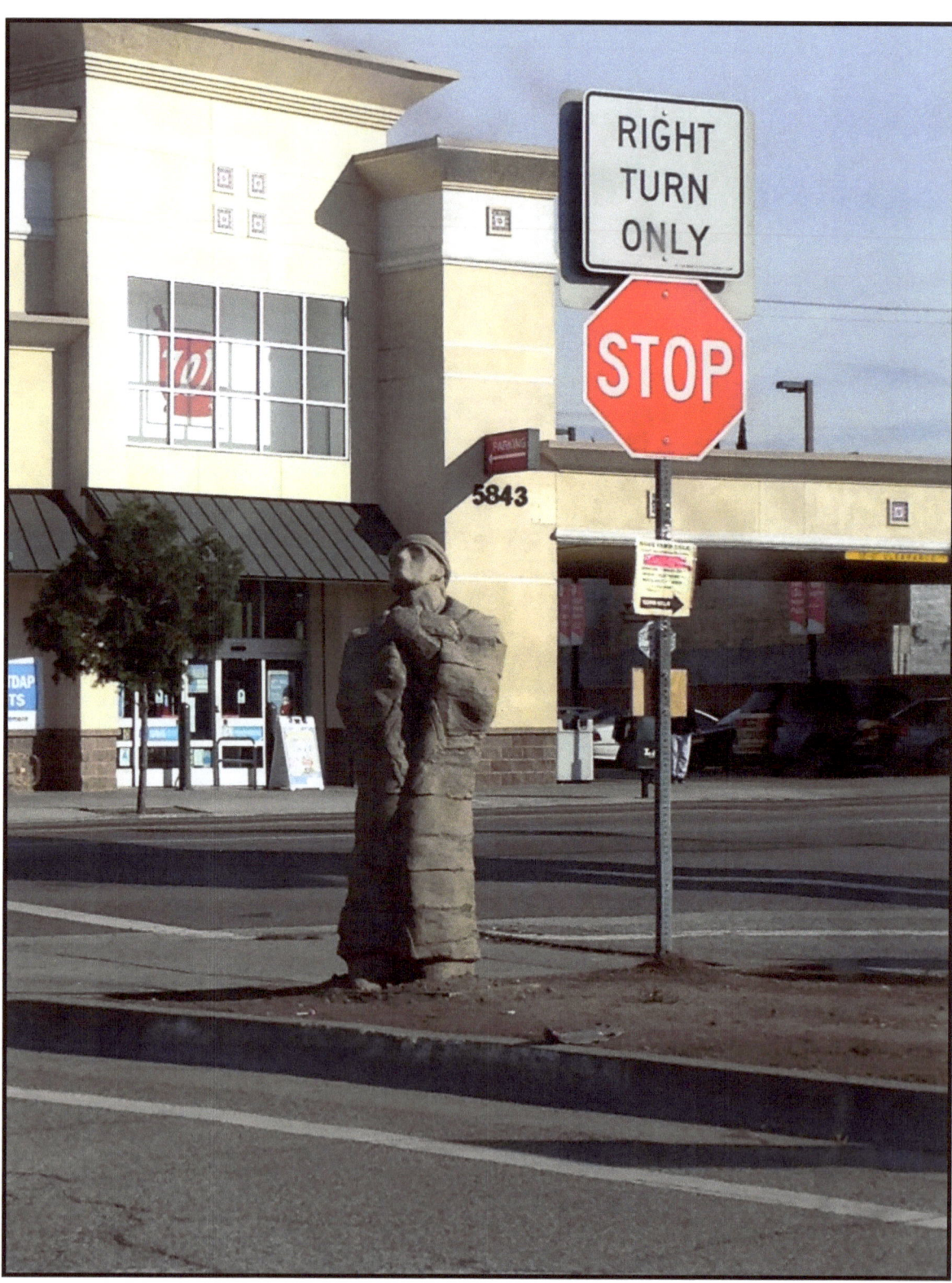

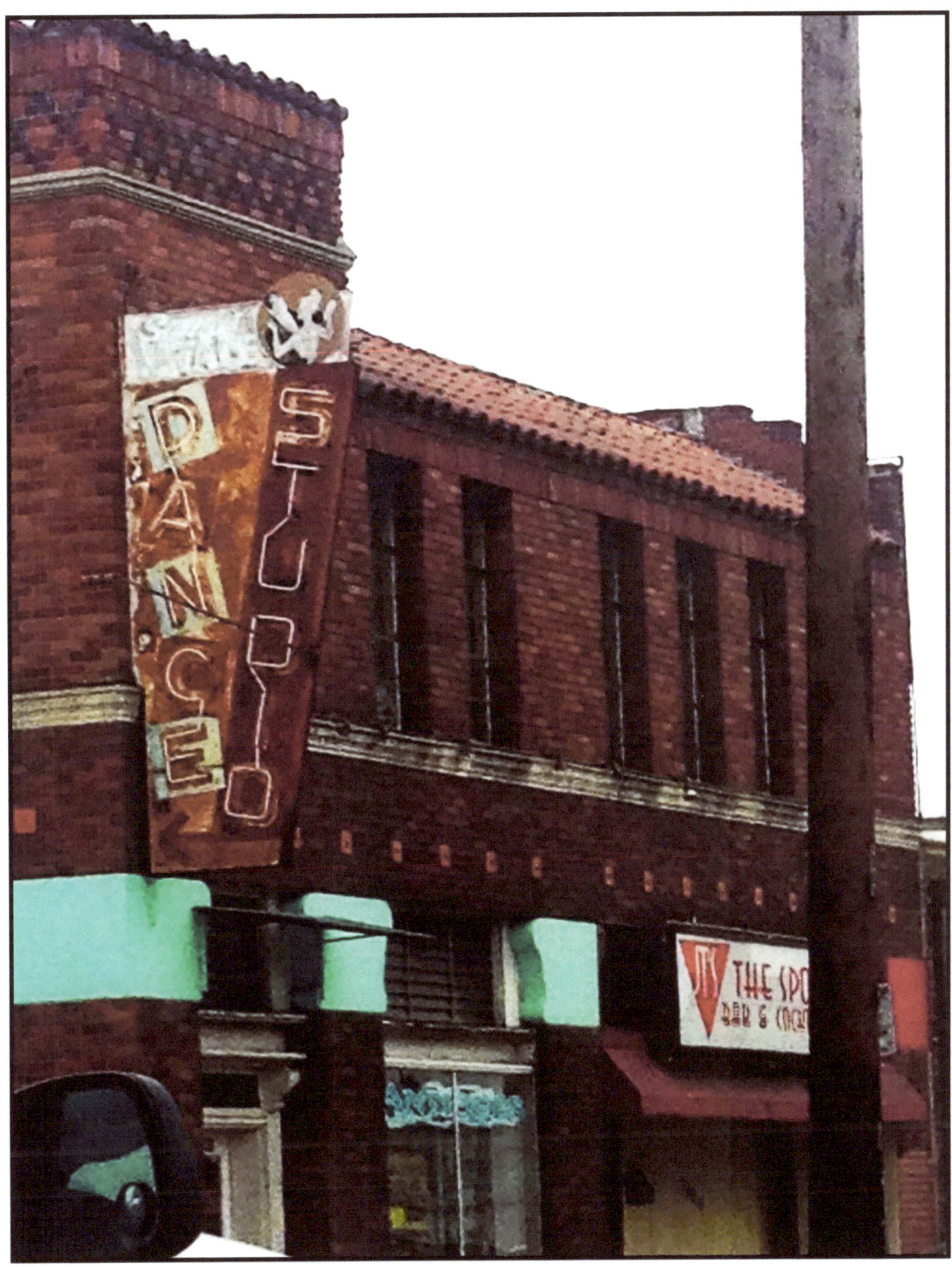

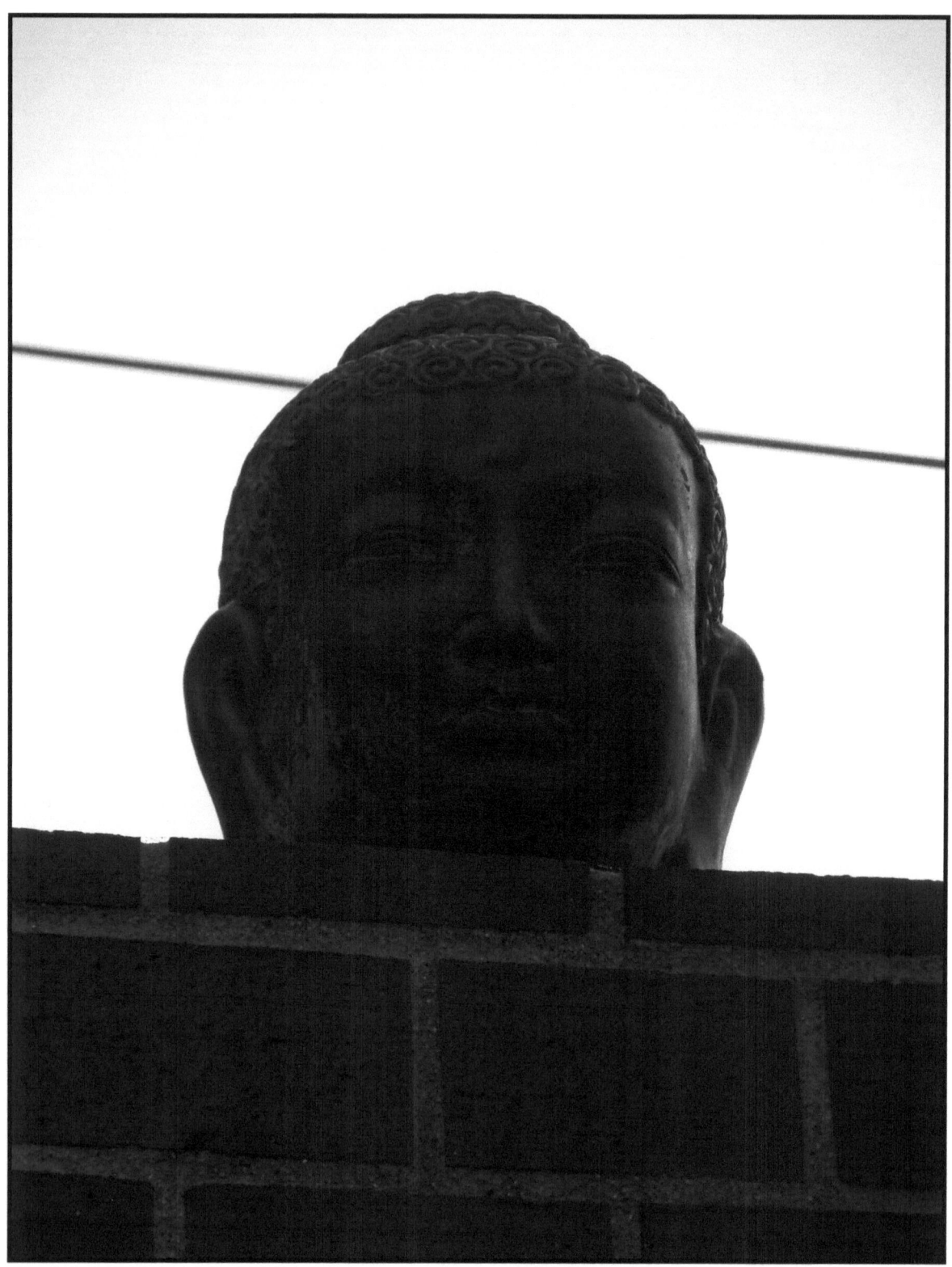

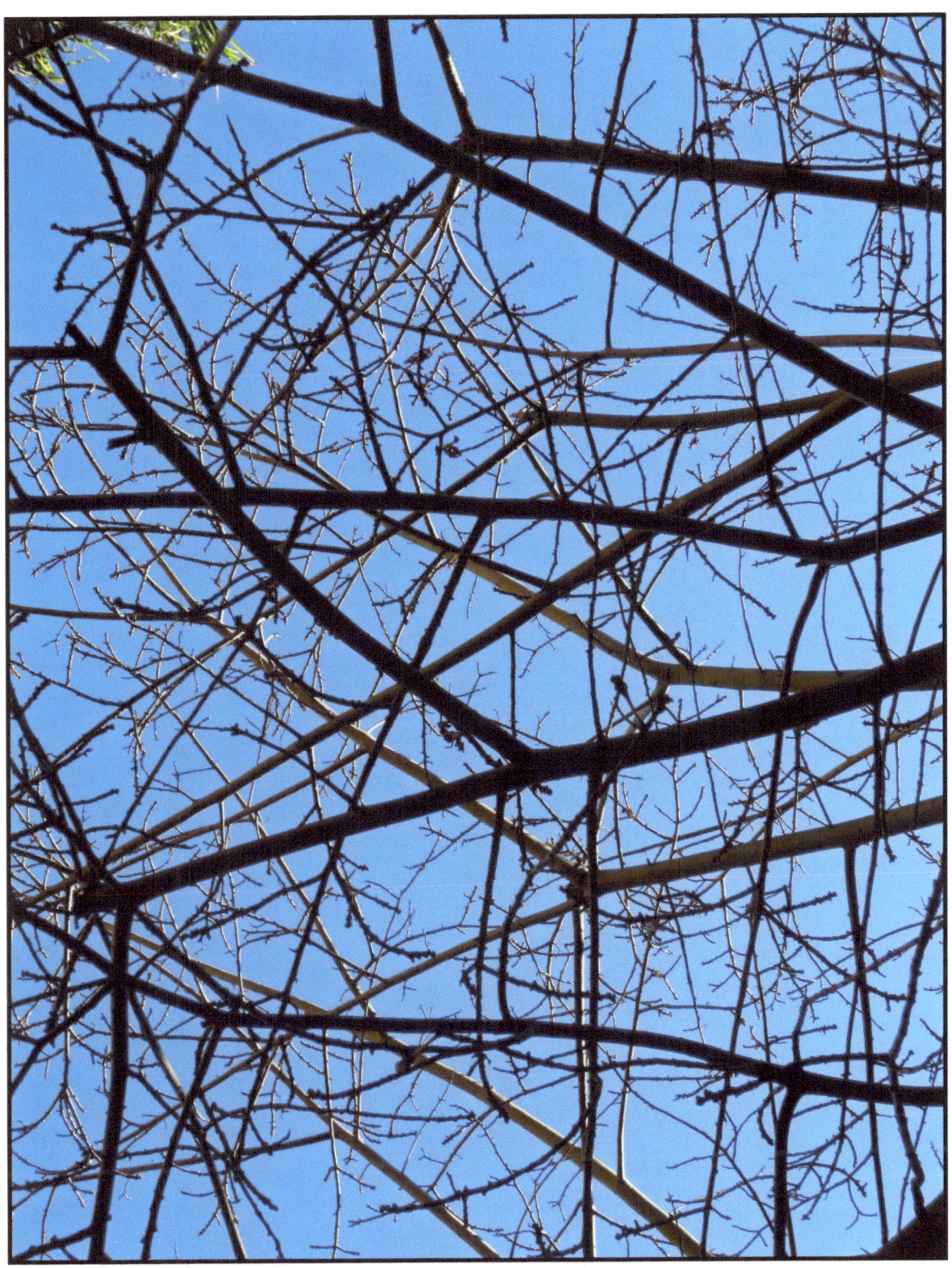

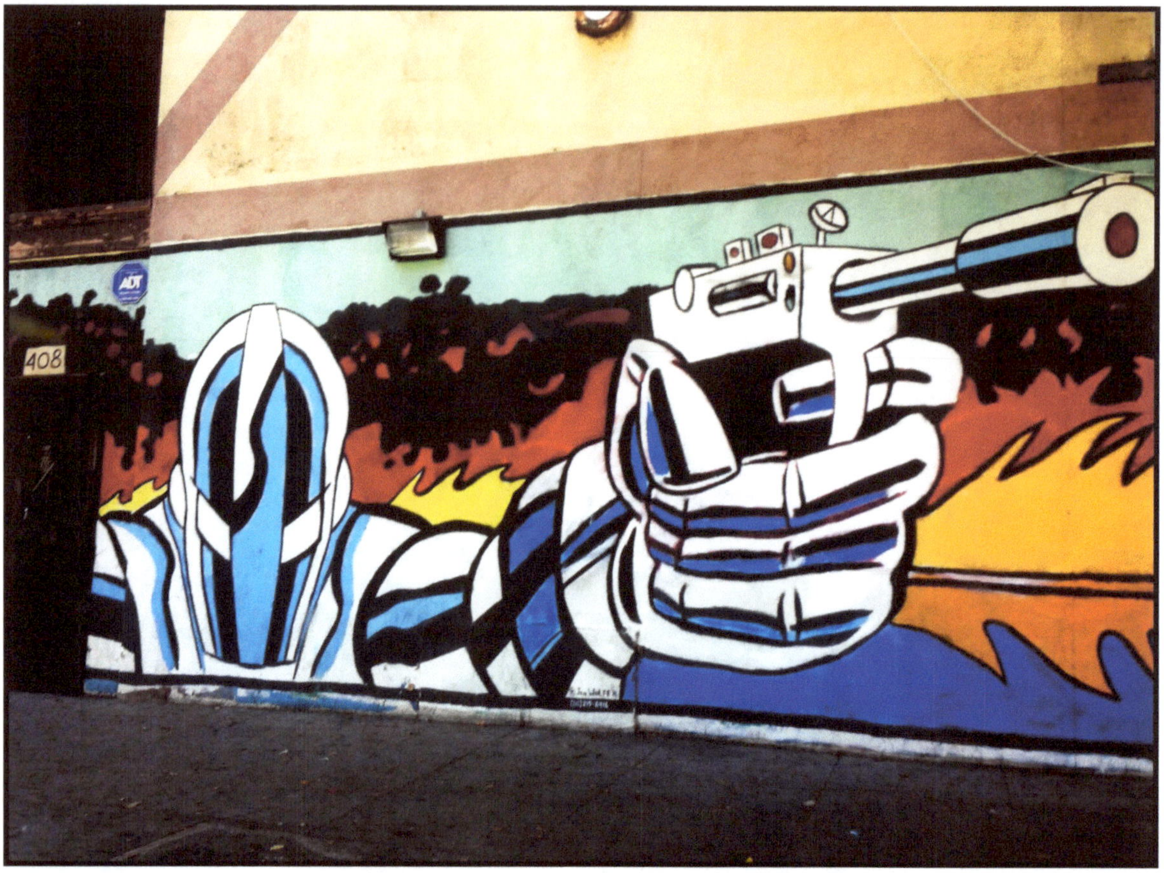

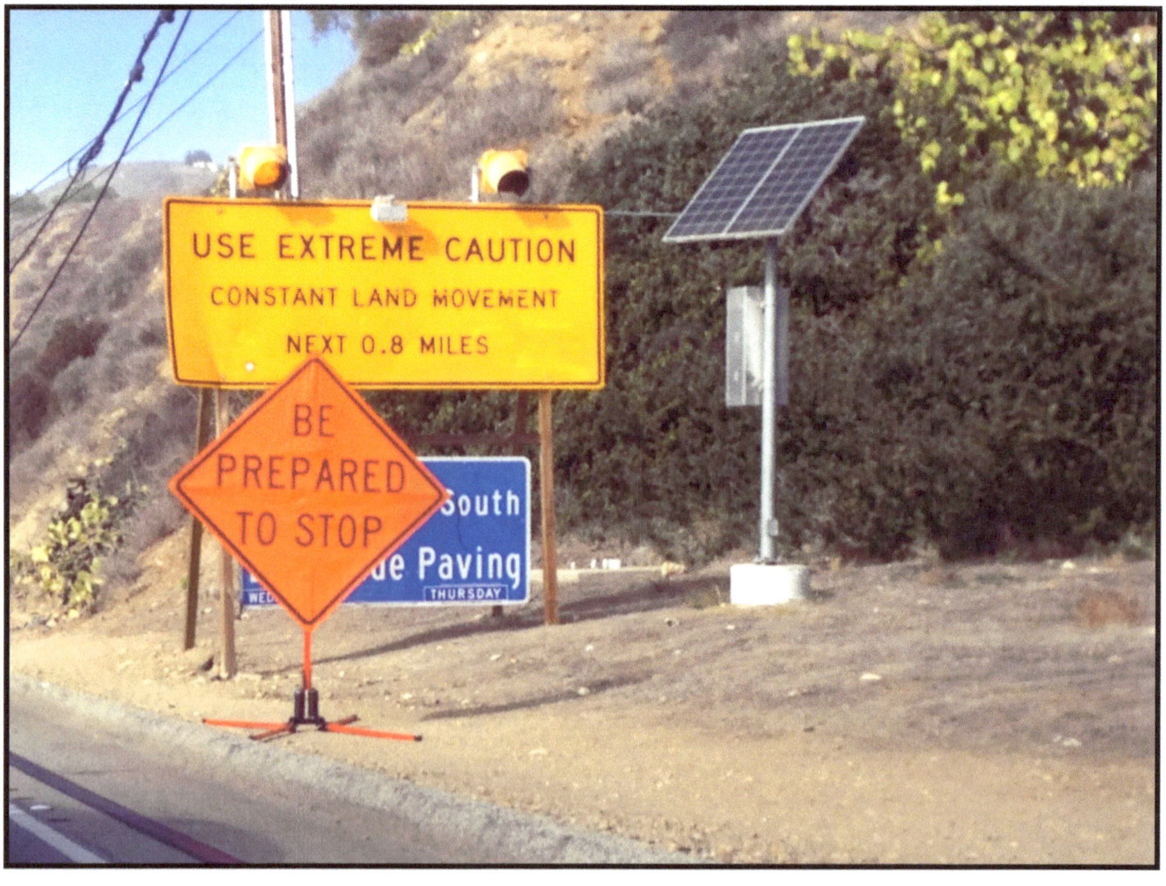

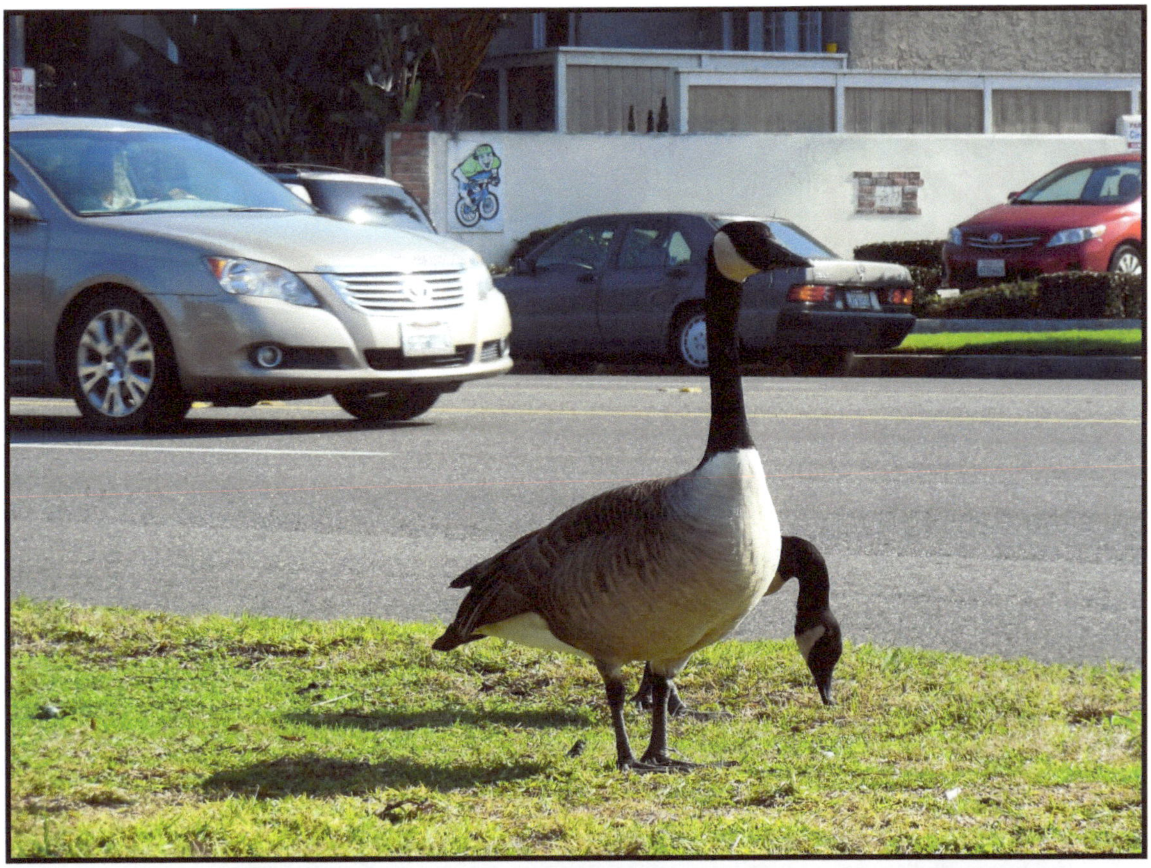

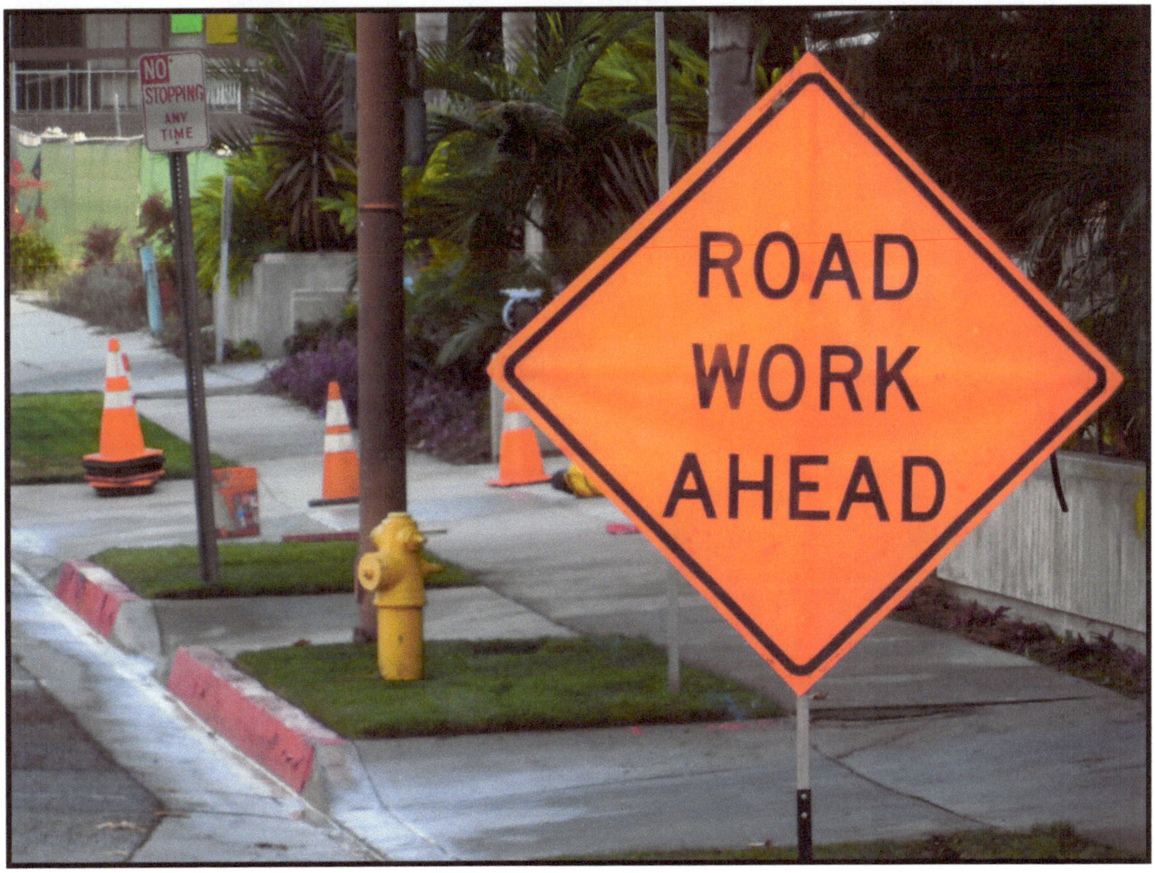

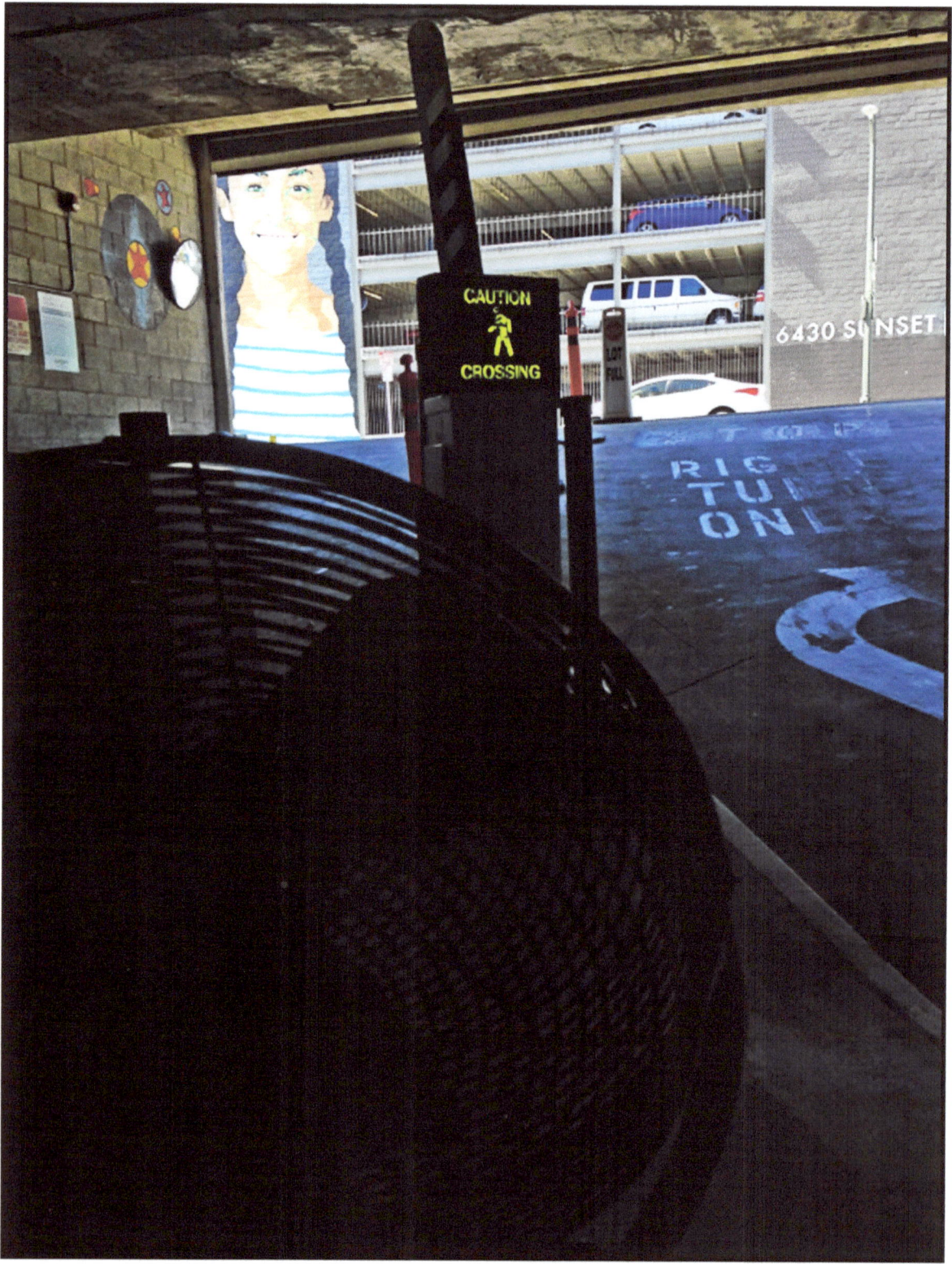

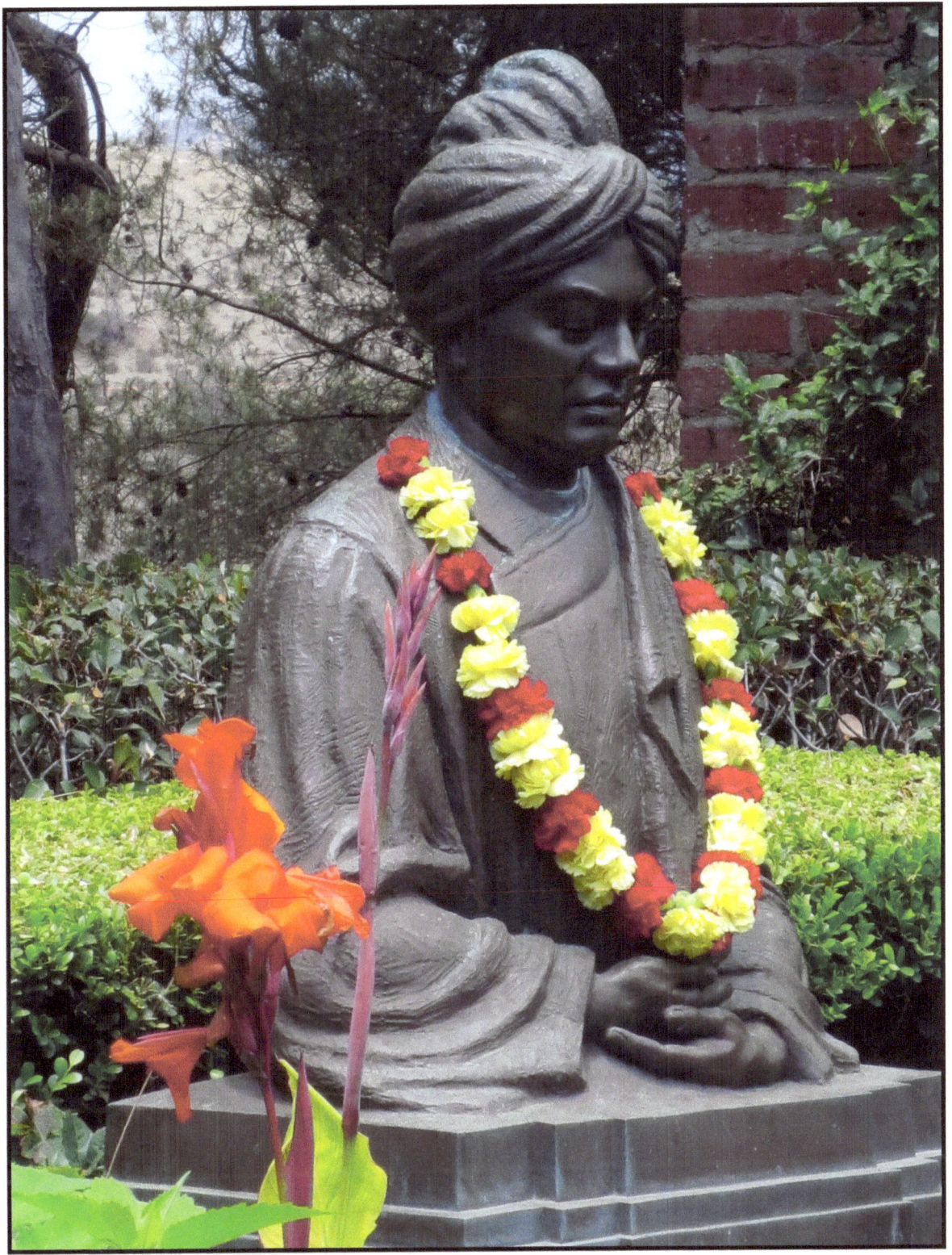

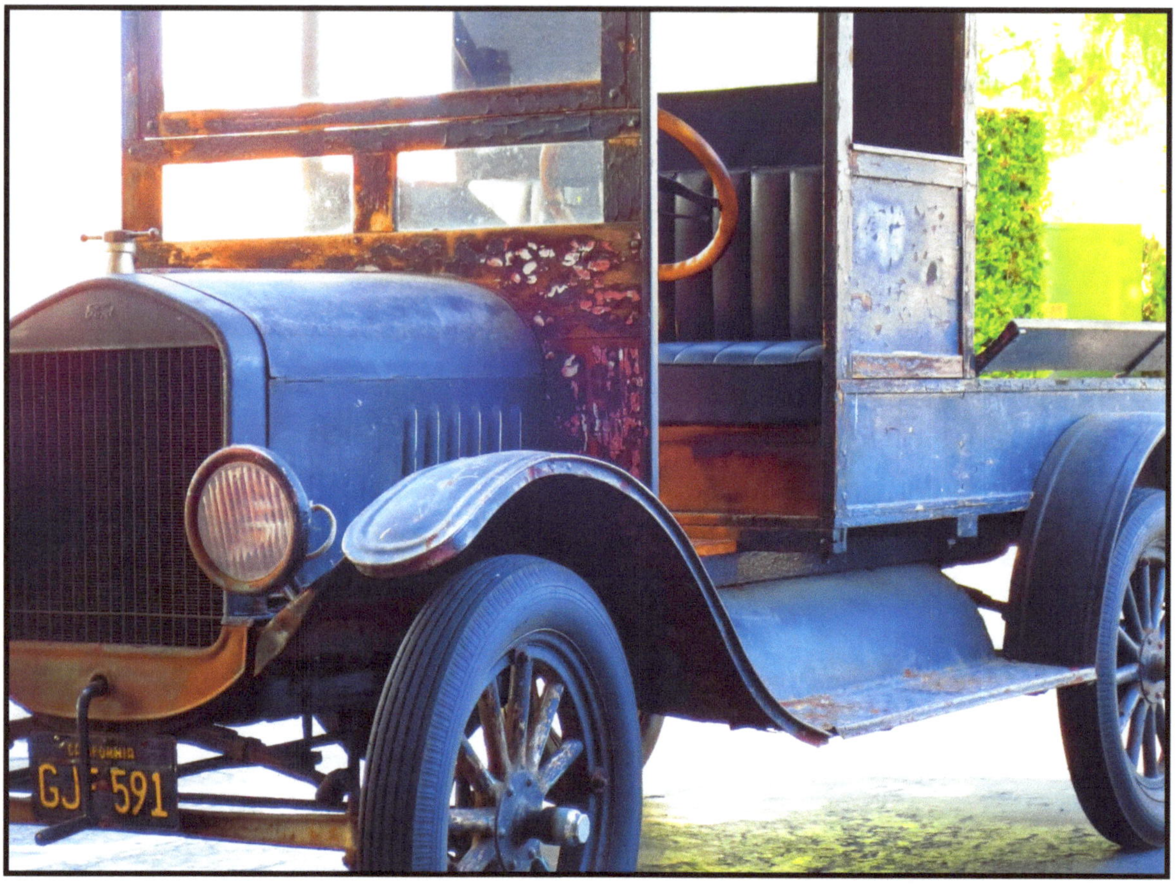

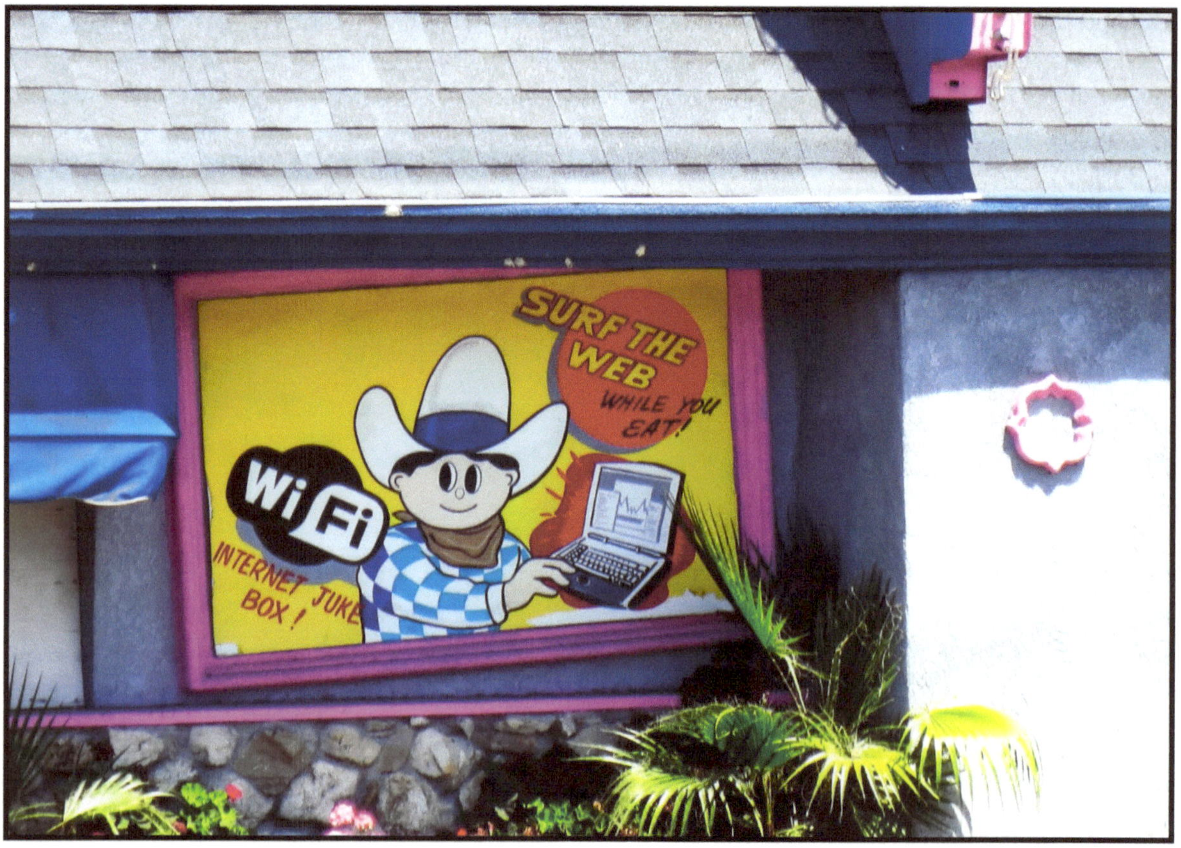

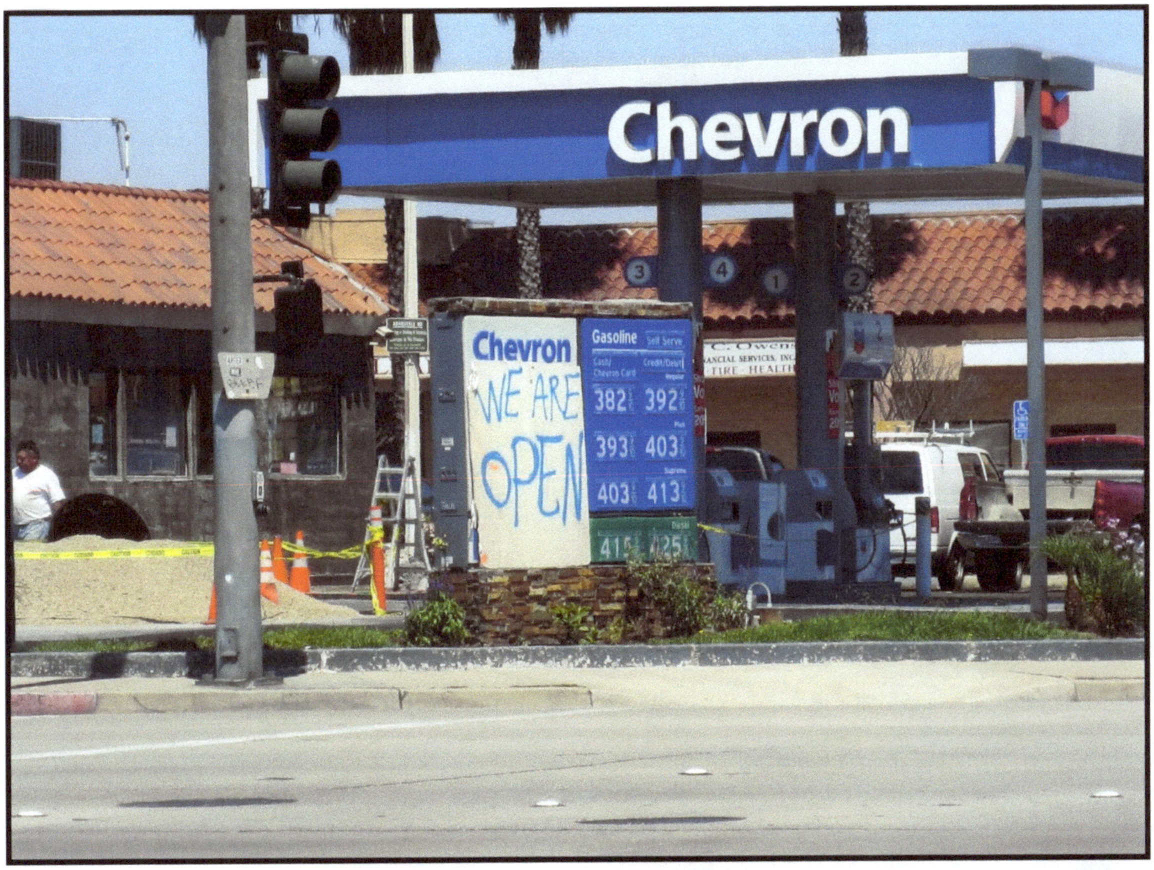

Chevron

Gasoline — Self Serve

	Cash/Chevron Card	Credit/Debit
Regular	382	392
Plus	393	403
Supreme	403	413
Diesel	415	425

WE ARE OPEN

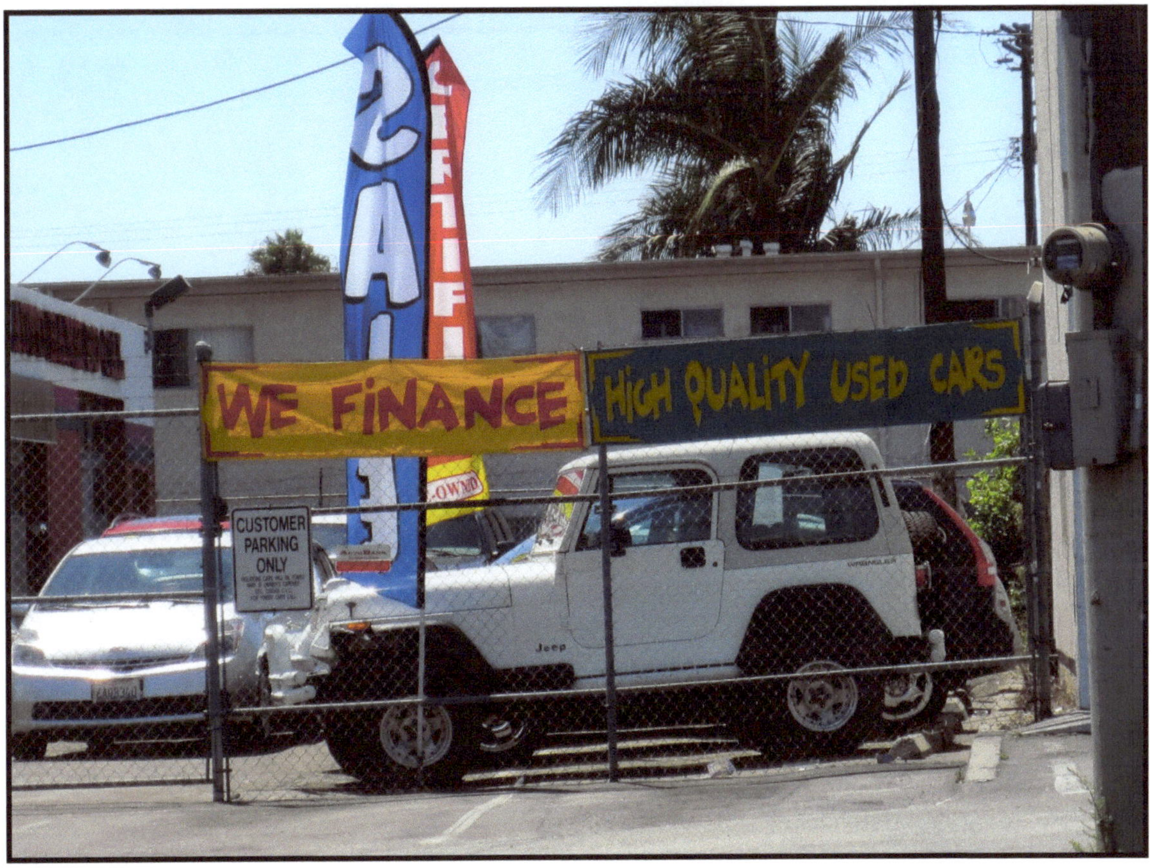

WE FINANCE — HIGH QUALITY USED CARS

CUSTOMER PARKING ONLY

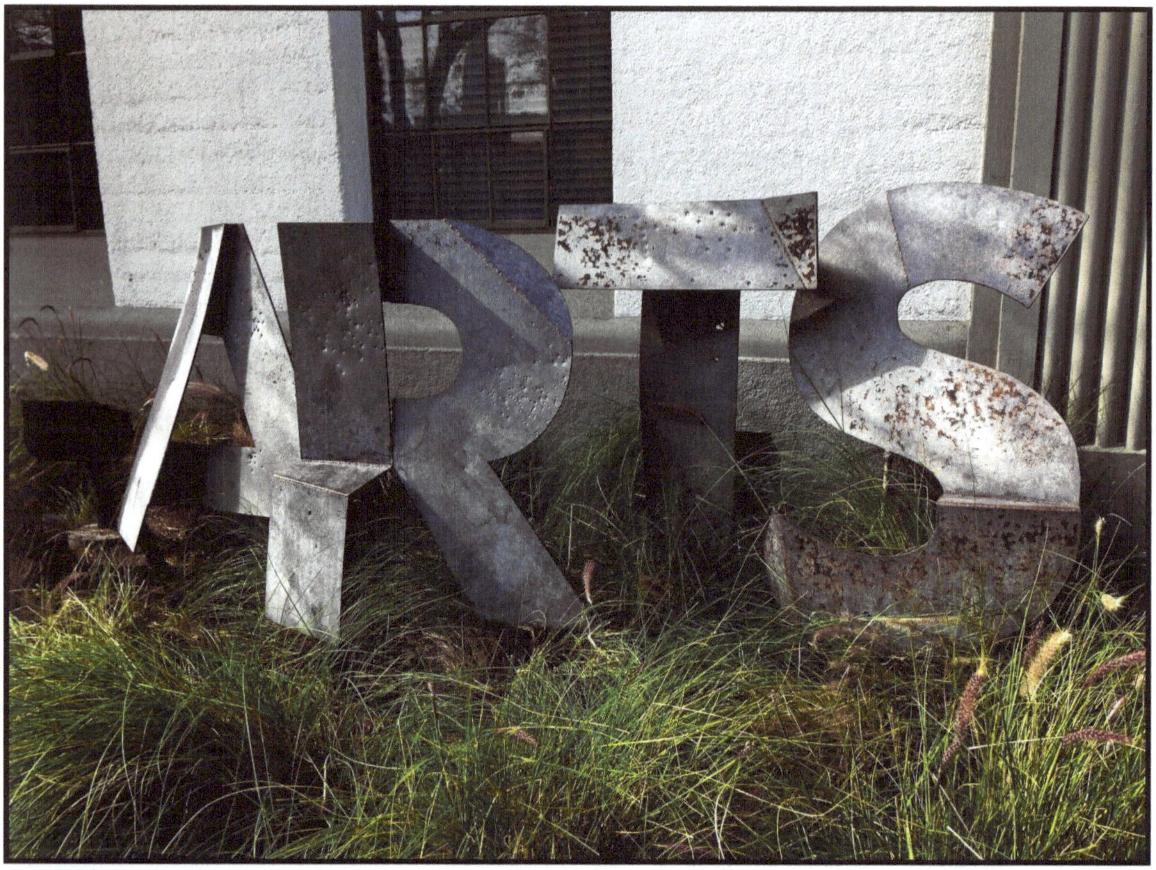

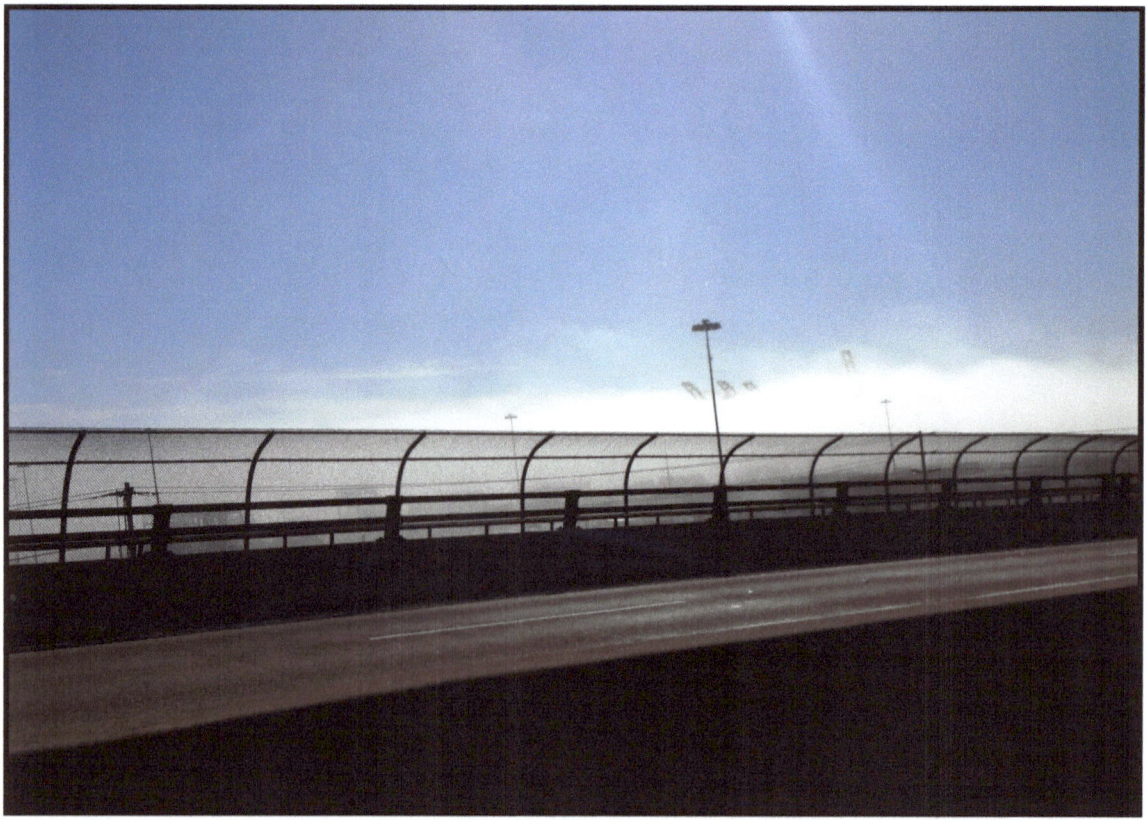

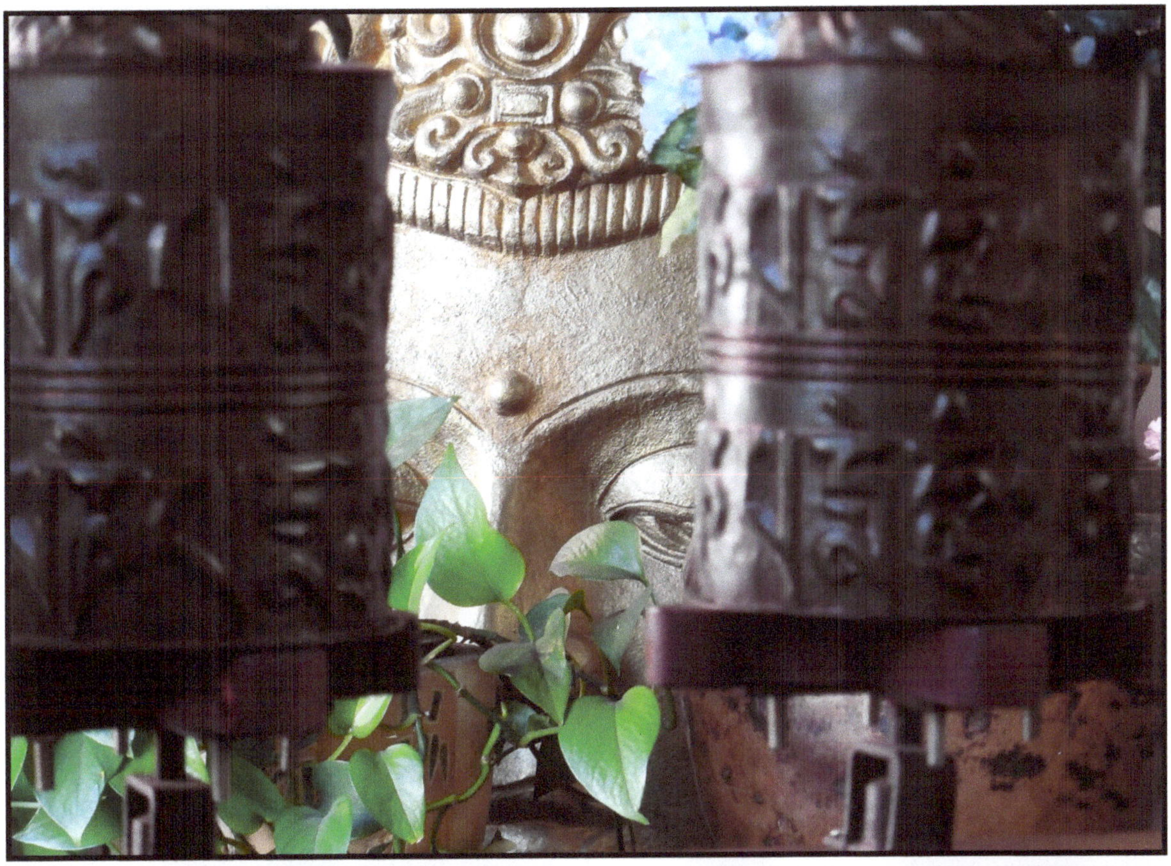

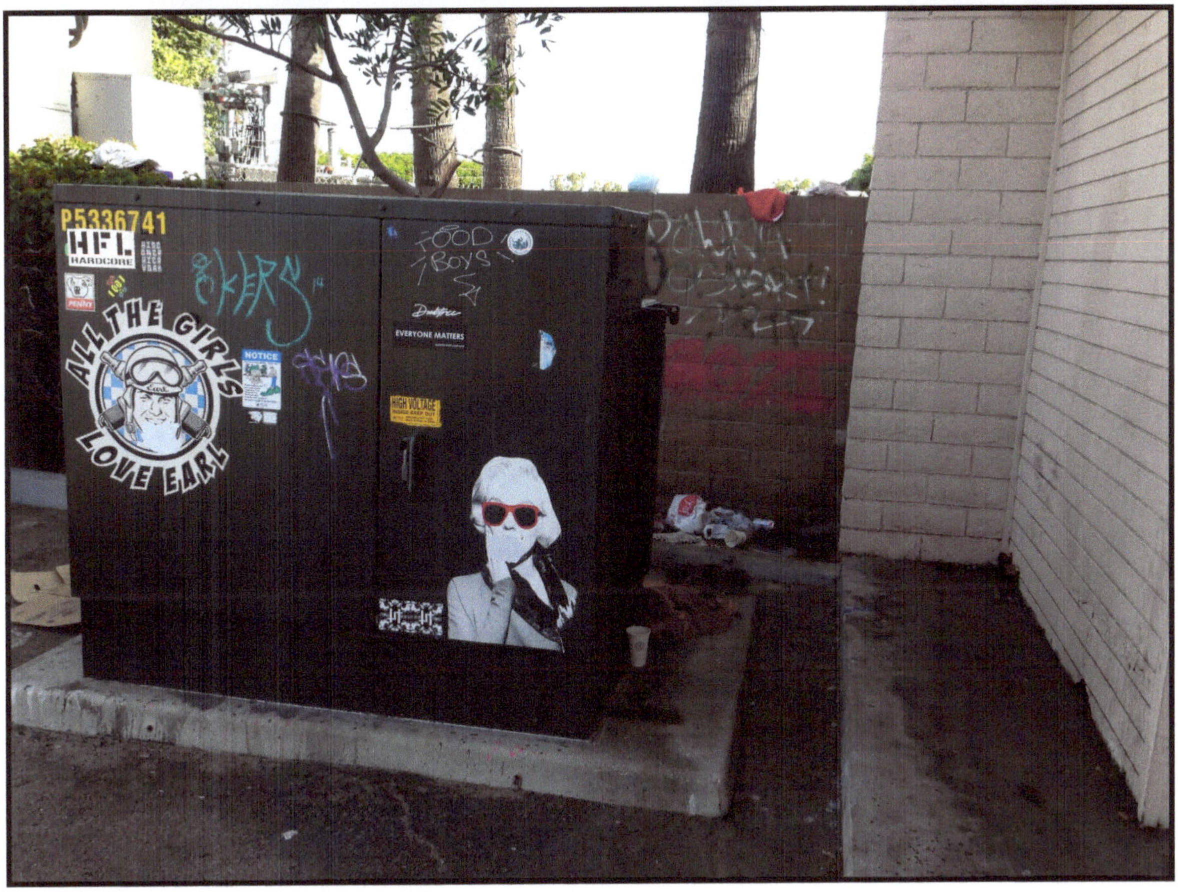

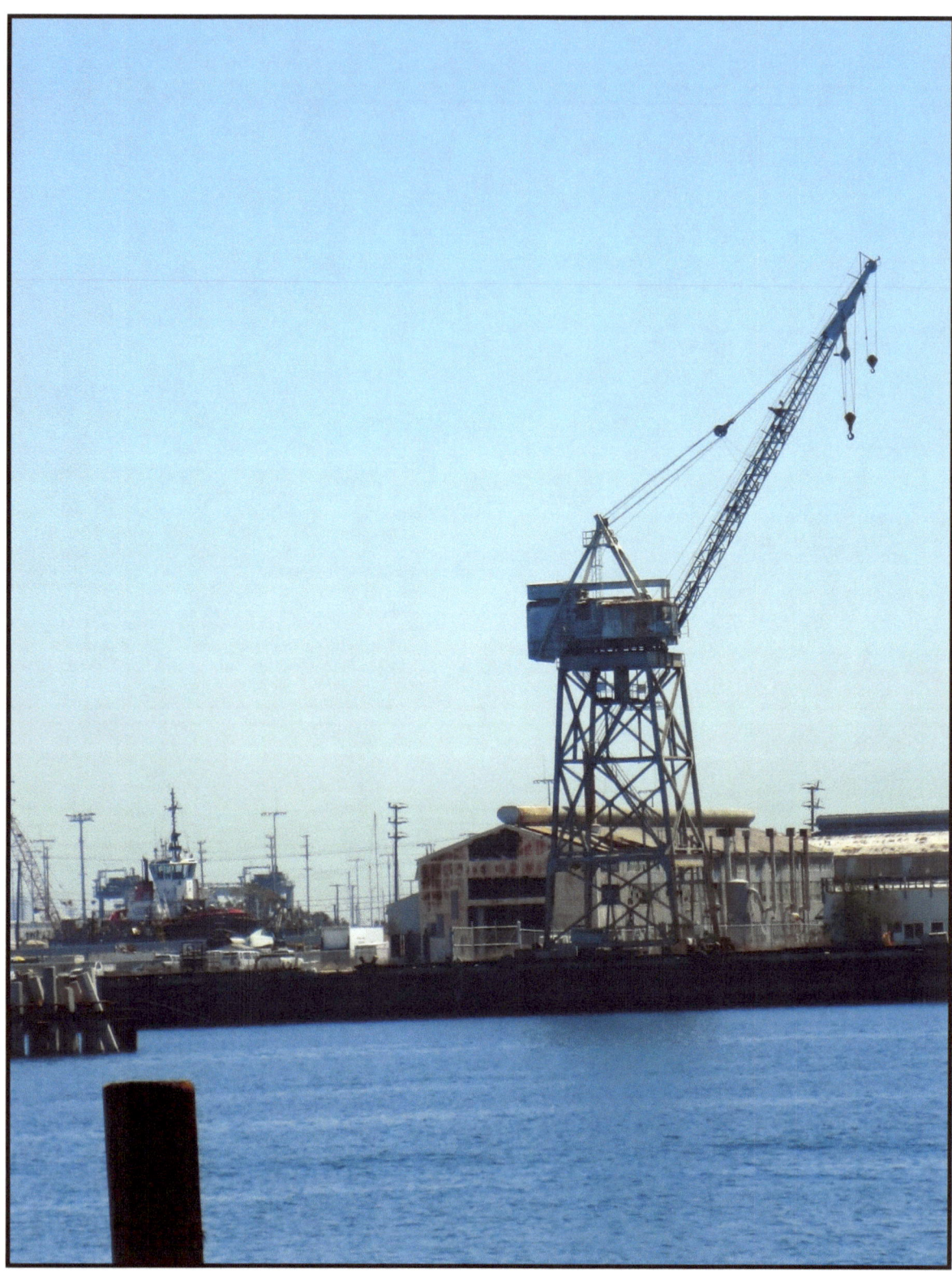

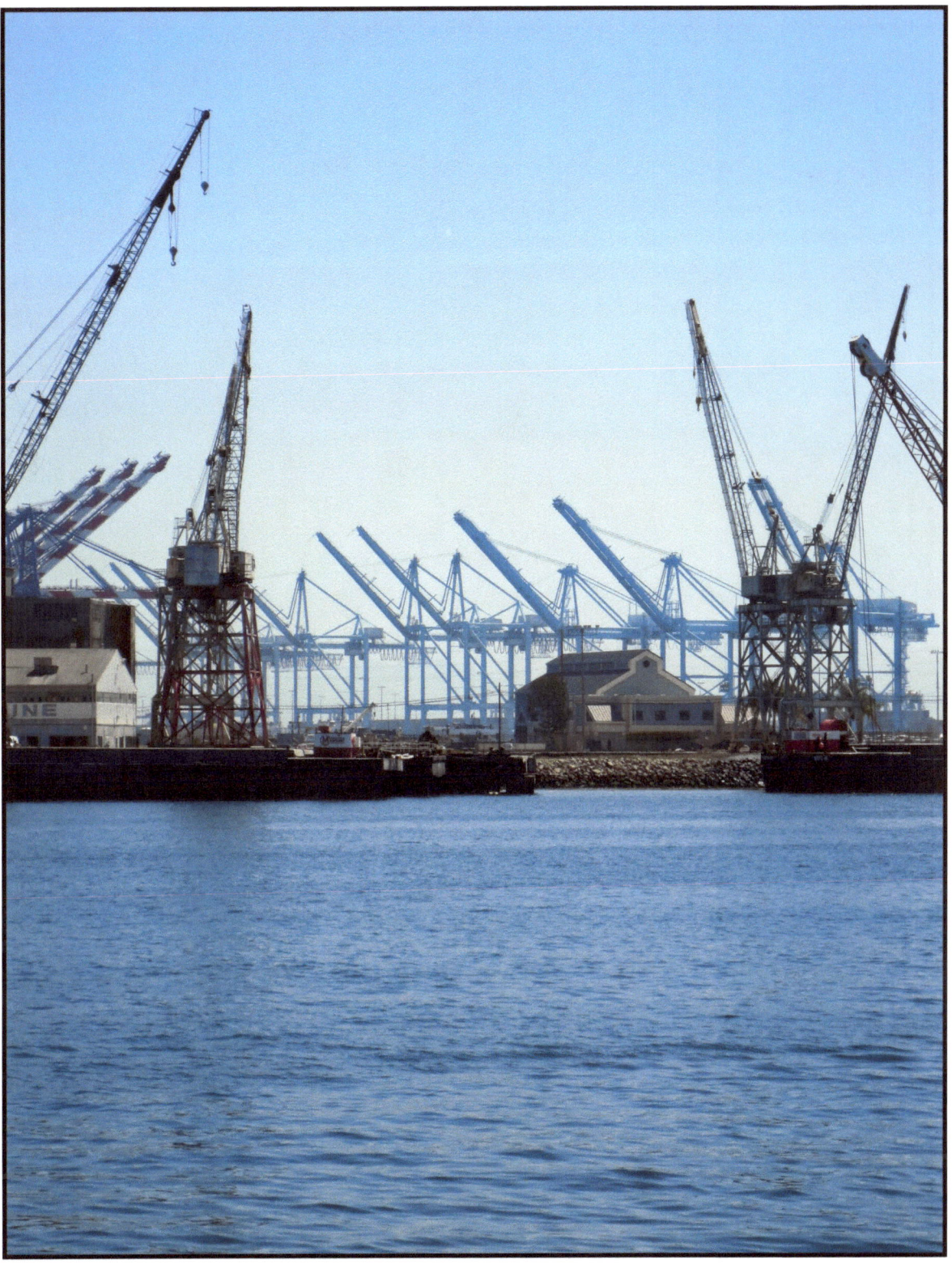

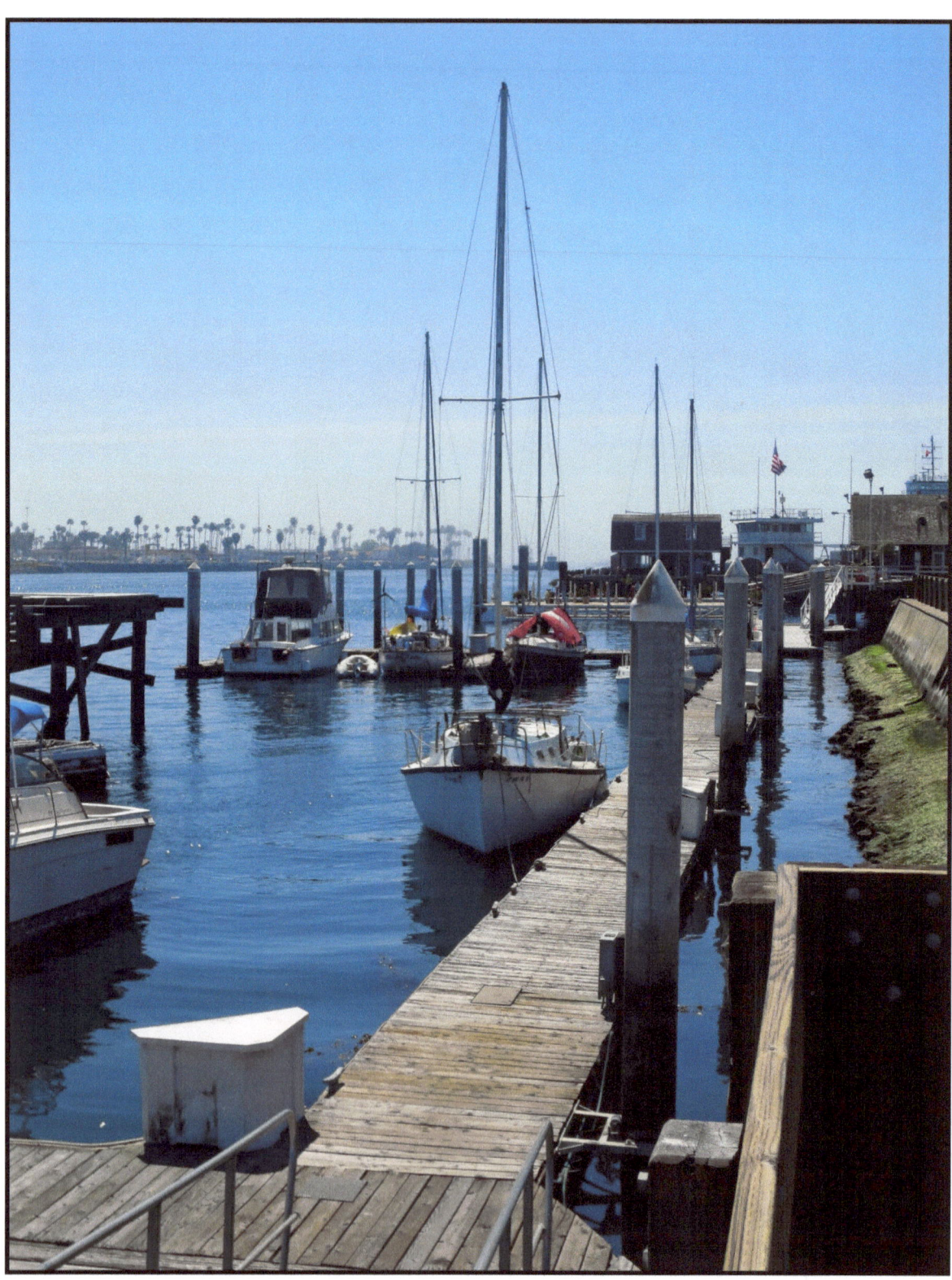

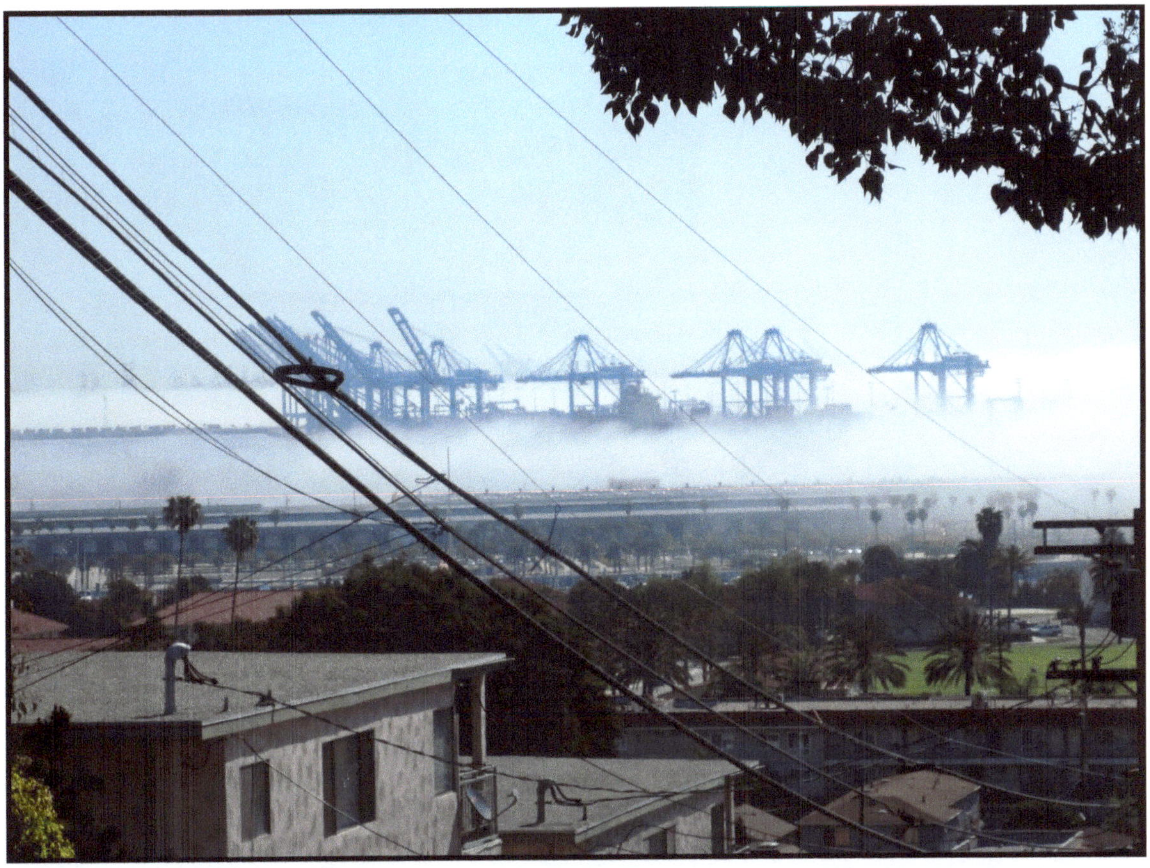

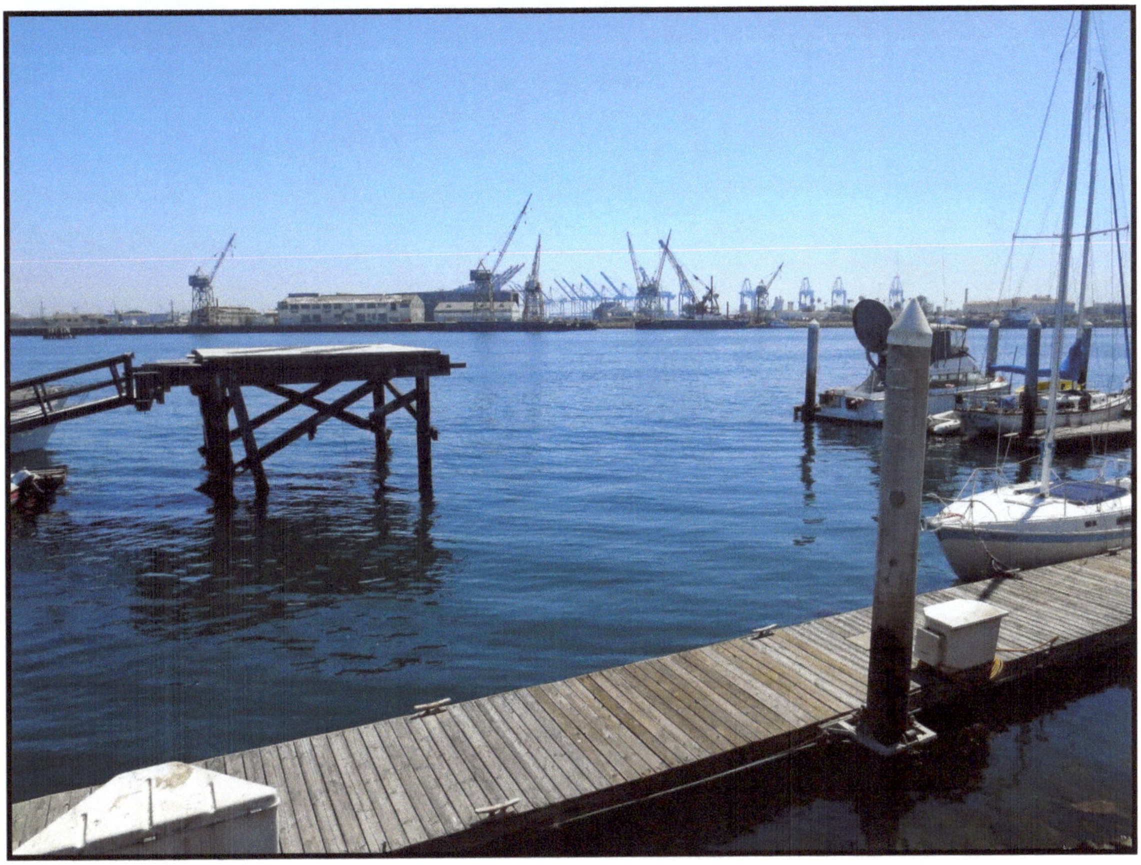

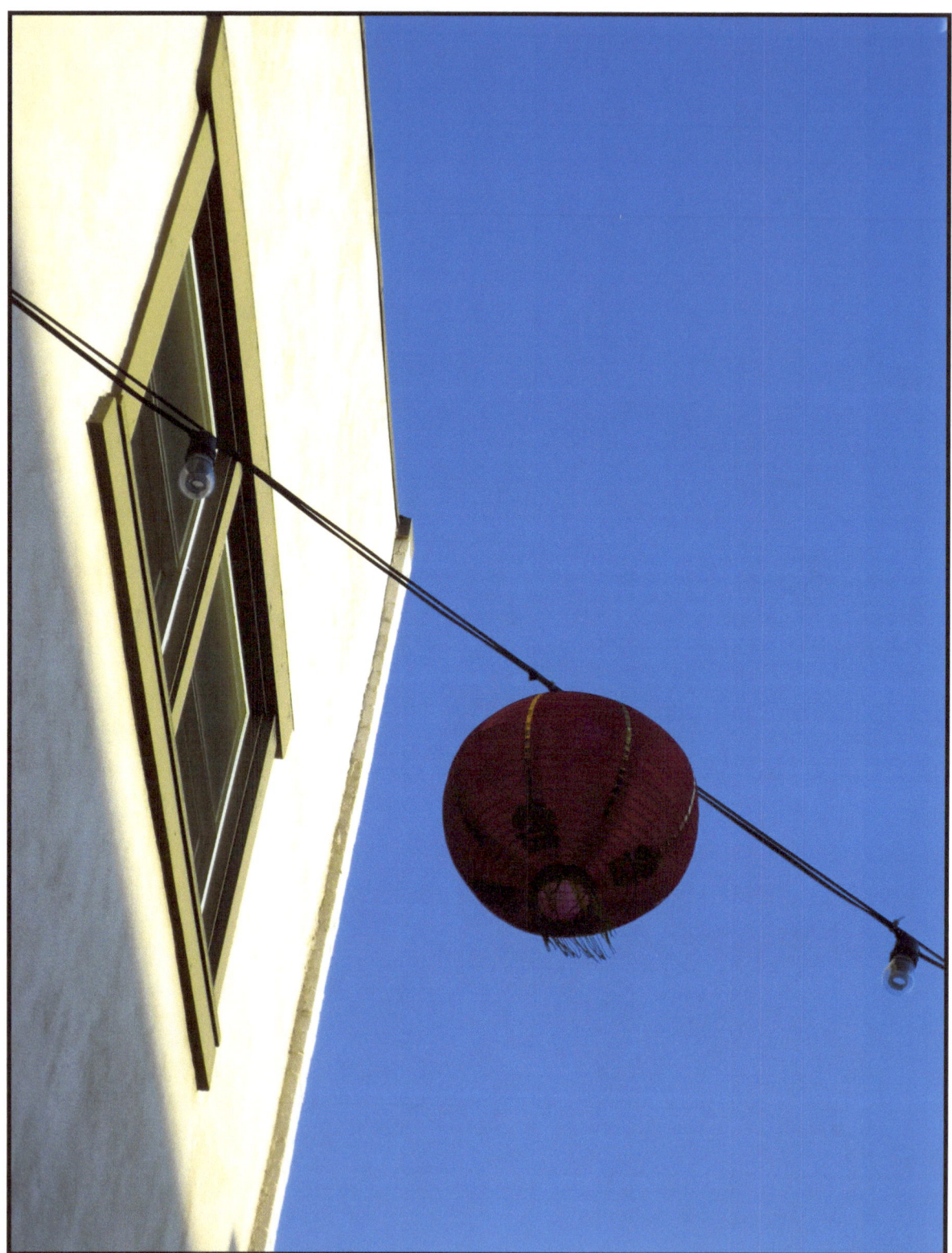

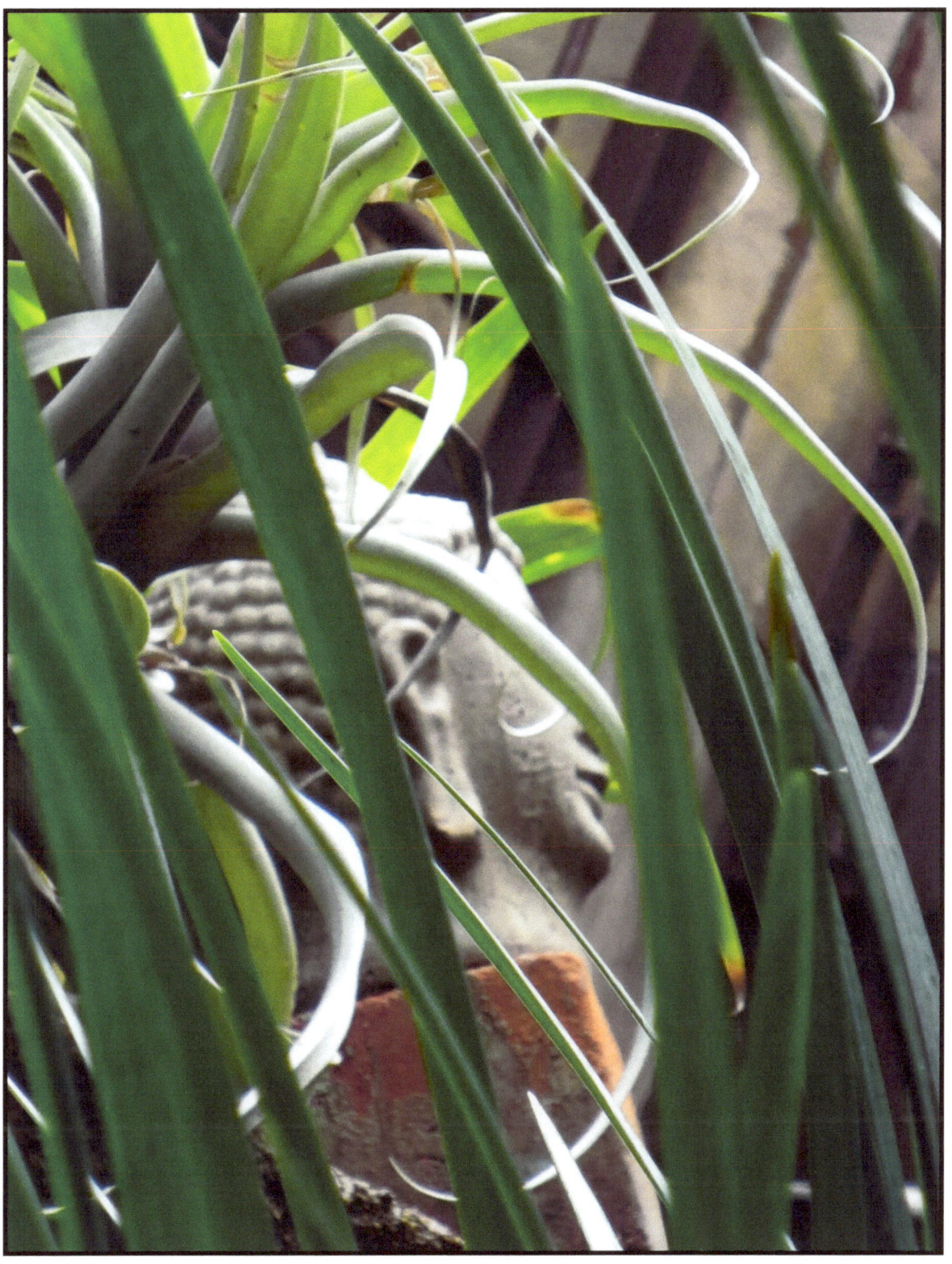

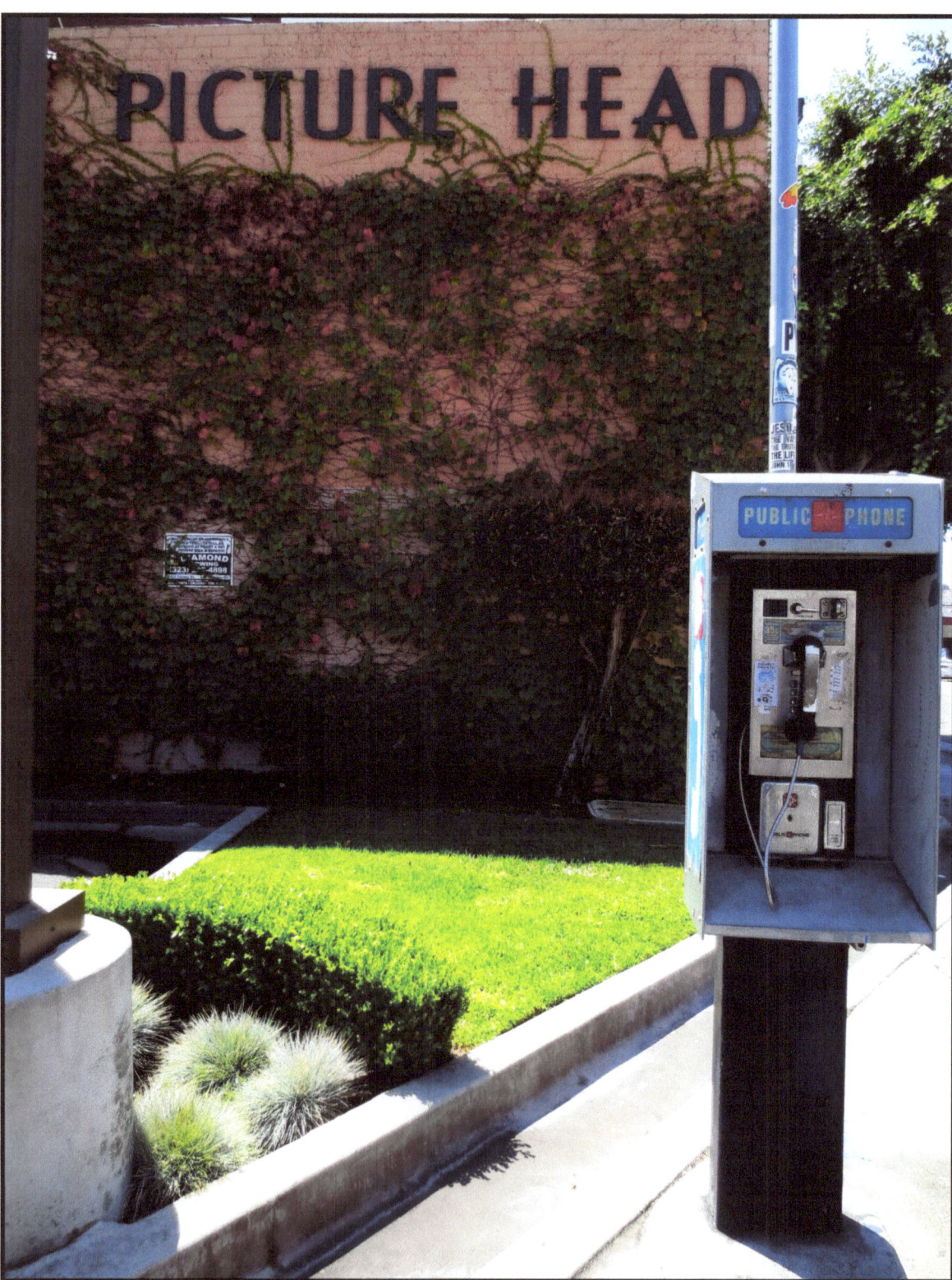

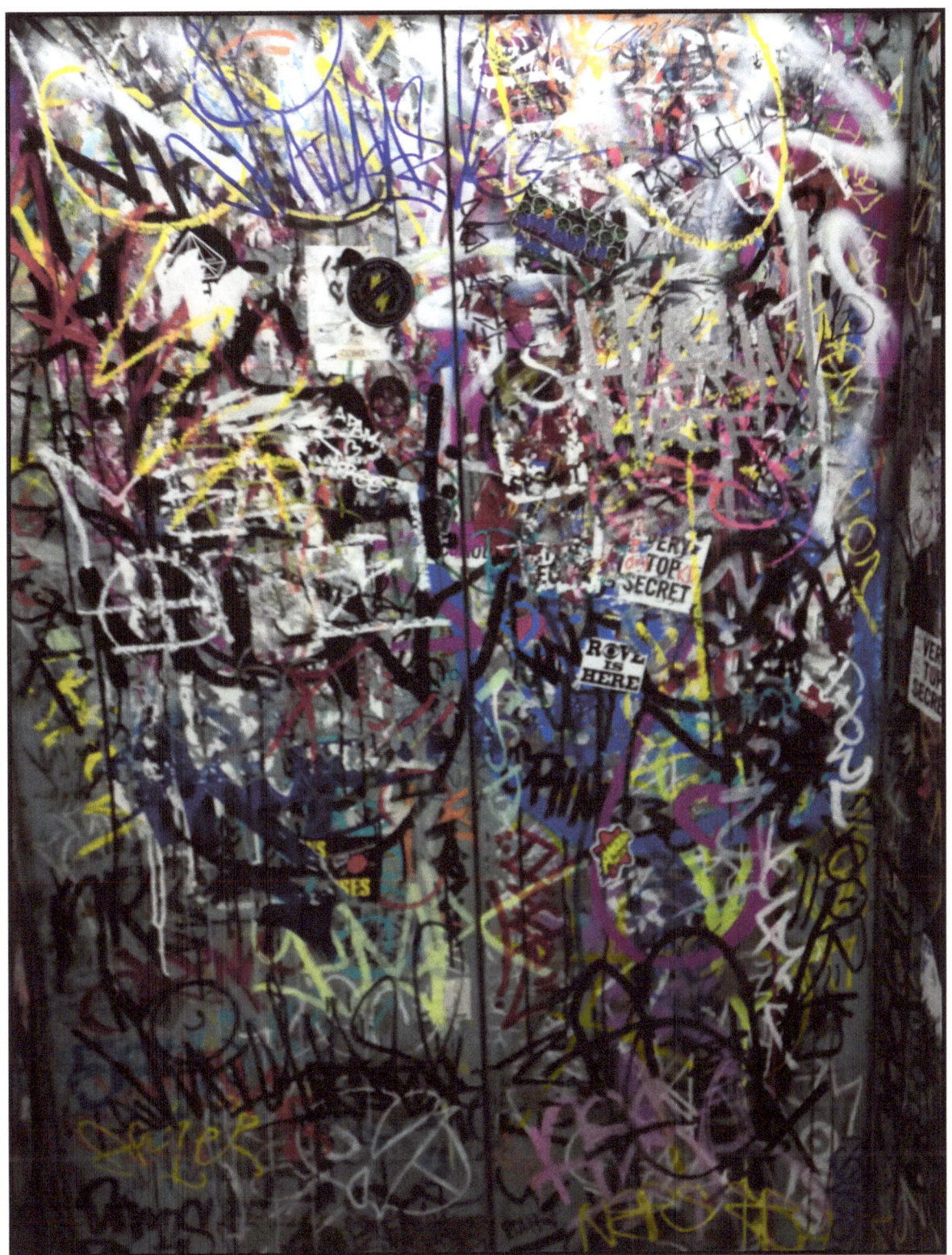

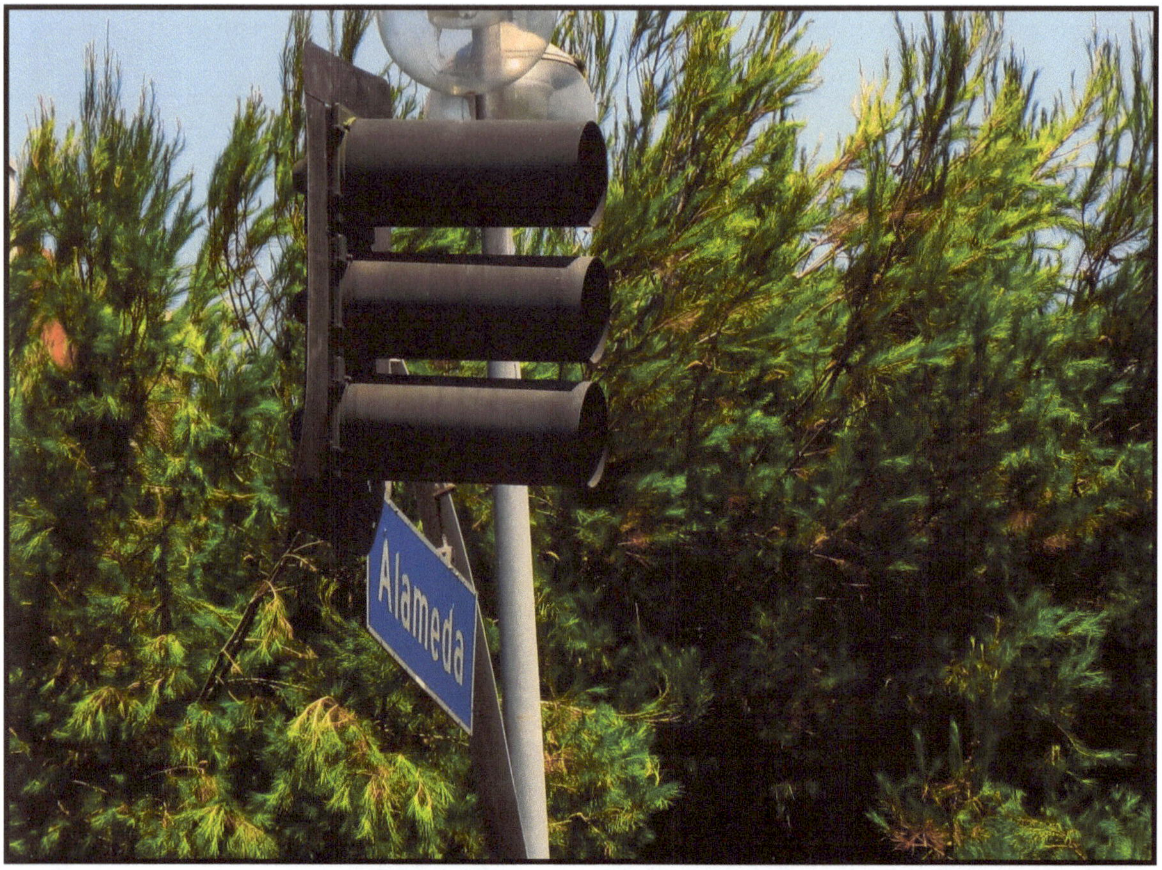

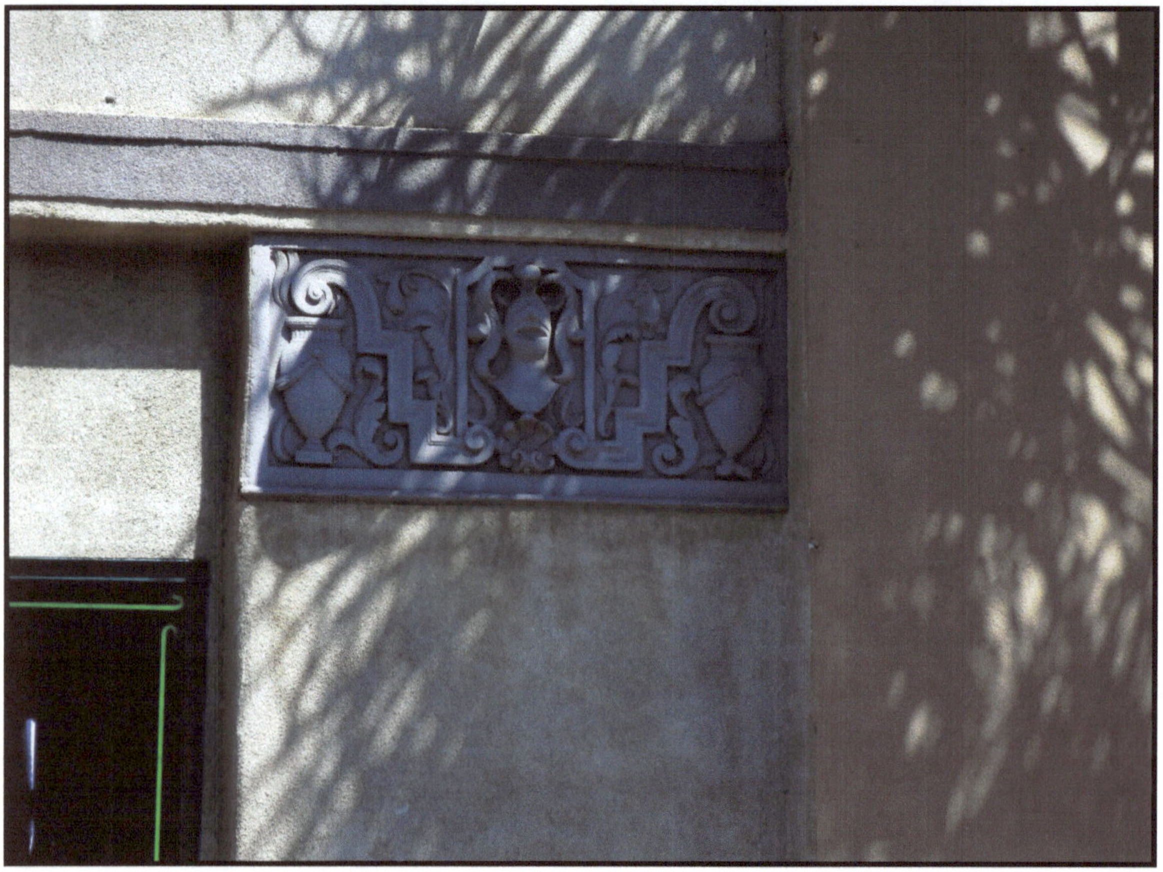

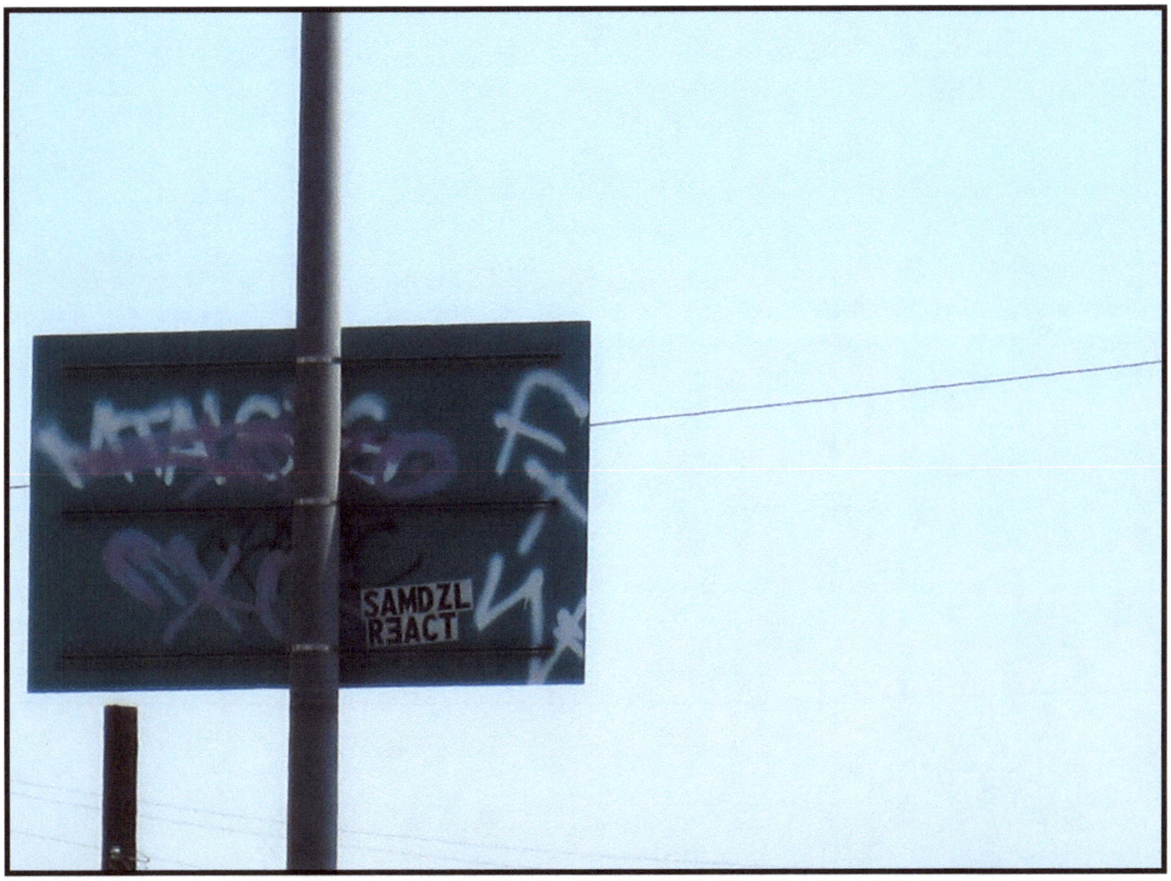

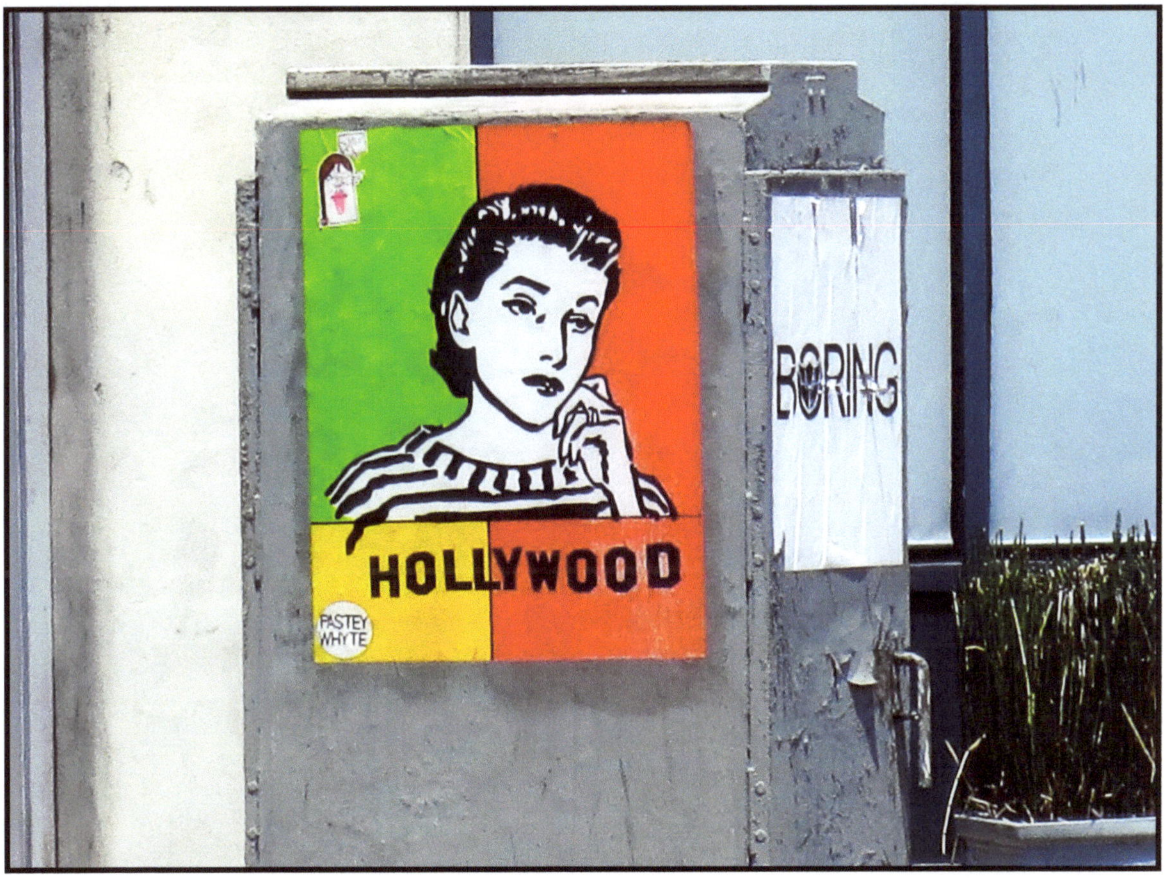

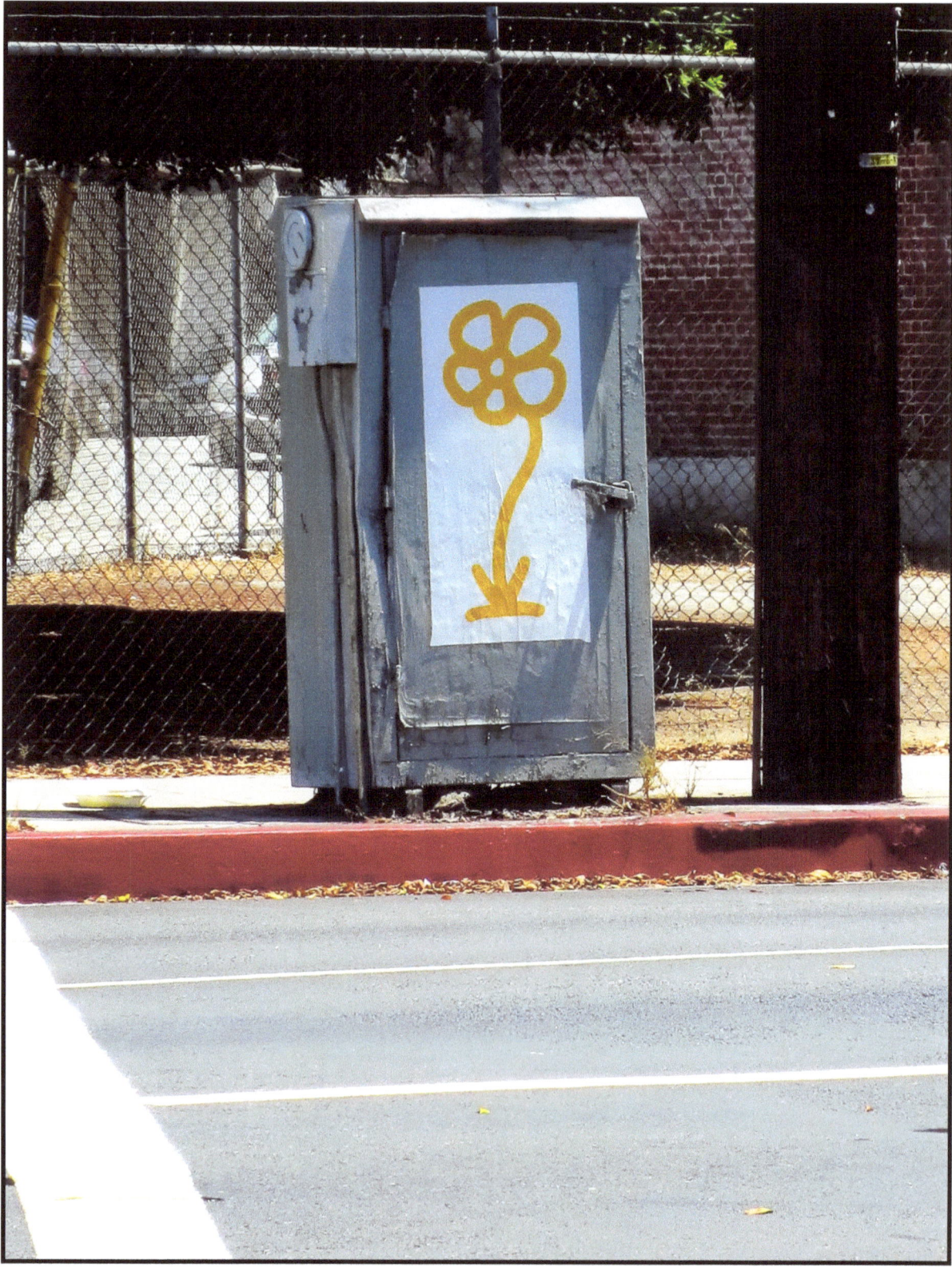

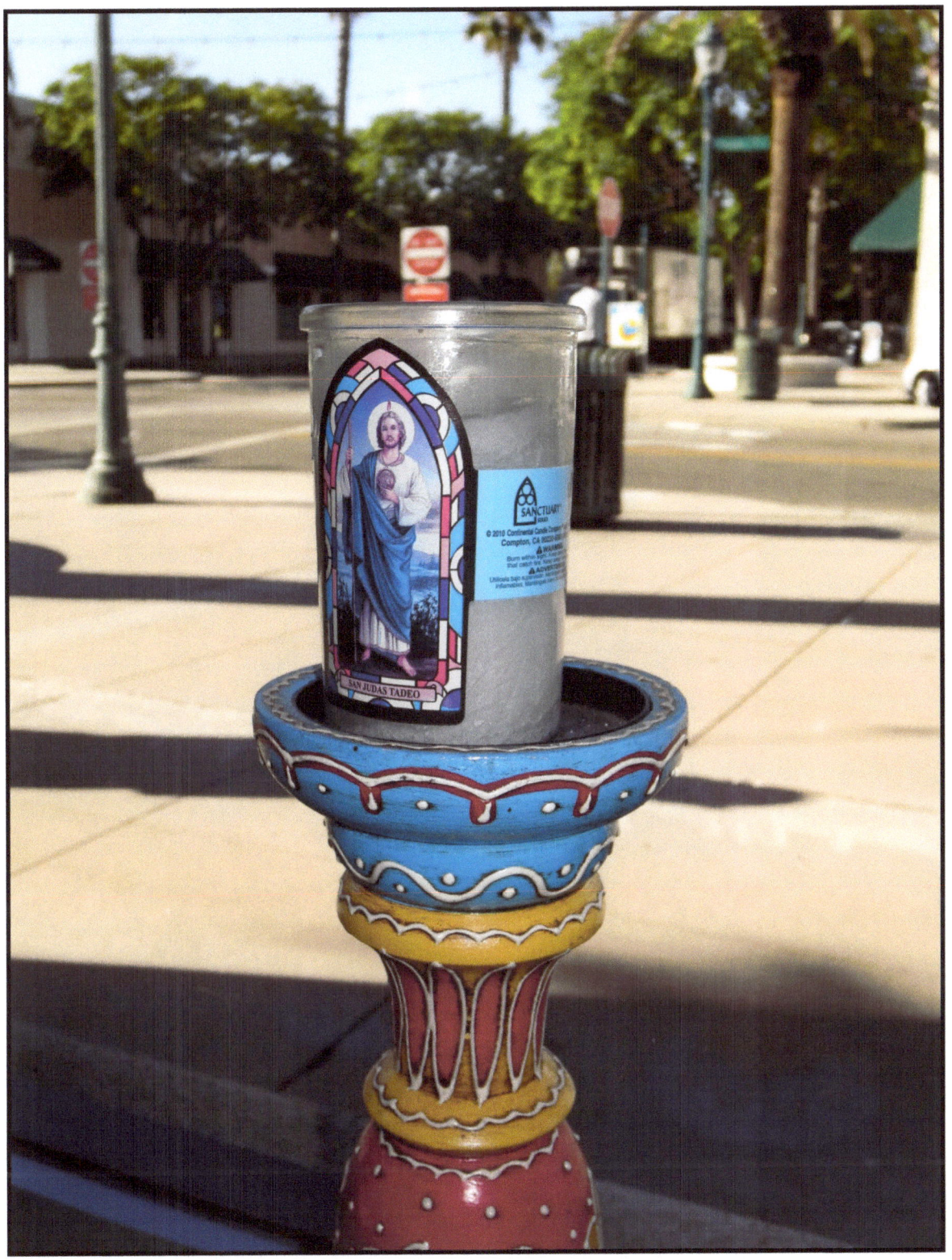

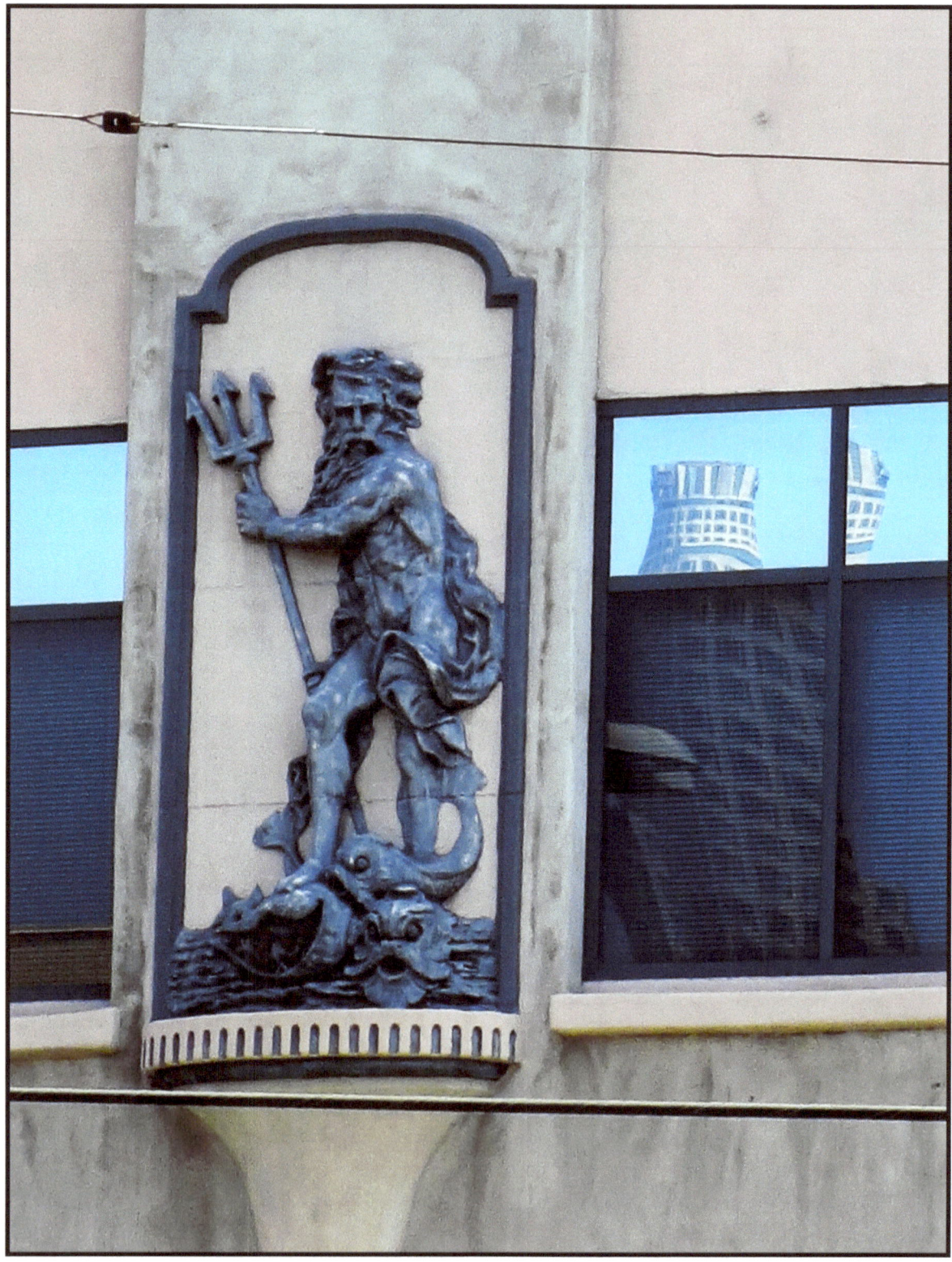

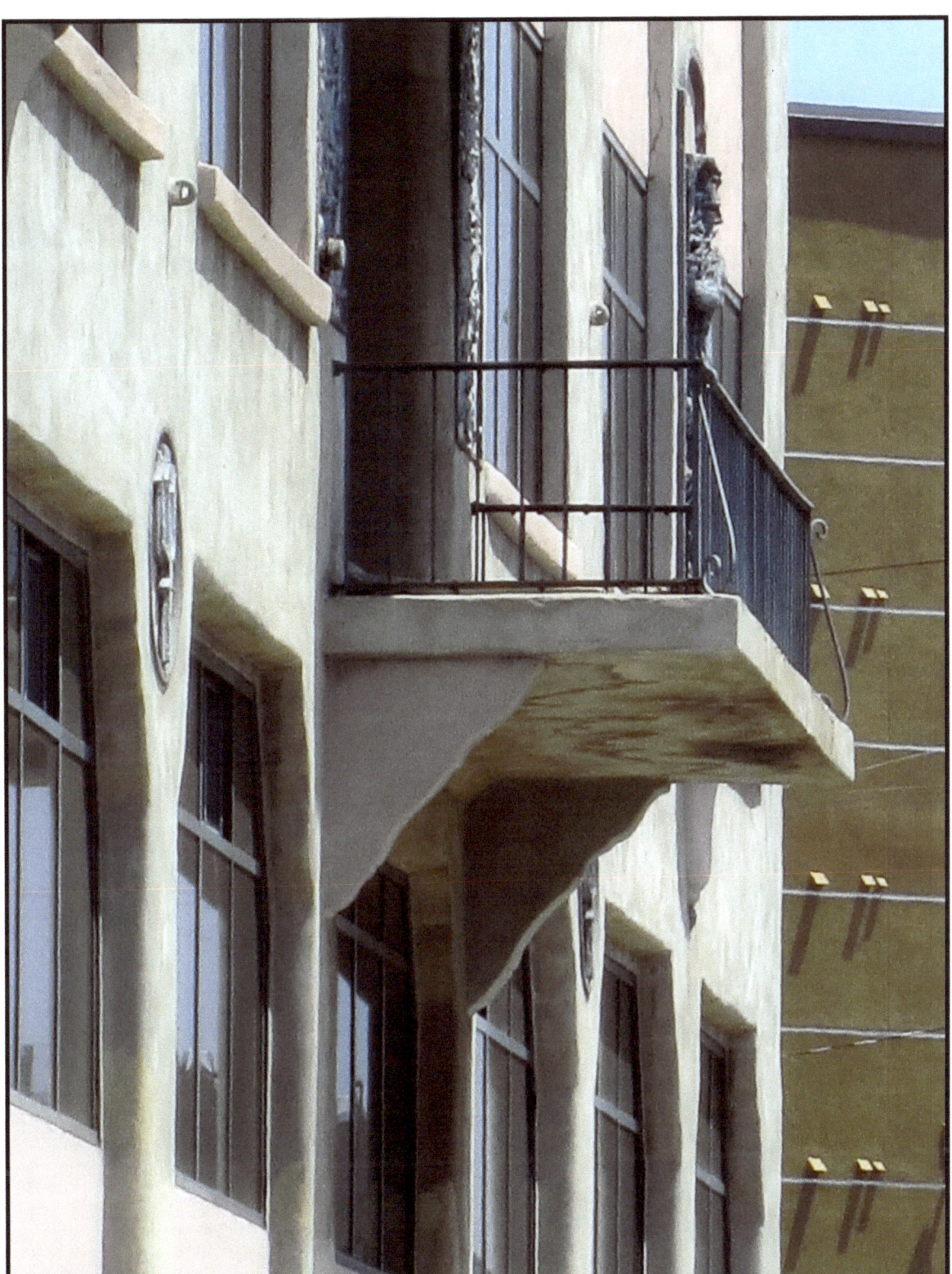

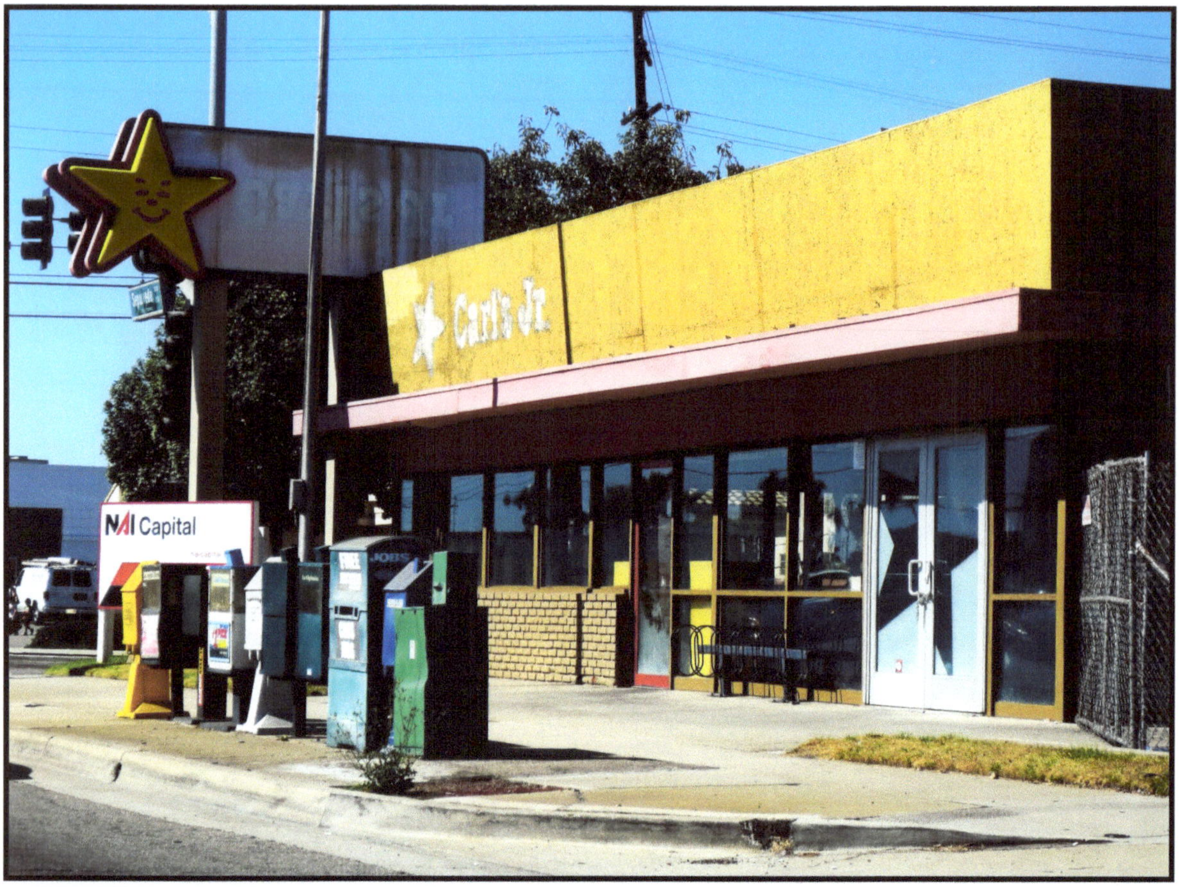

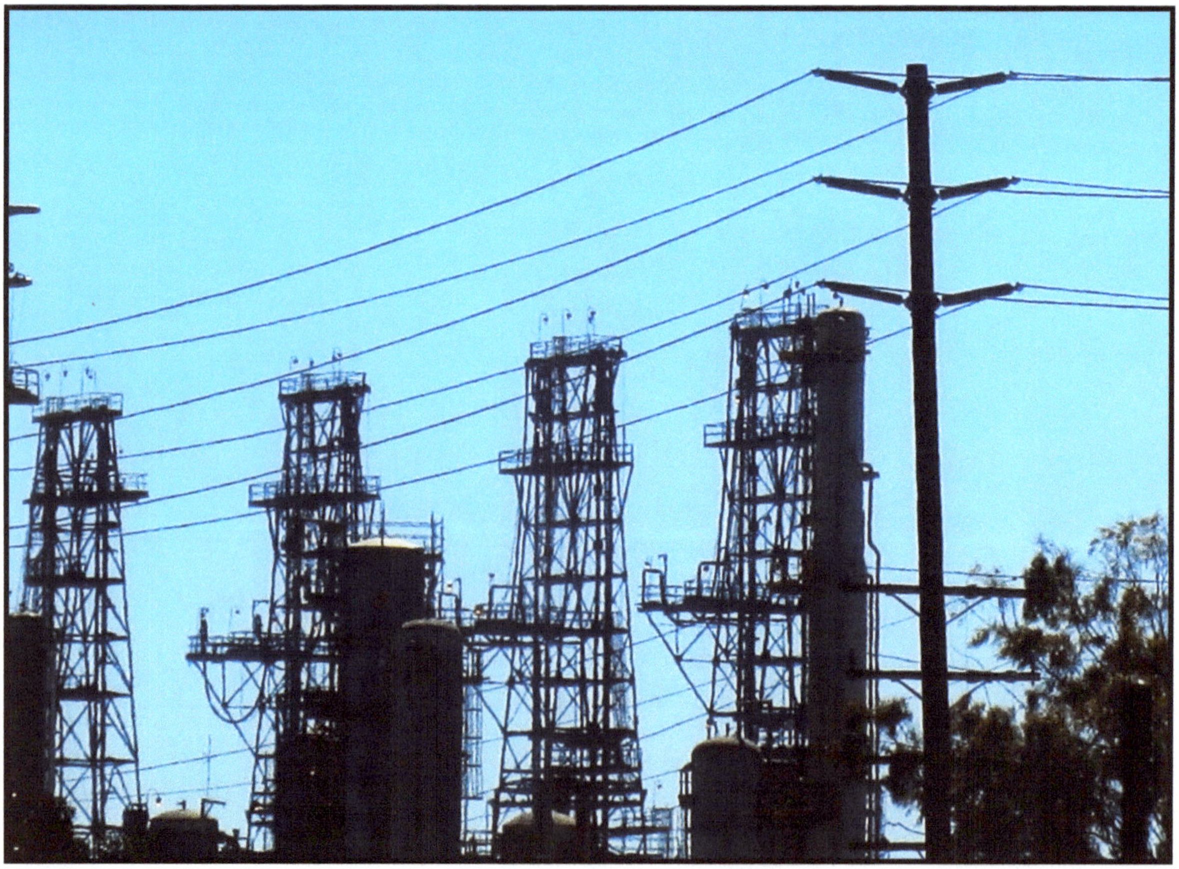

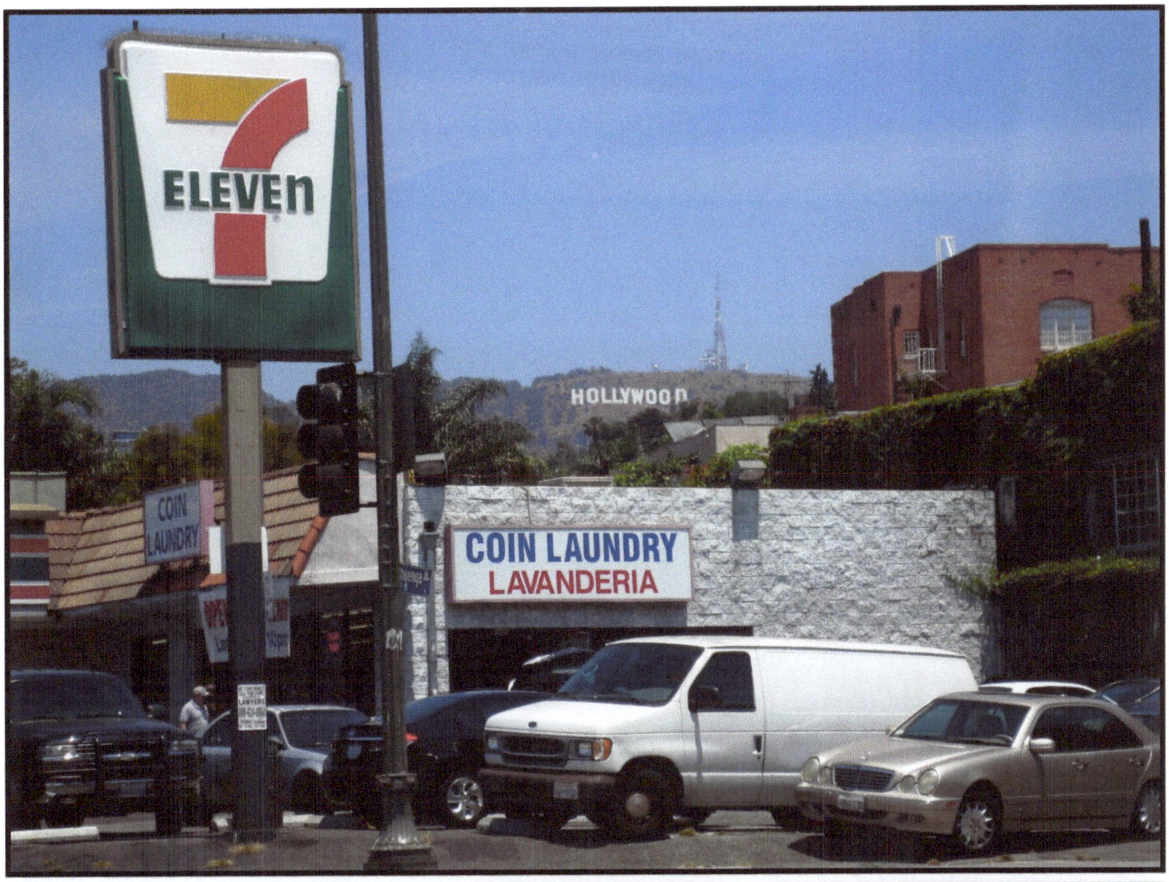

COIN LAUNDRY
COIN LAUNDRY
LAVANDERIA
HOLLYWOOD

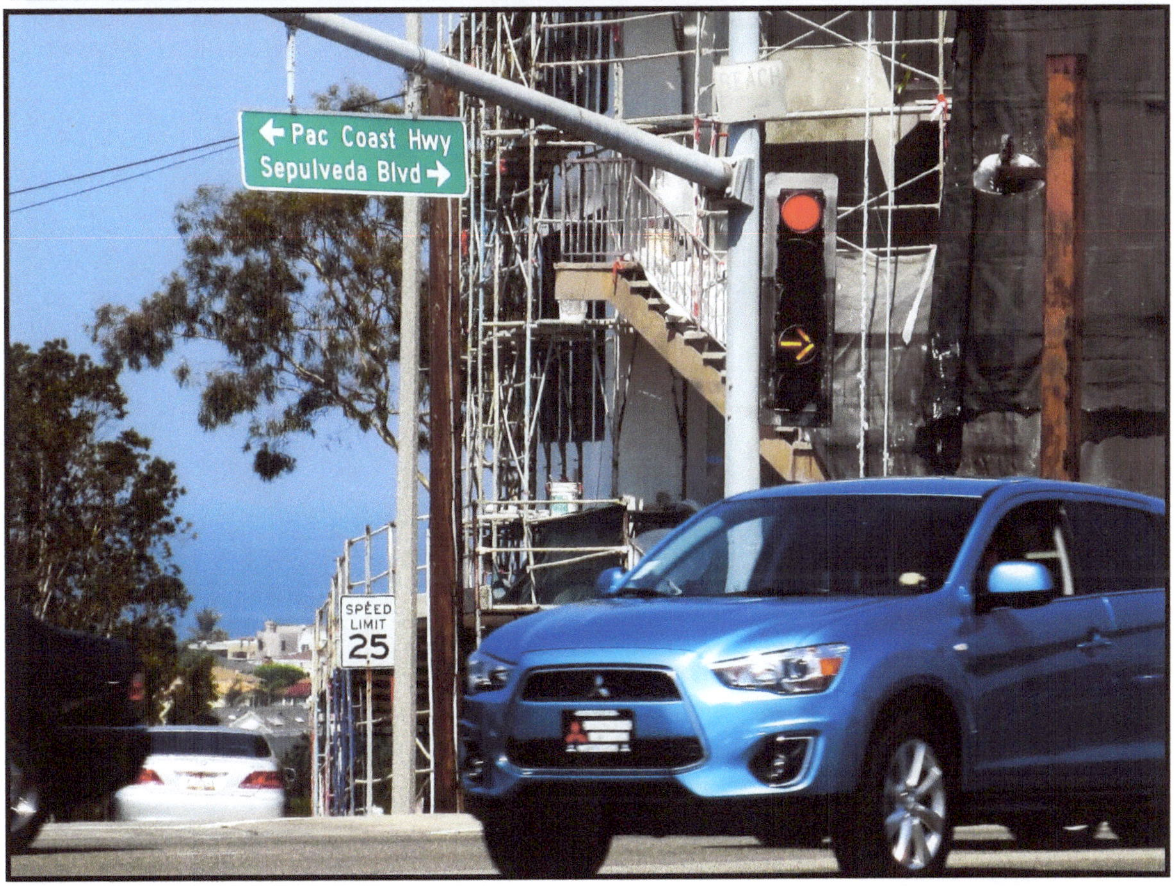

← Pac Coast Hwy
Sepulveda Blvd →

SPEED
LIMIT
25

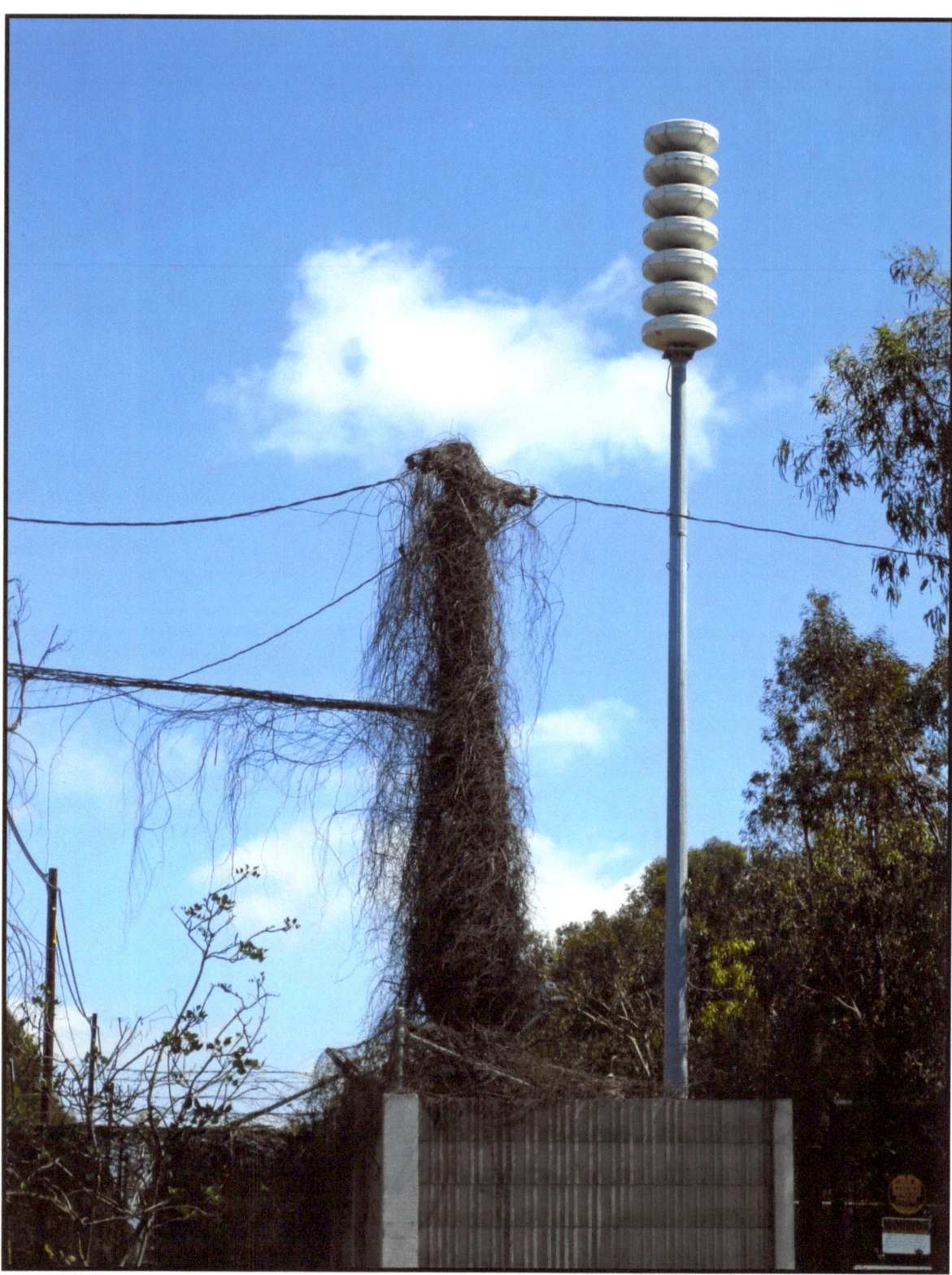

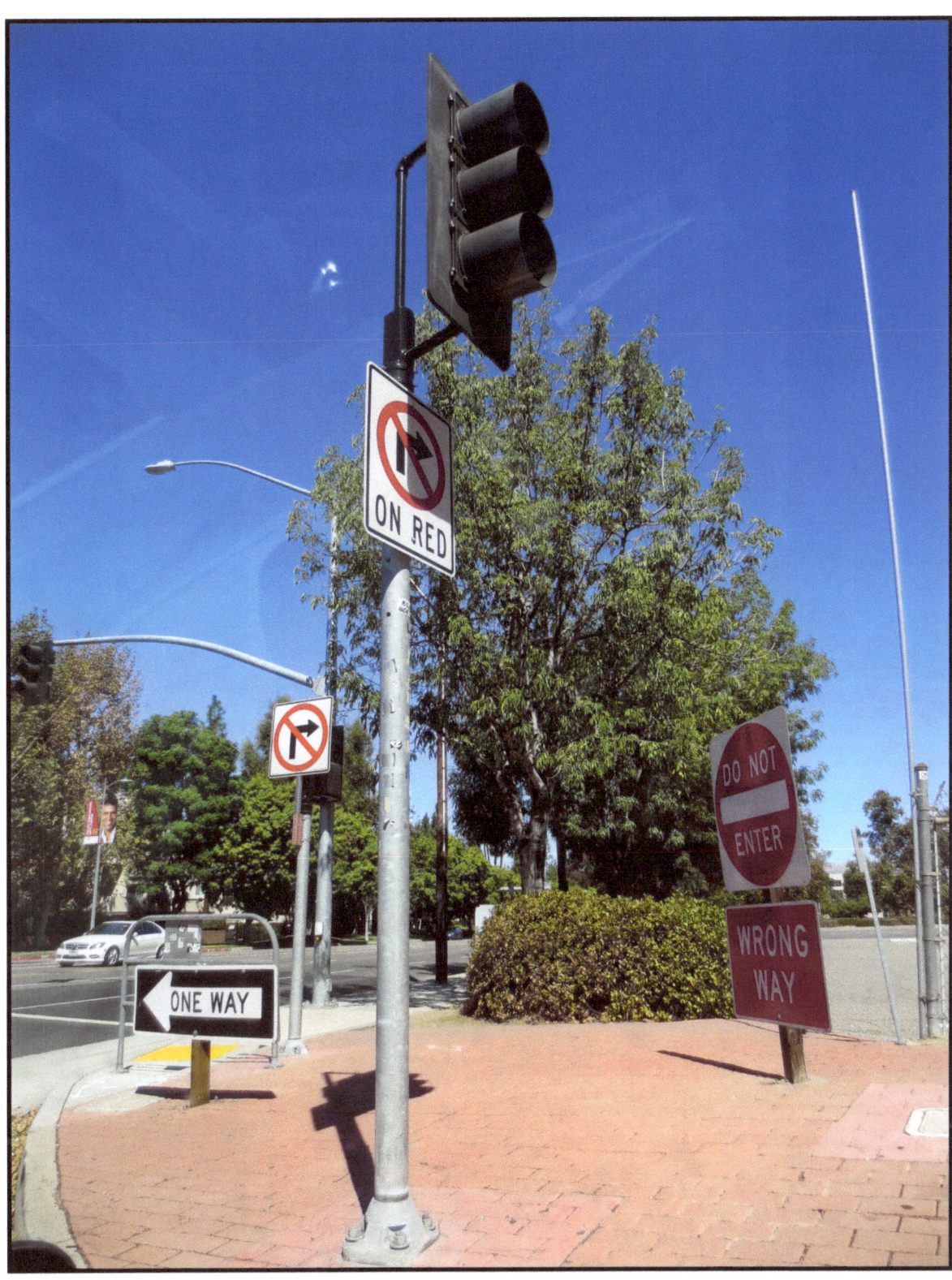

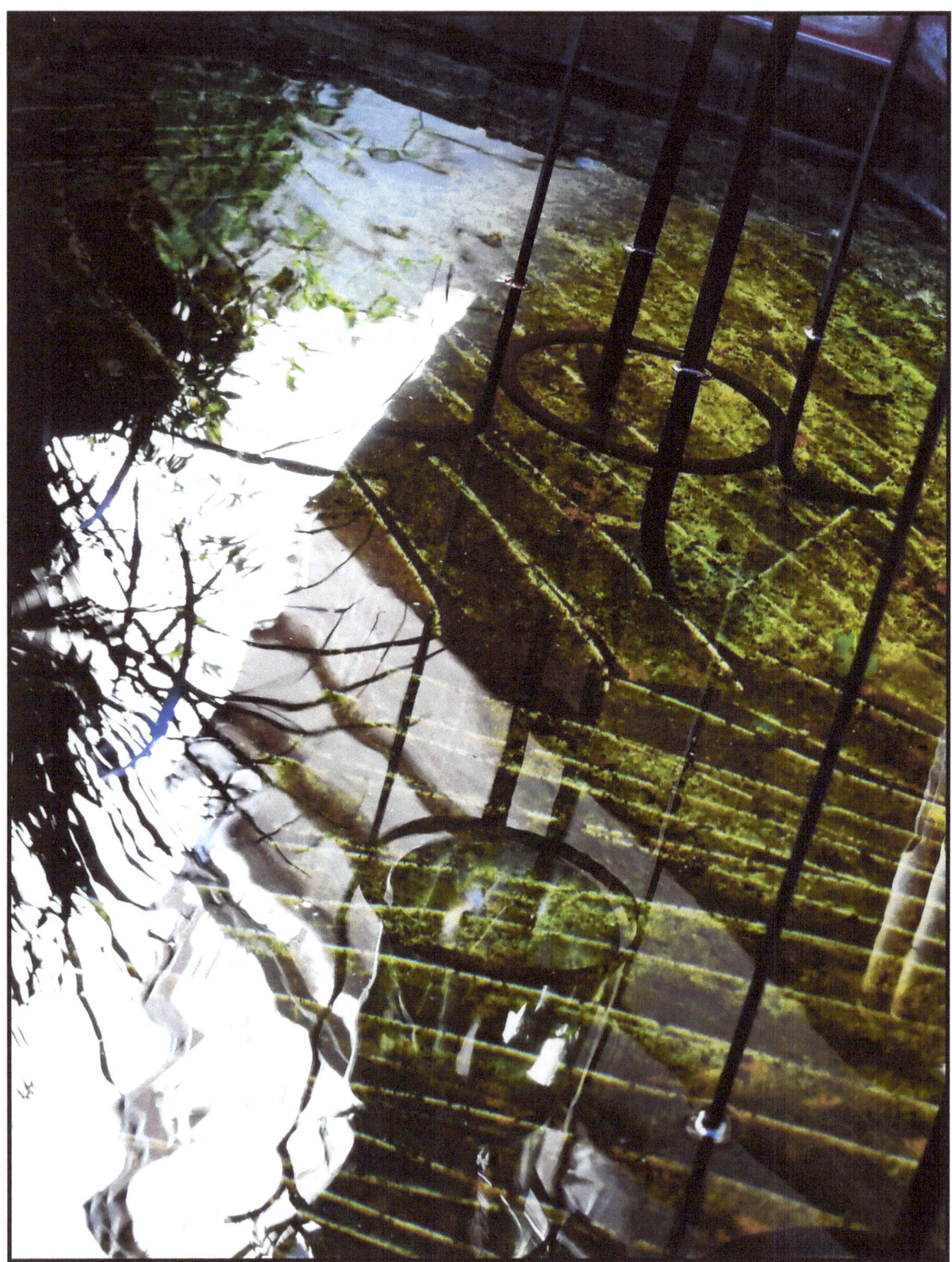

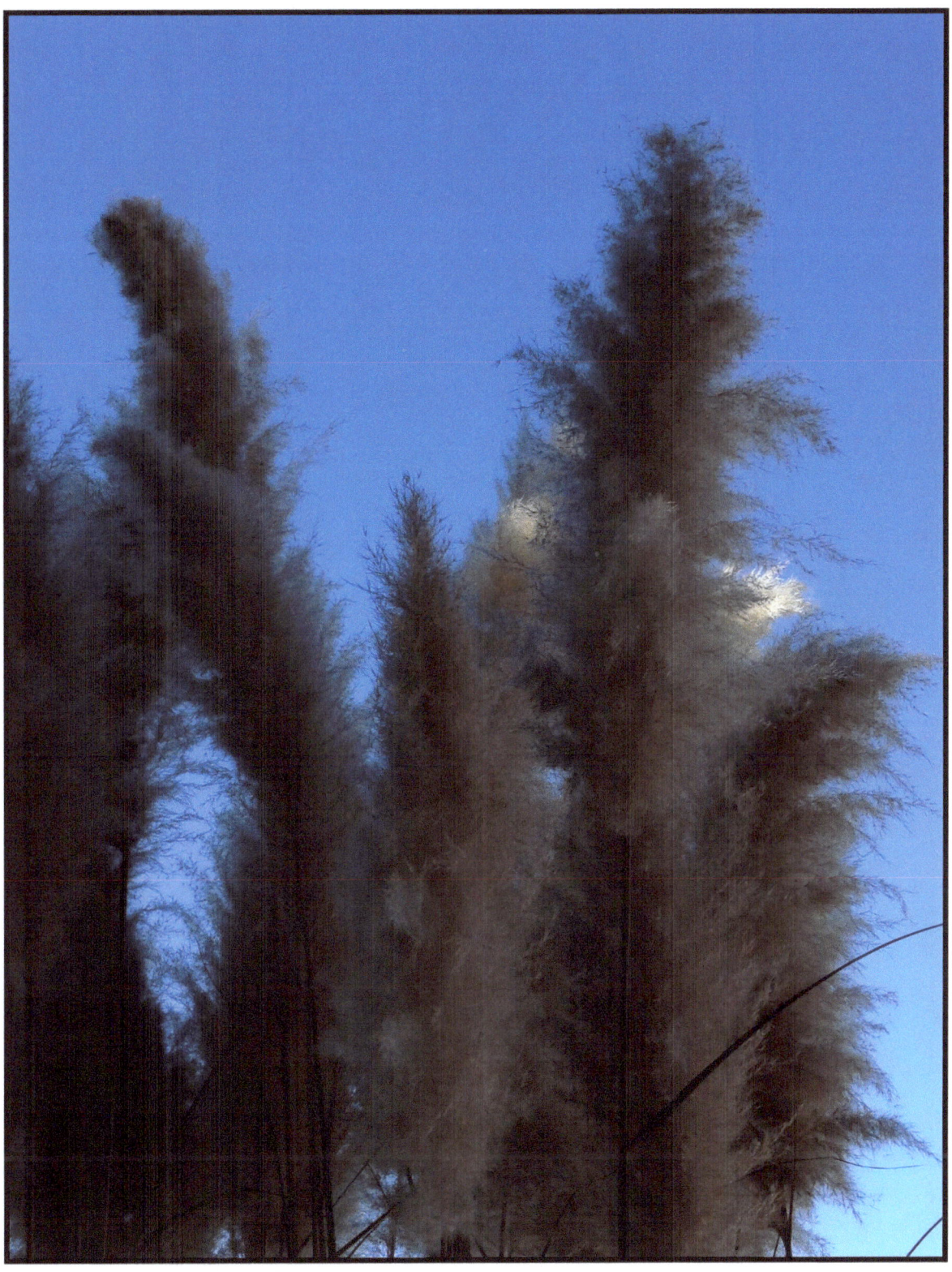

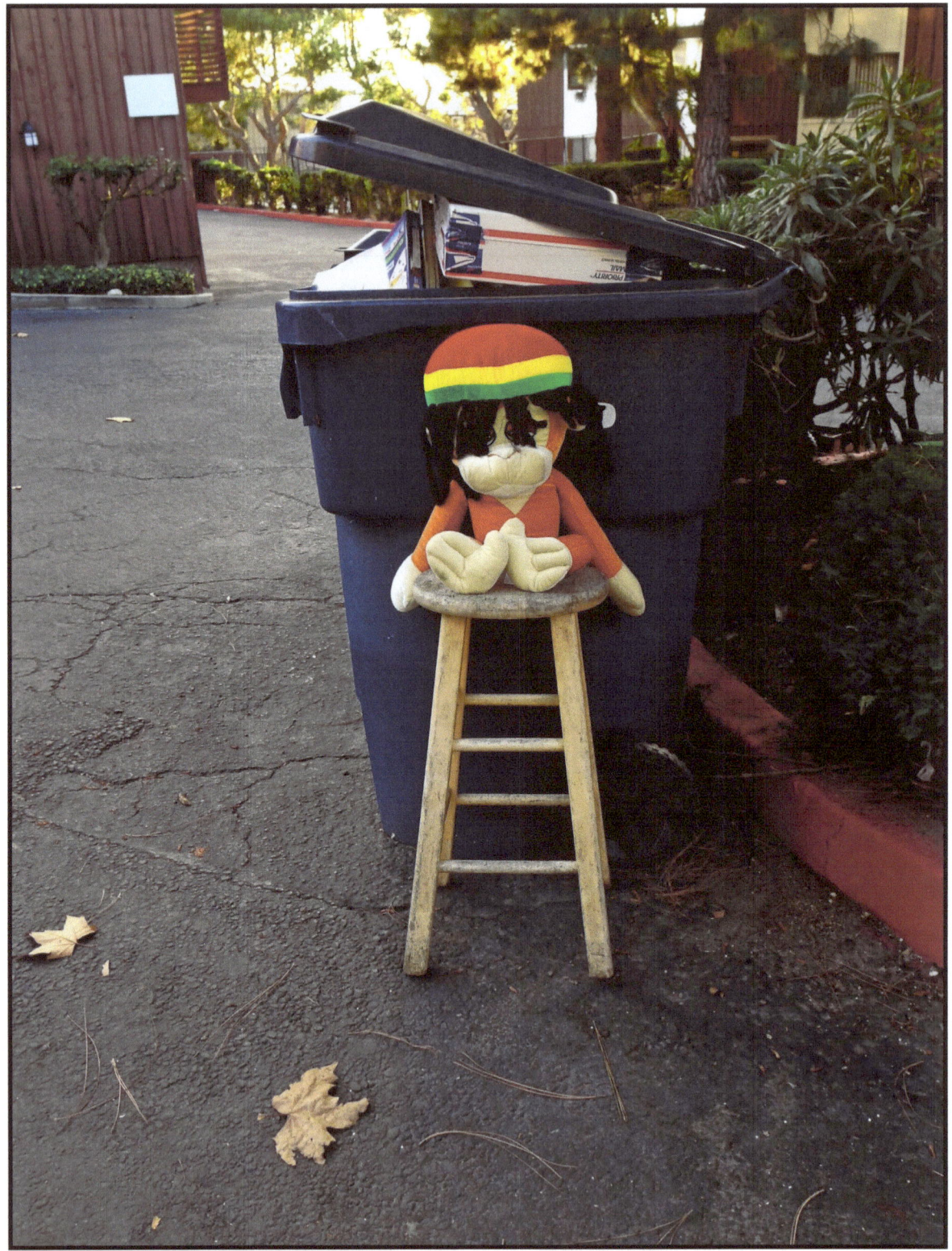

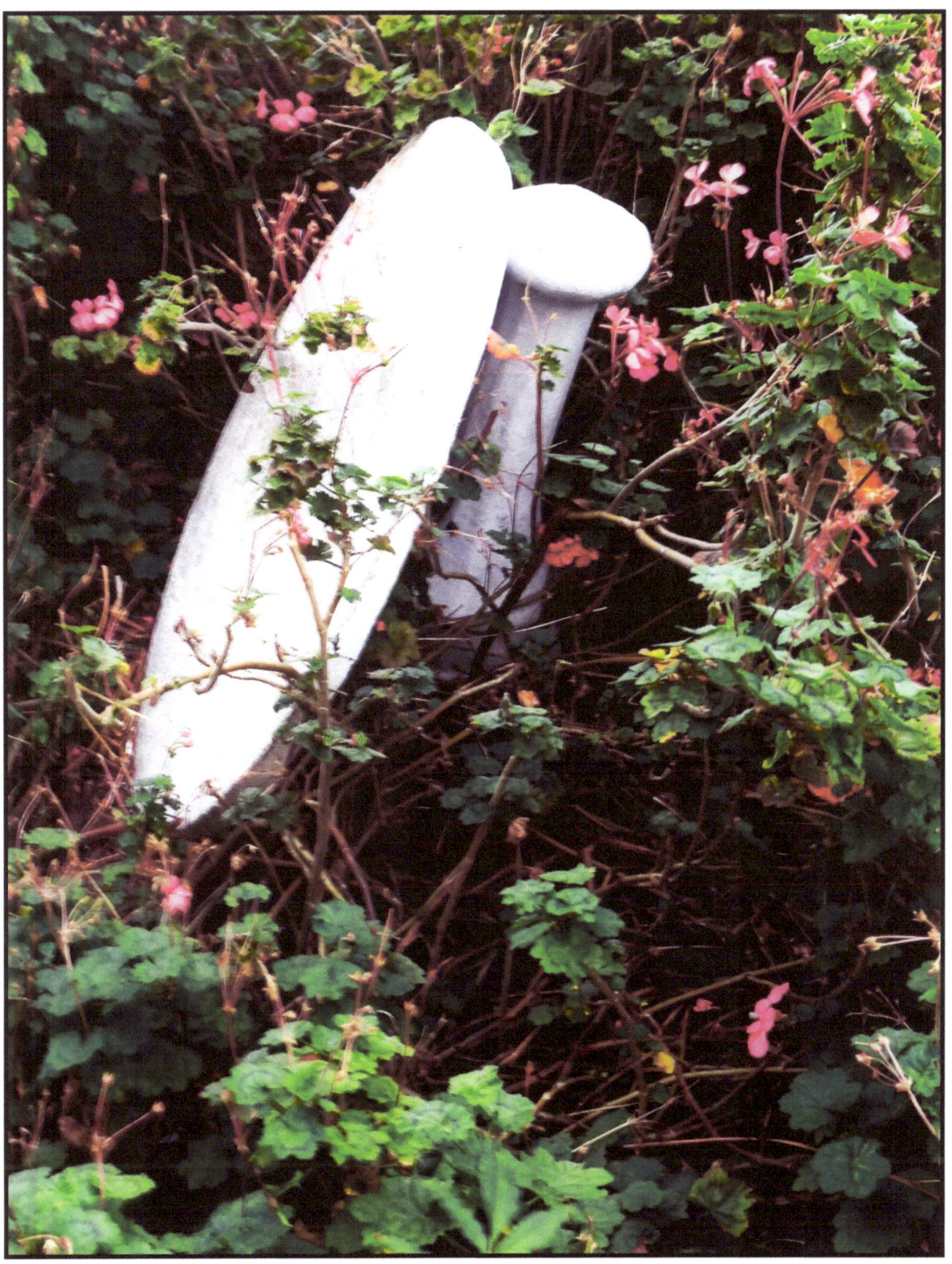

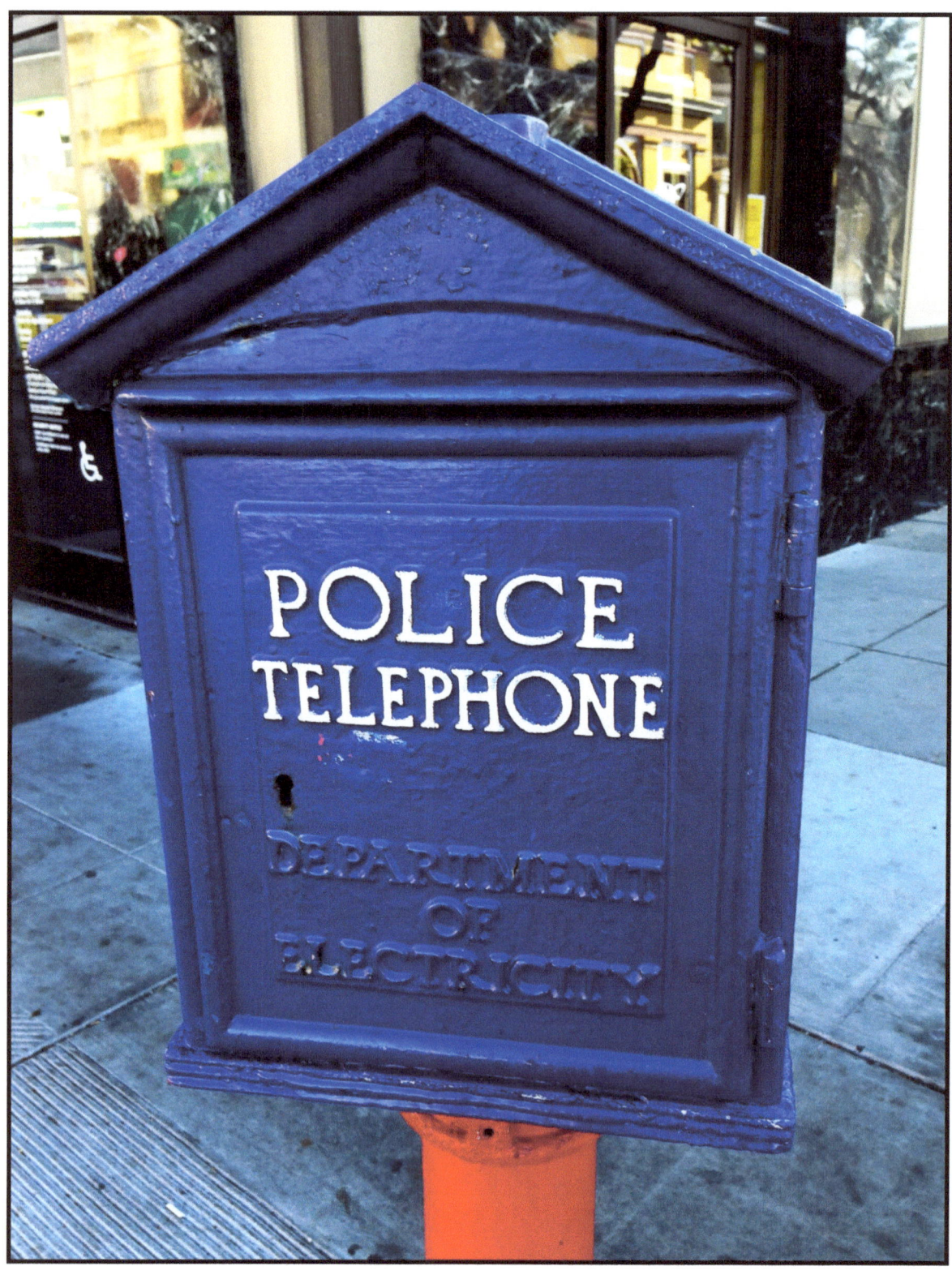

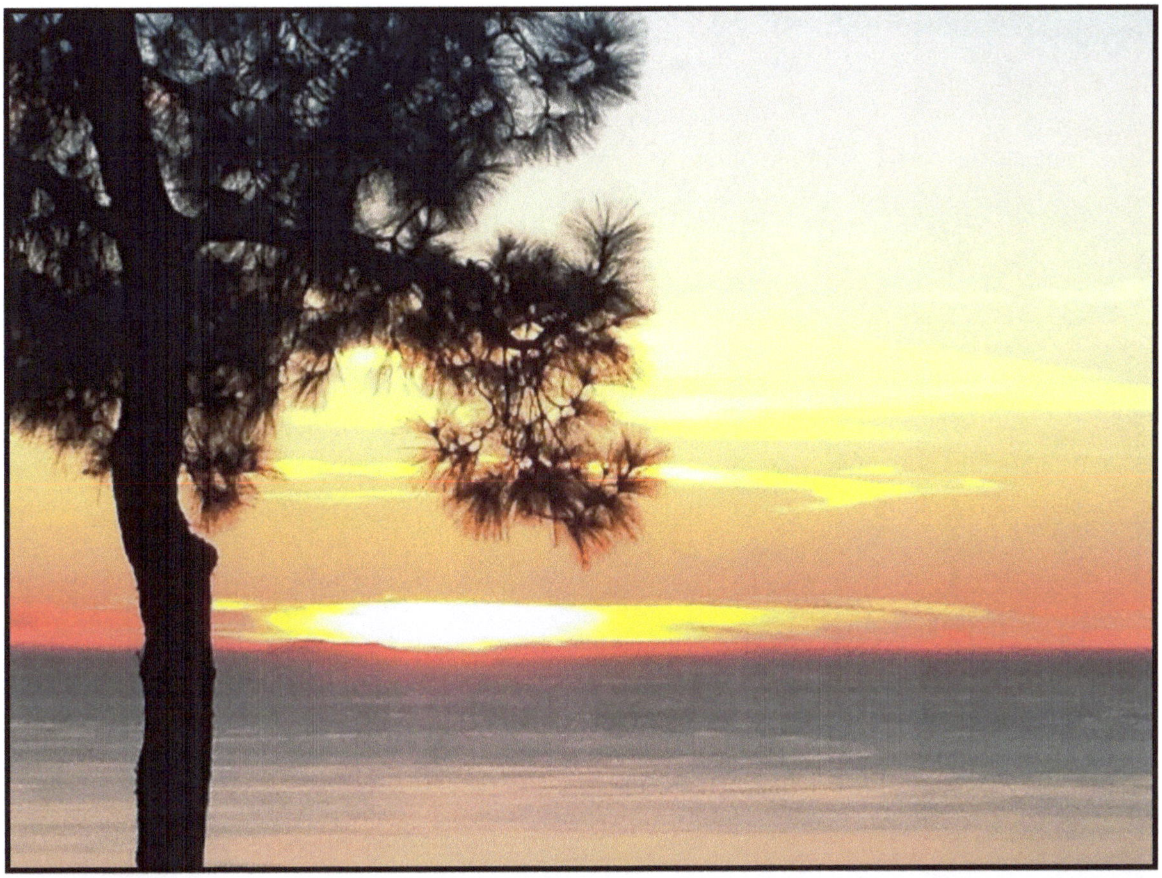

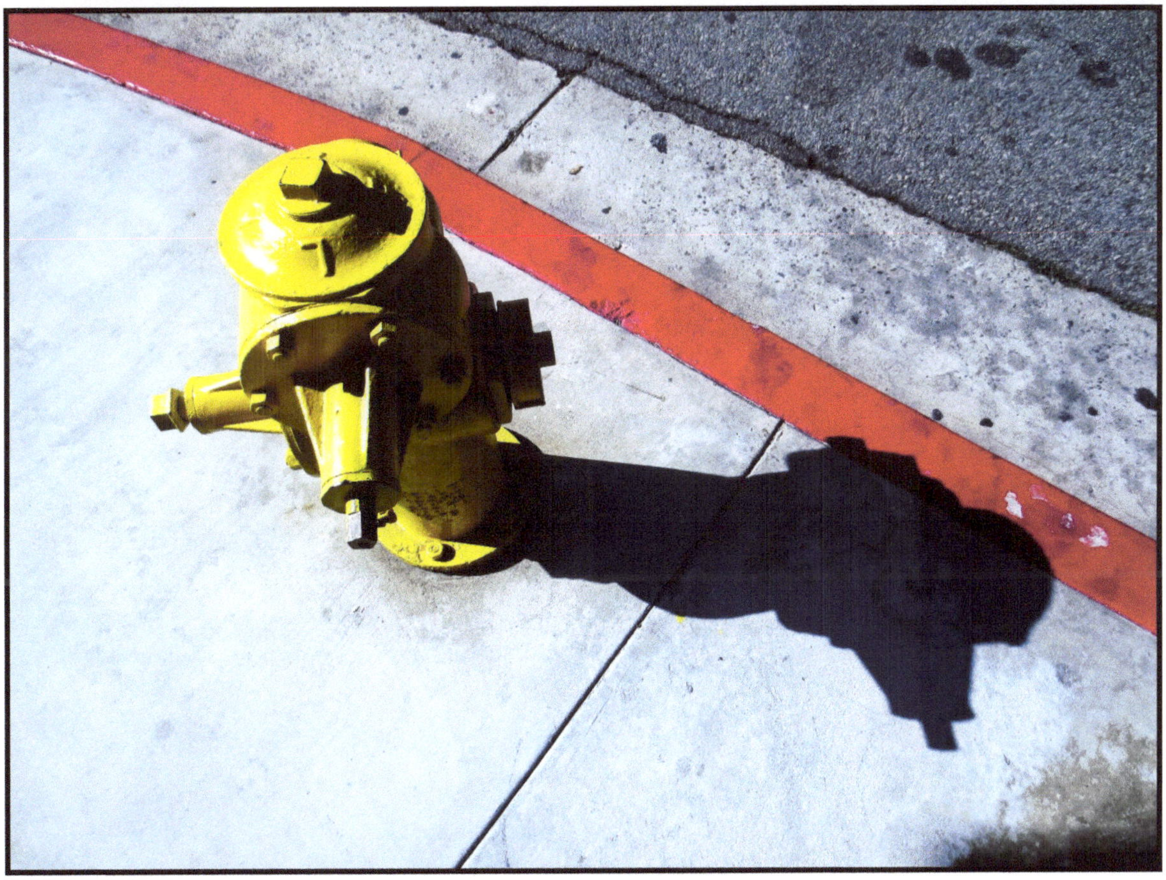

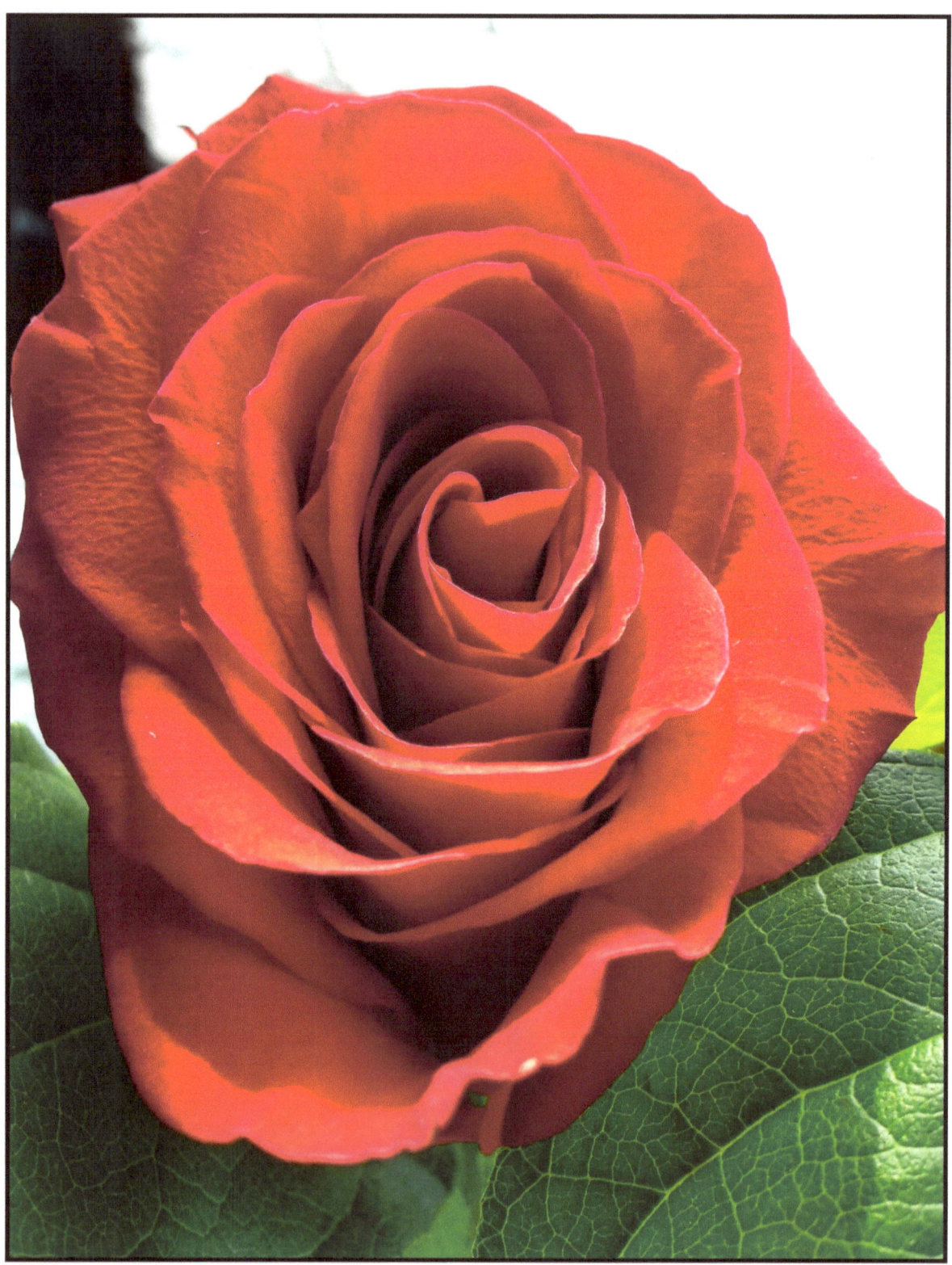

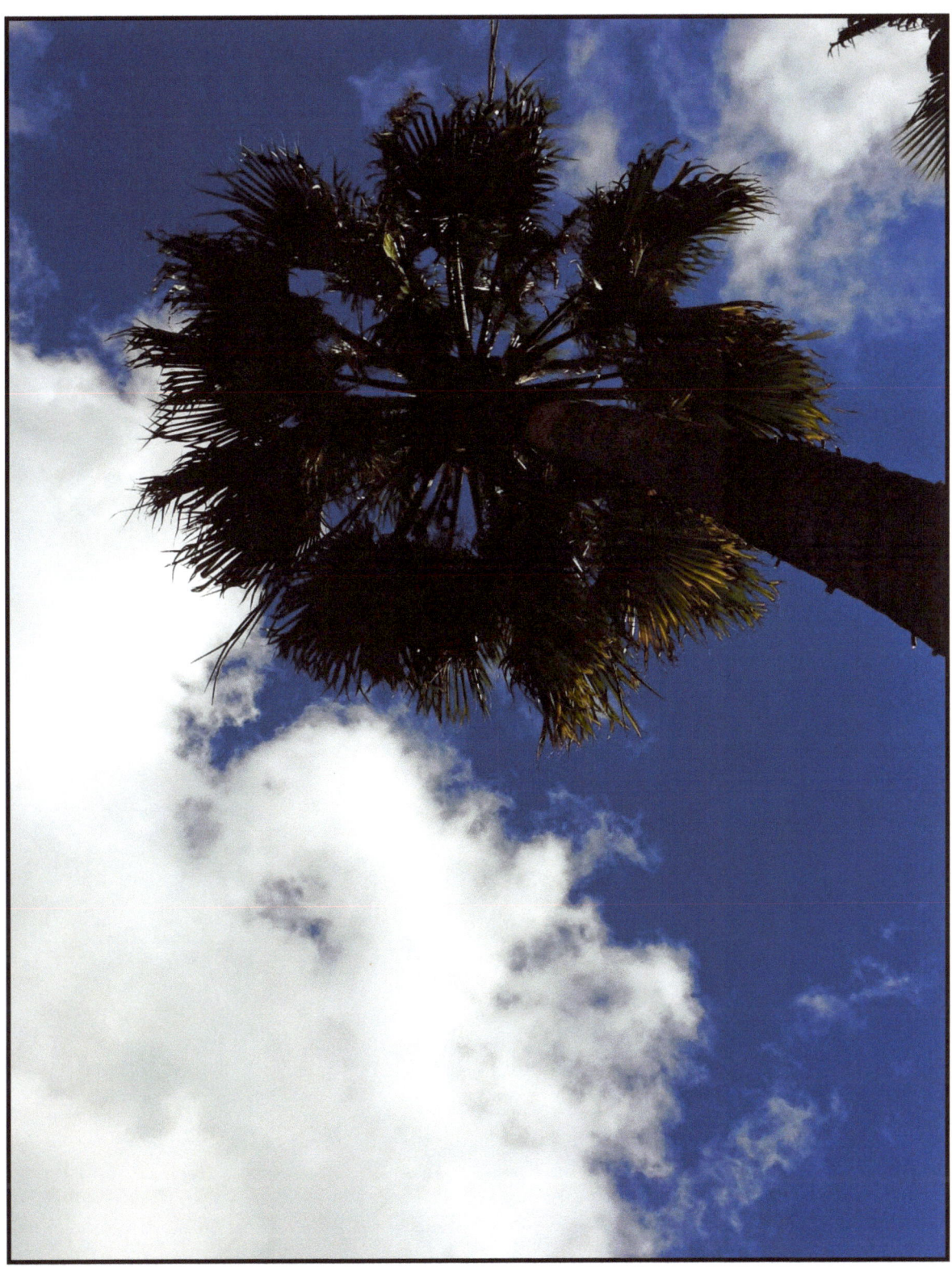

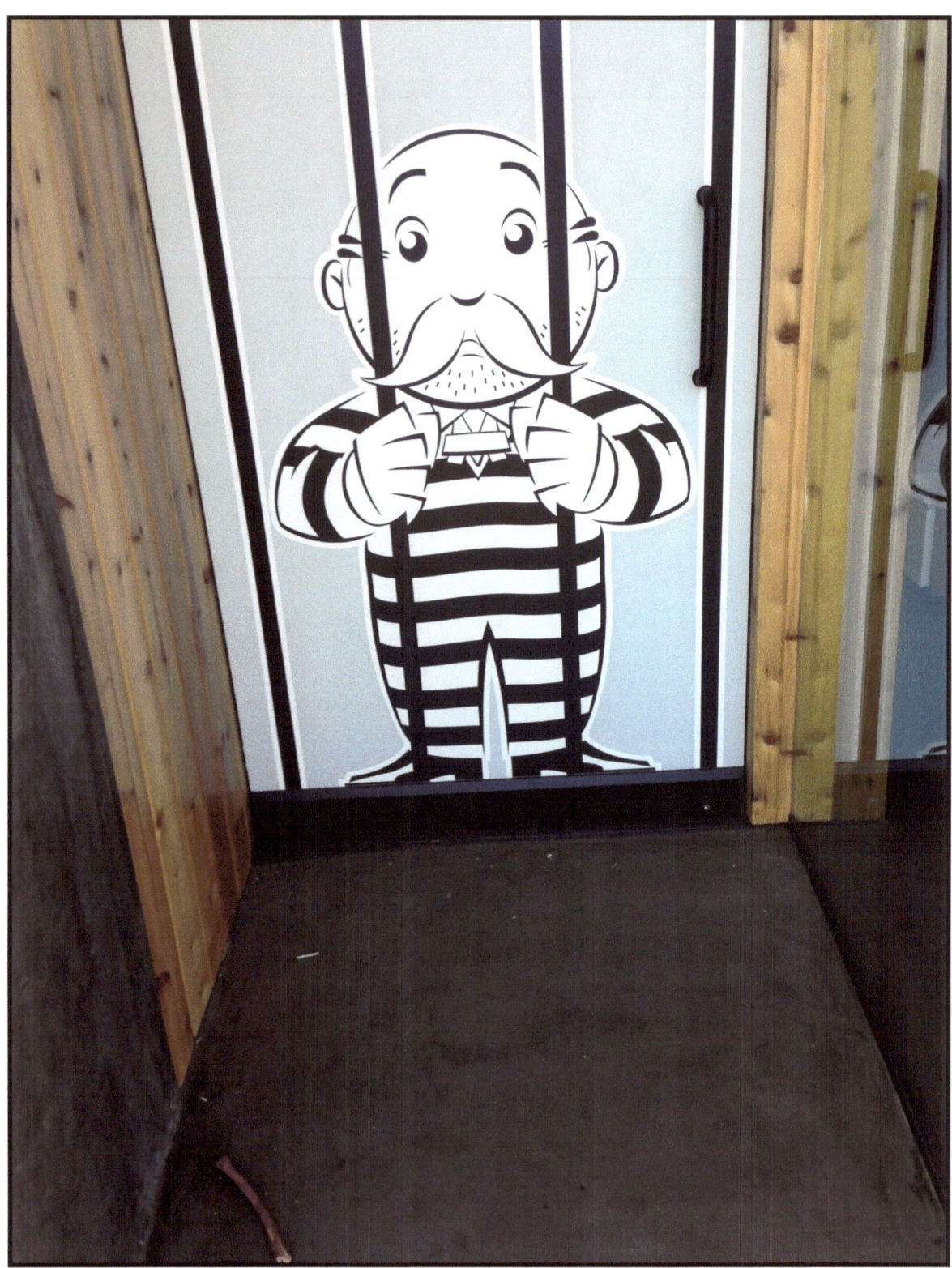

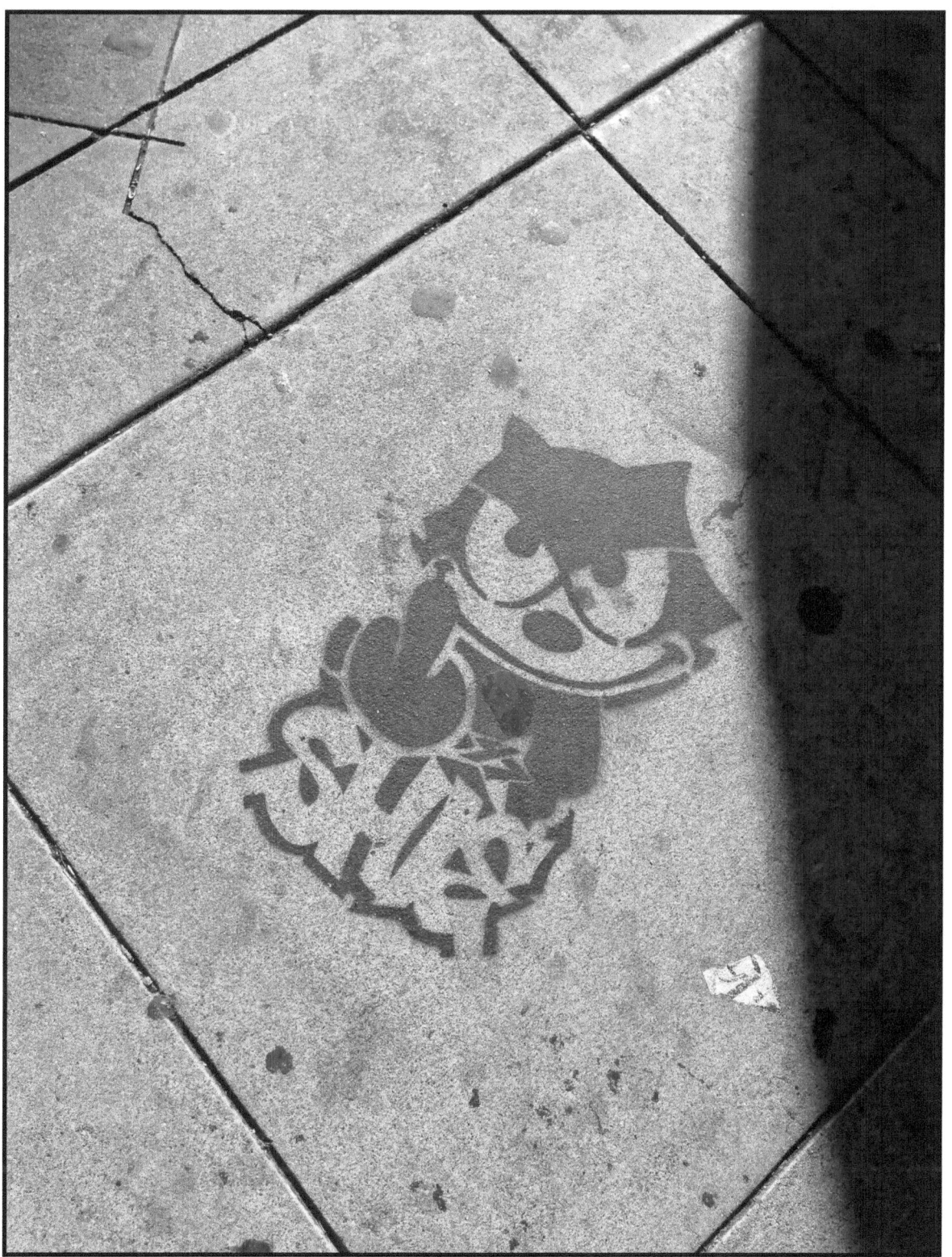

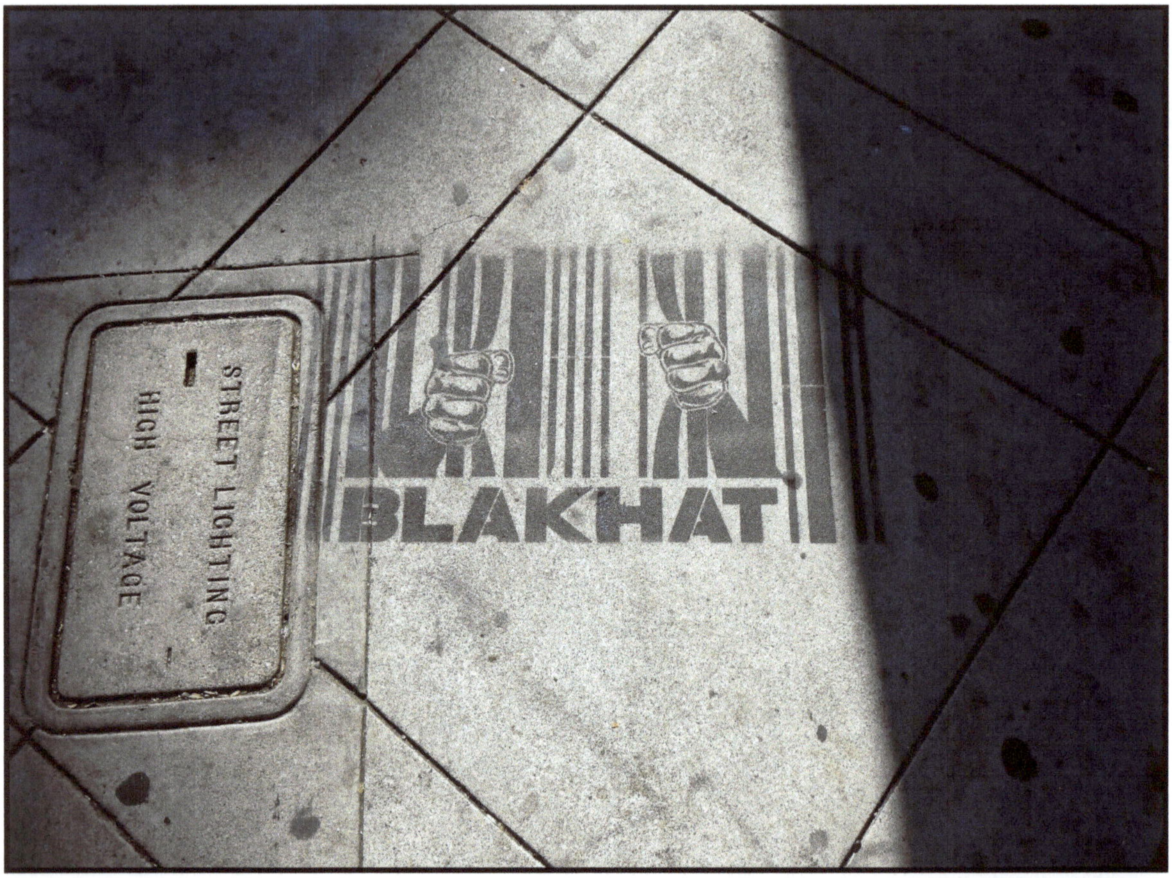

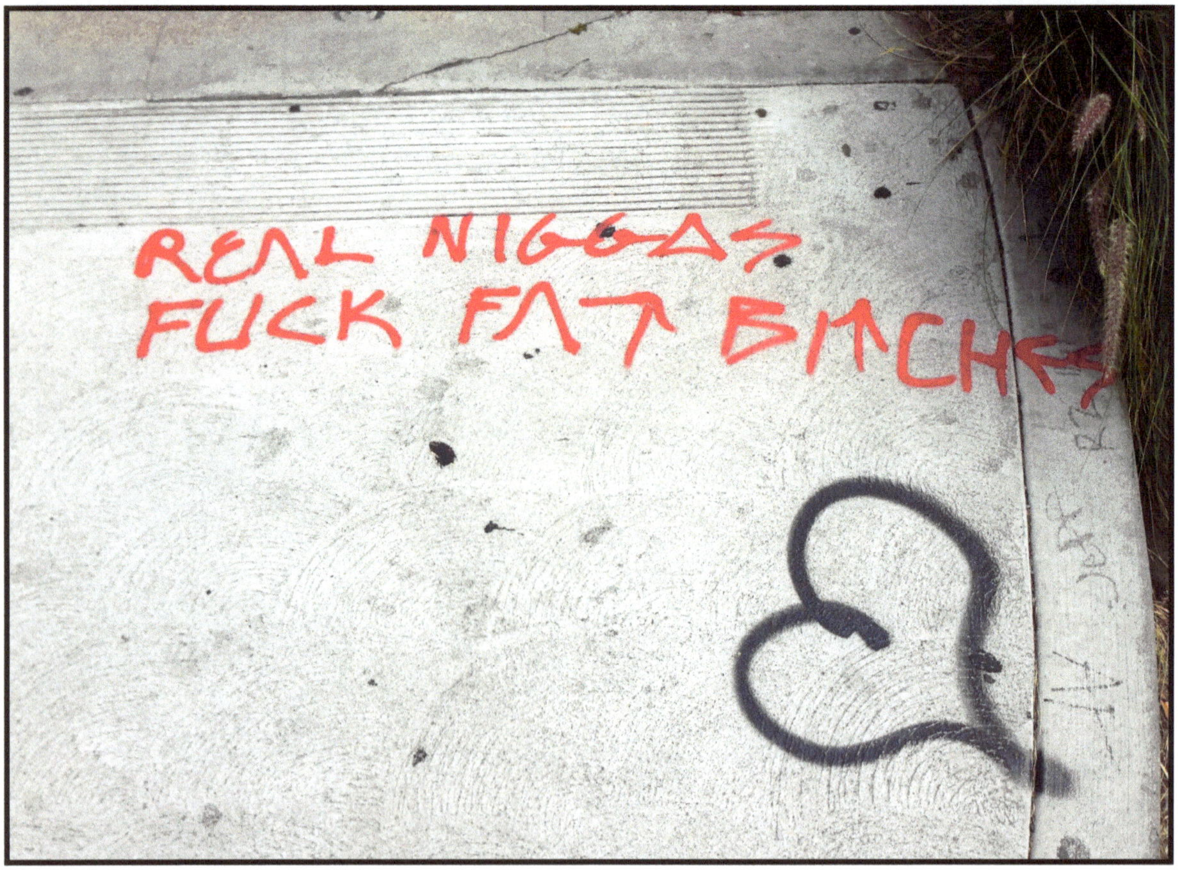

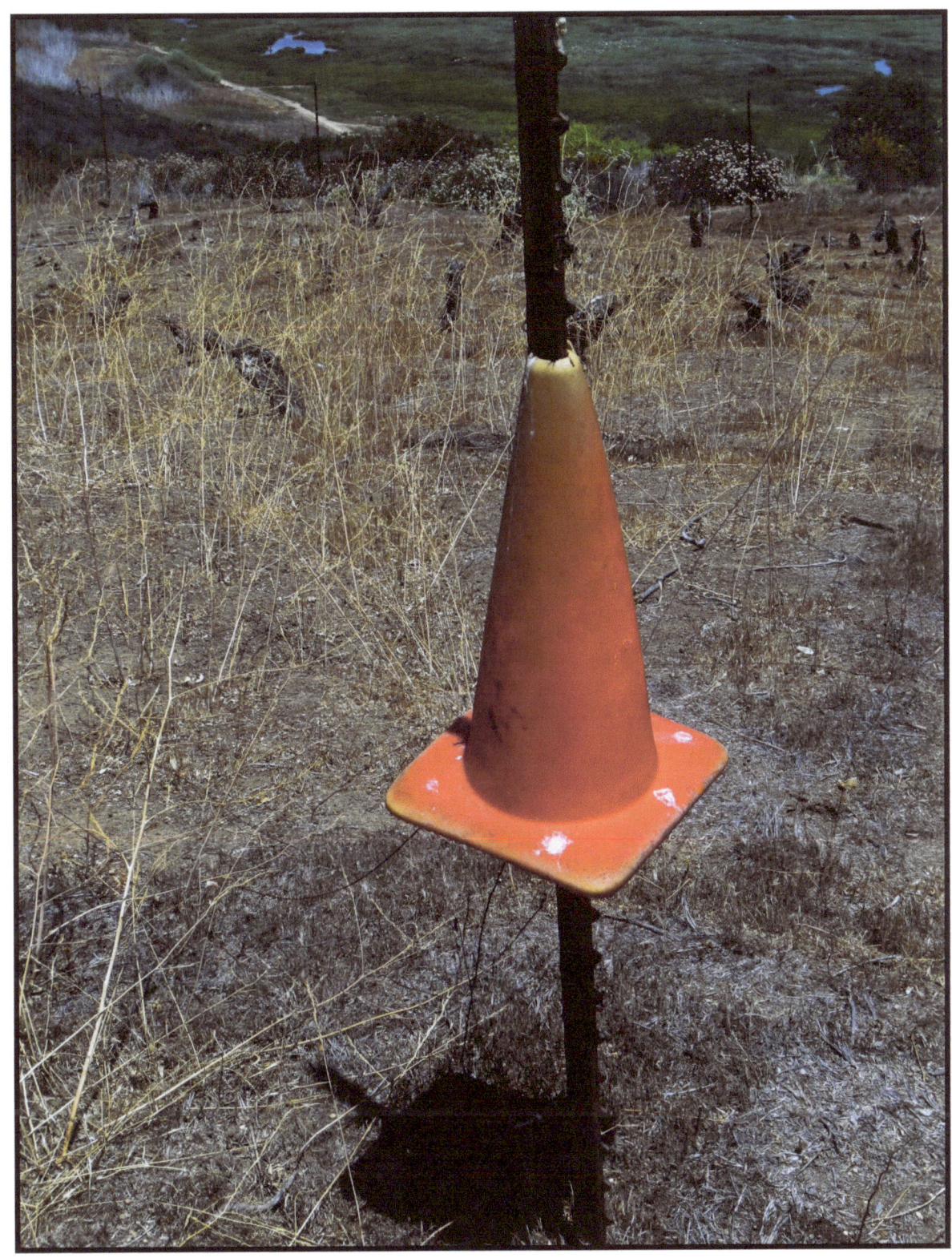

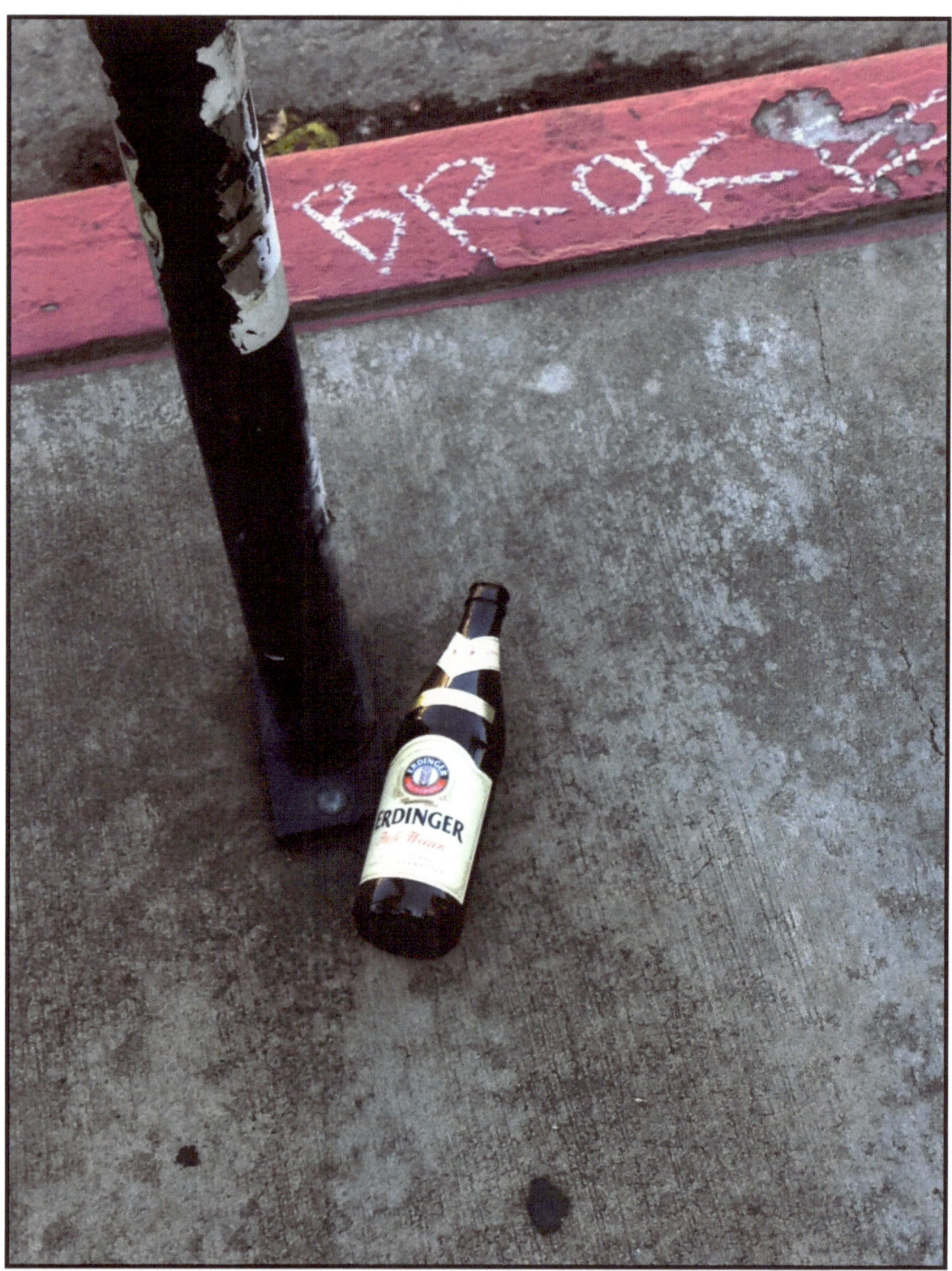

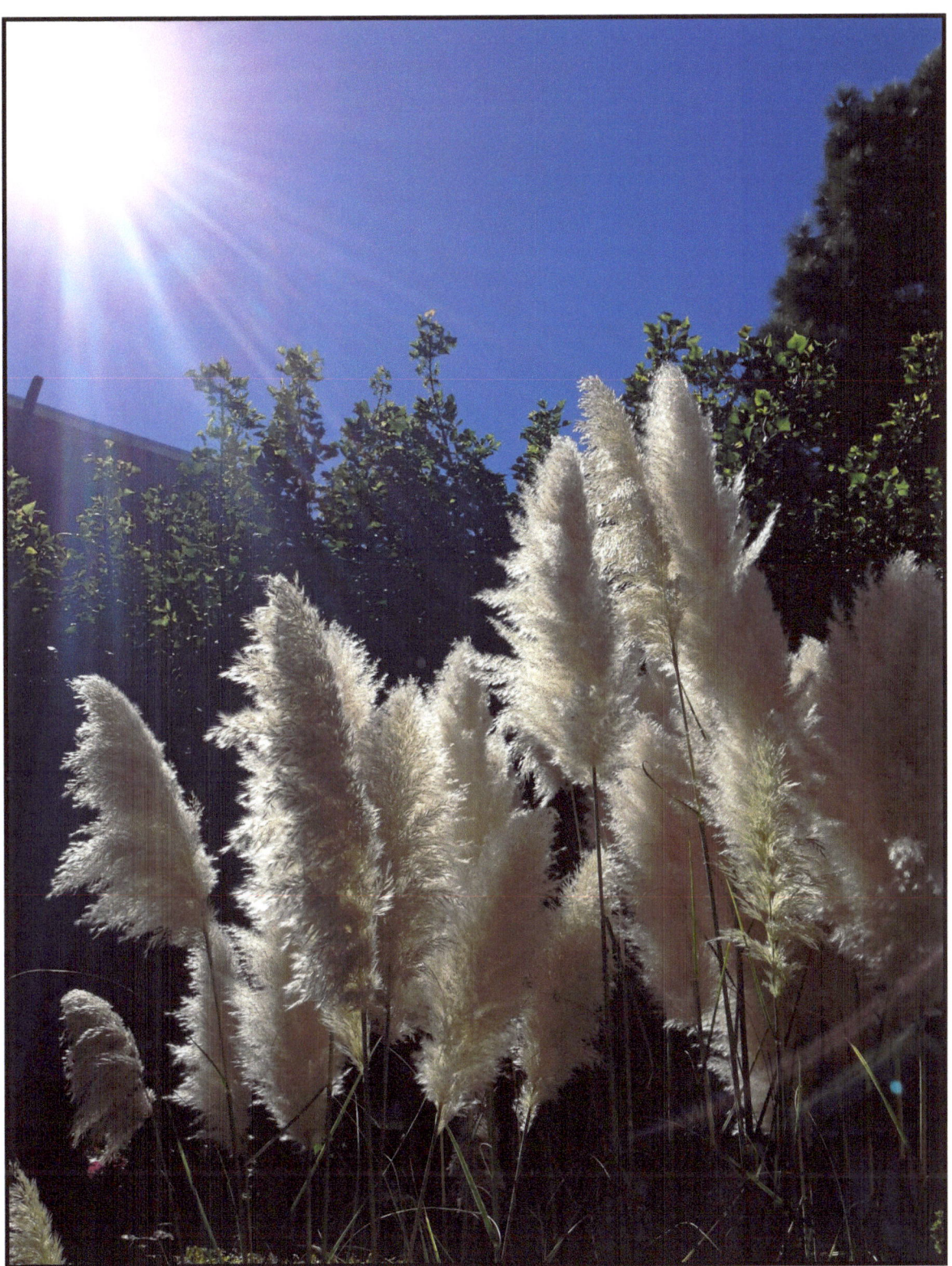

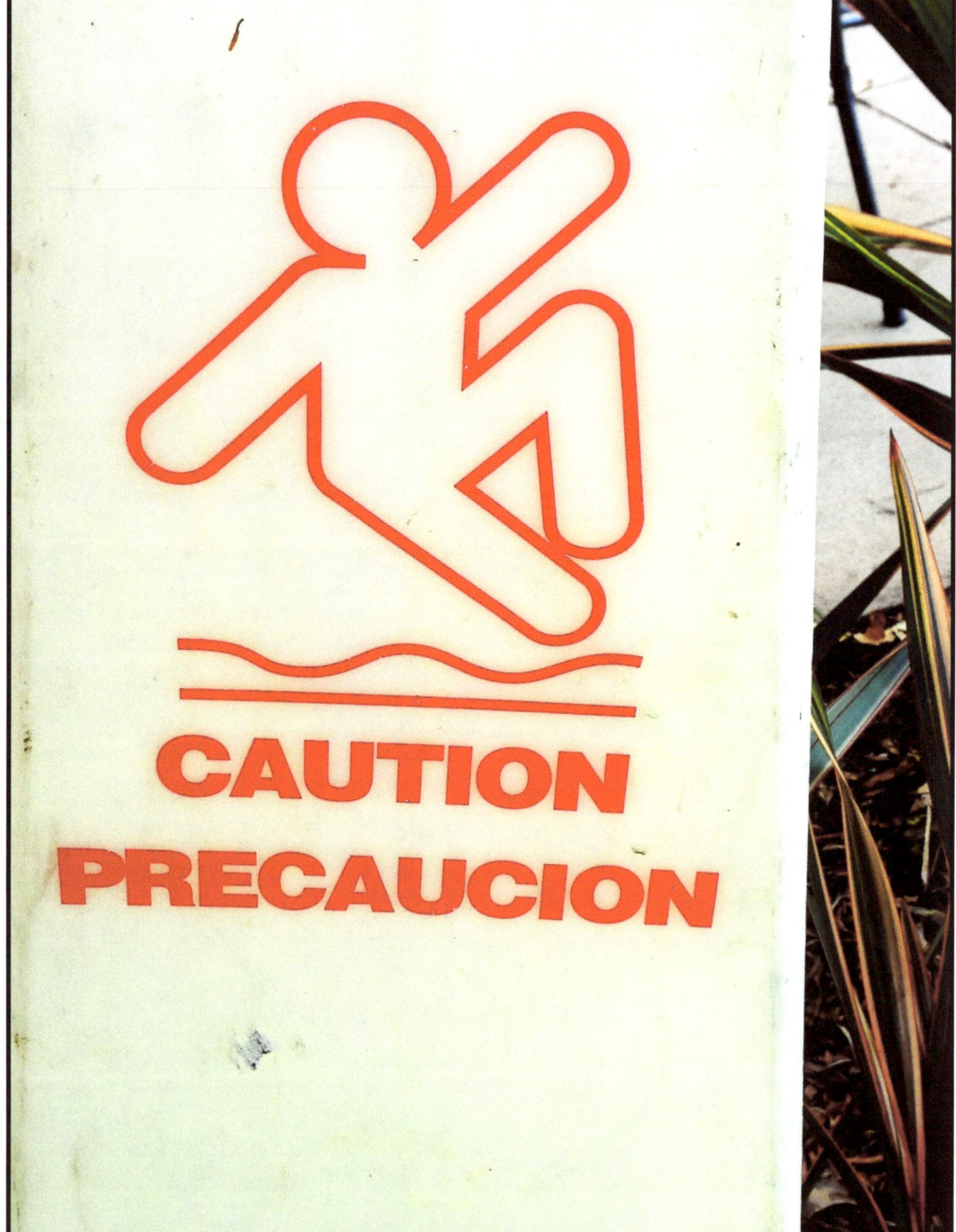

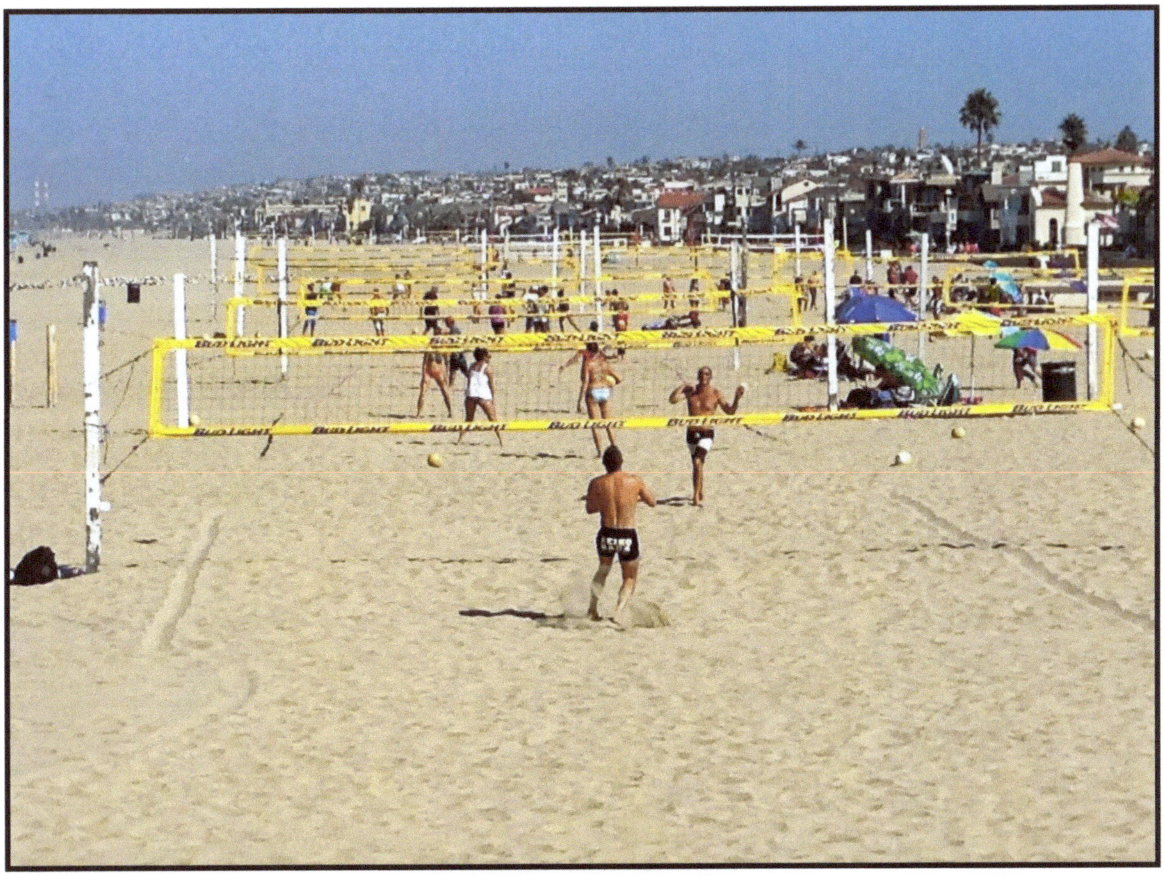

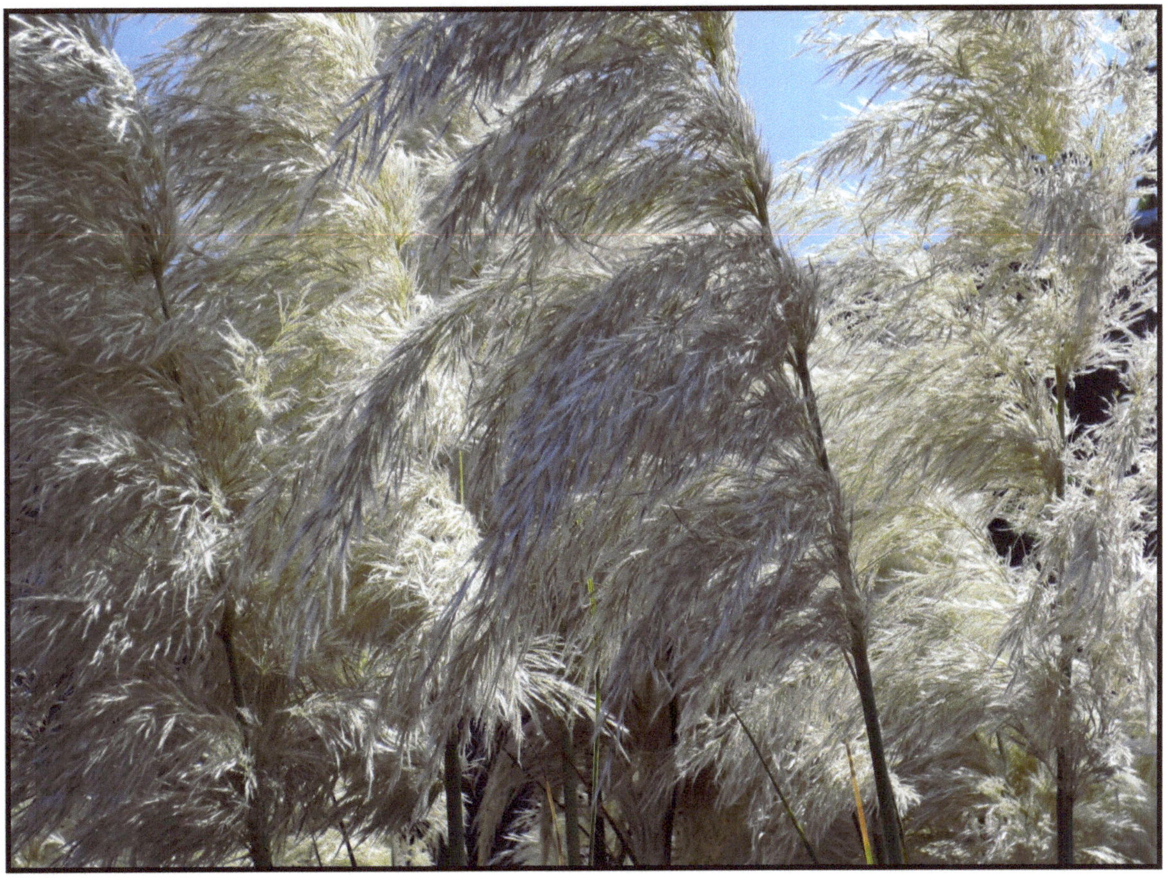

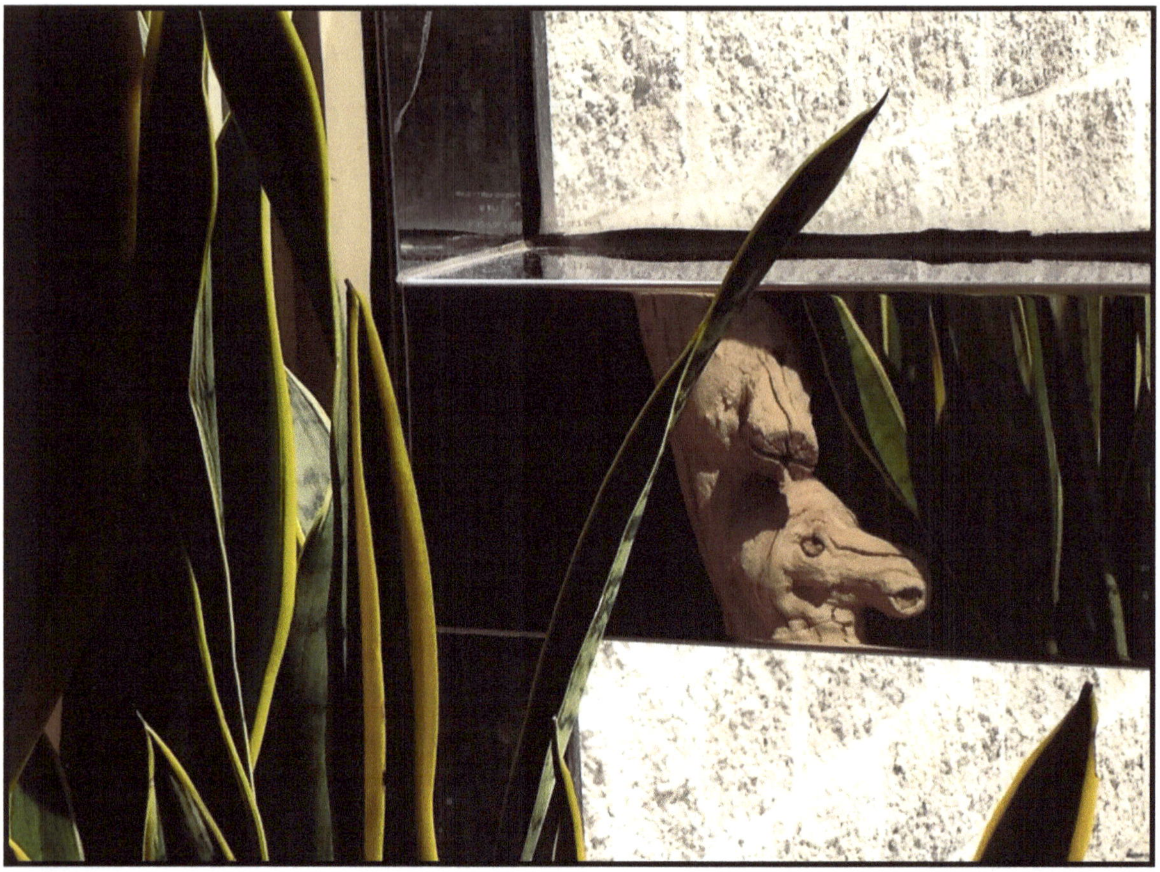

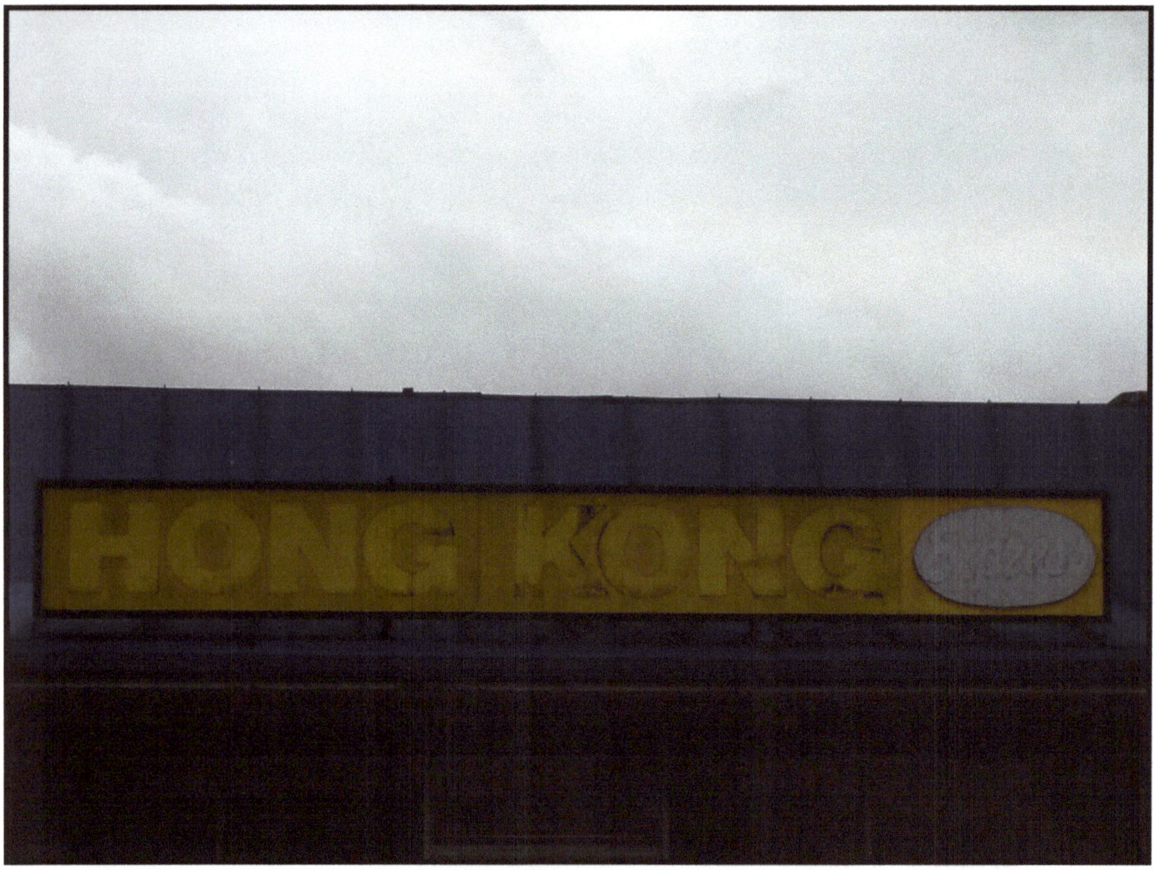

HONG KONG

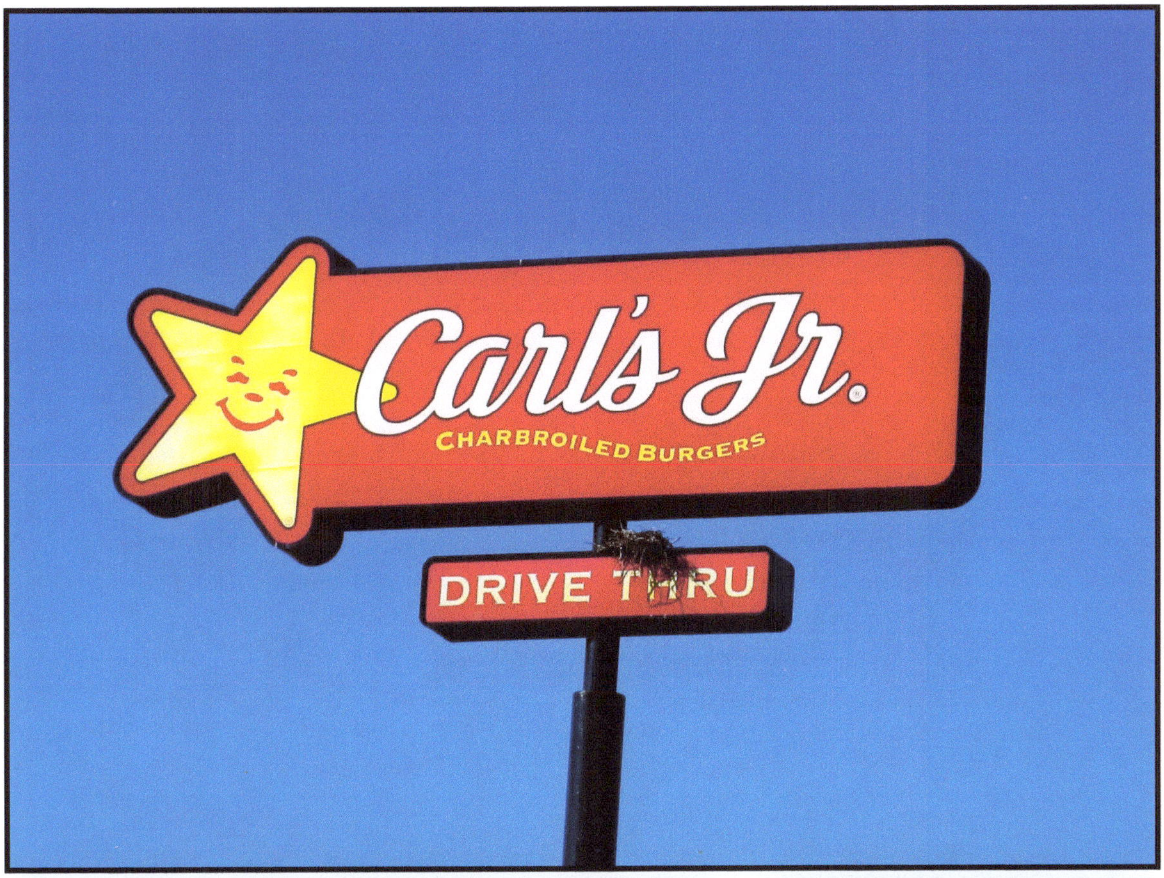

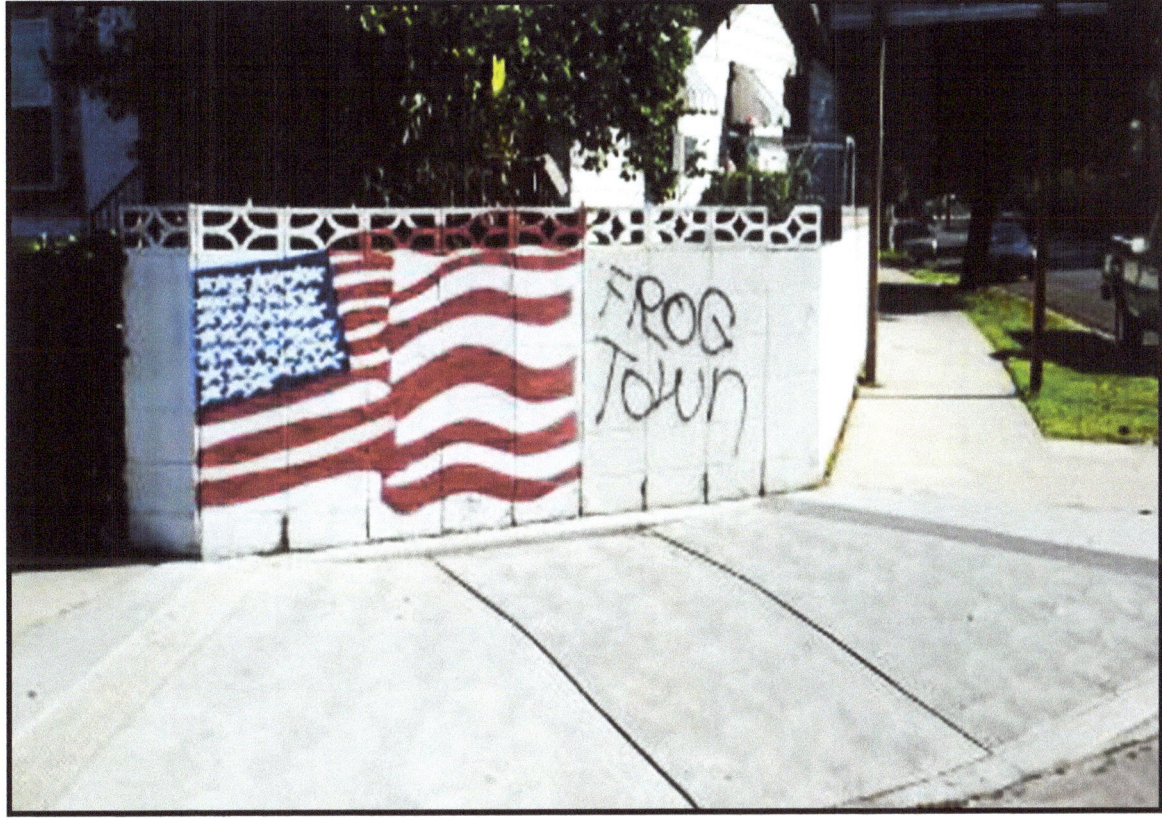

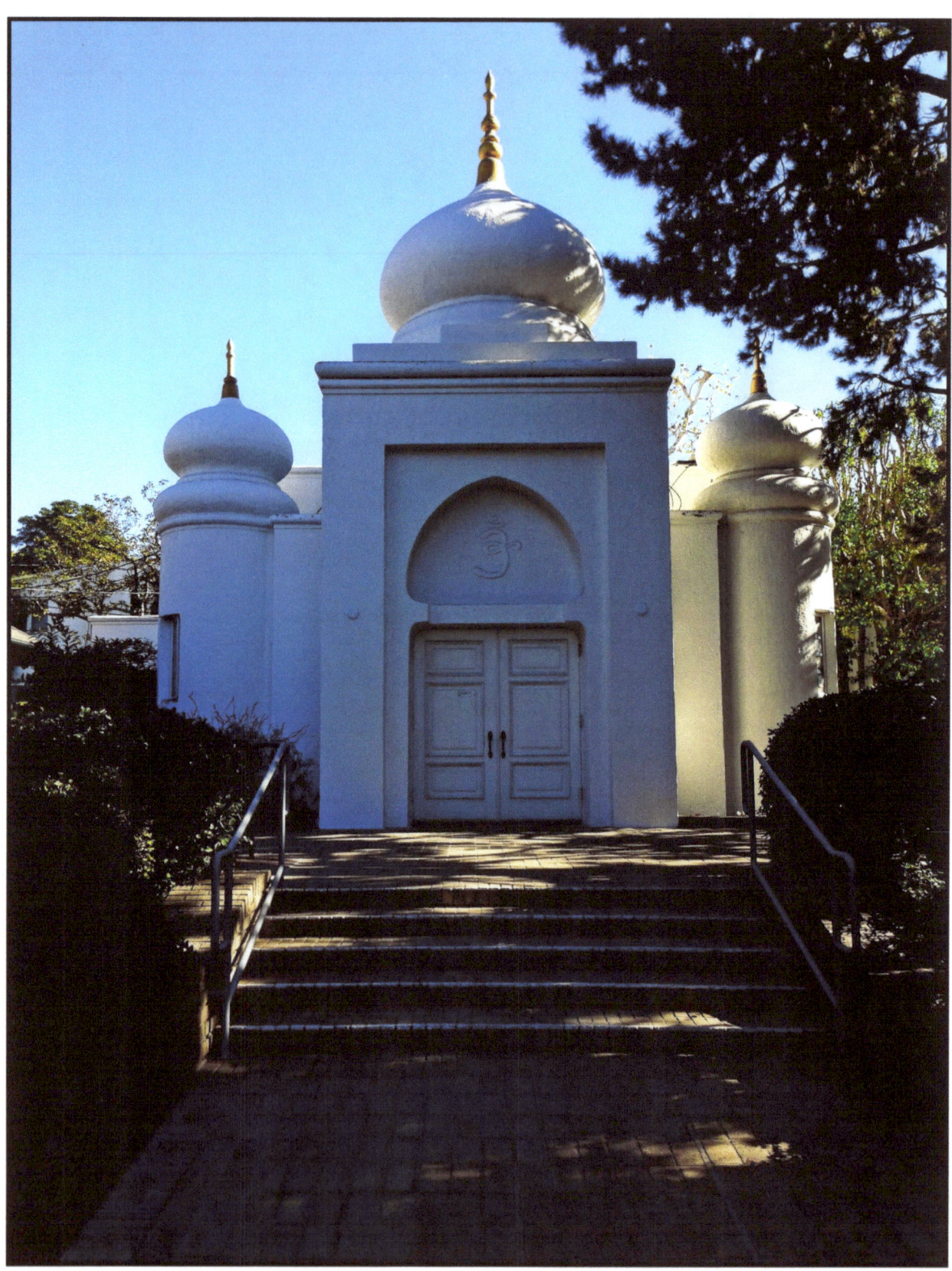

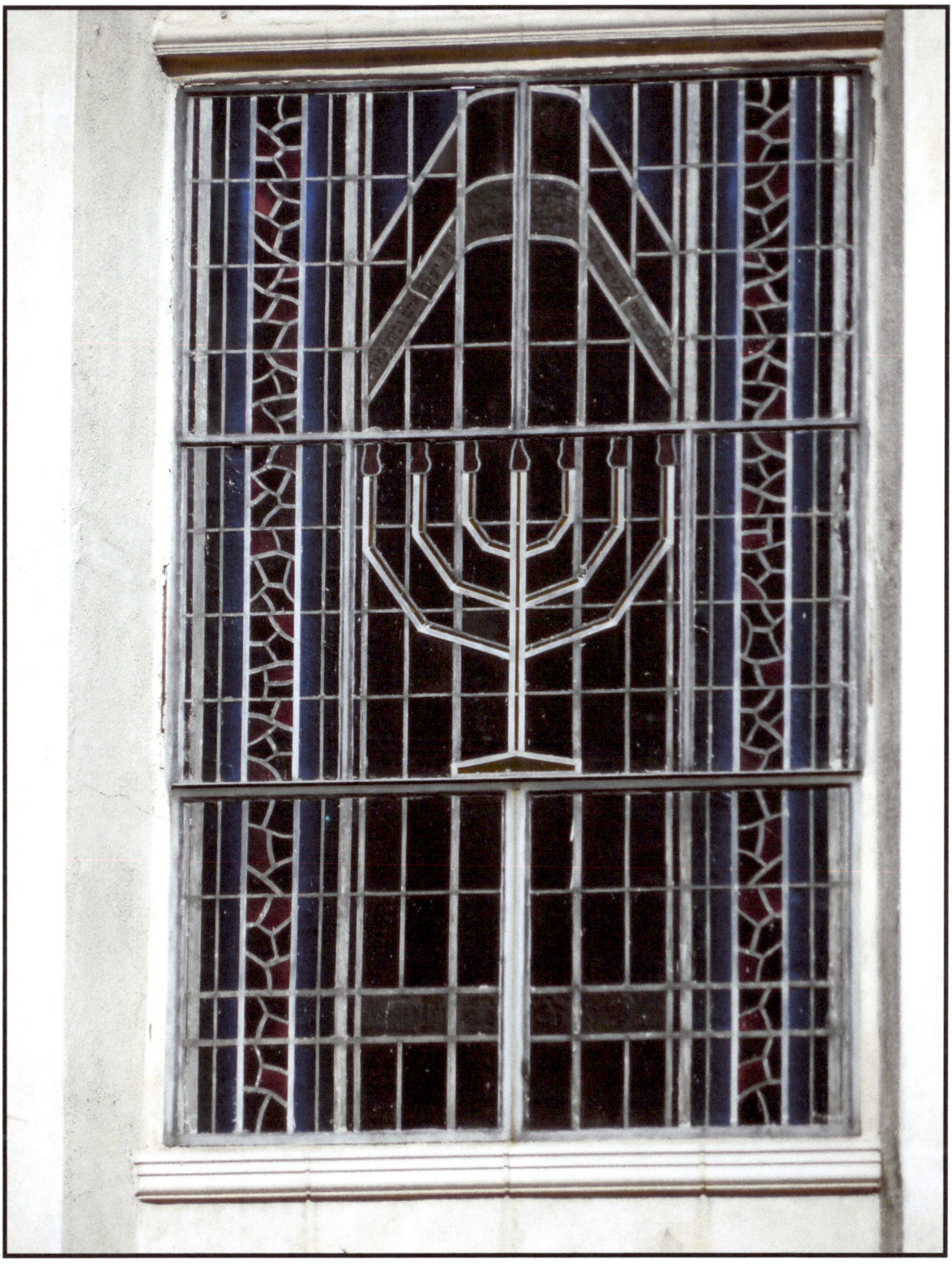

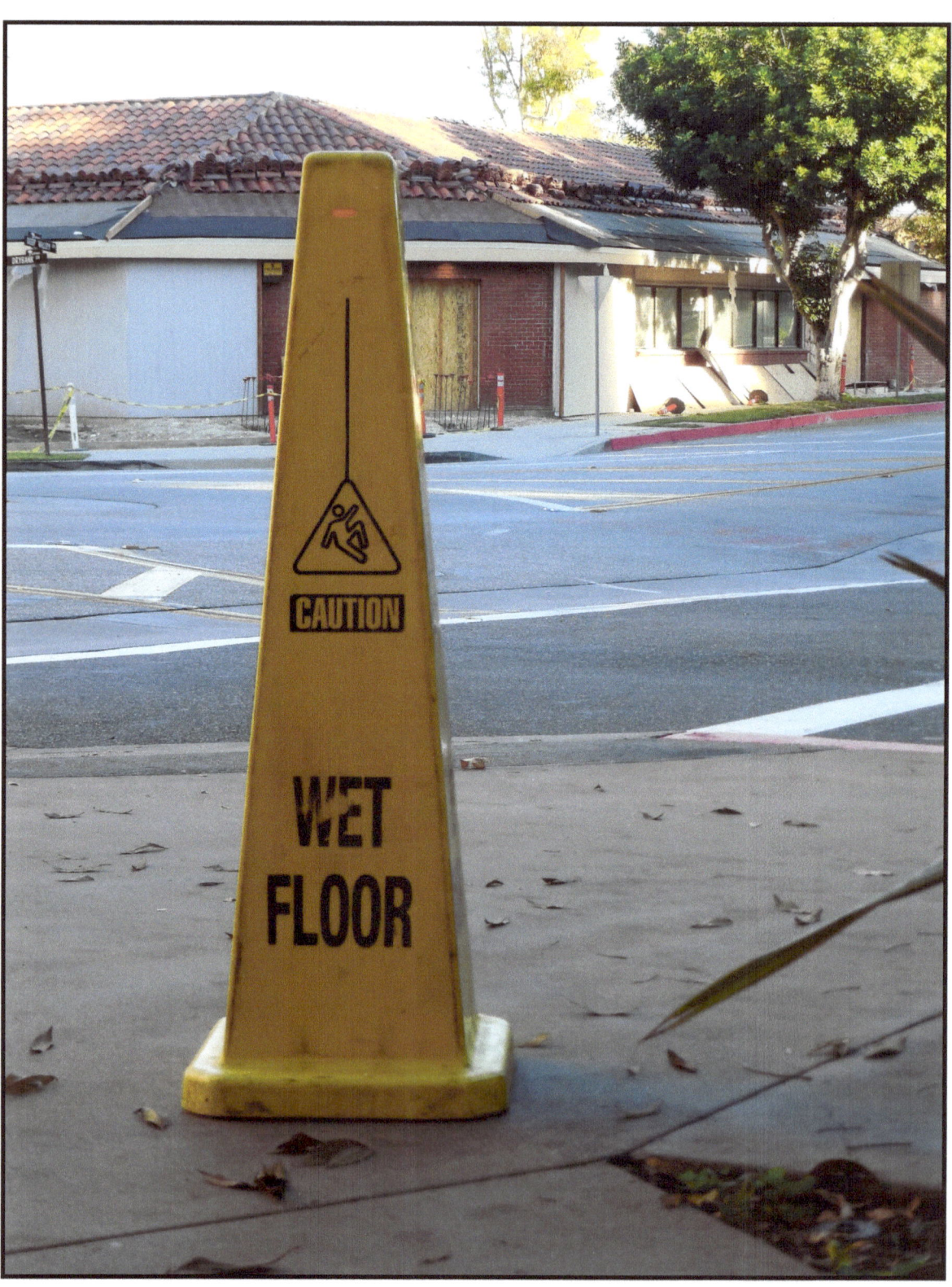

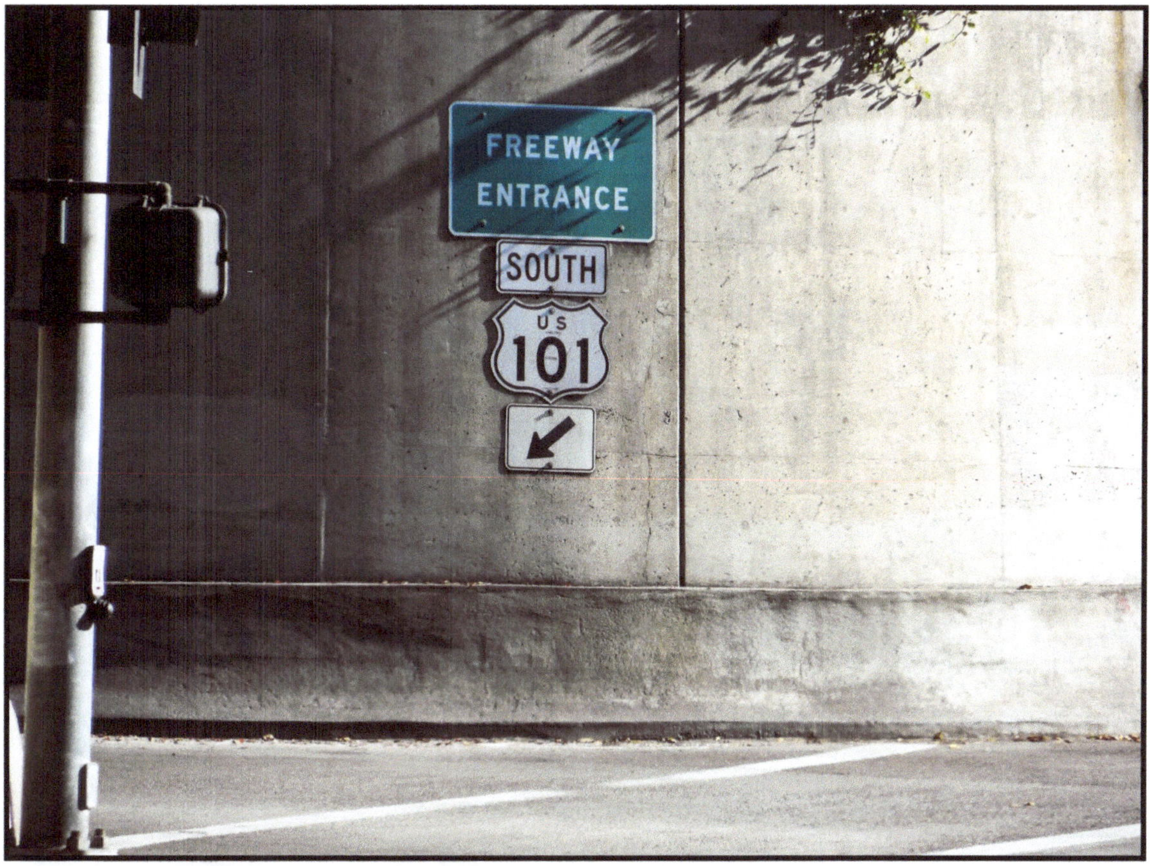

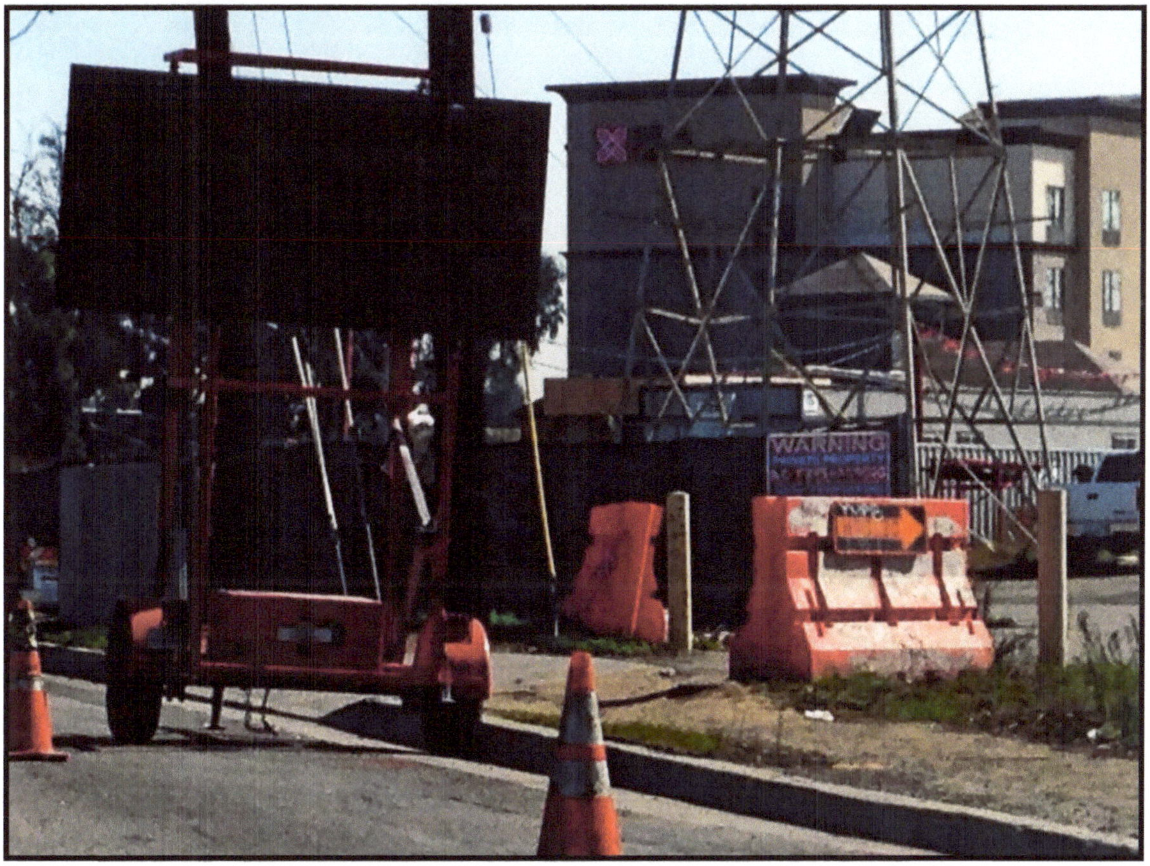

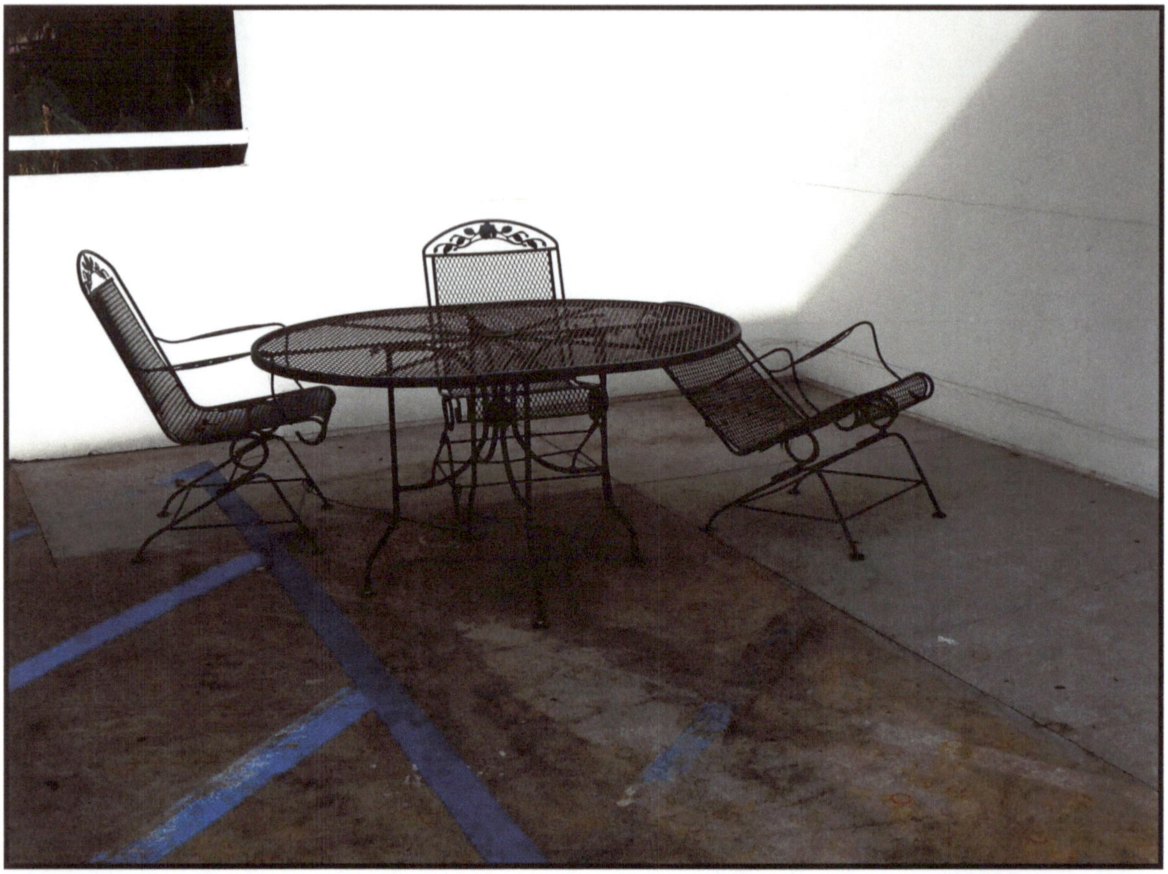

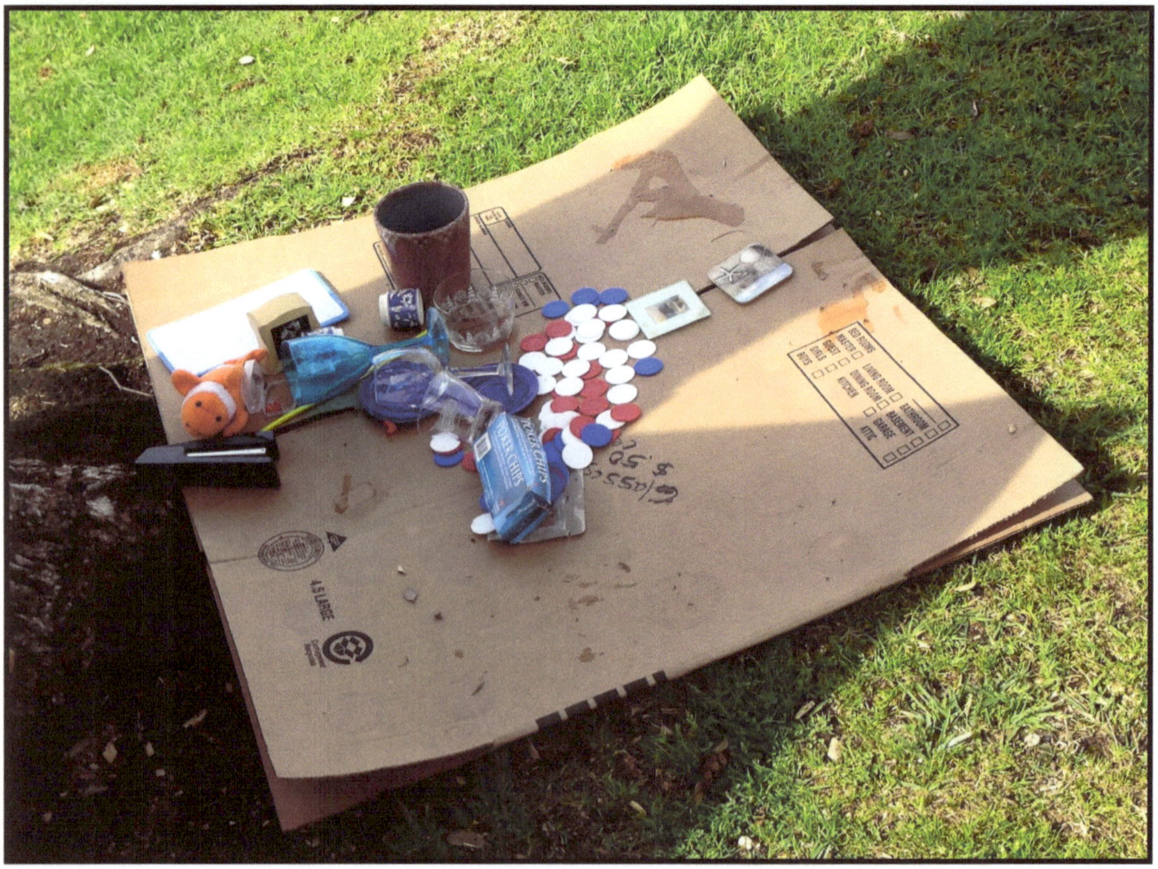

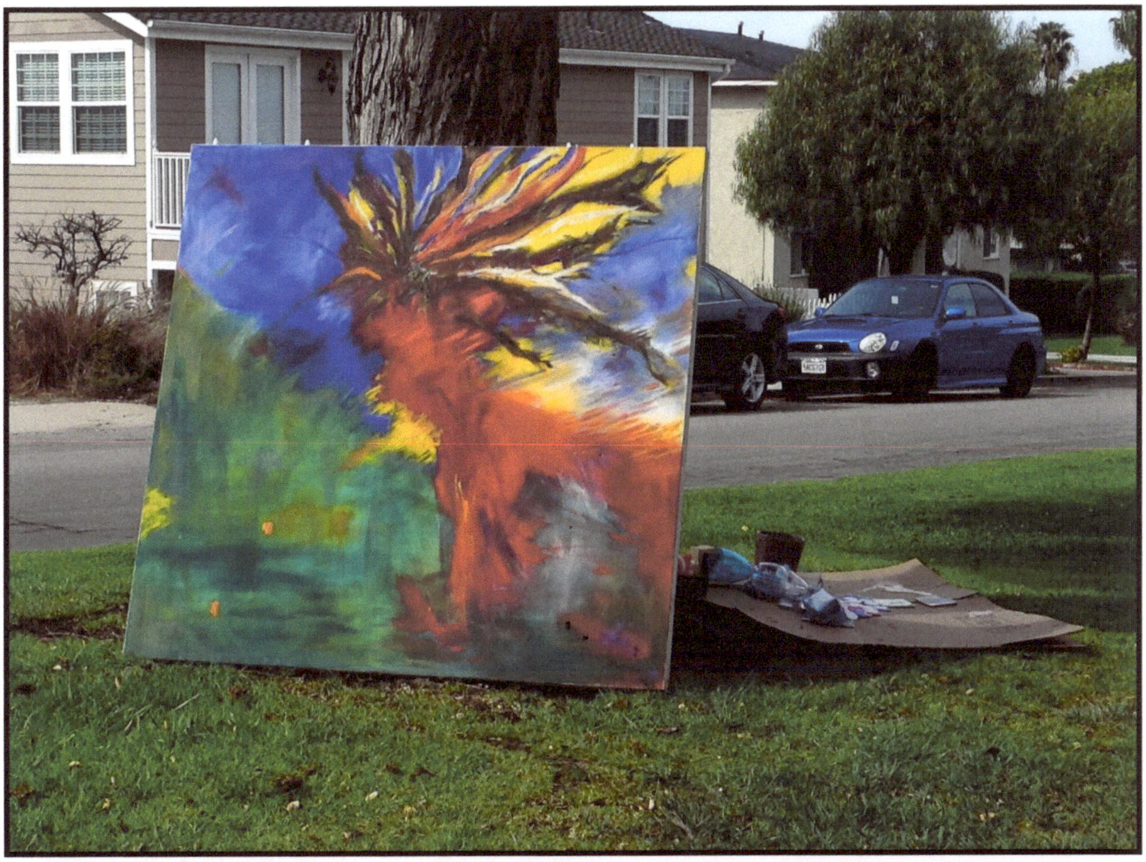

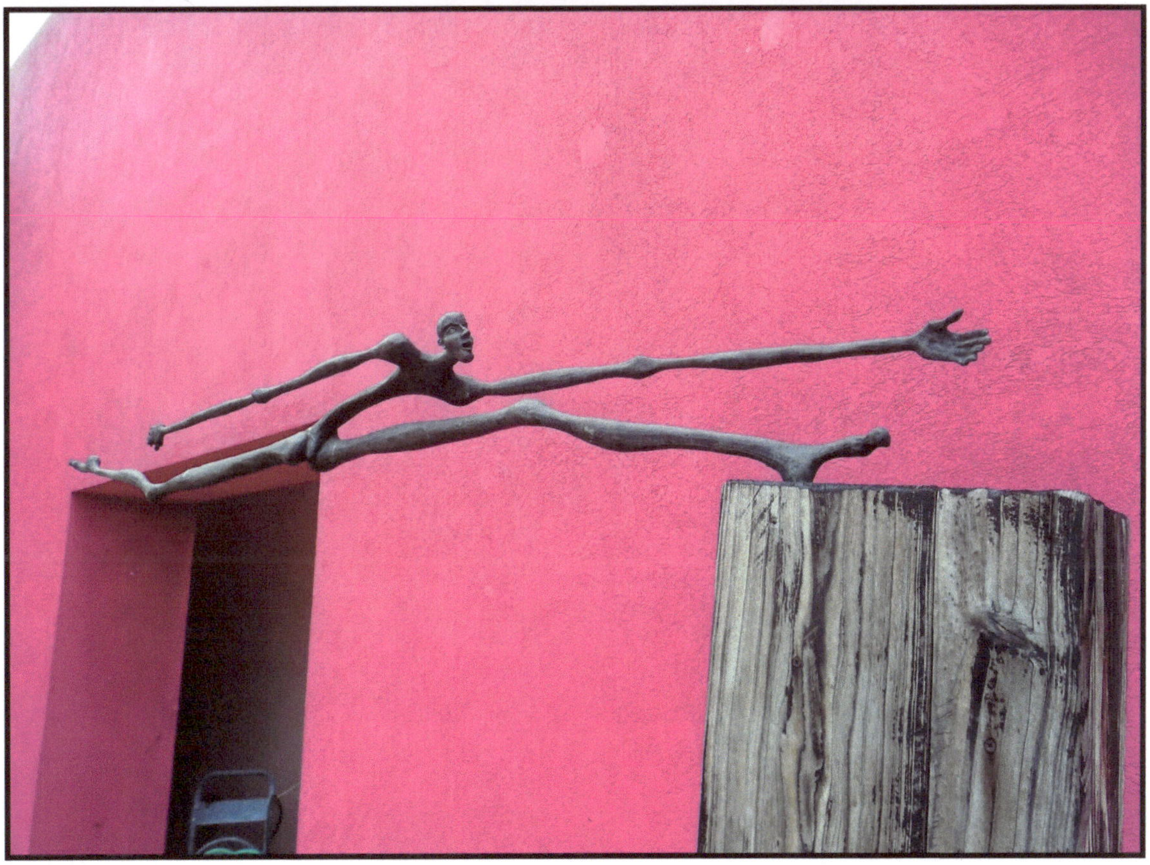

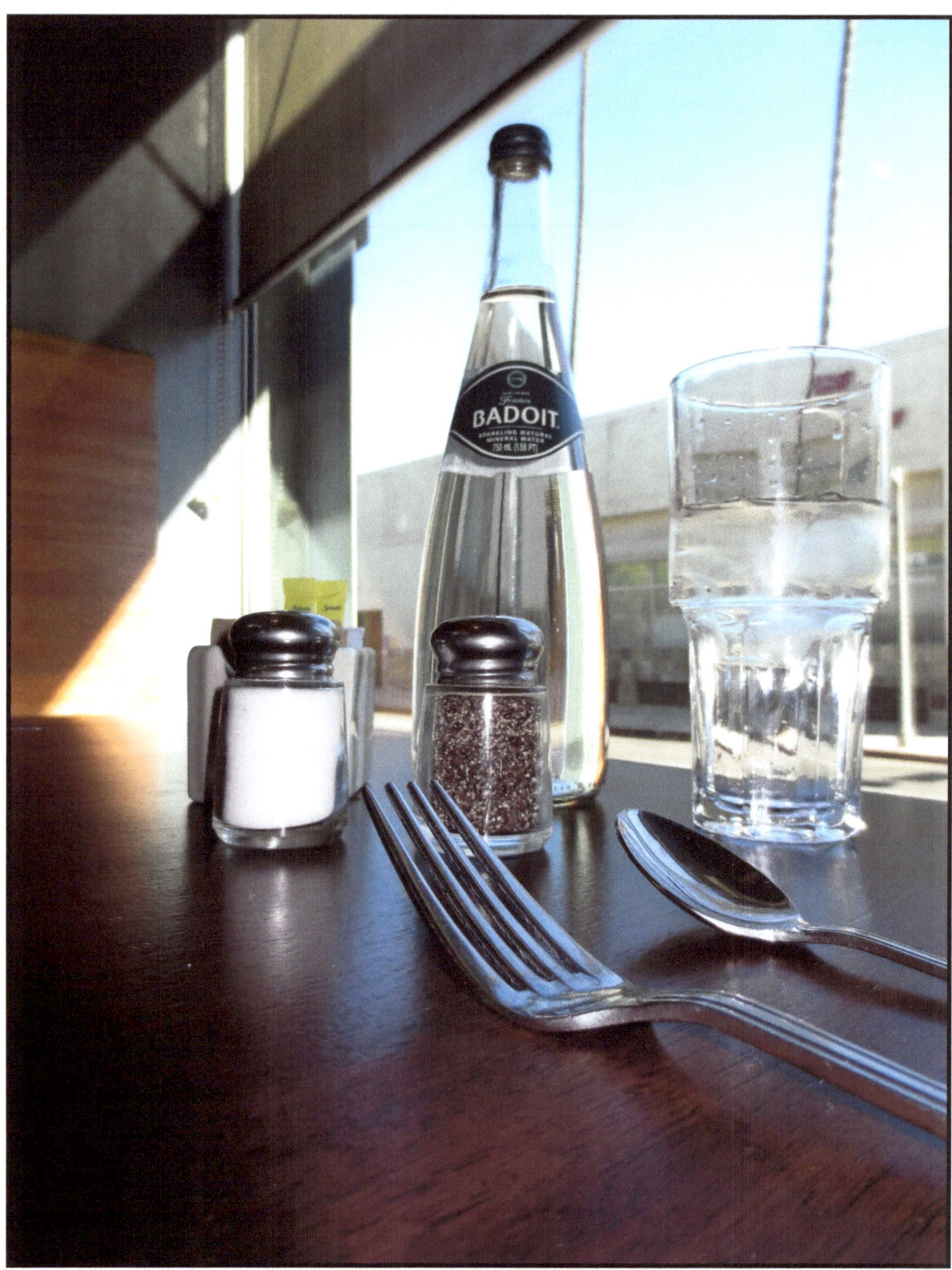

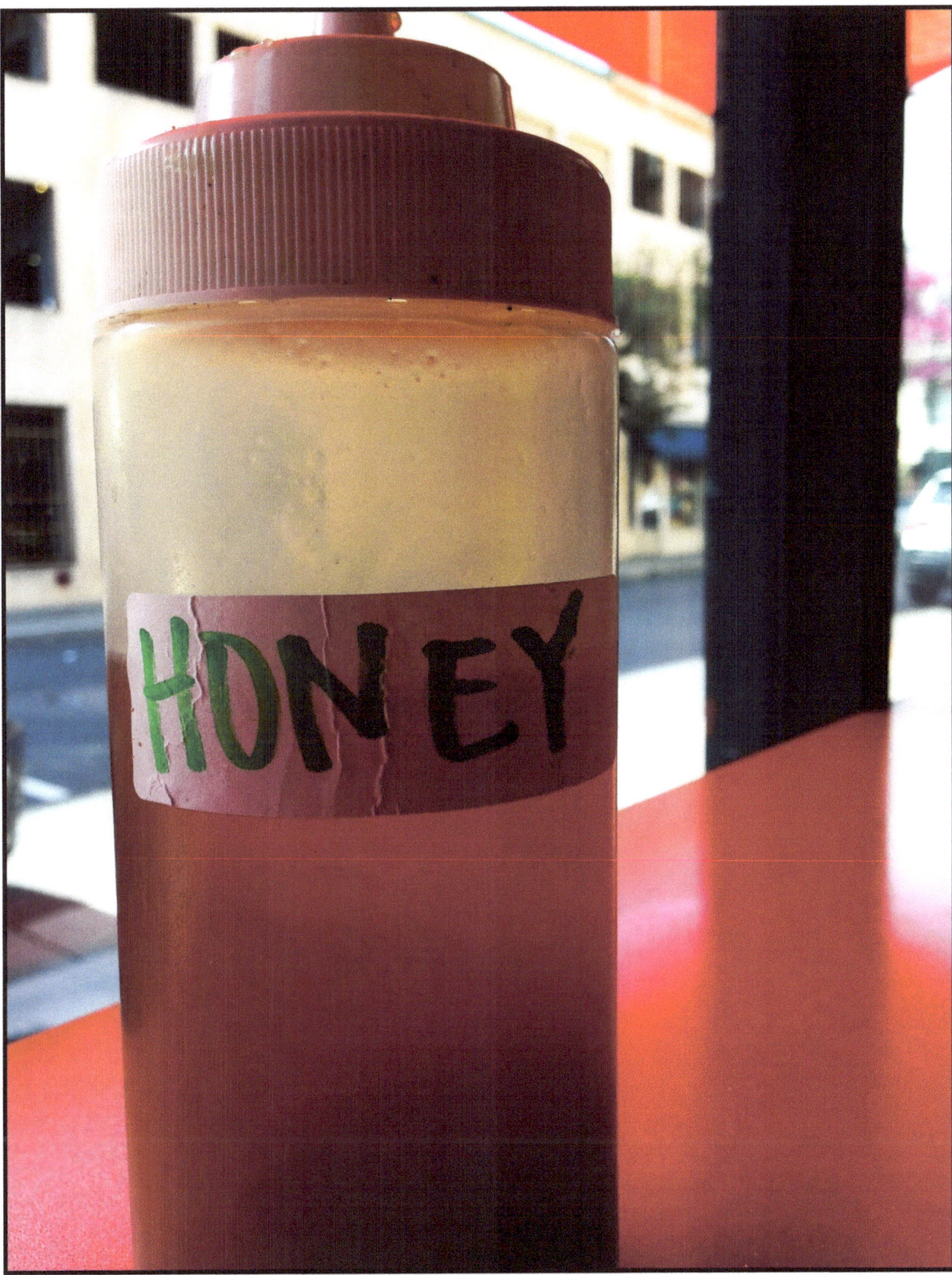

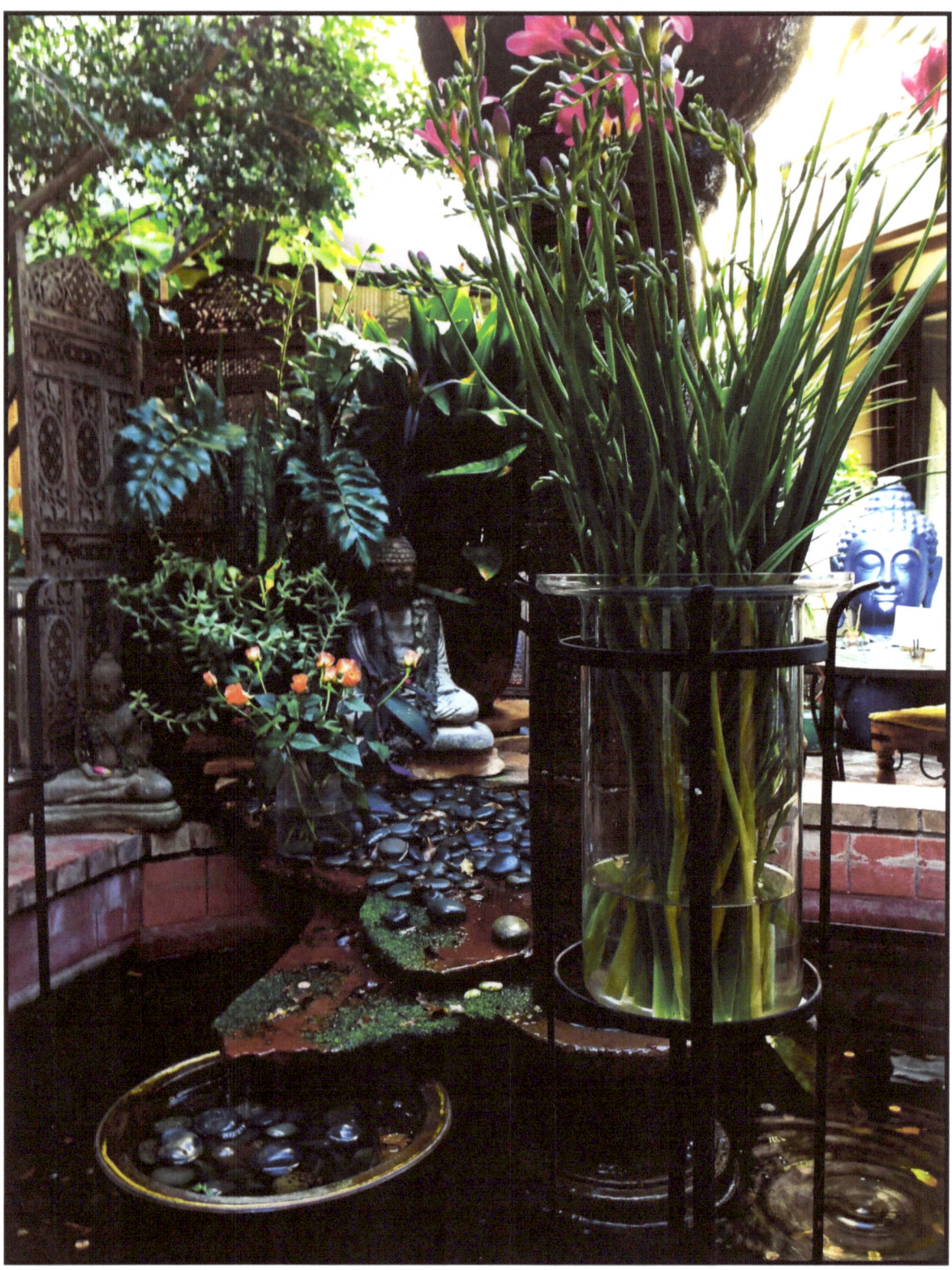

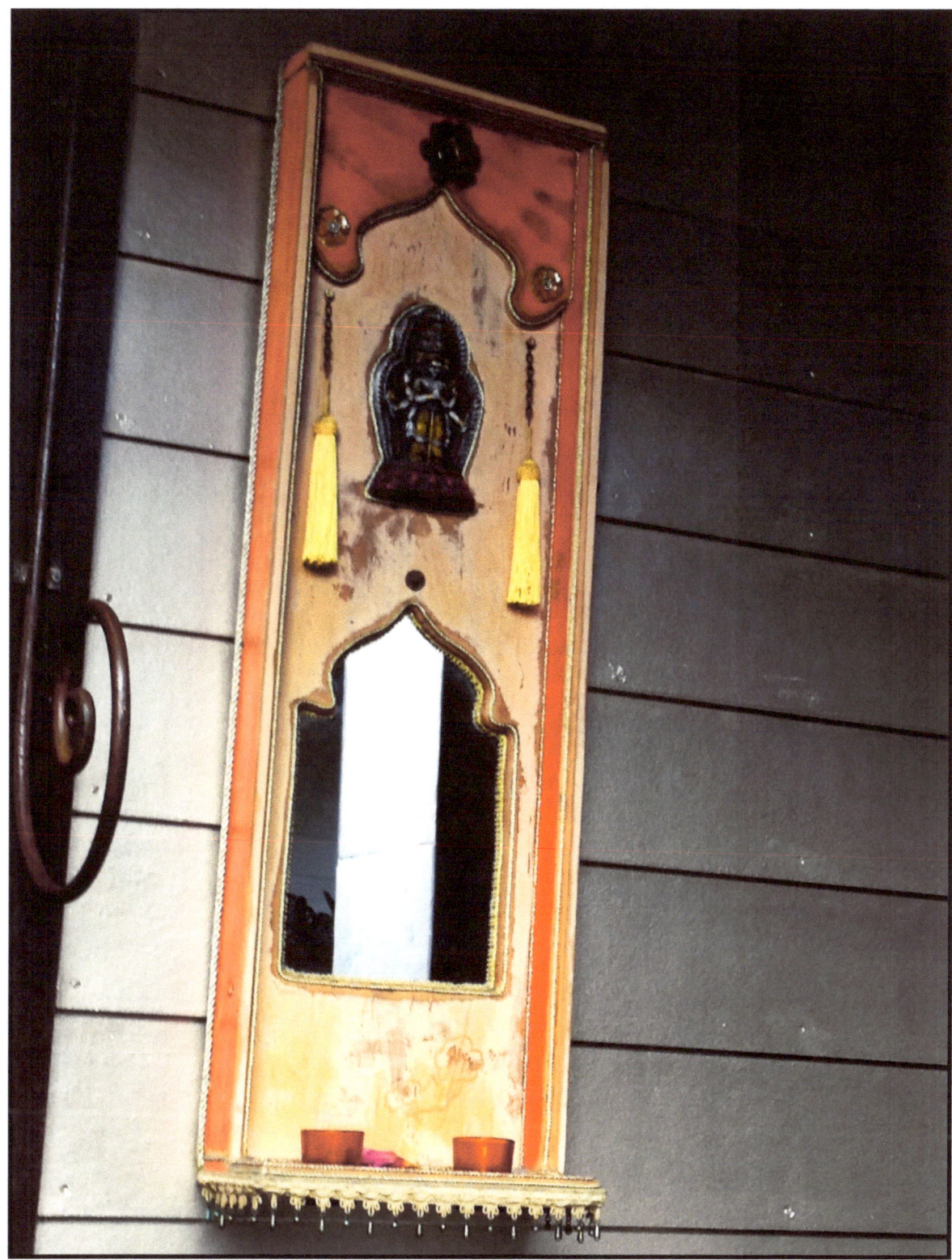

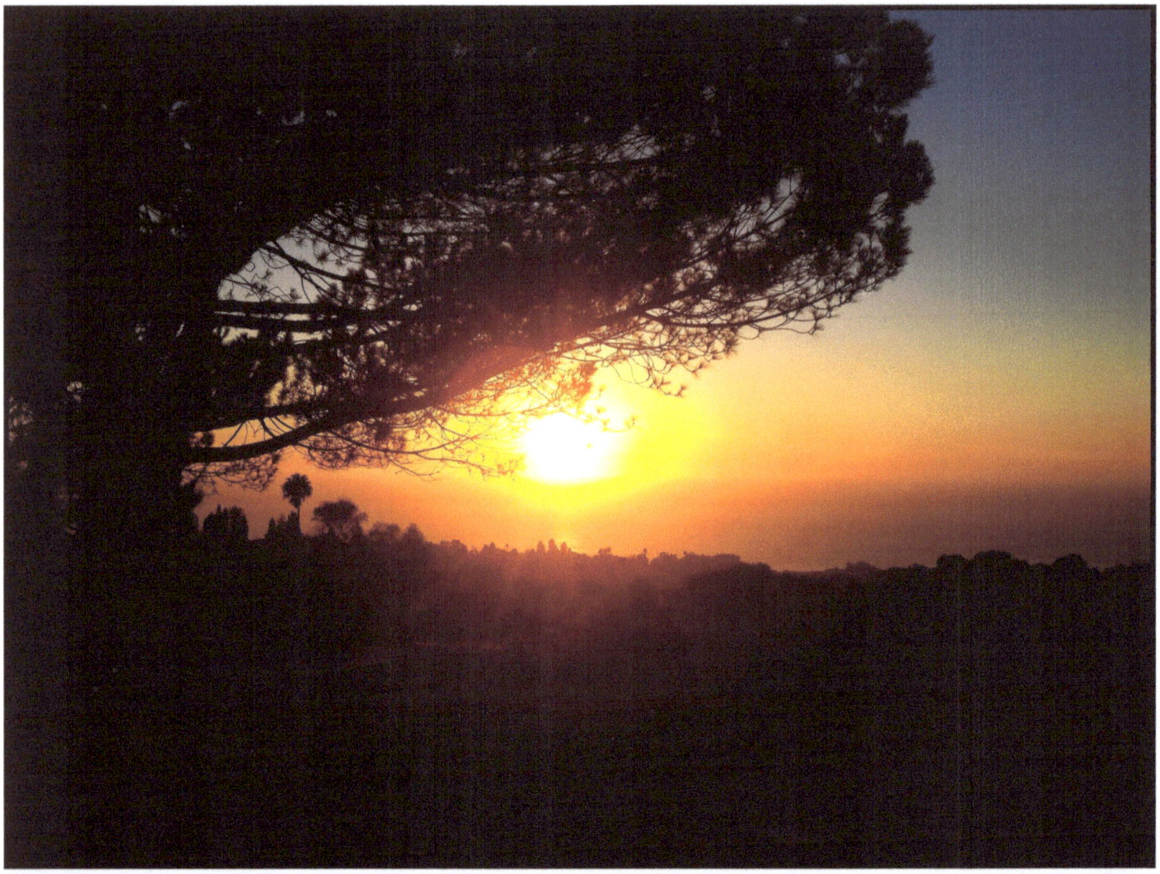

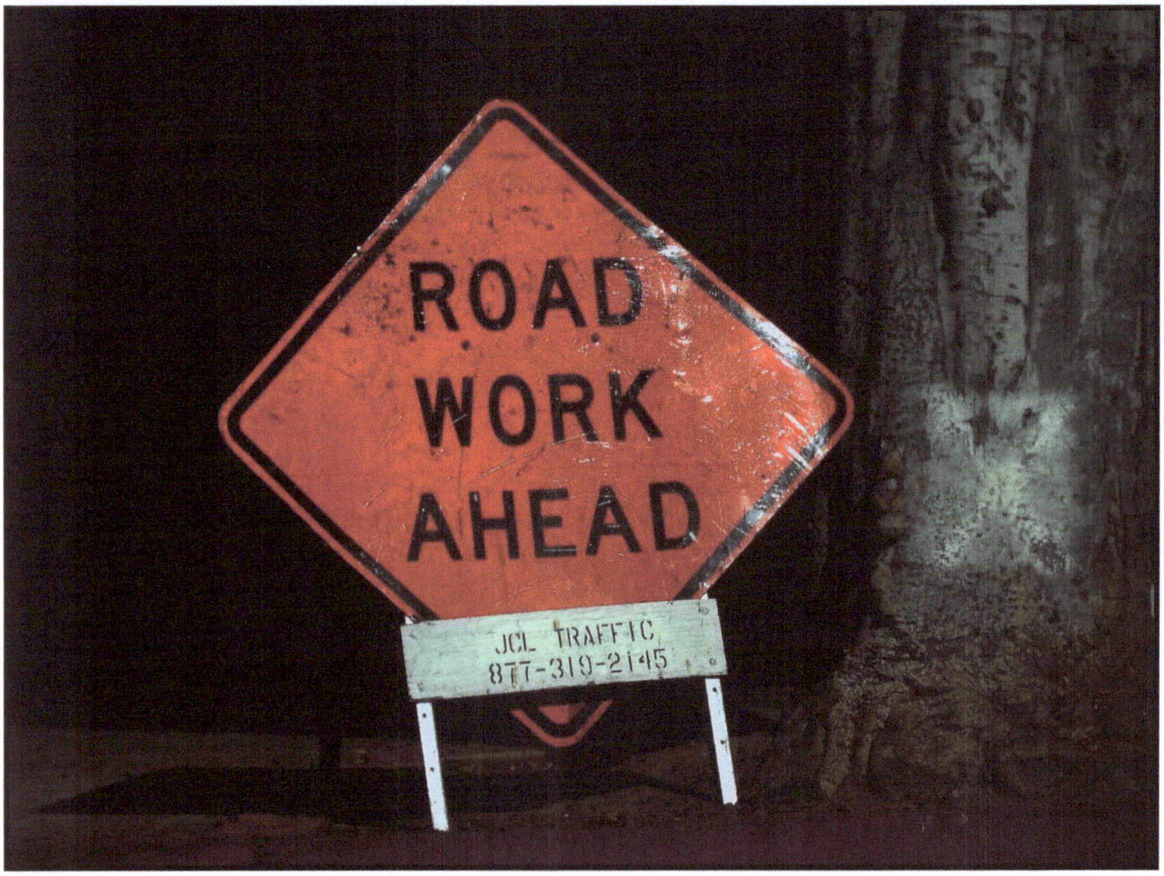

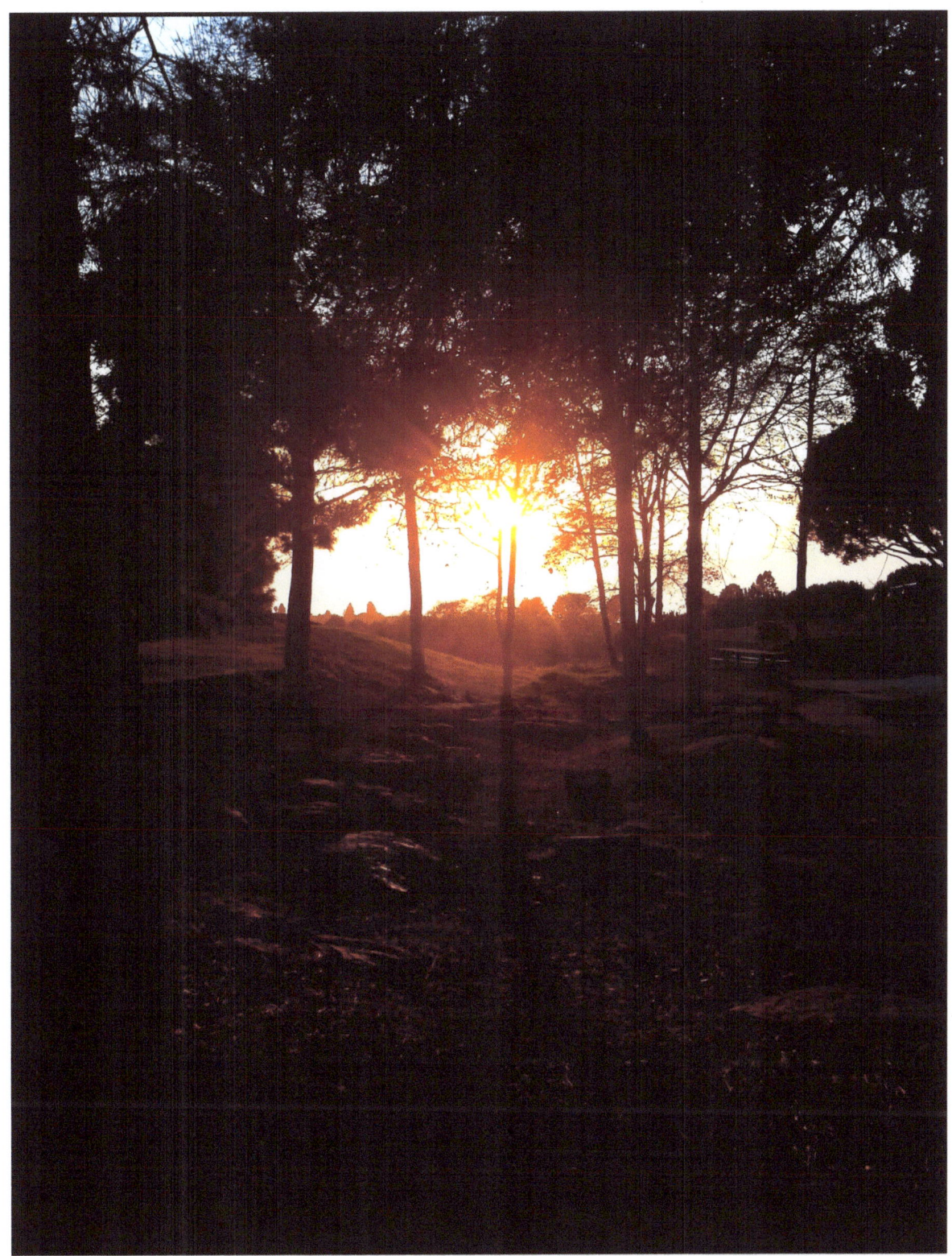

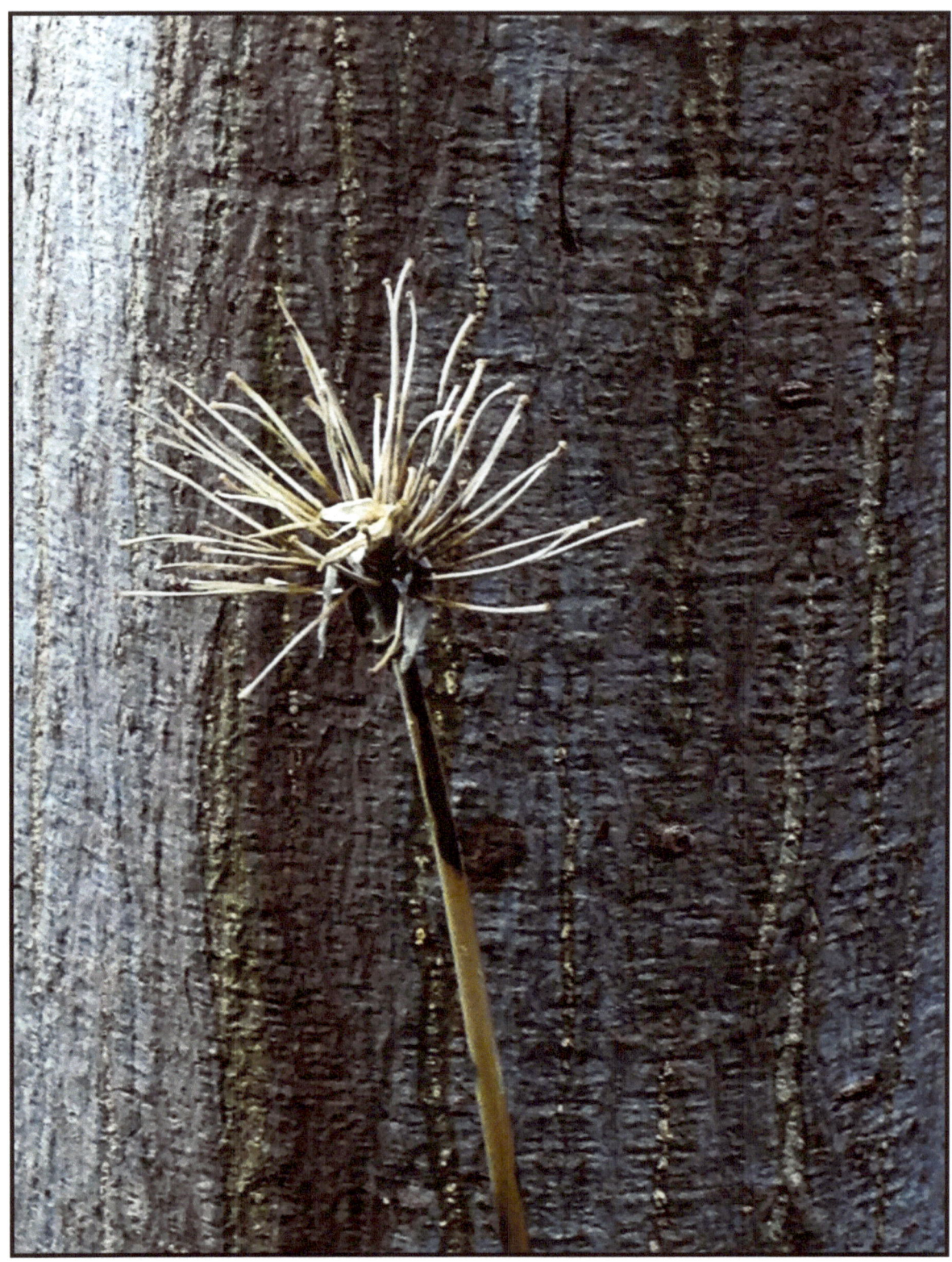

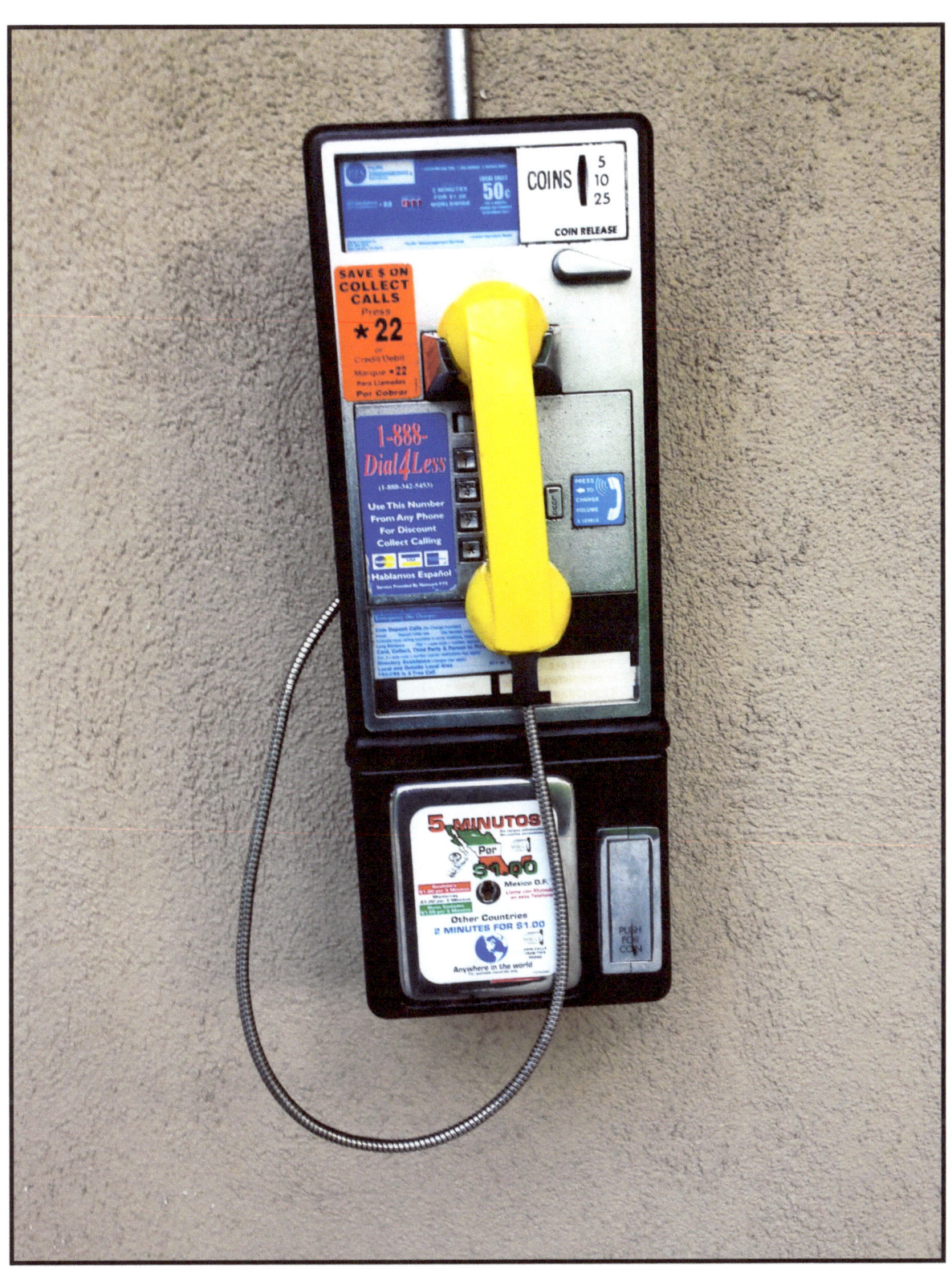

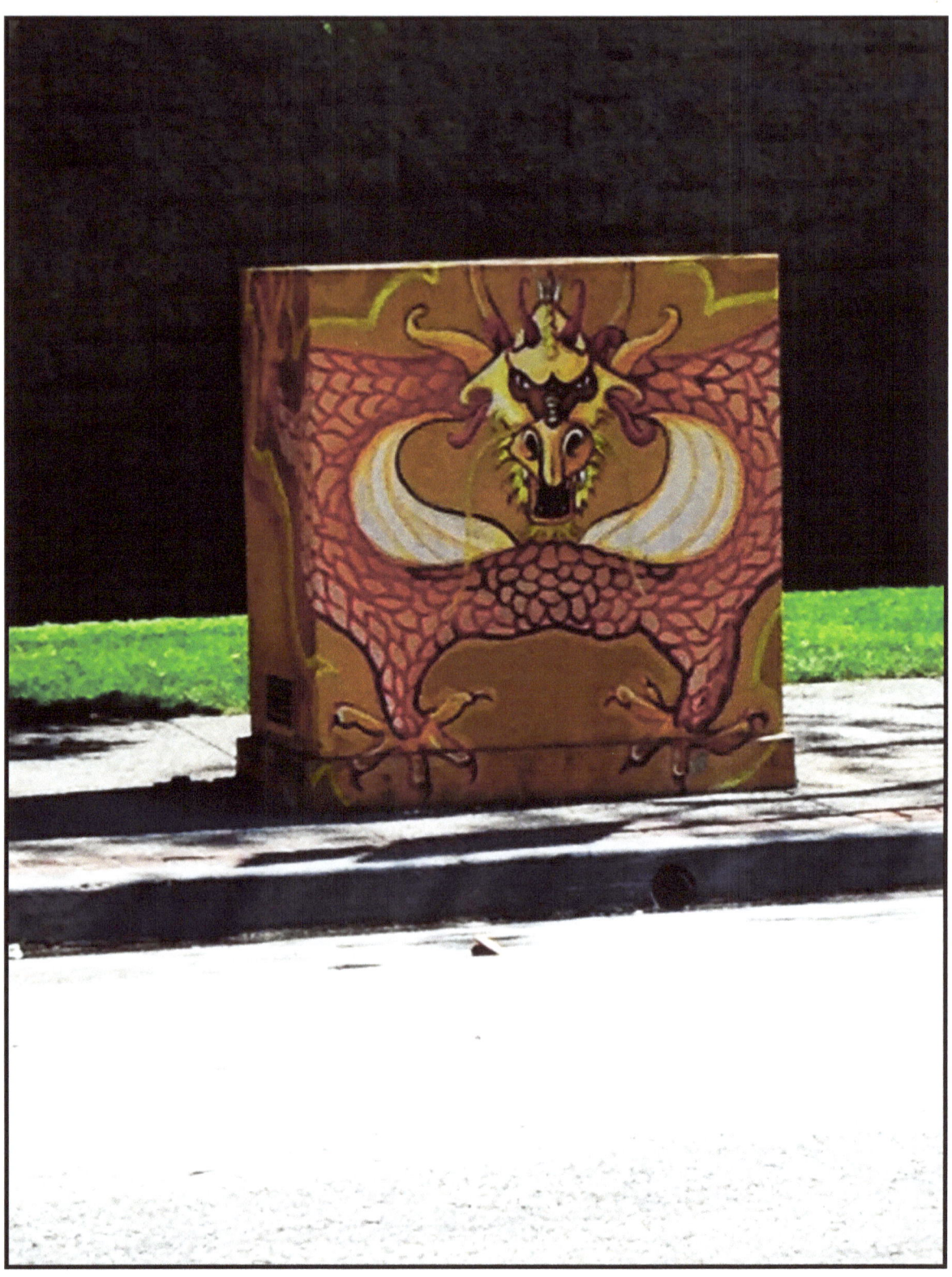

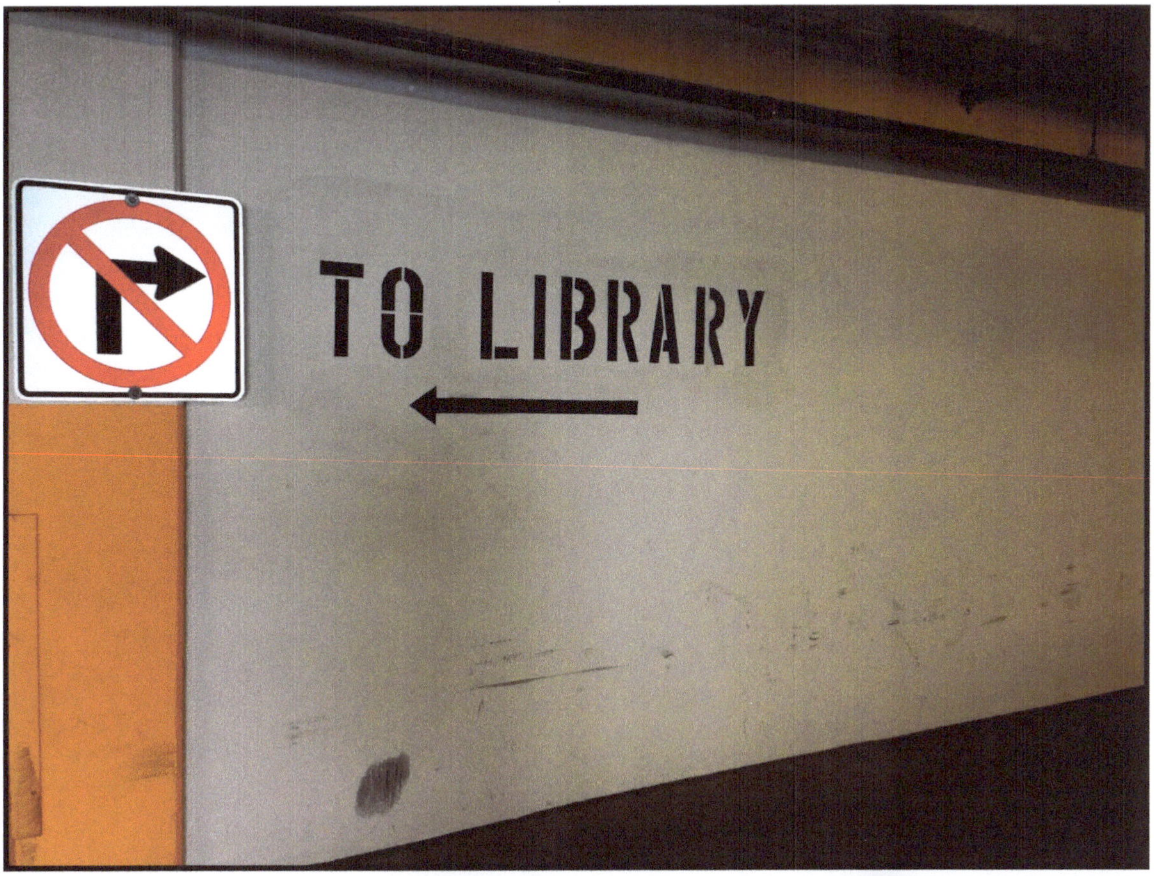

TO LIBRARY ←

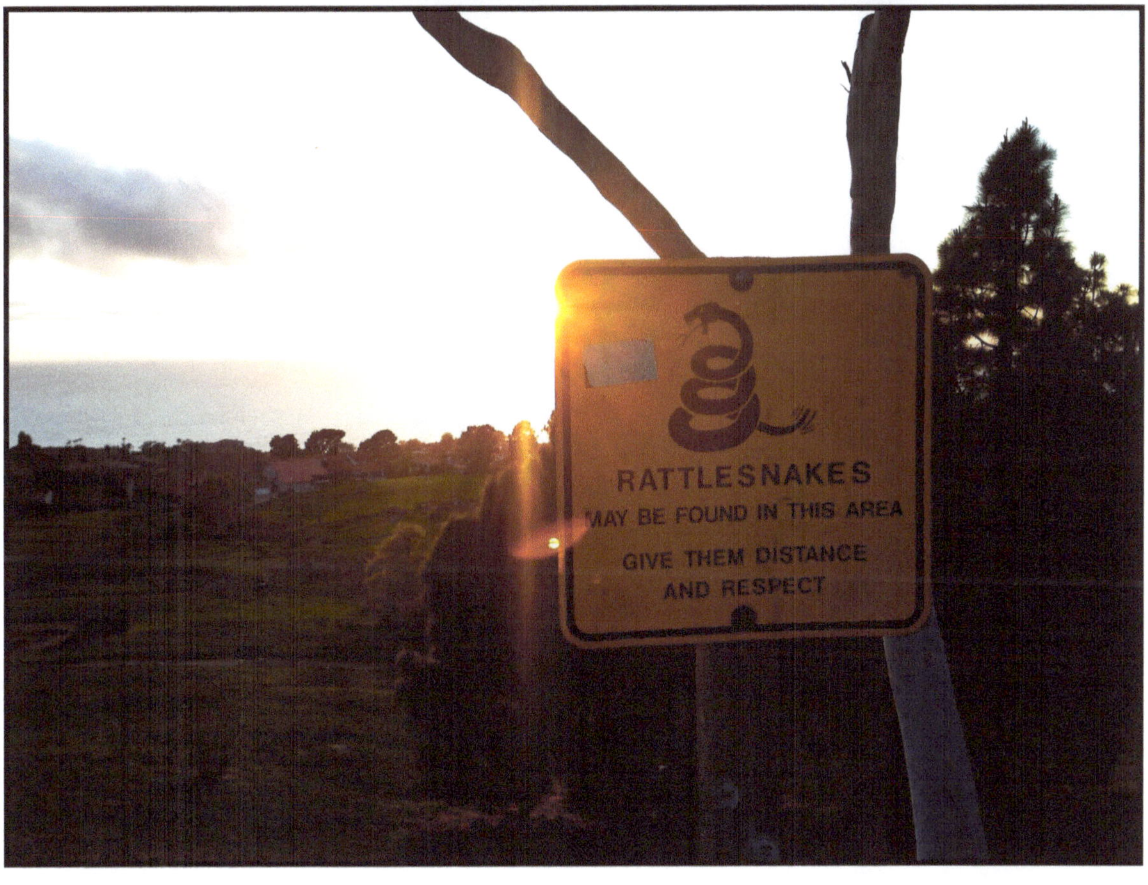

RATTLESNAKES
MAY BE FOUND IN THIS AREA

GIVE THEM DISTANCE
AND RESPECT

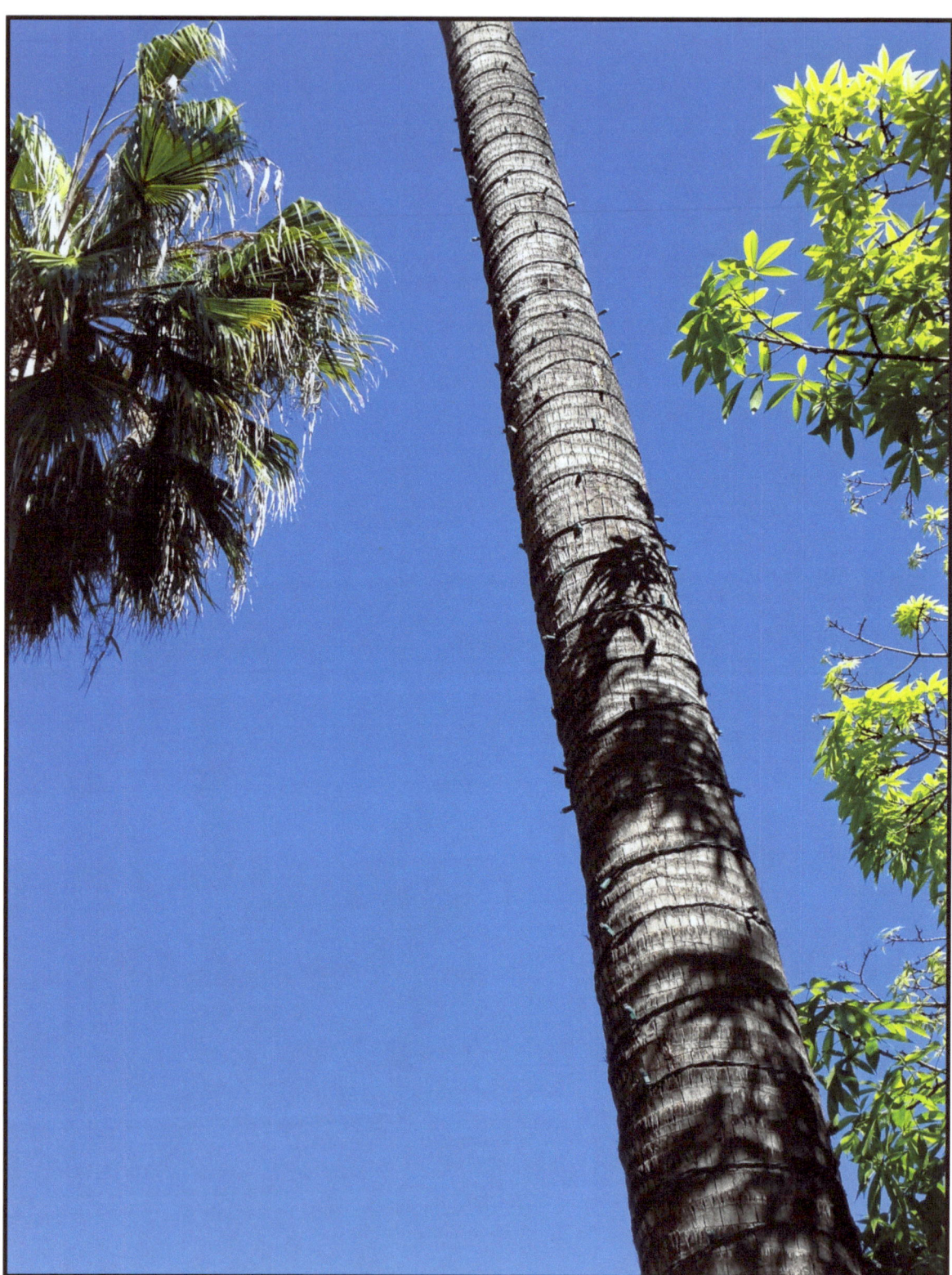

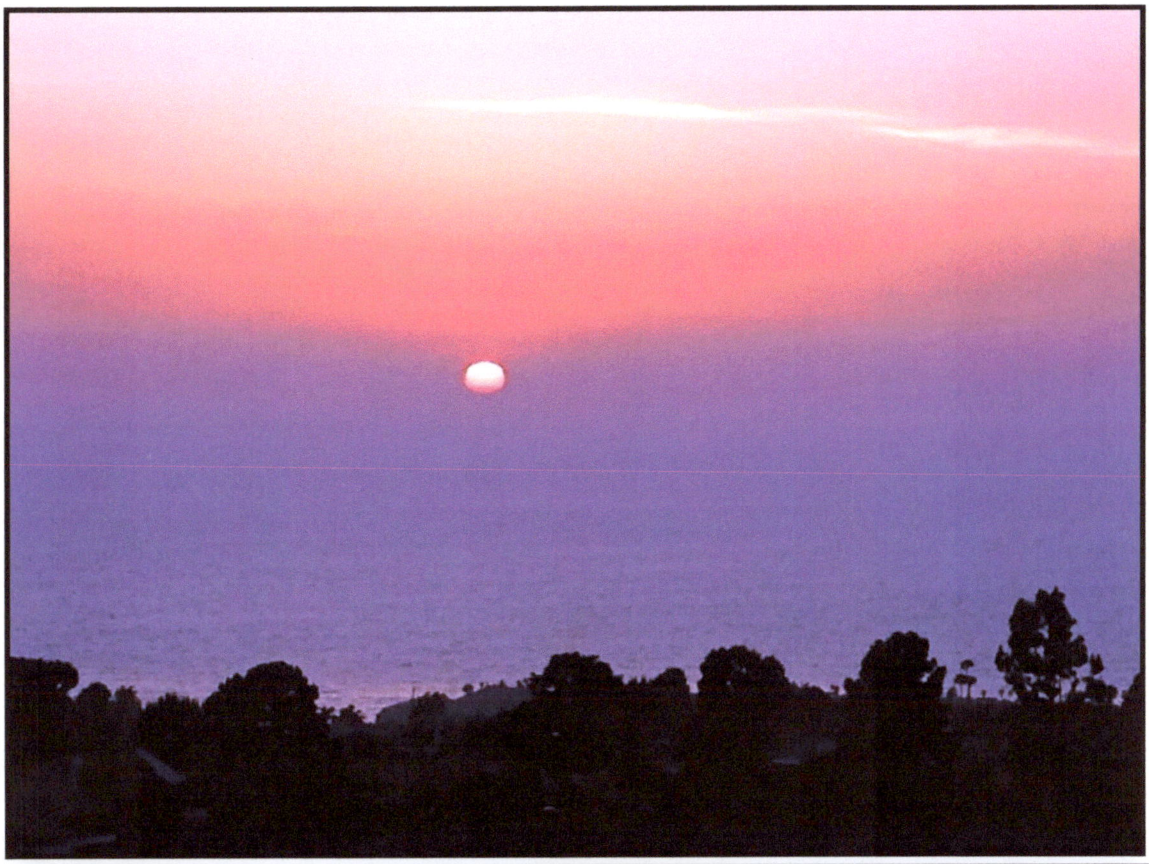

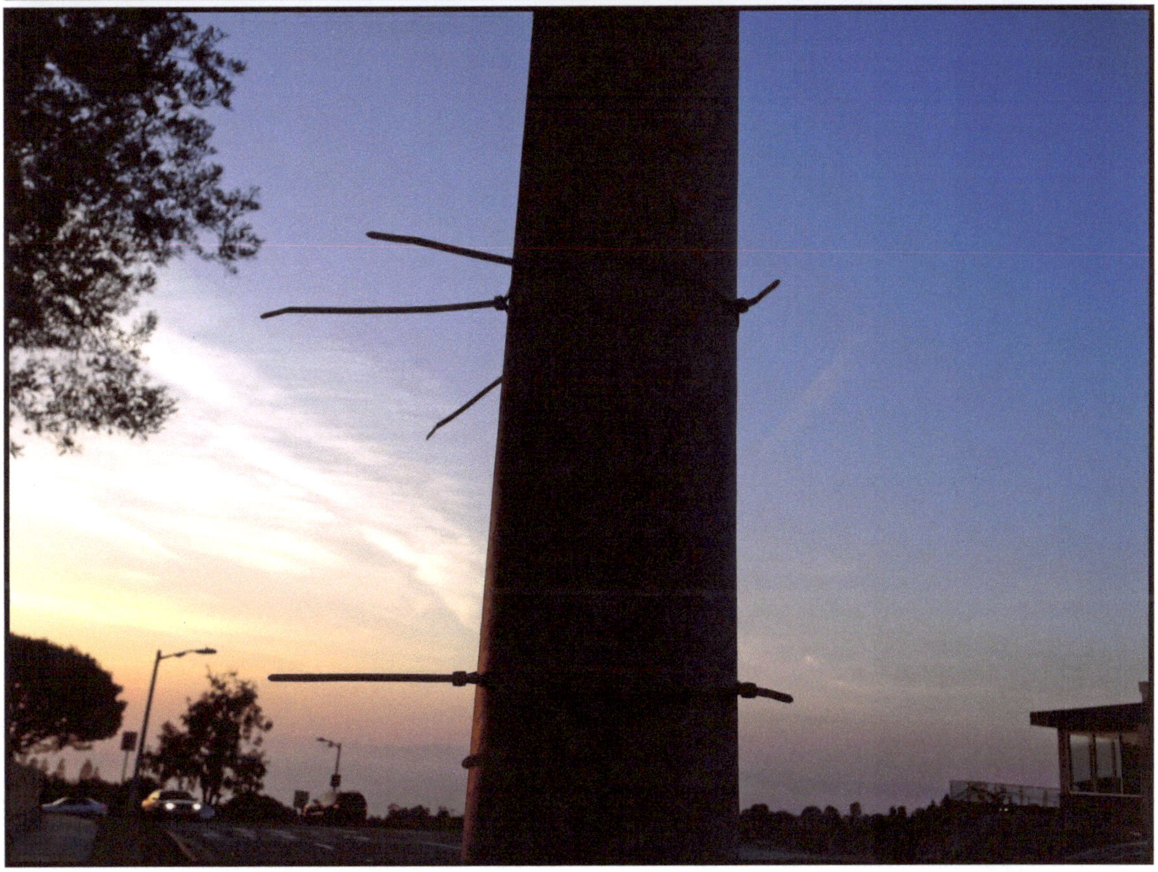

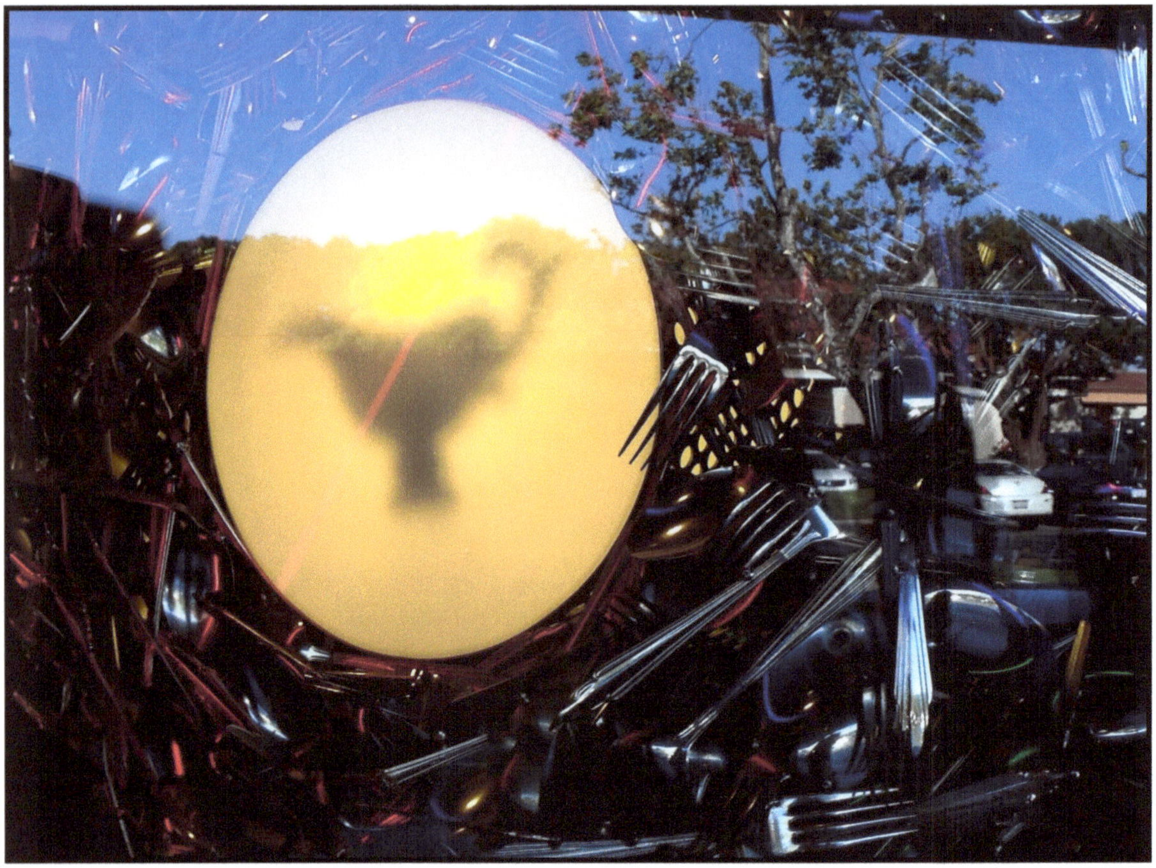

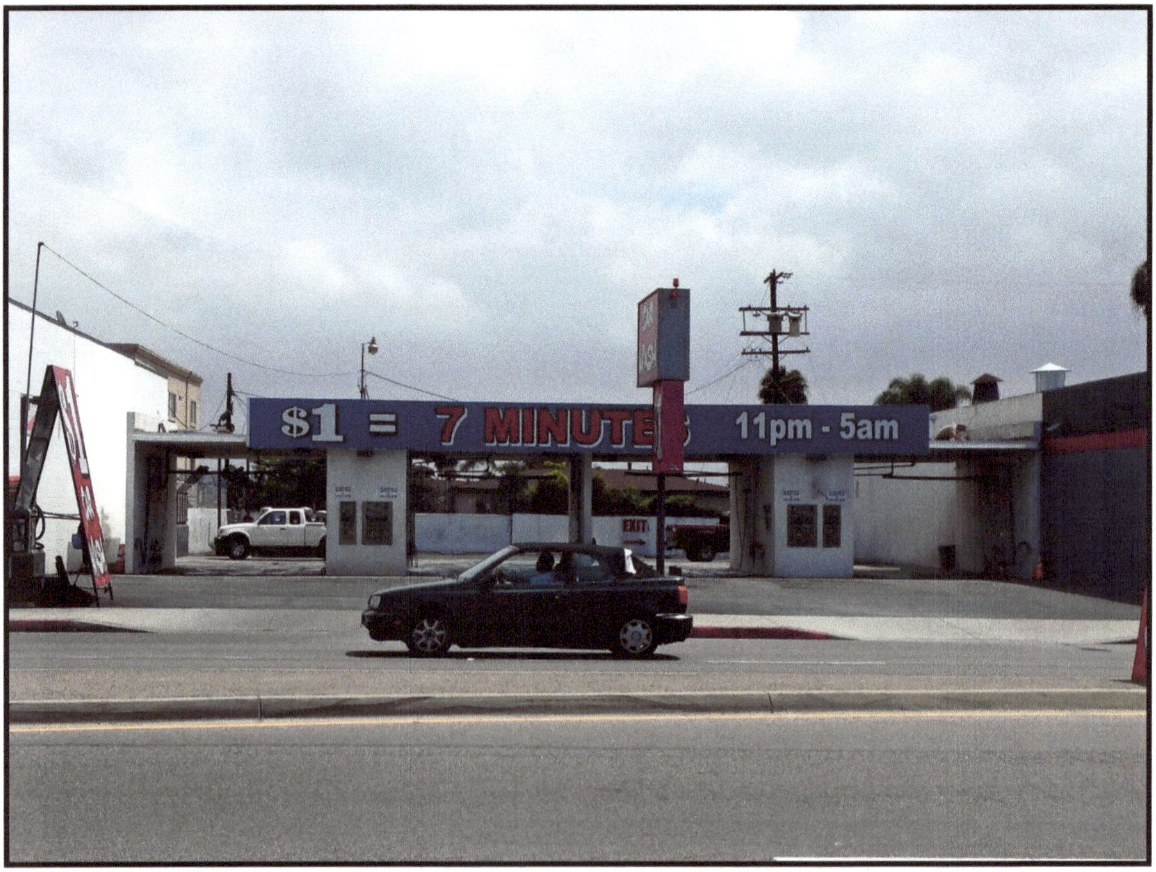

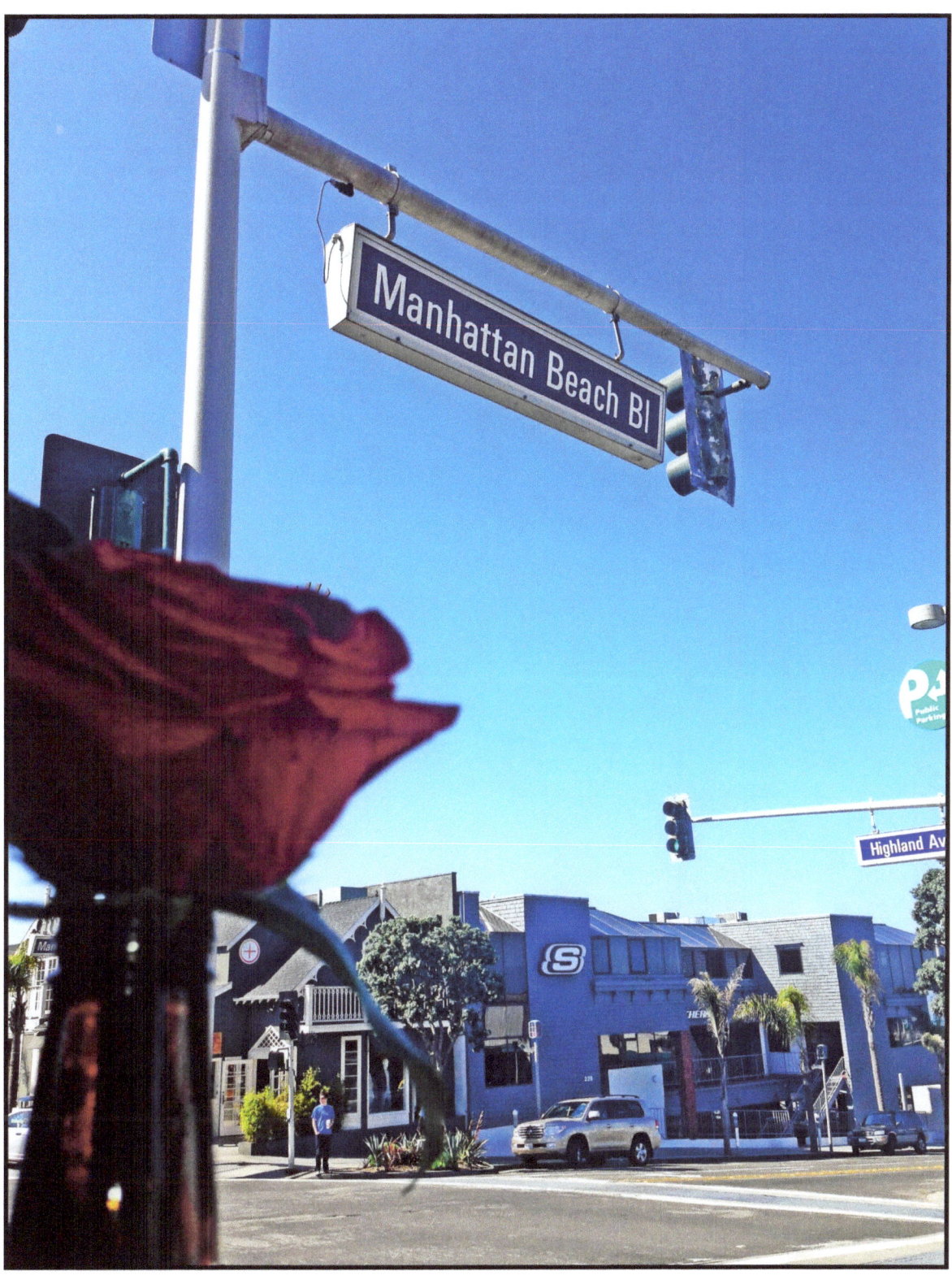

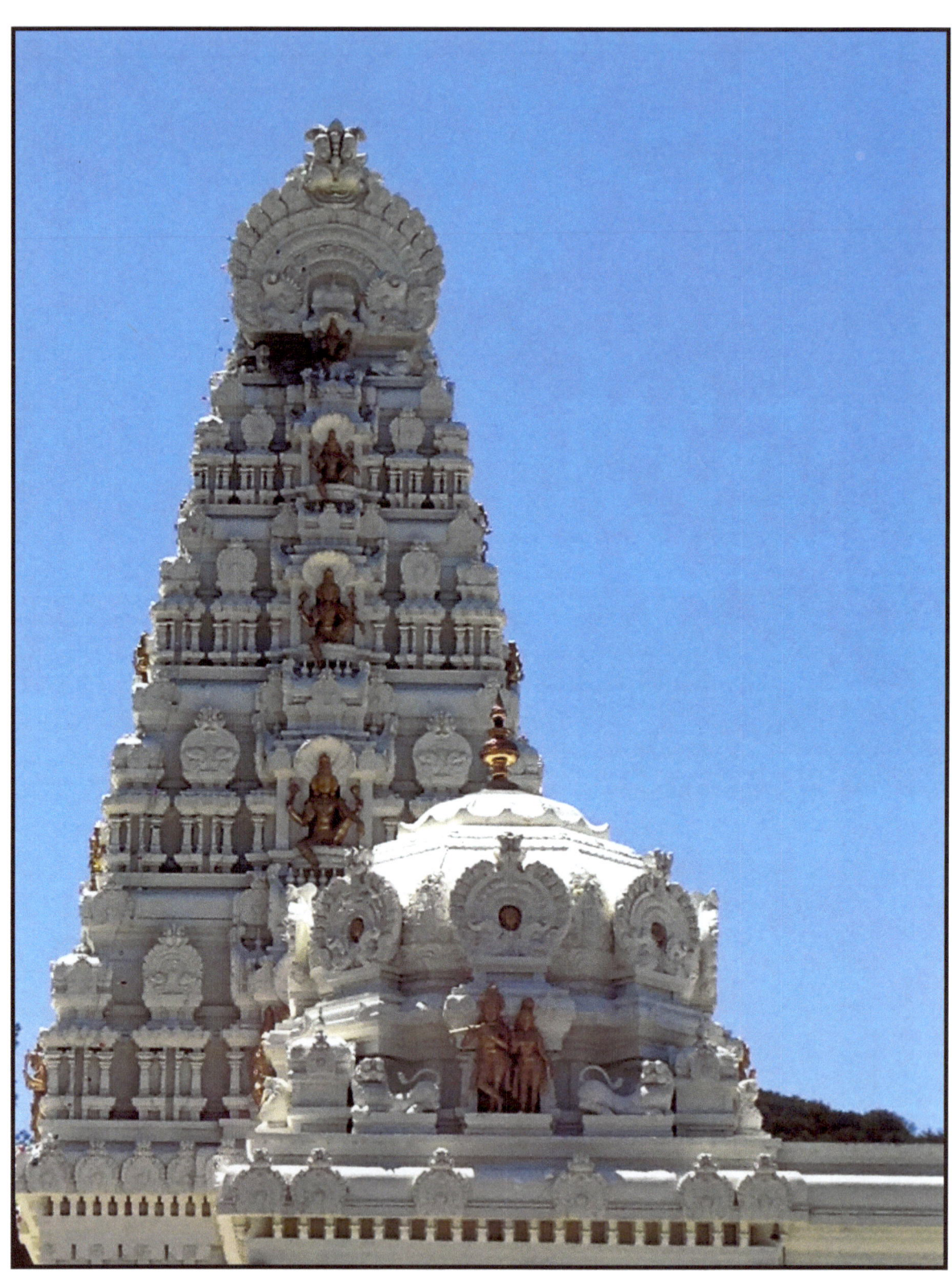

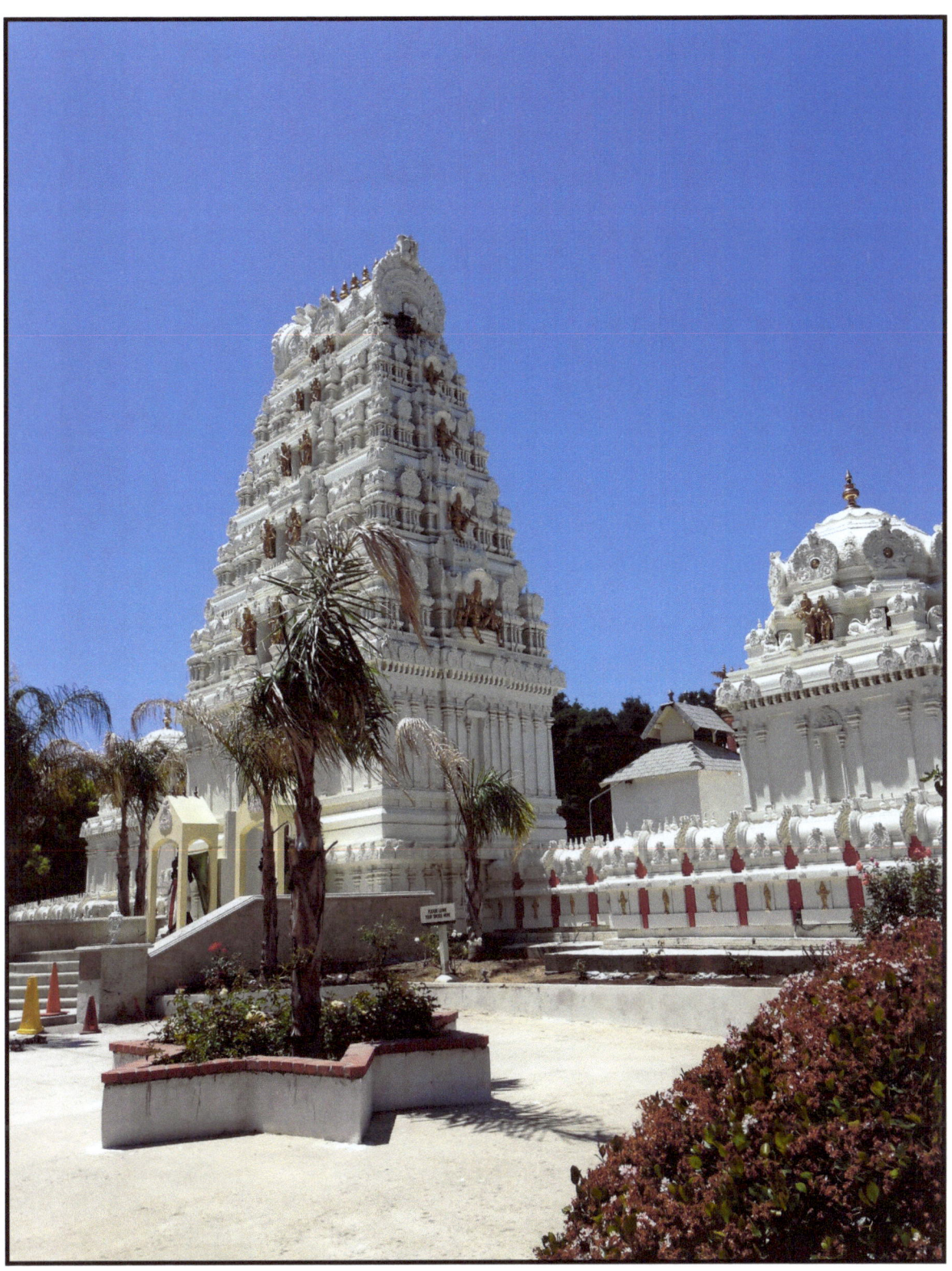

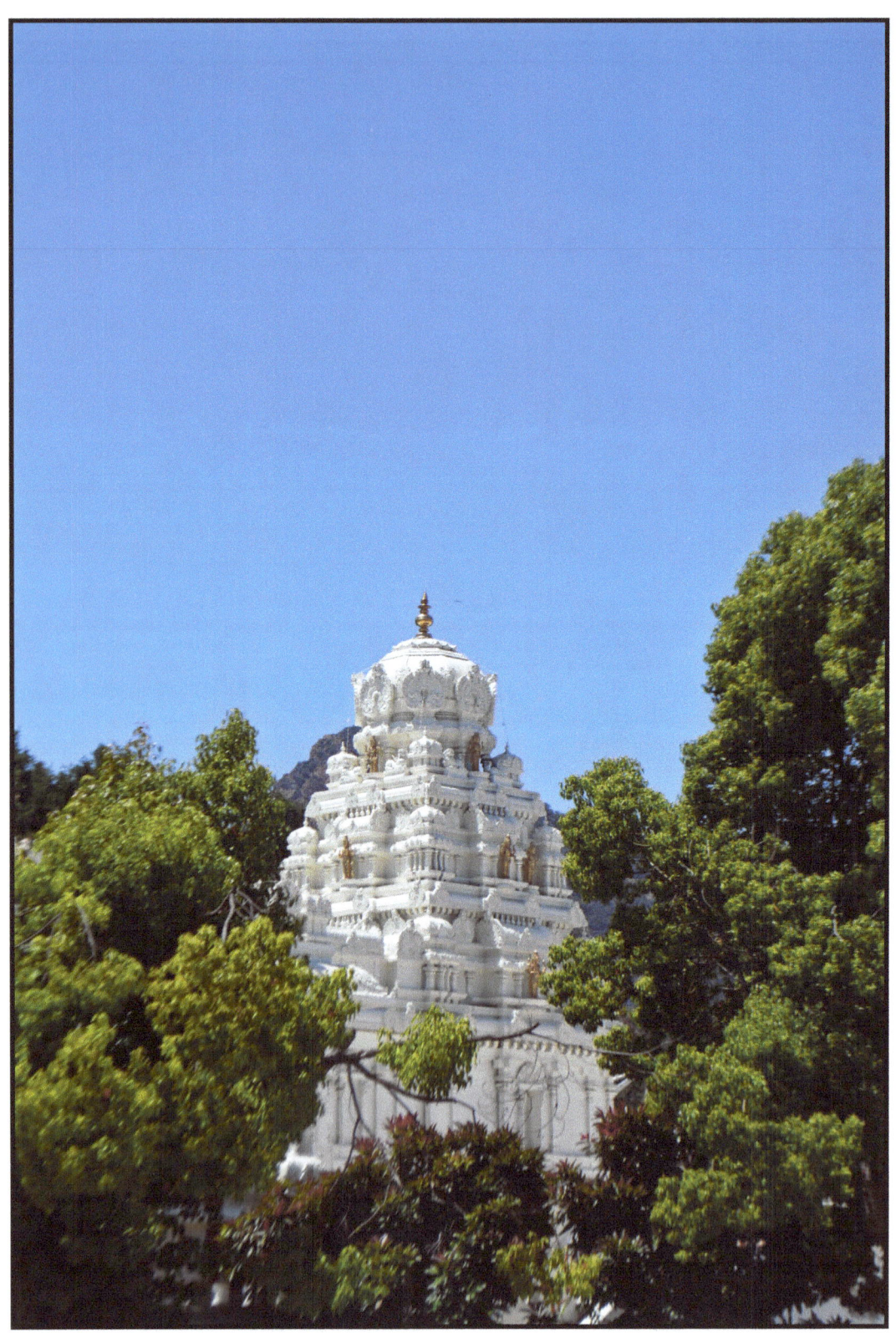

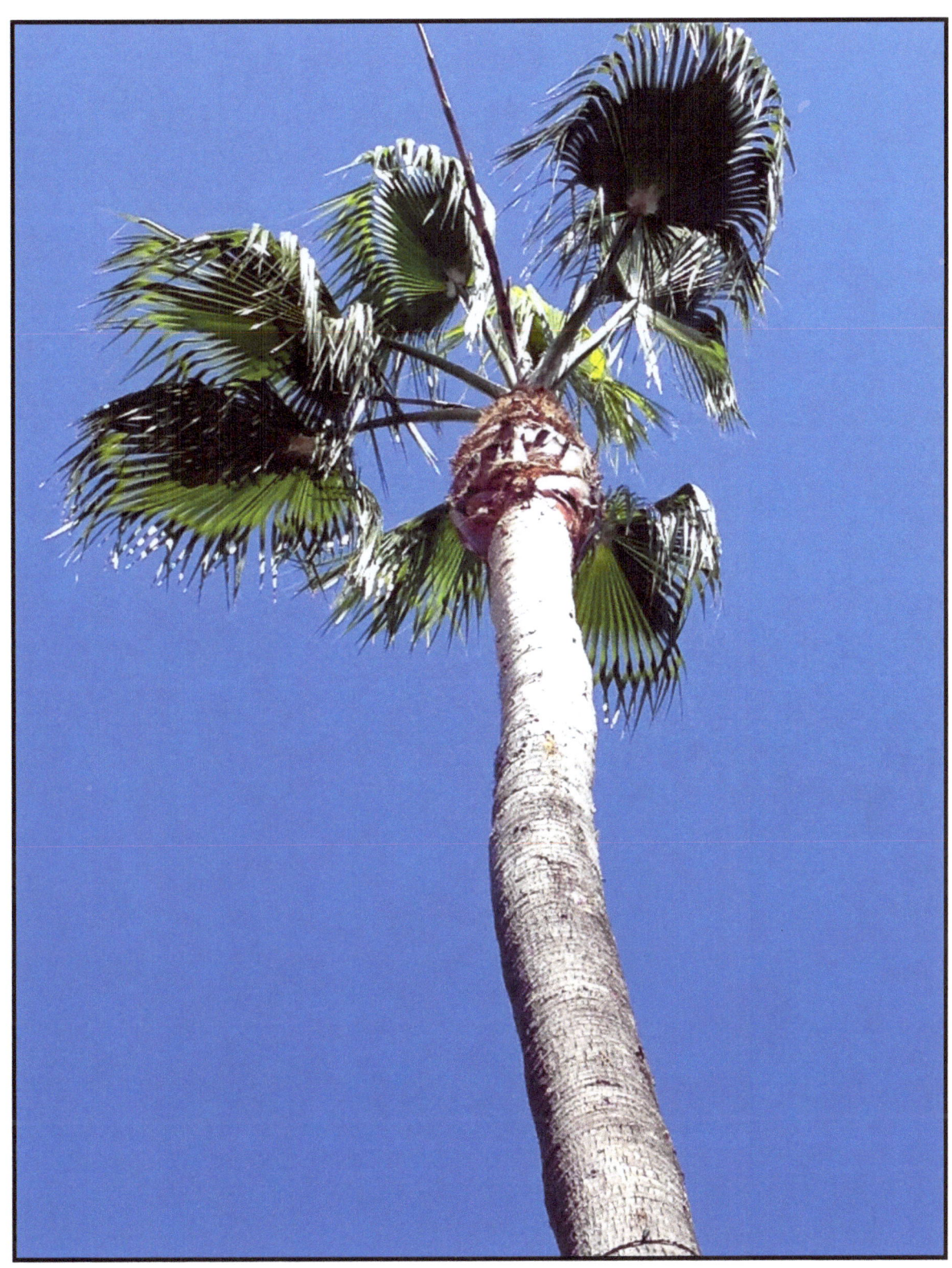

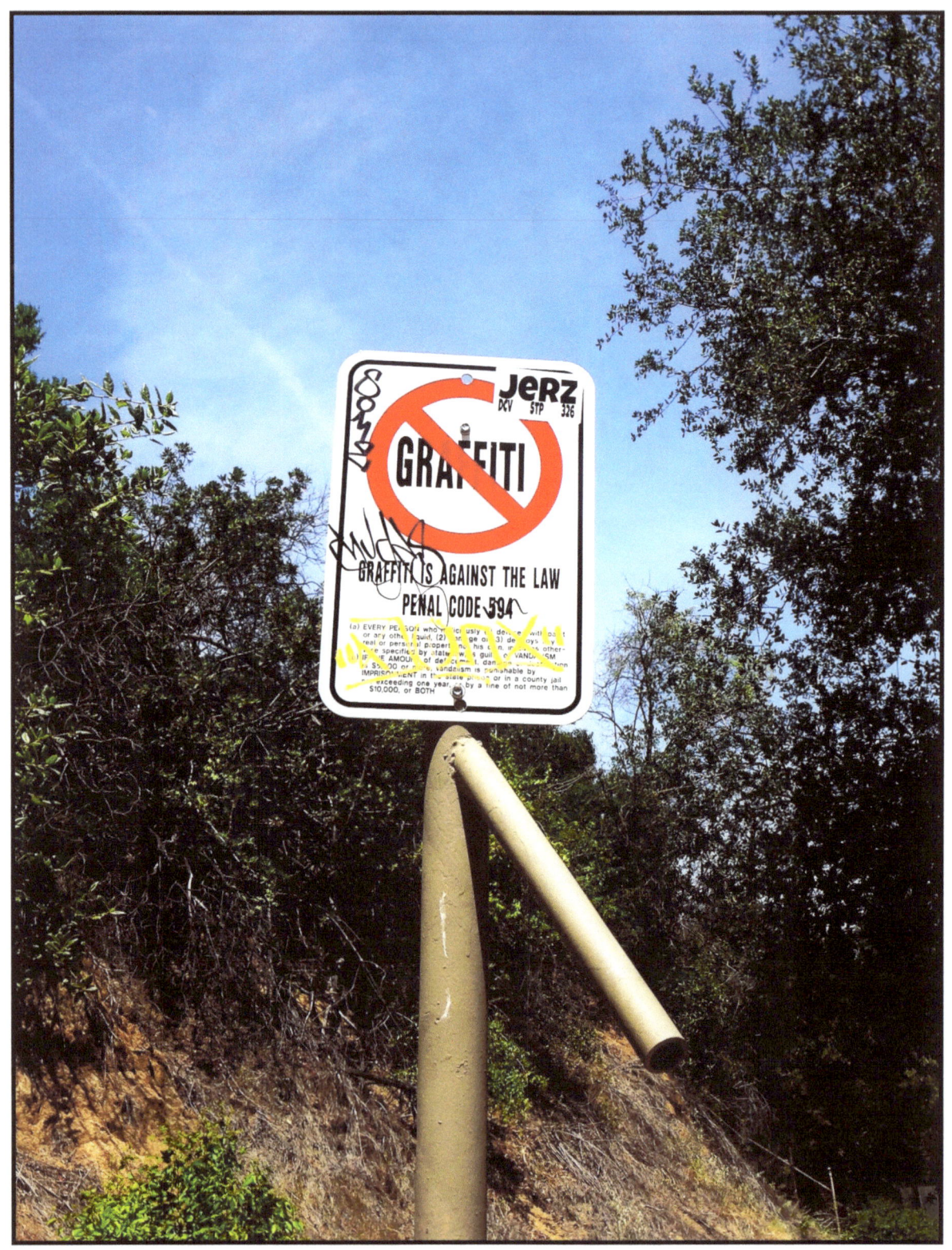

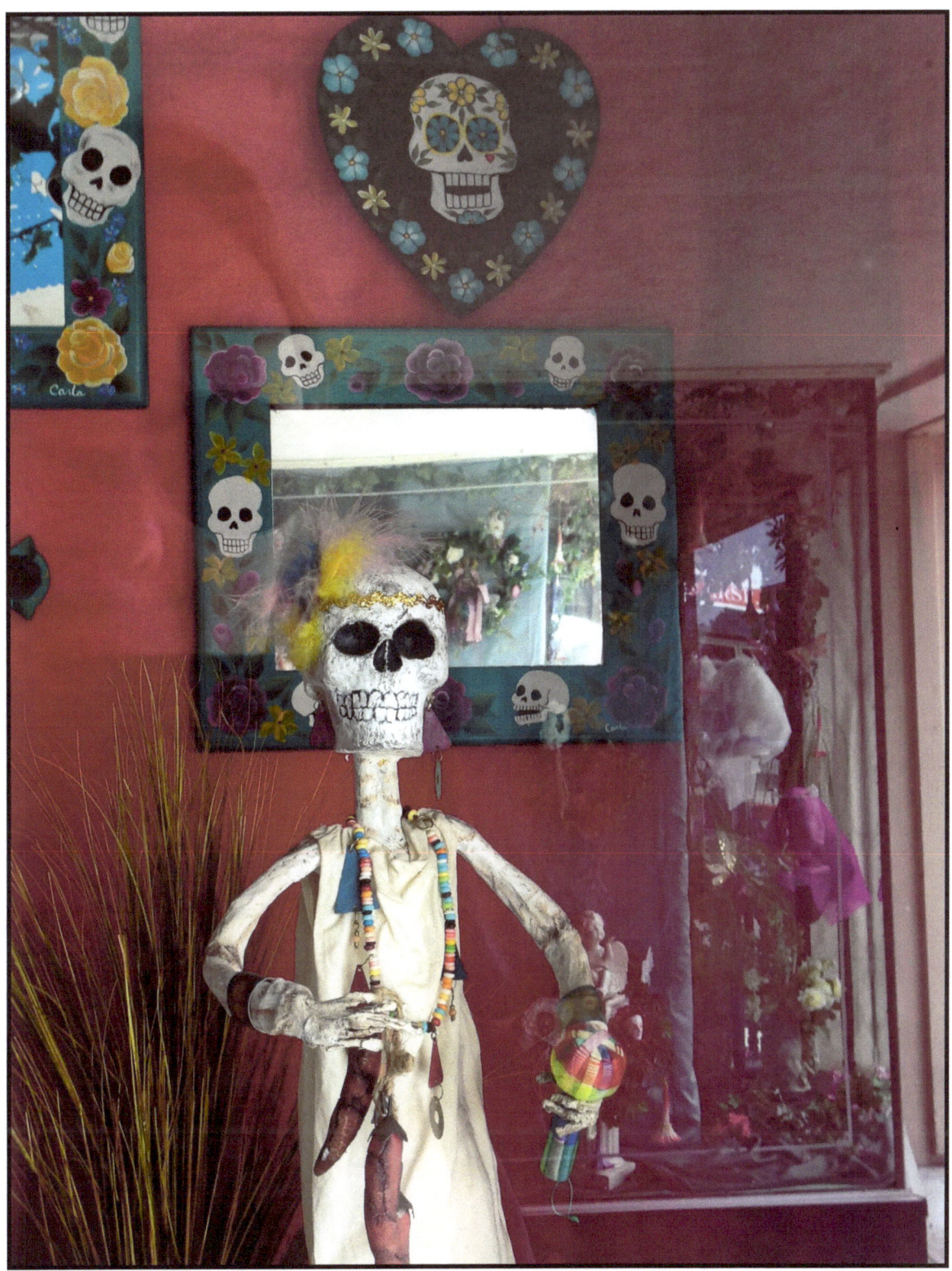

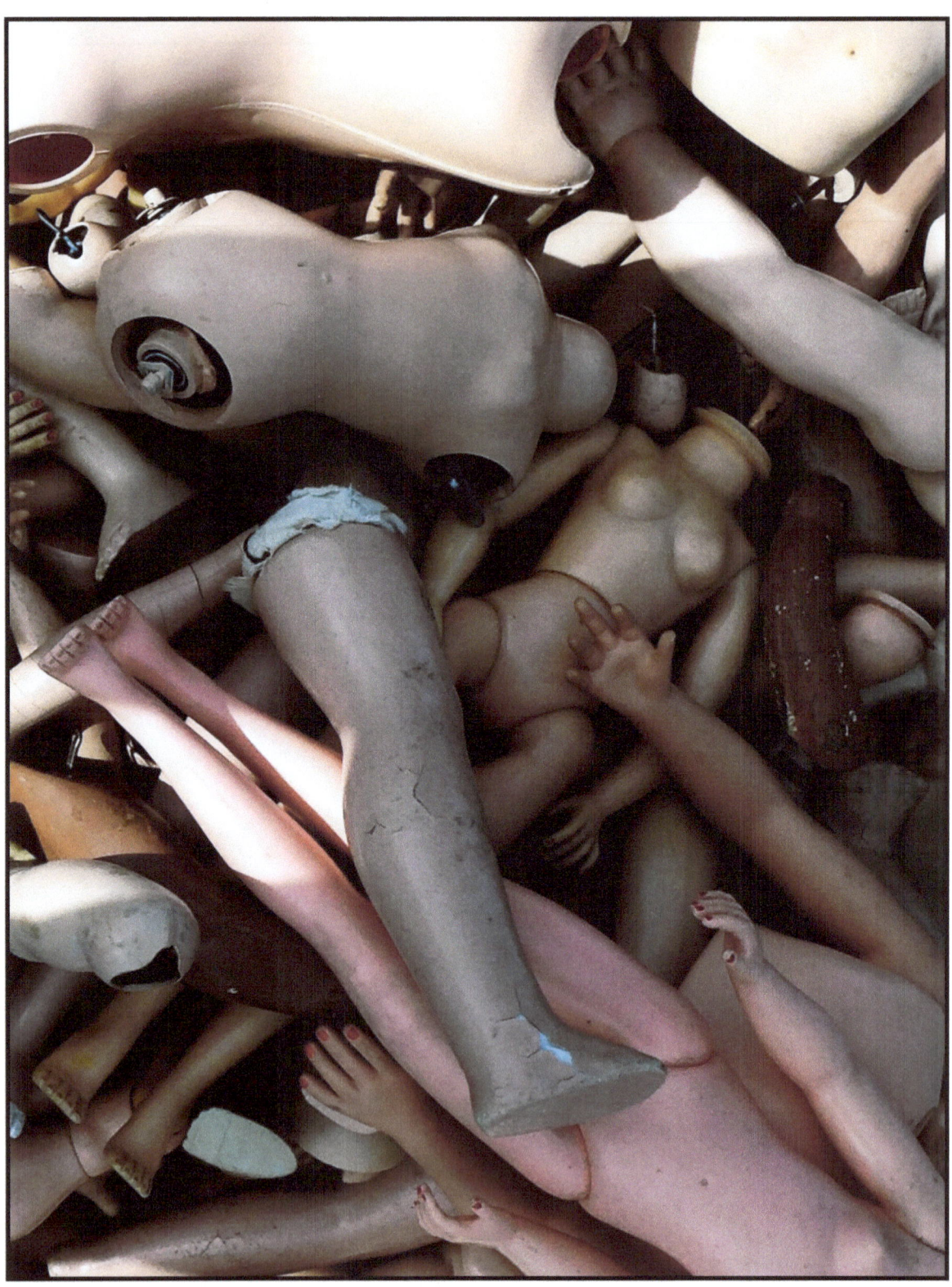

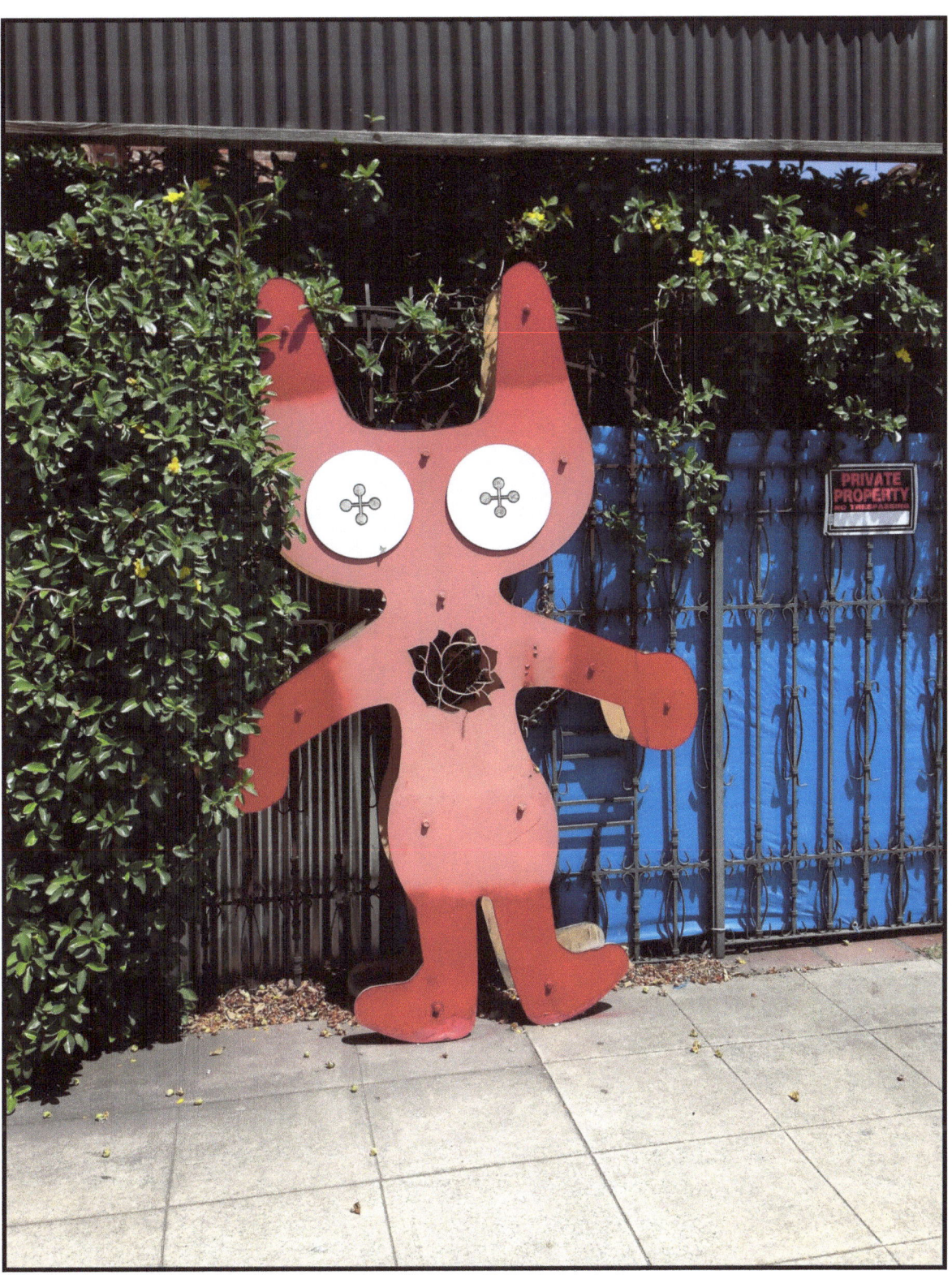

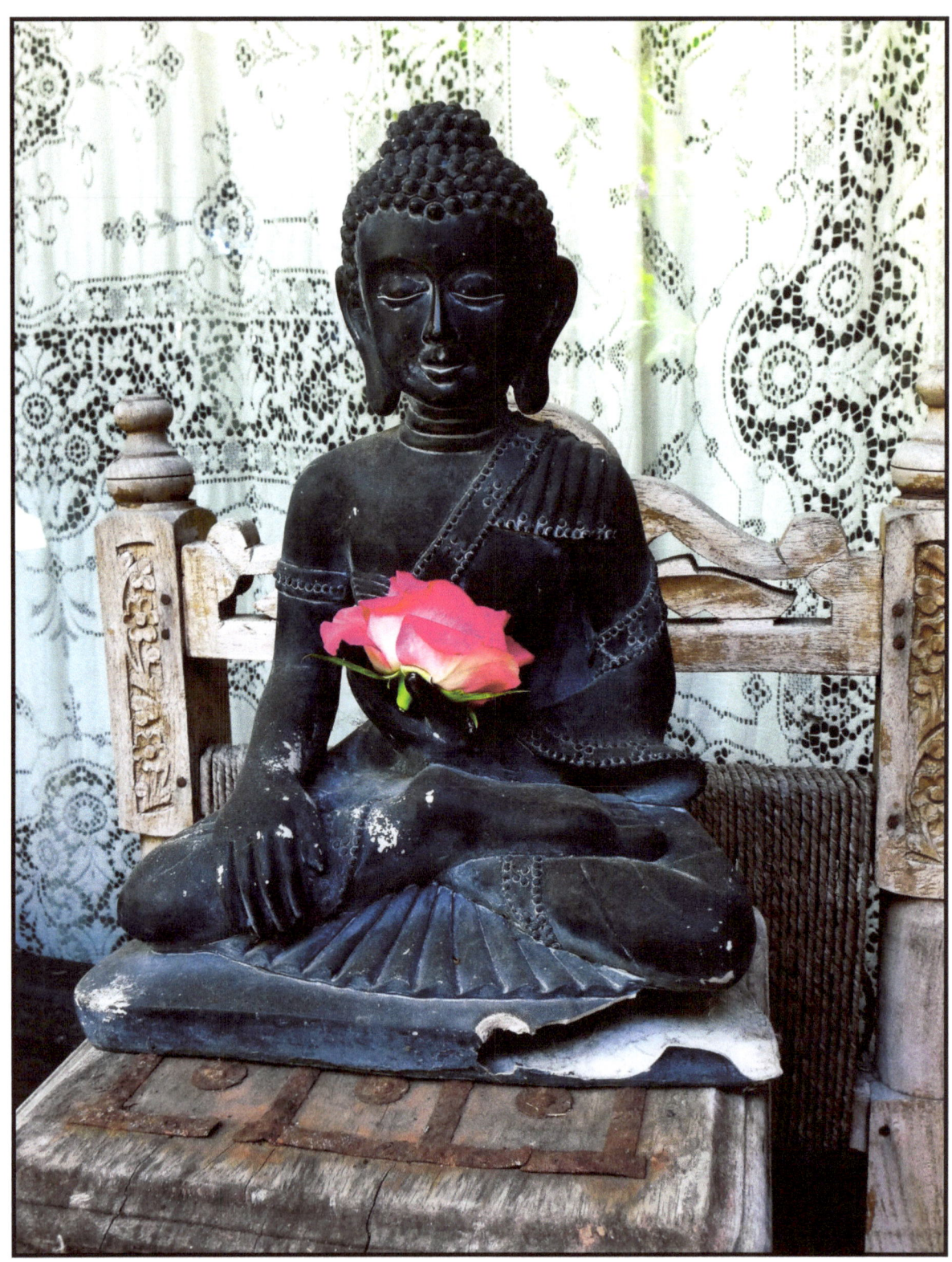

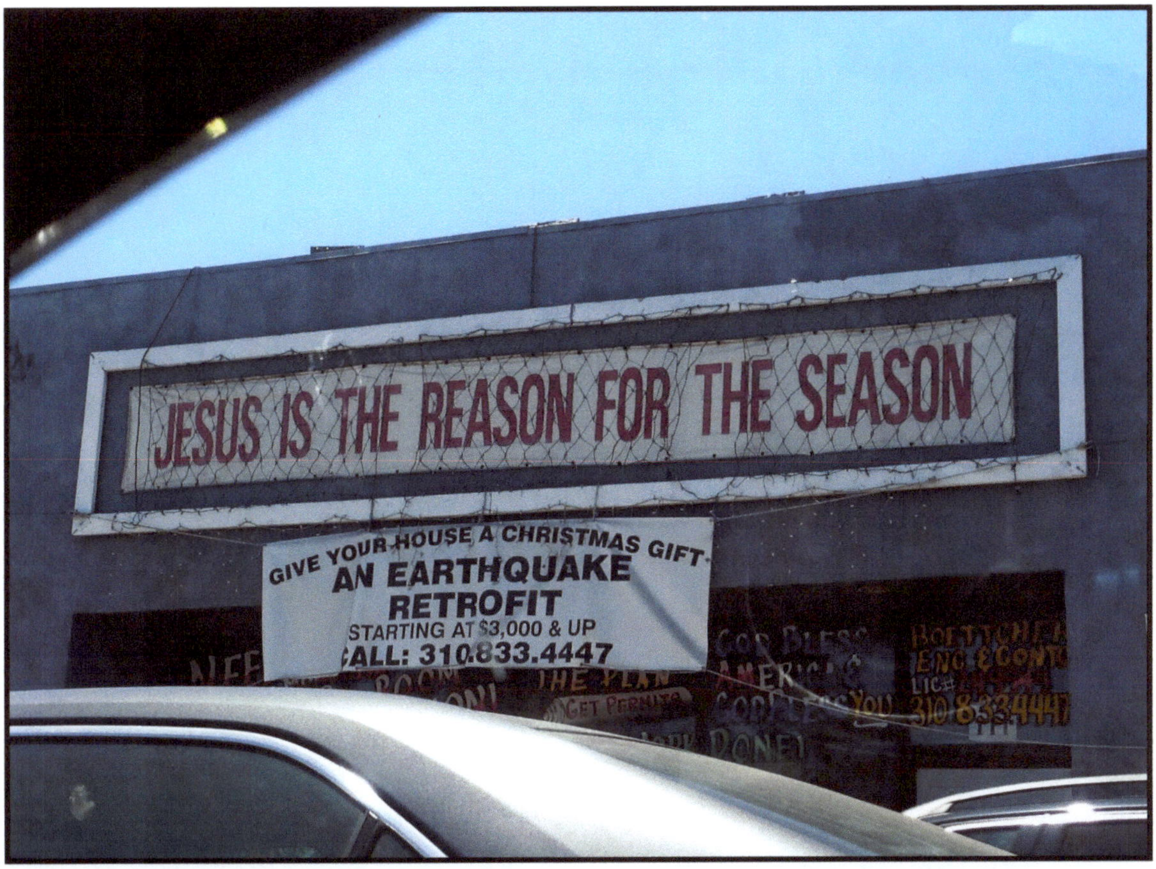

JESUS IS THE REASON FOR THE SEASON

GIVE YOUR HOUSE A CHRISTMAS GIFT
AN EARTHQUAKE RETROFIT
STARTING AT $3,000 & UP
CALL: 310.833.4447

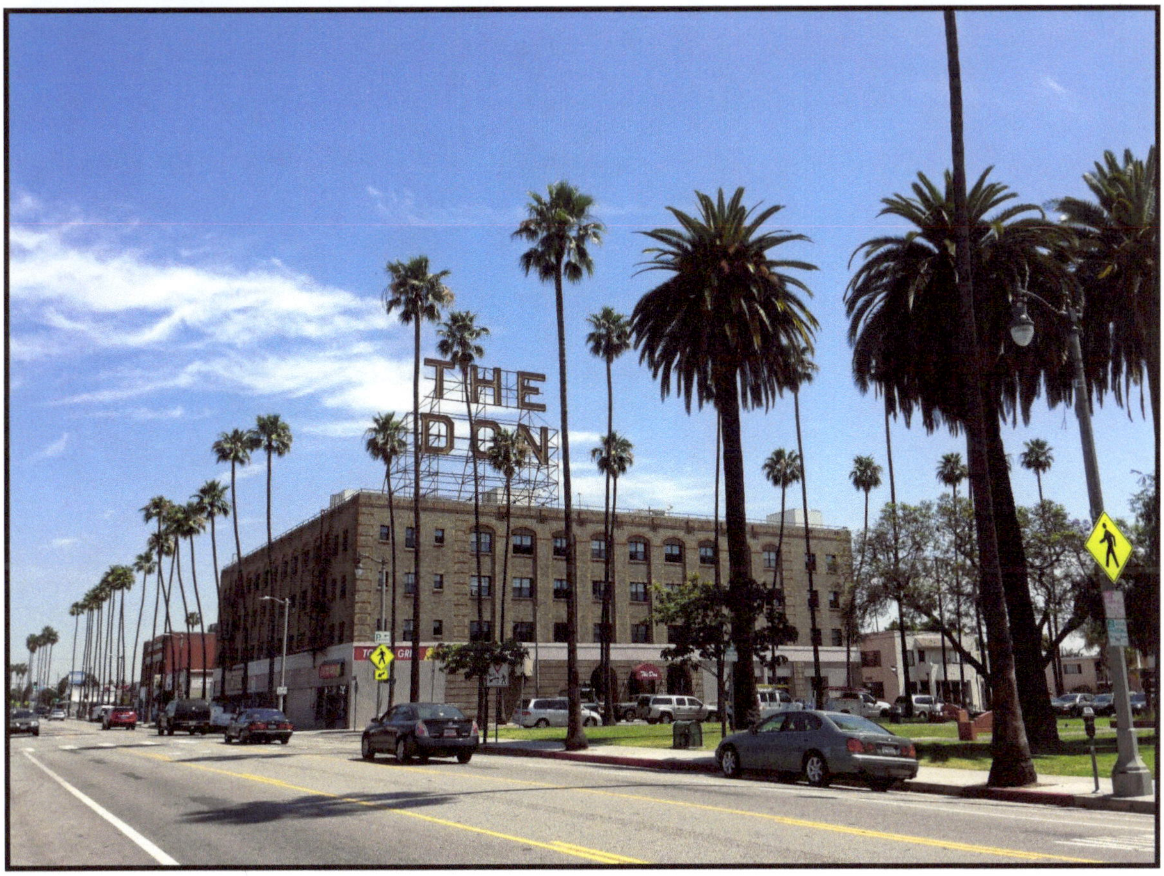

THE DON

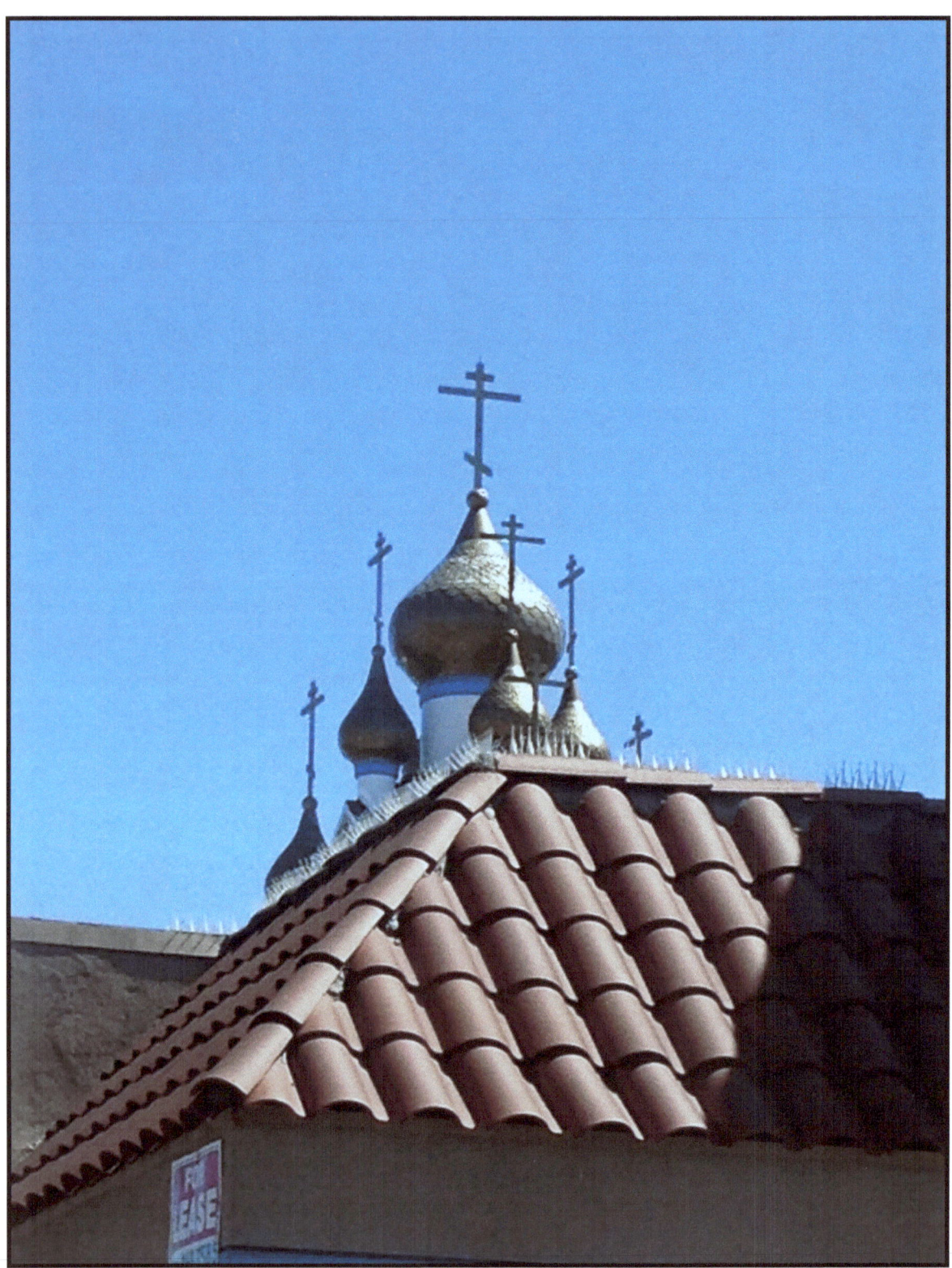

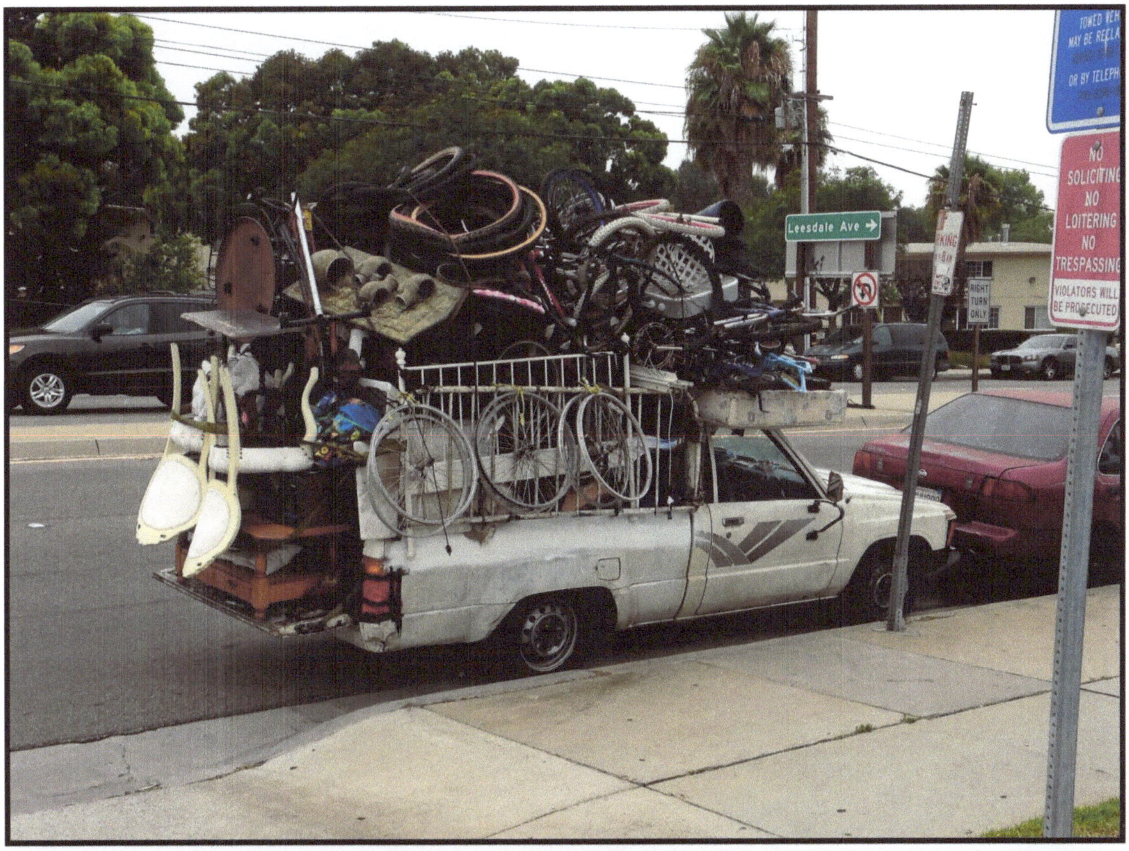

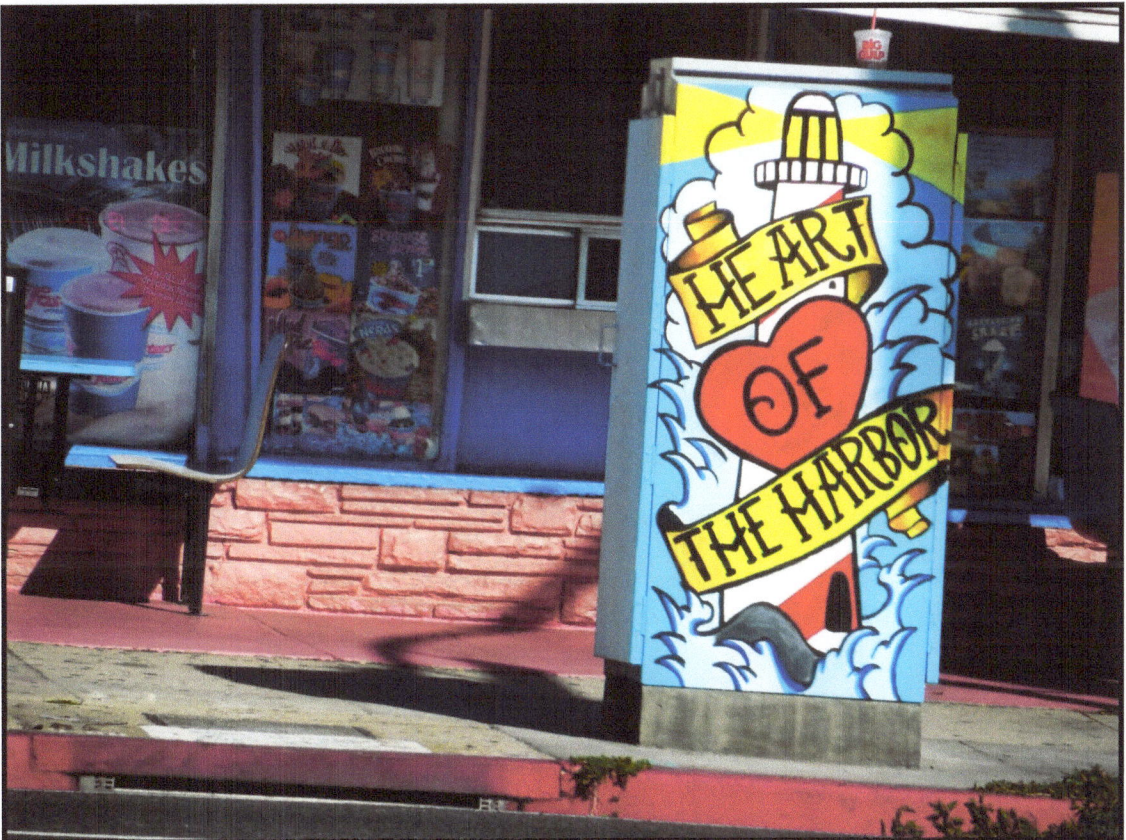

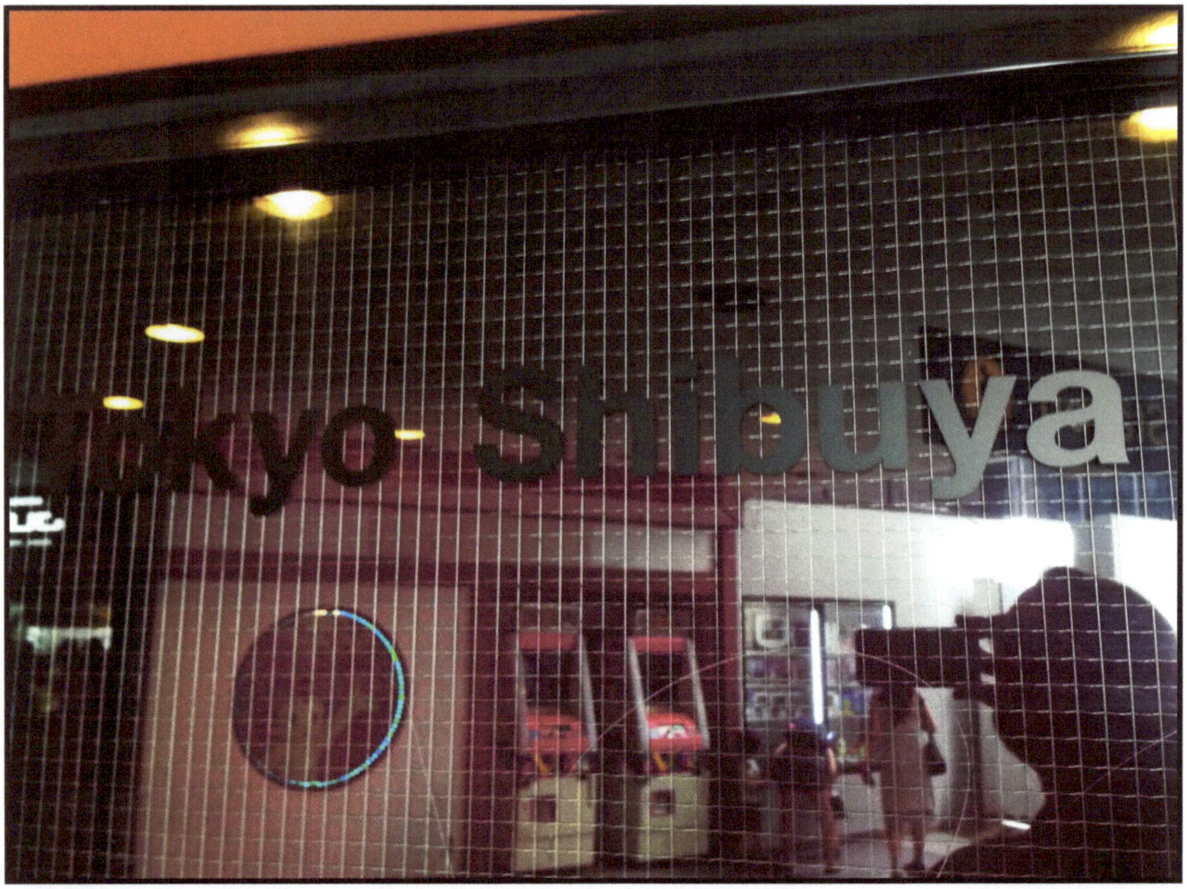

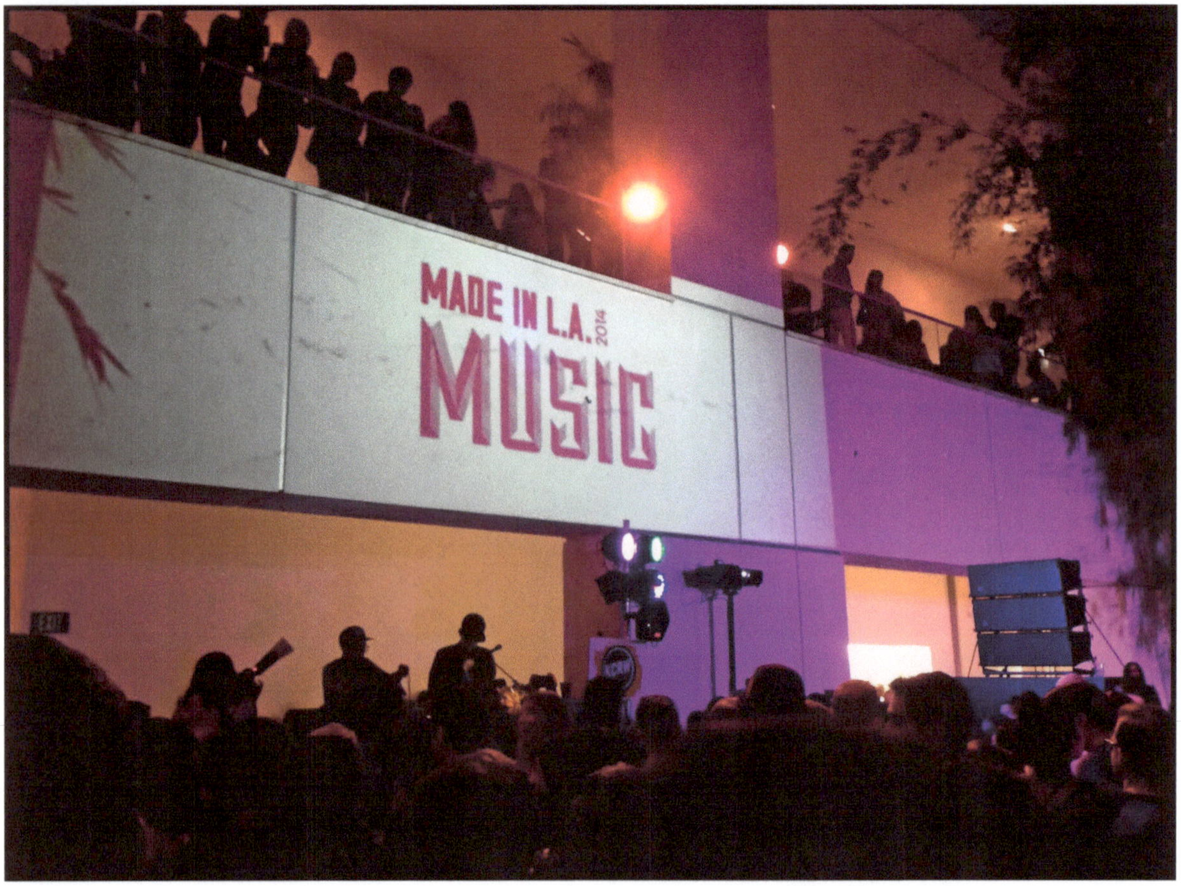

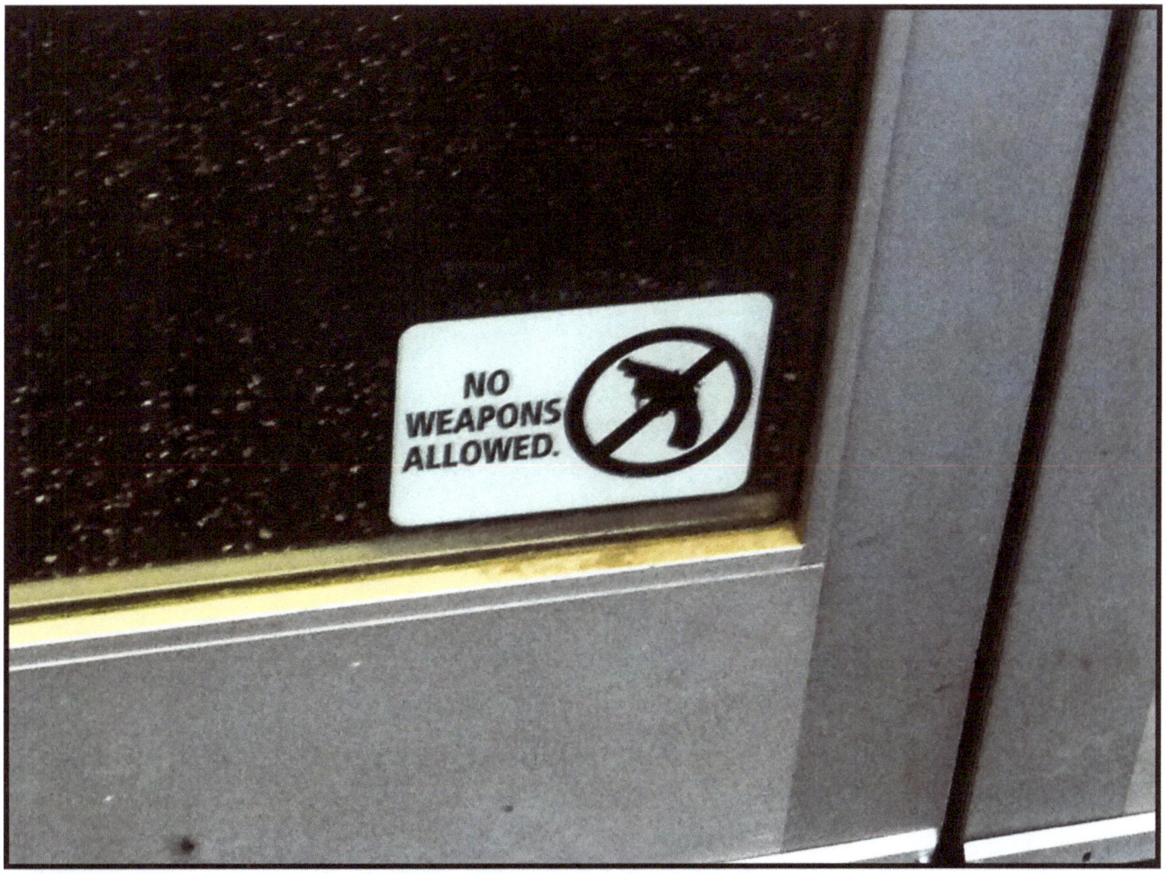

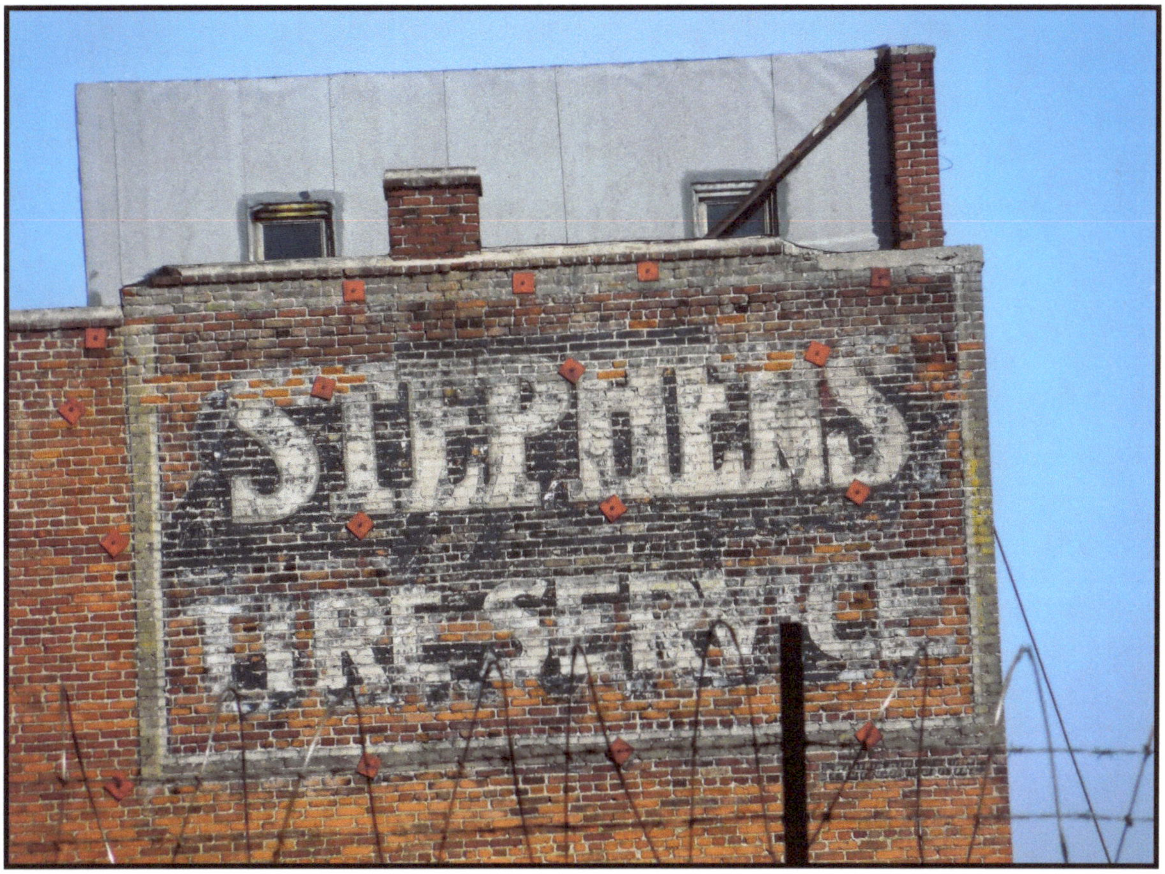

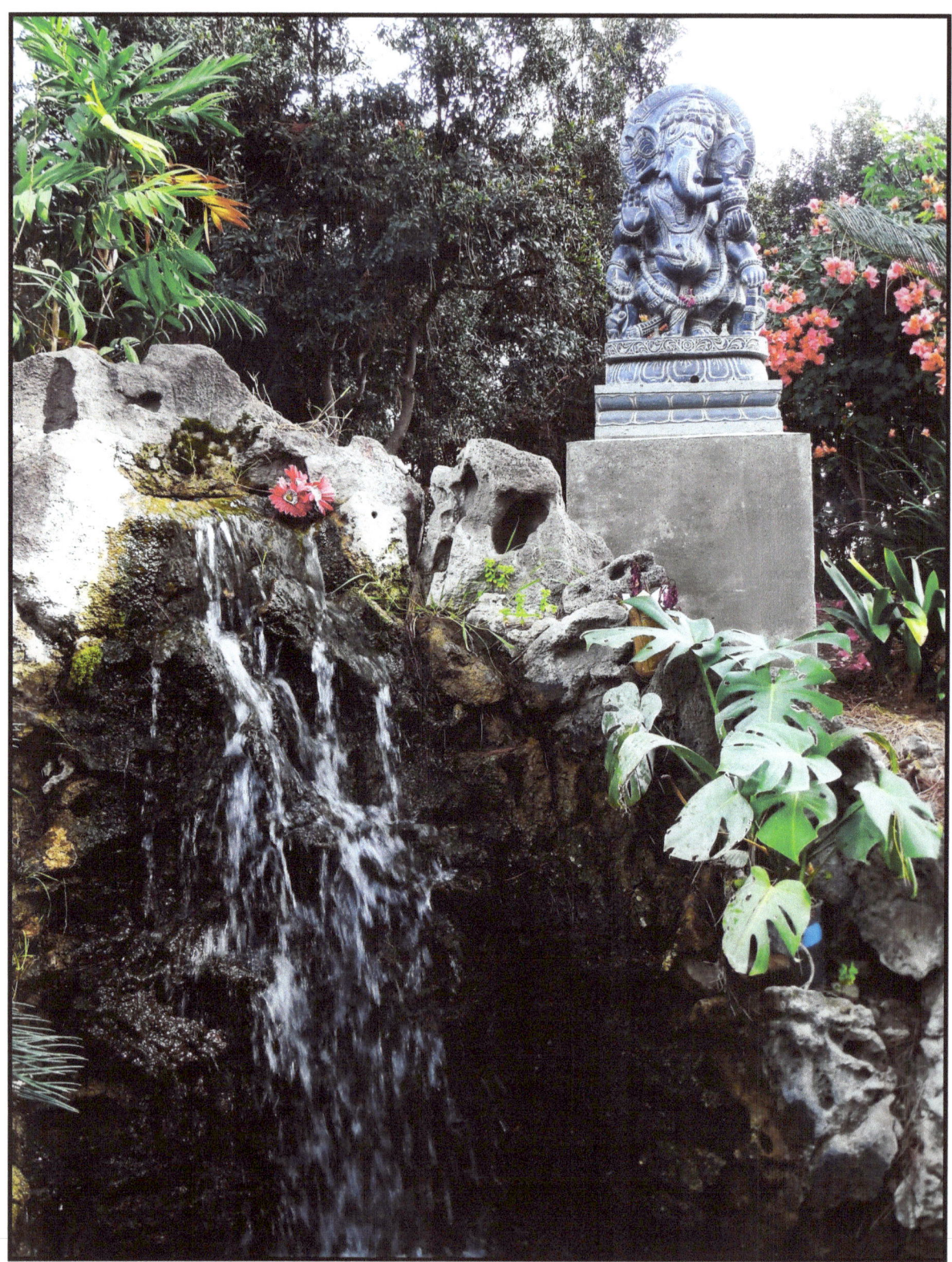

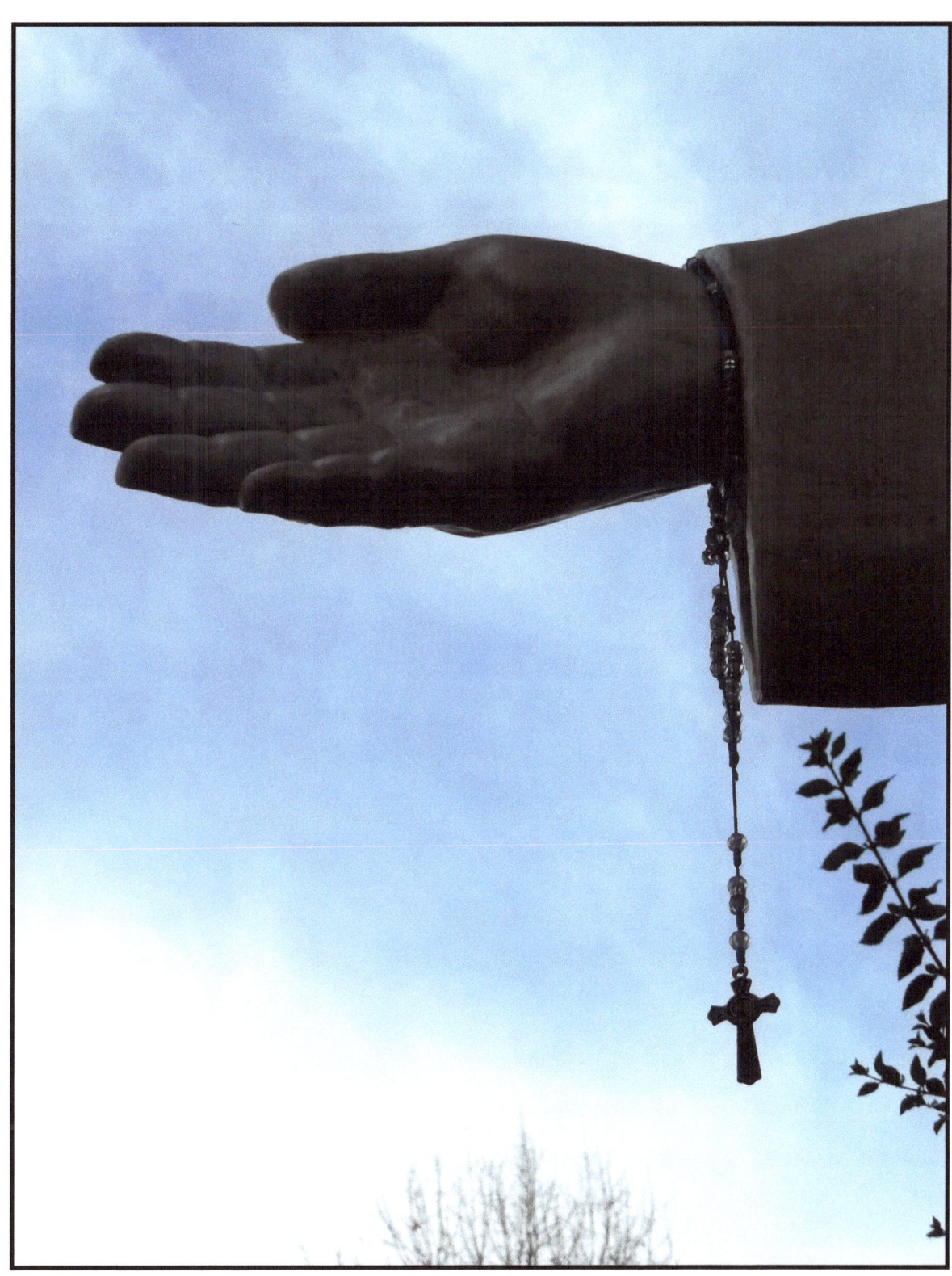

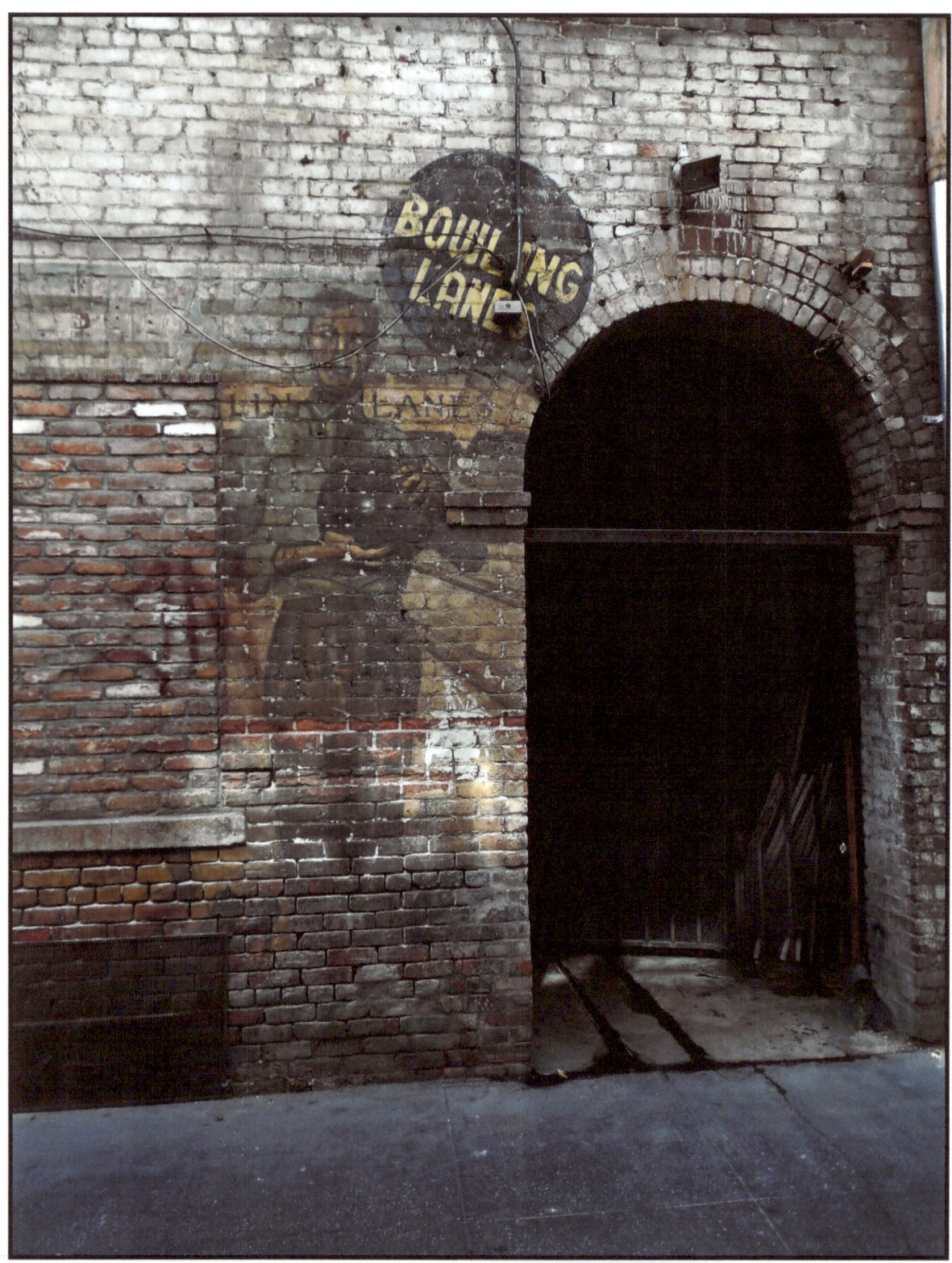

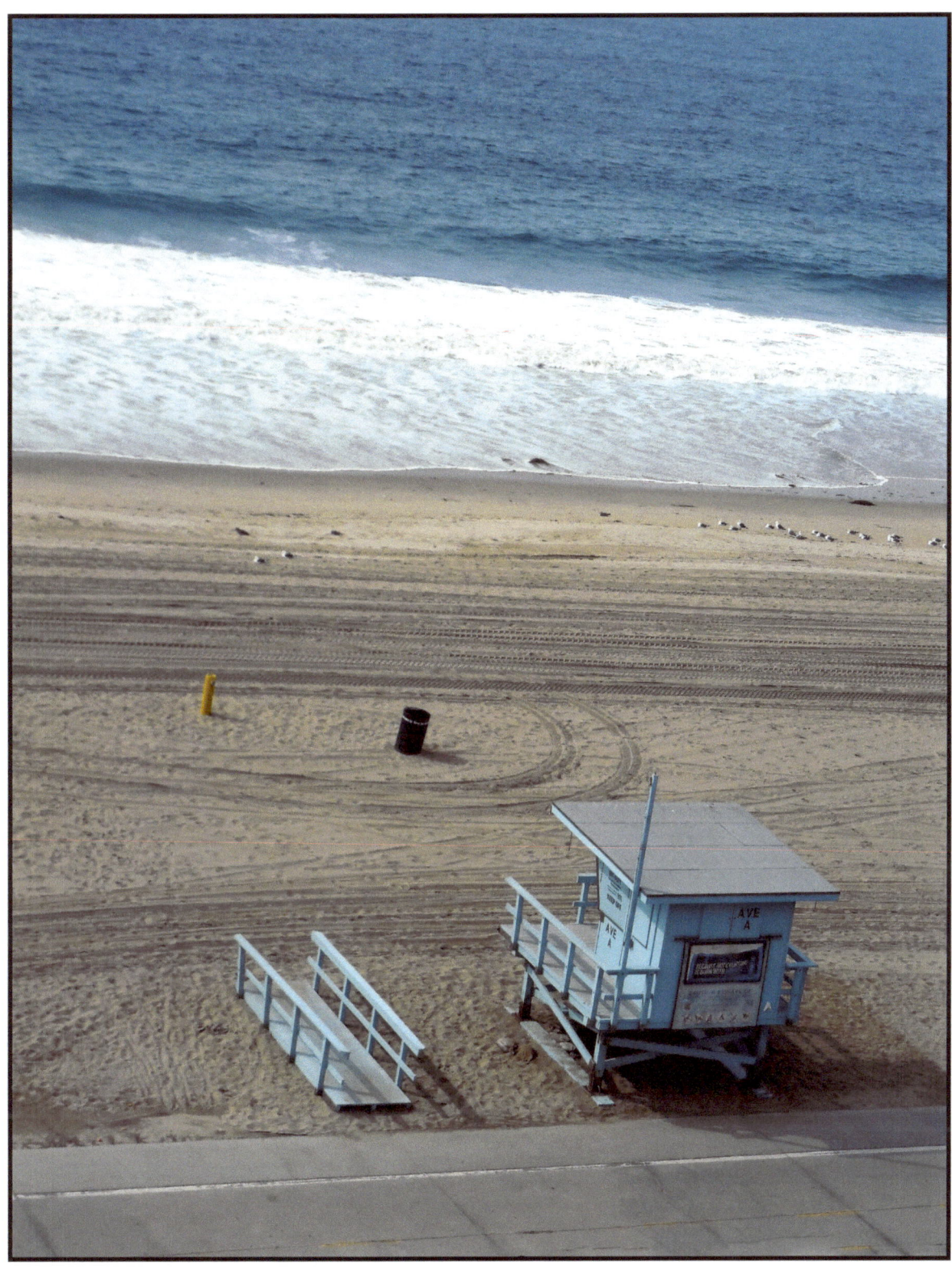

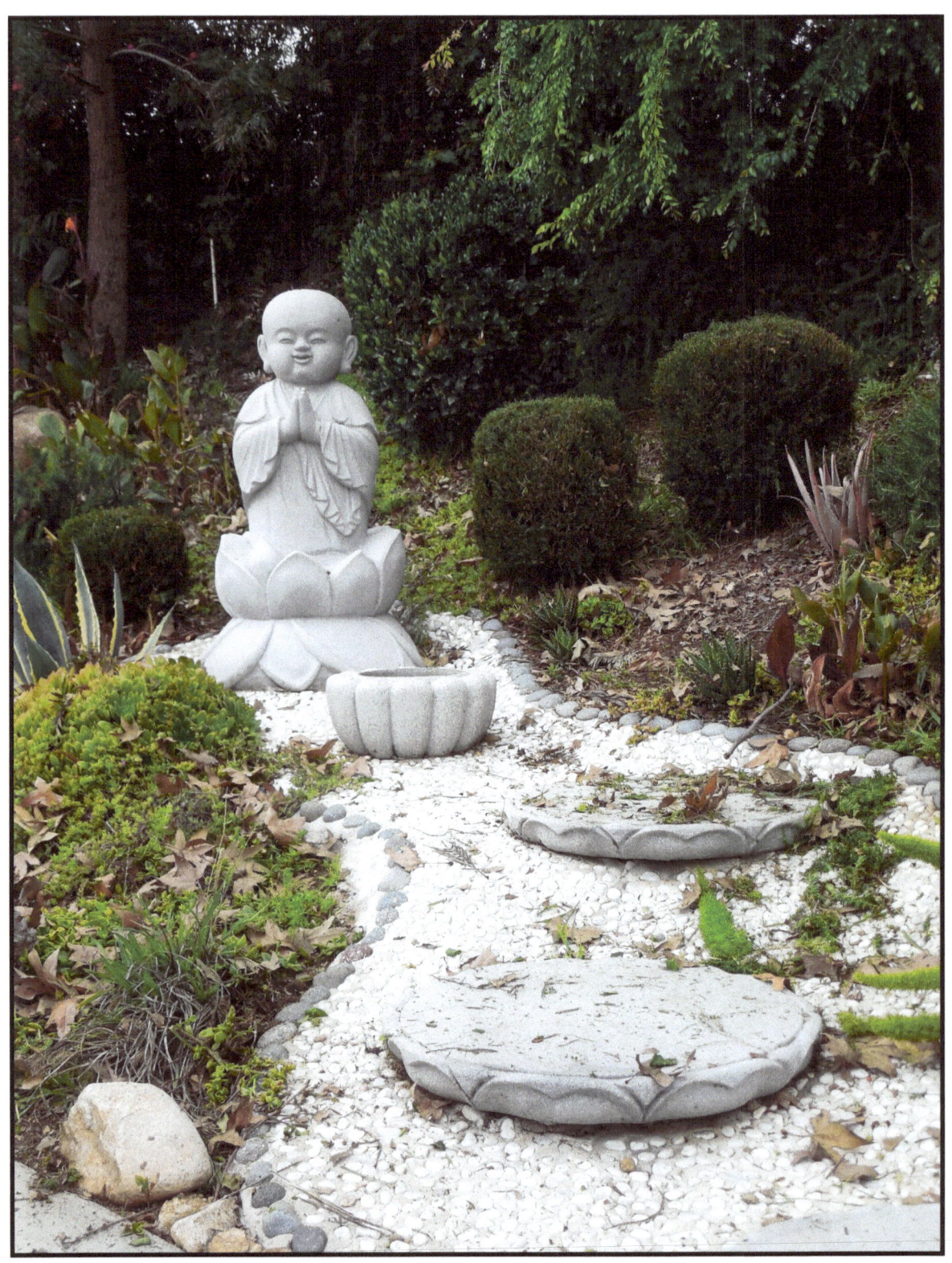

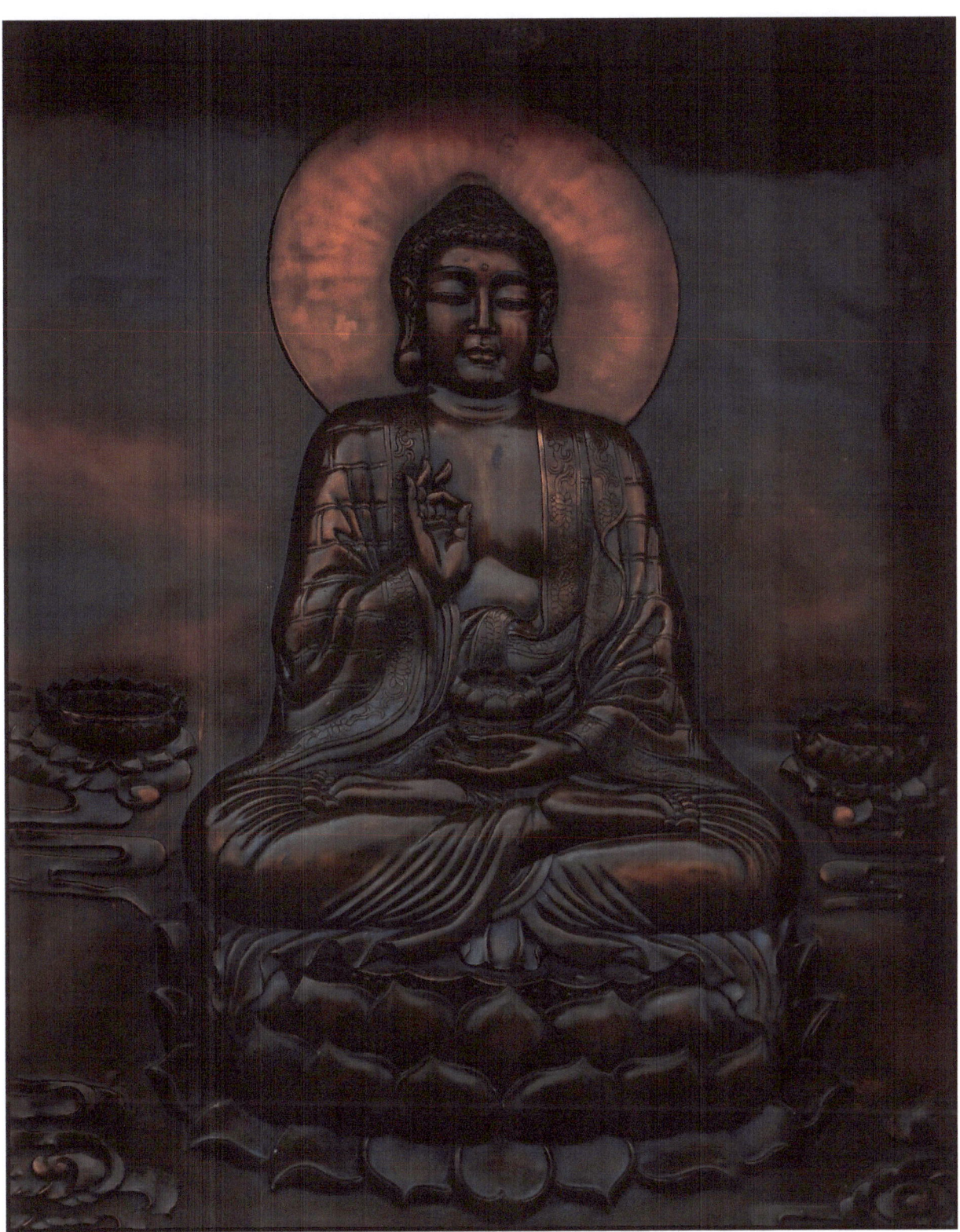

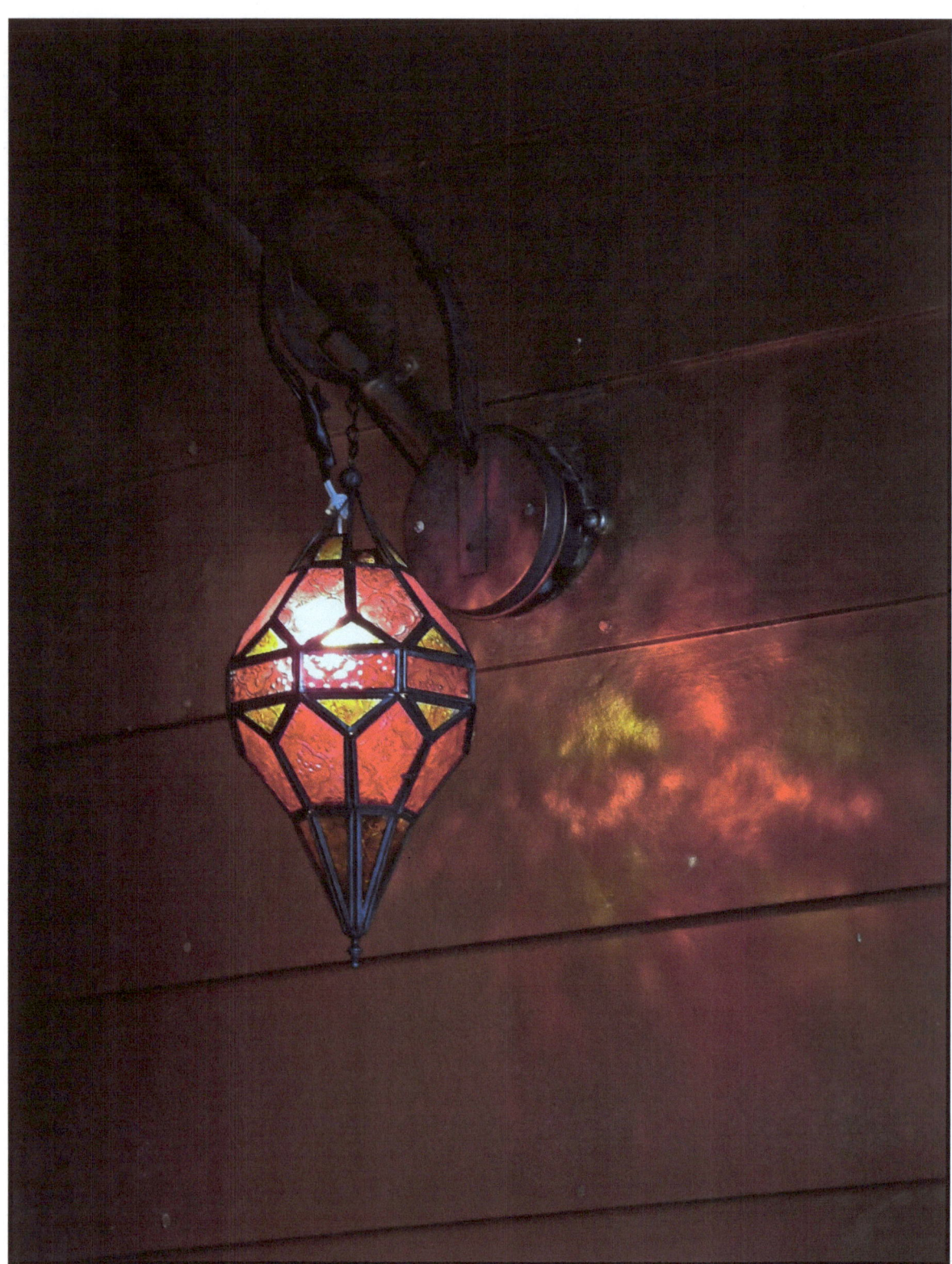

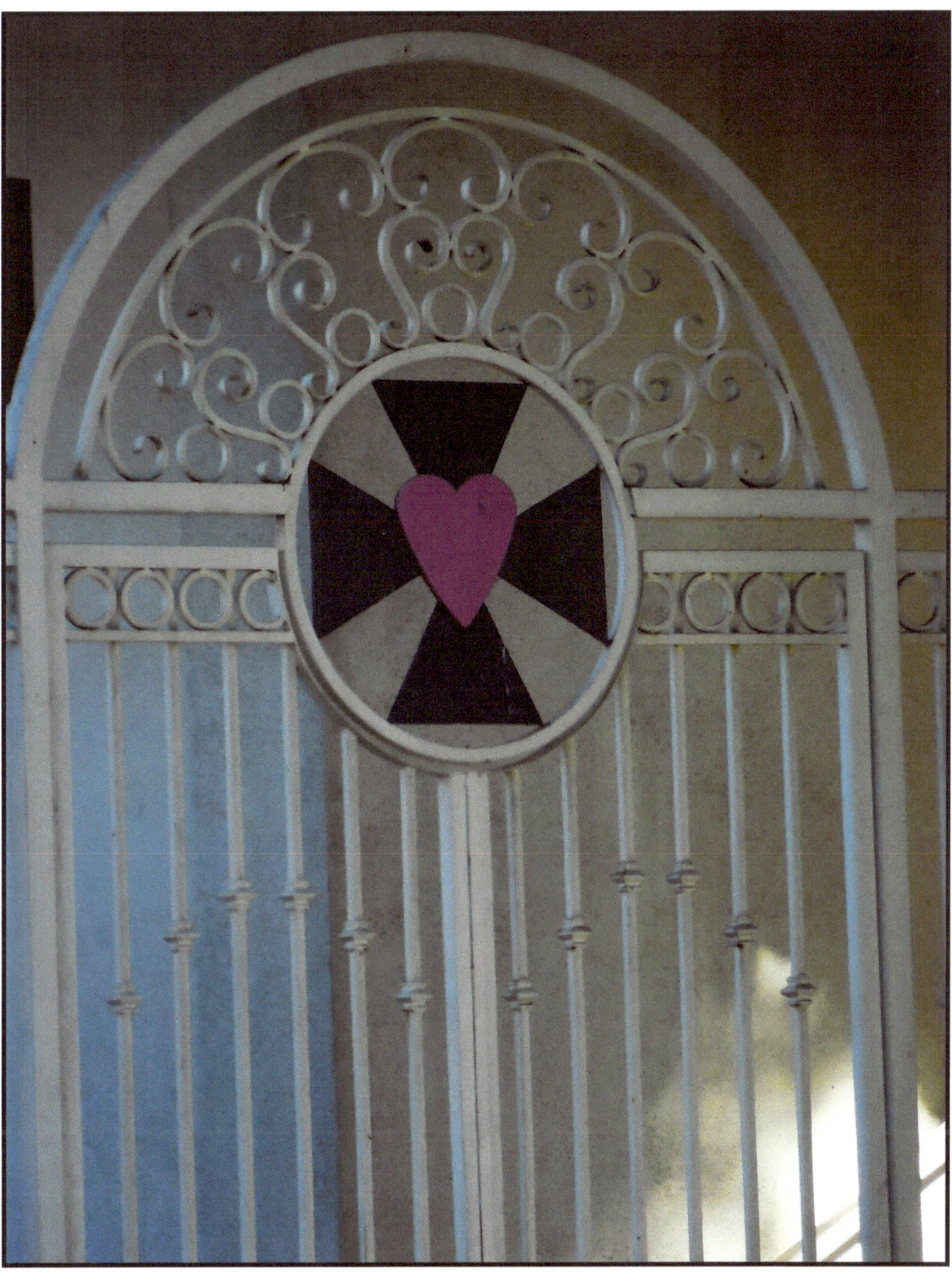

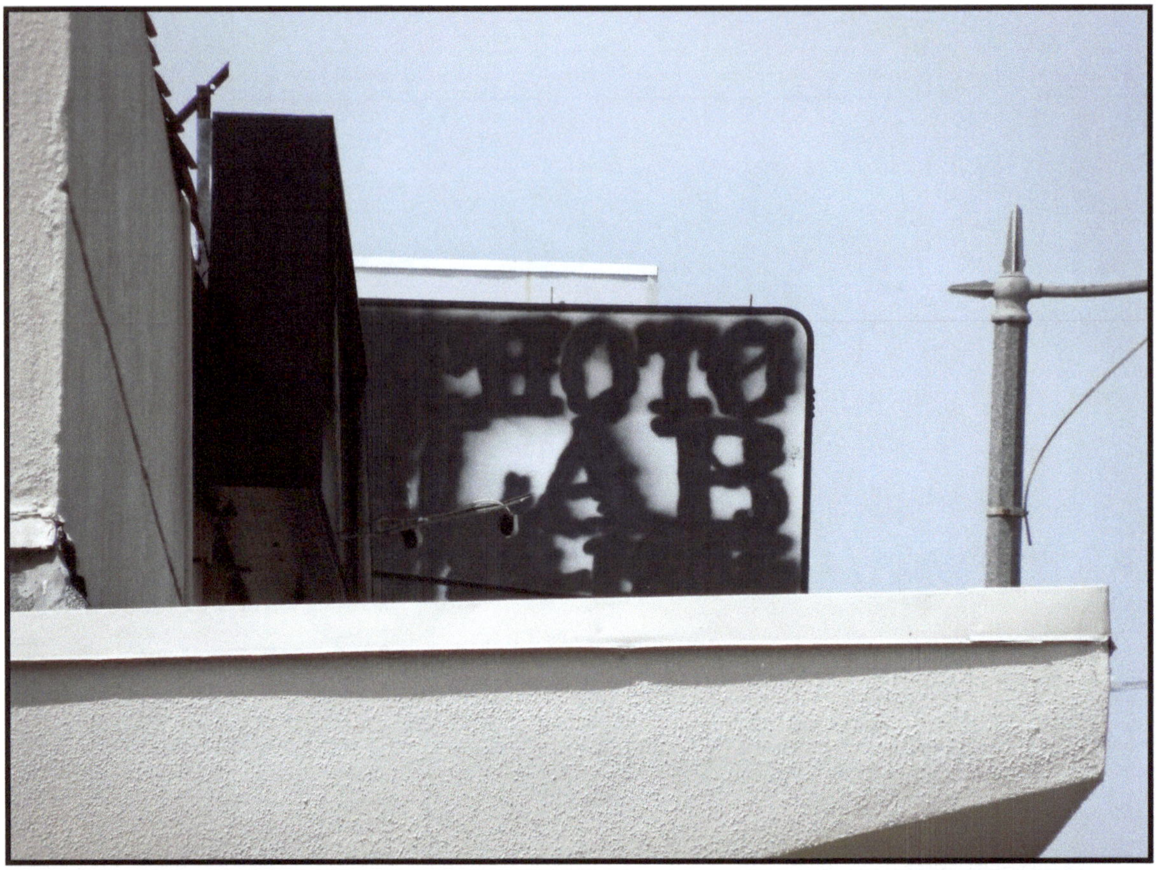

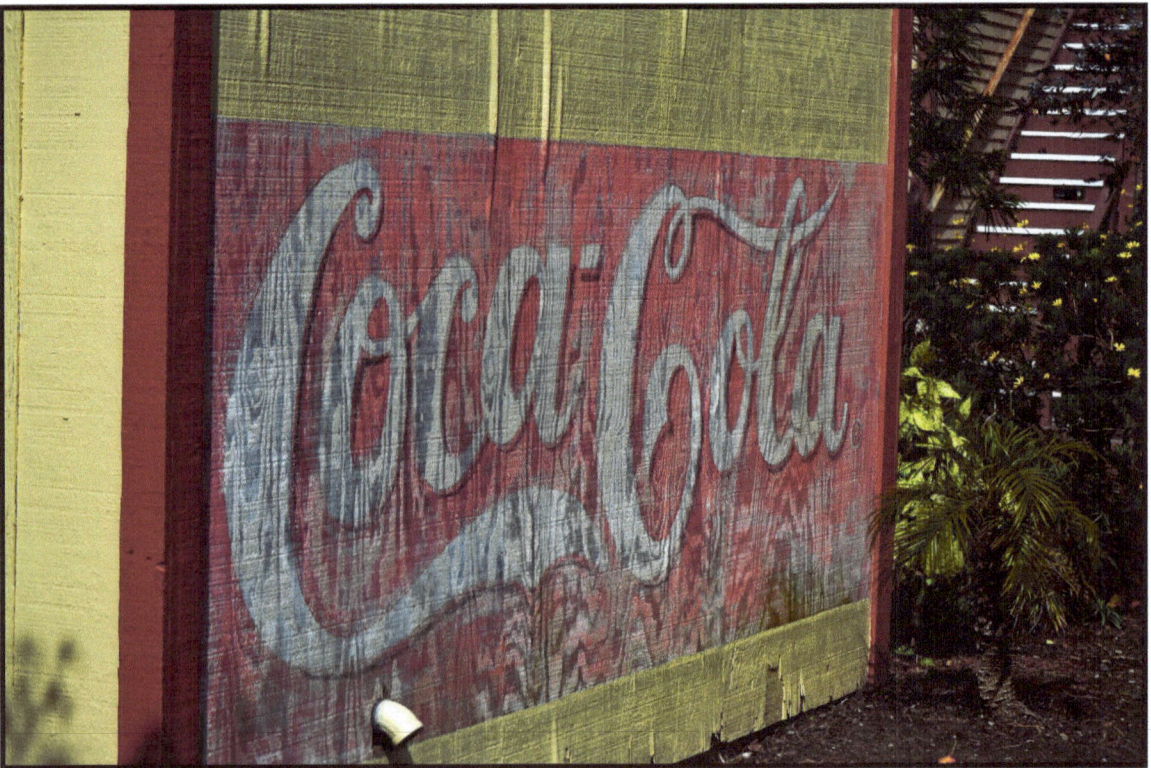

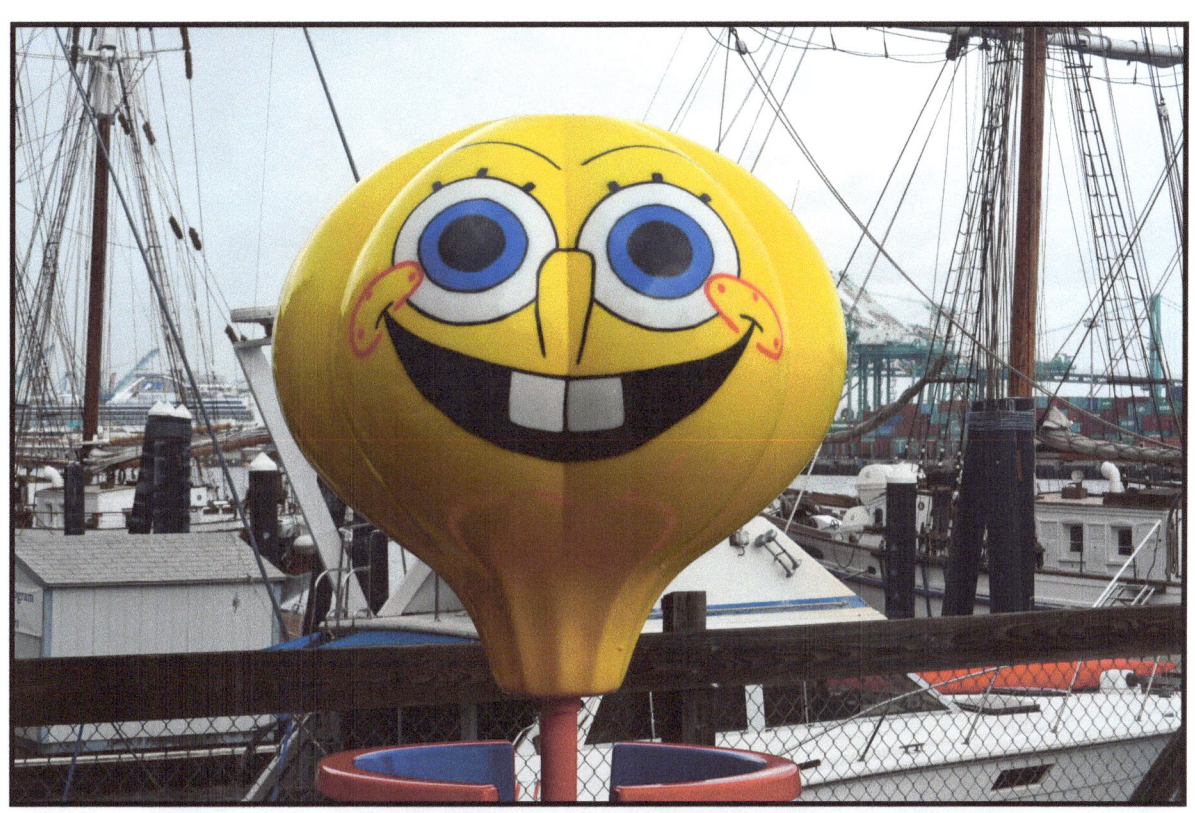
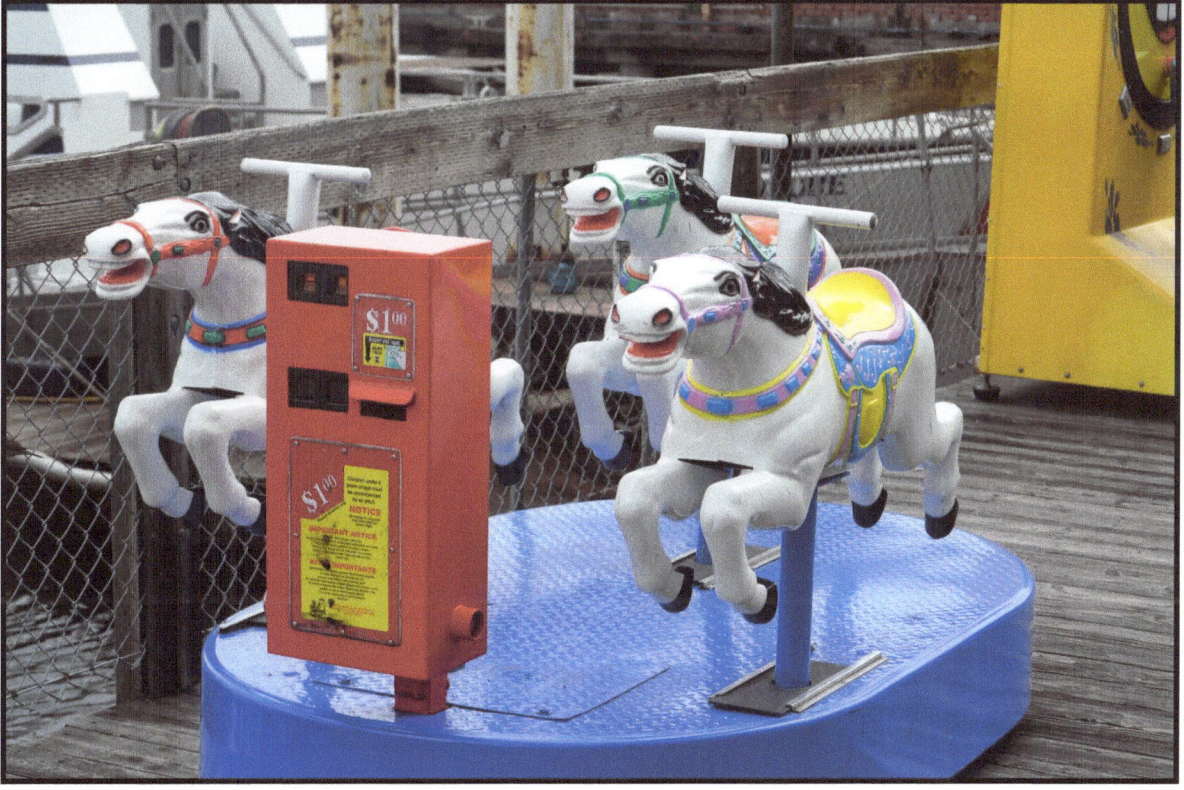

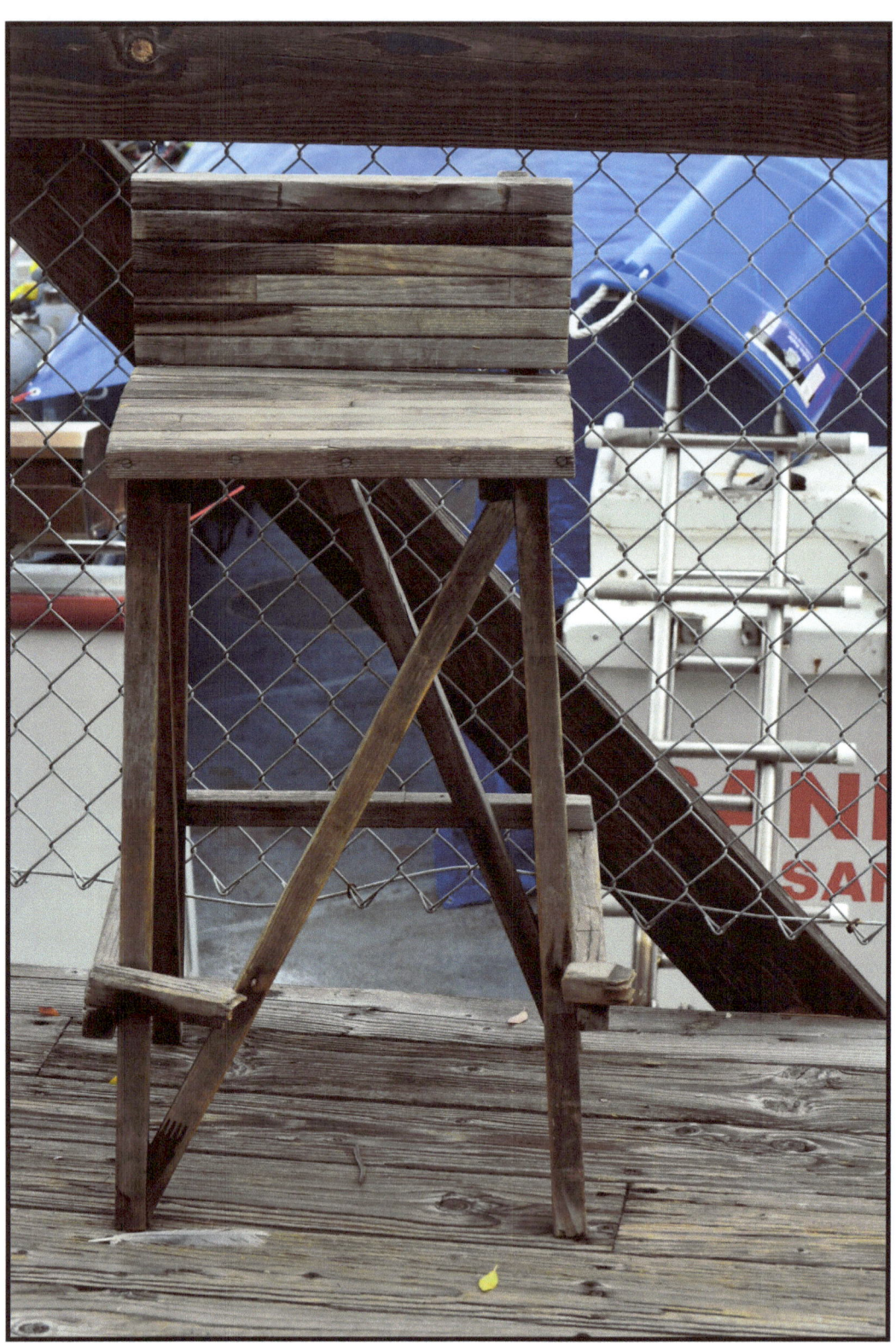

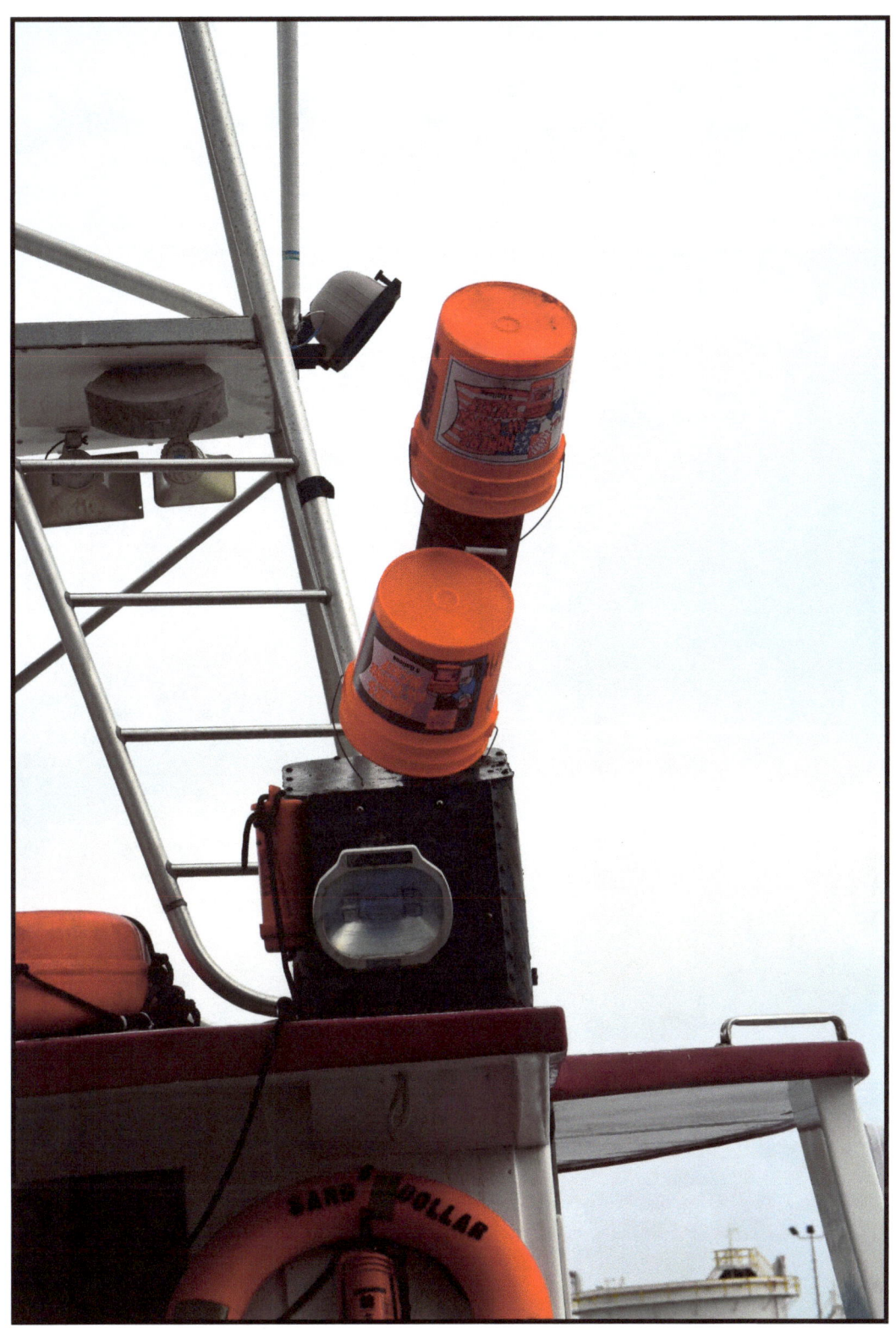

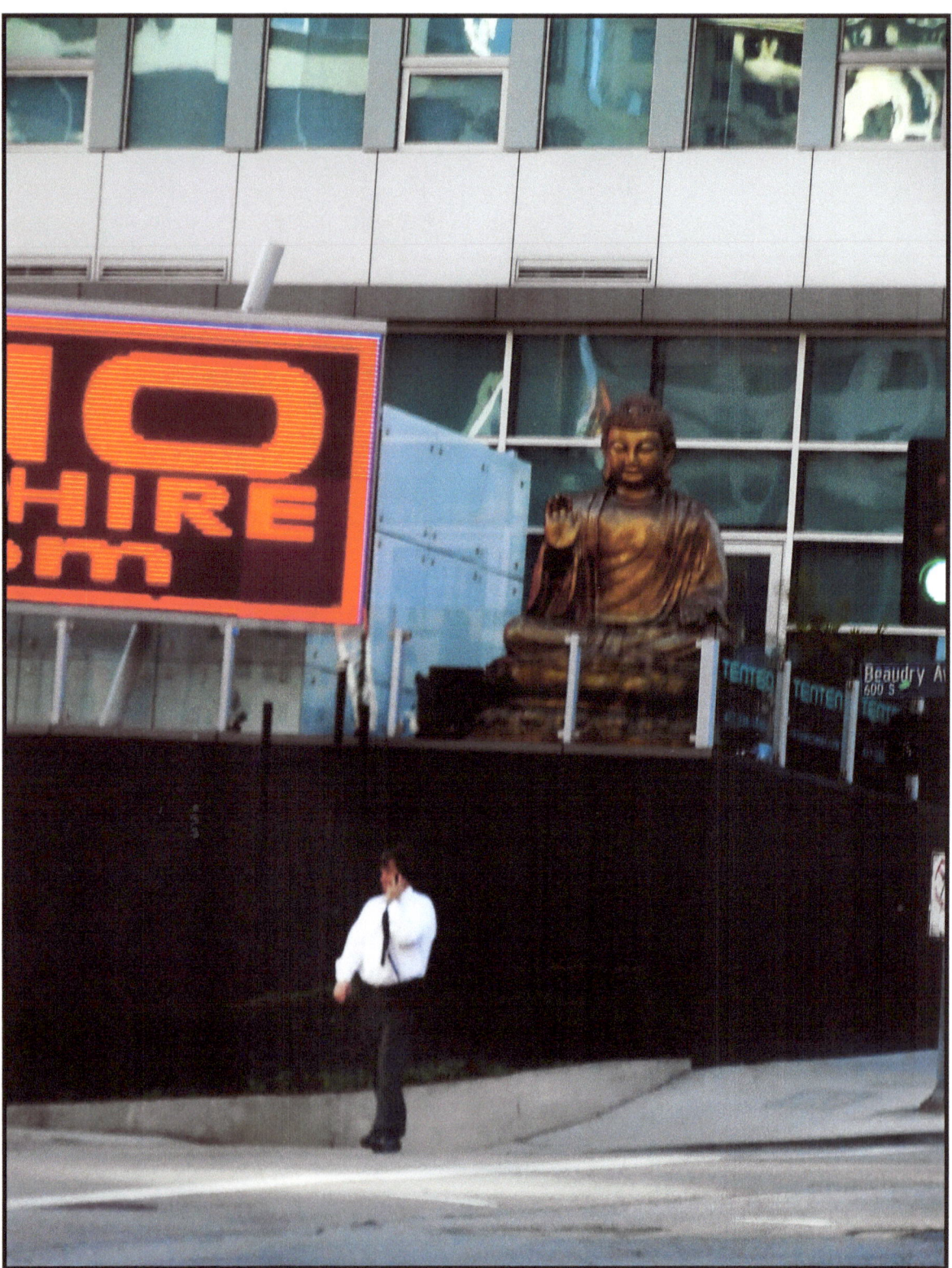

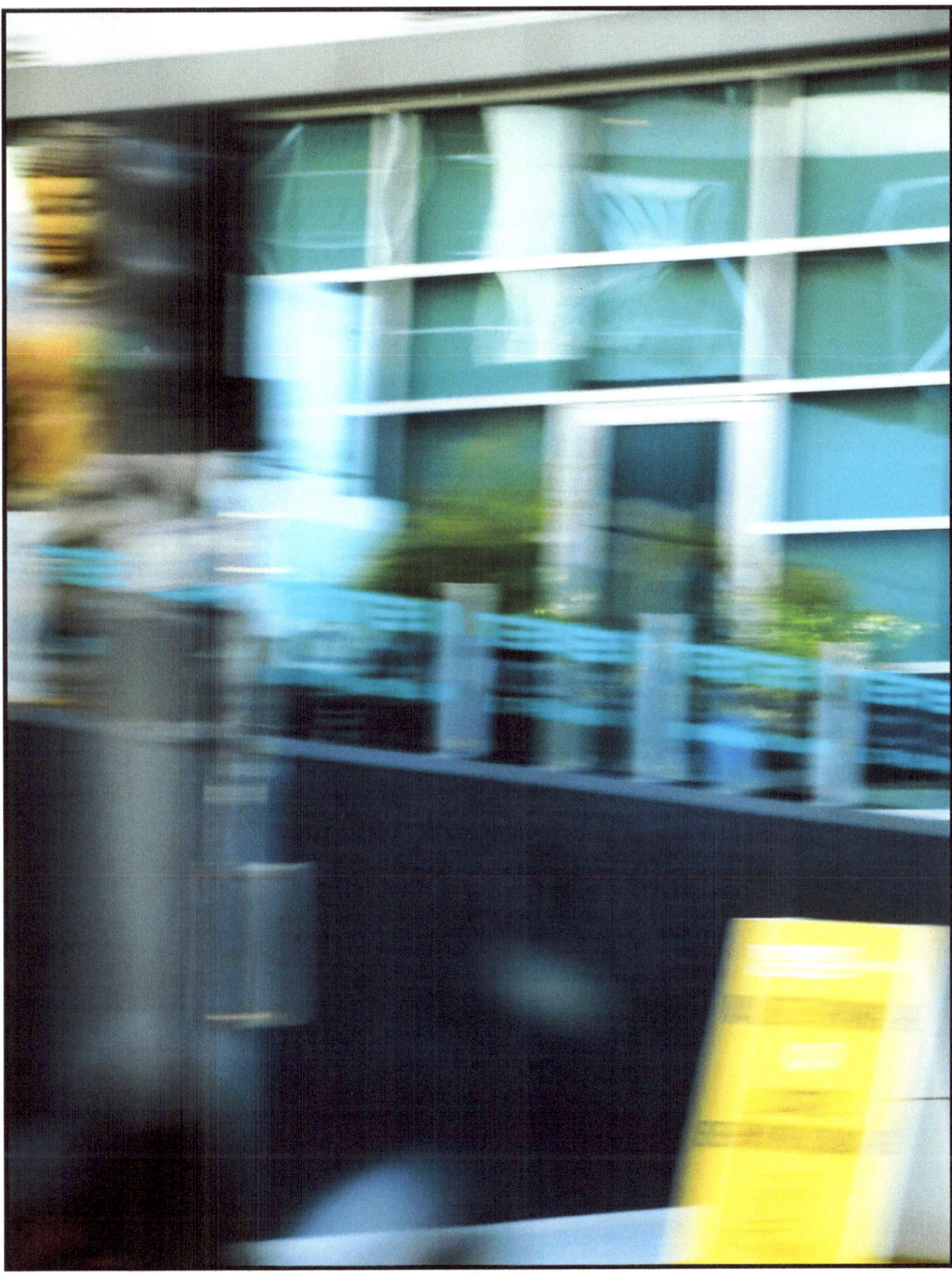

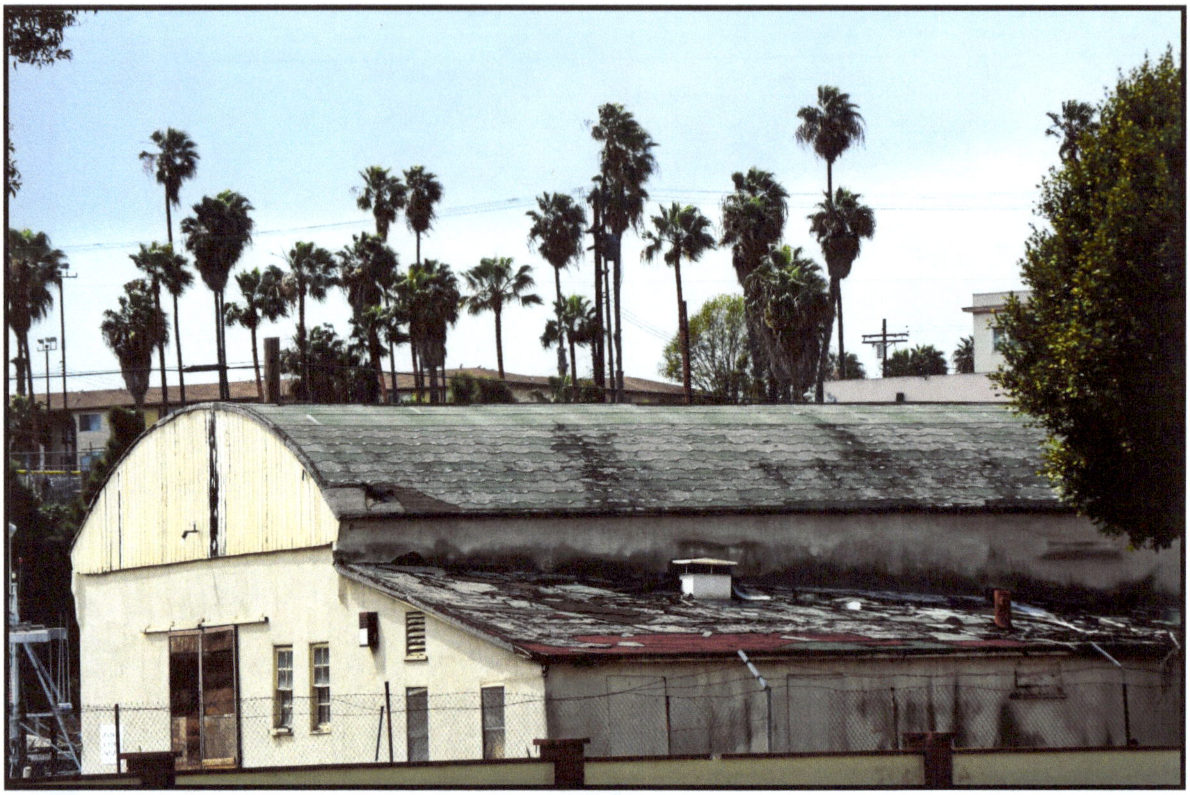

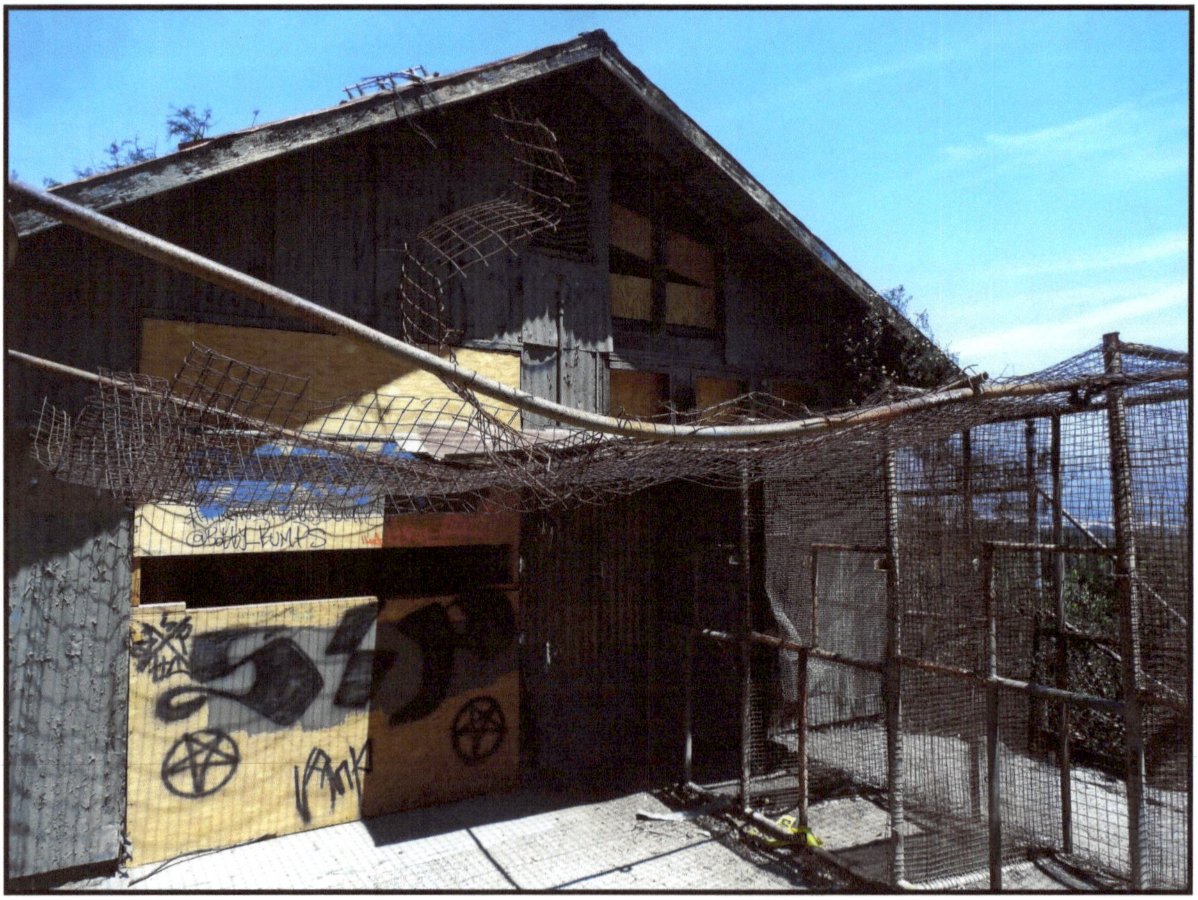

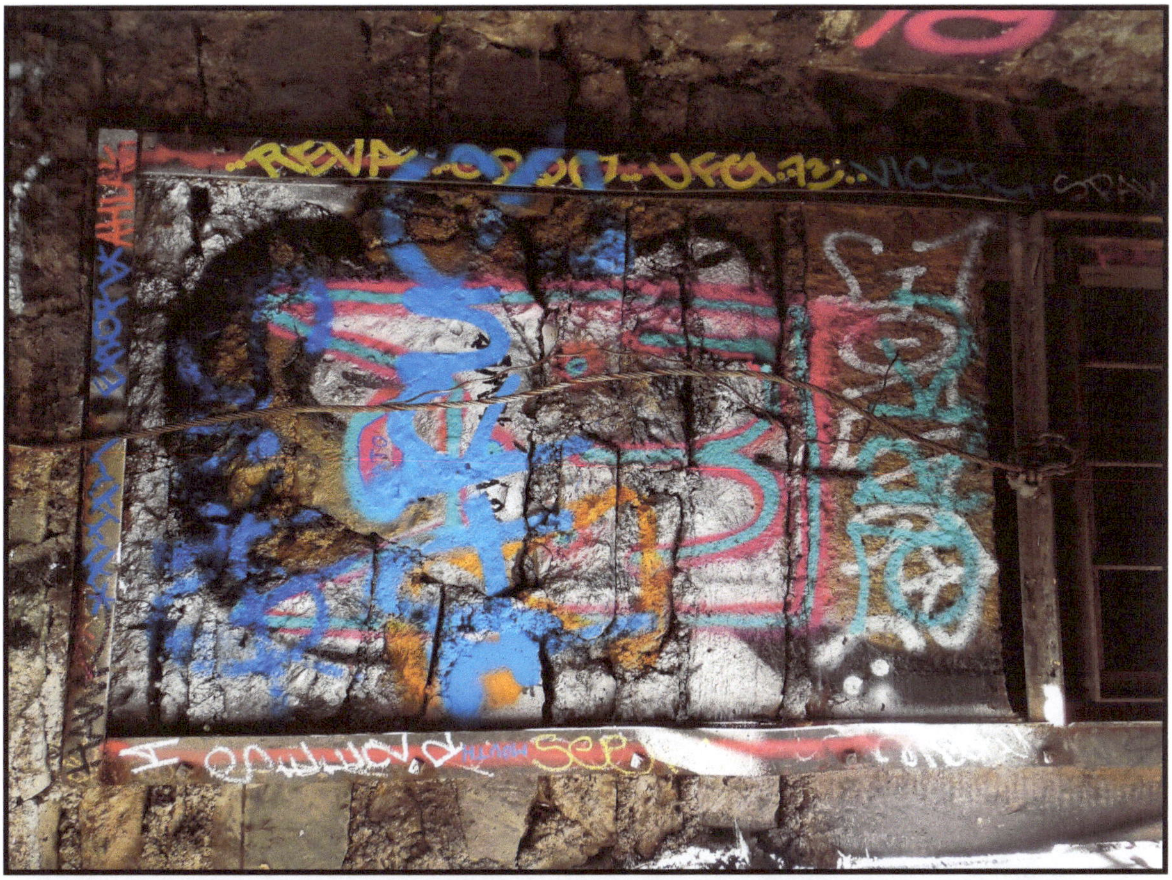

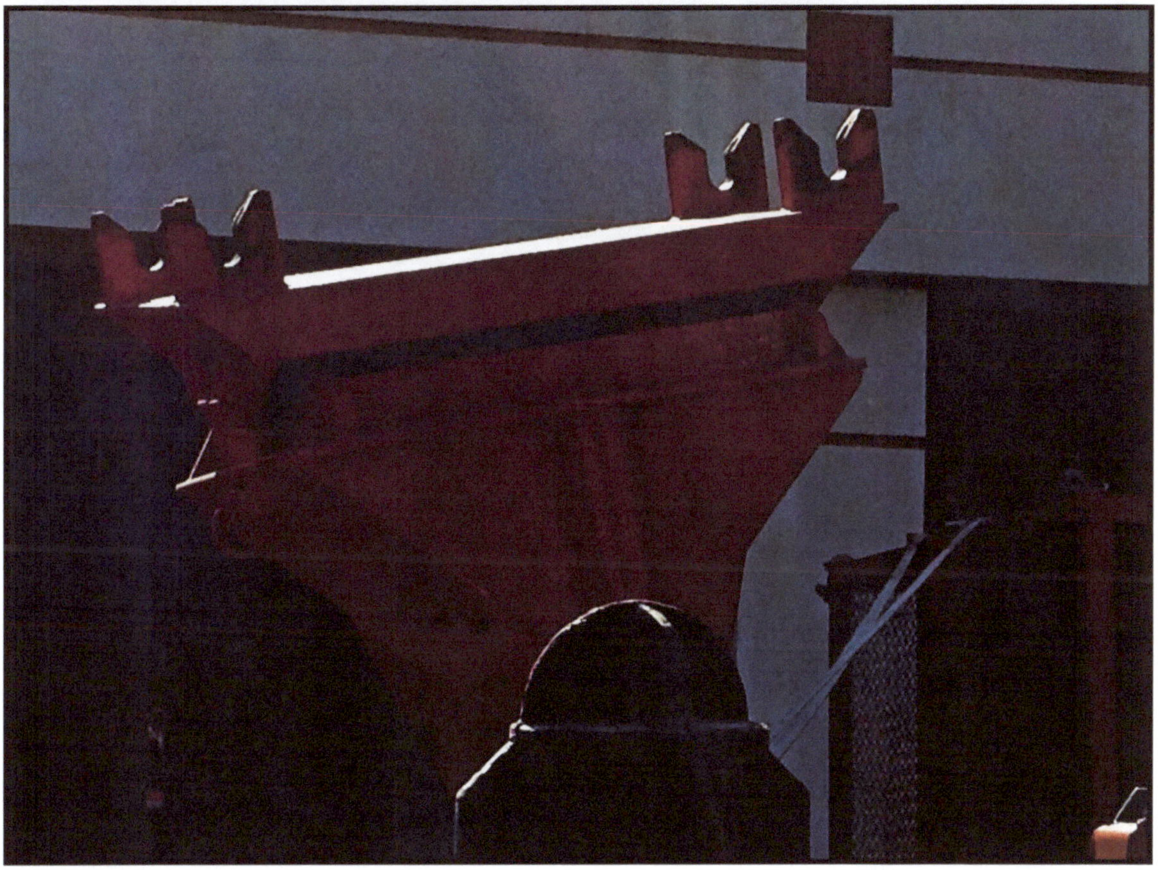

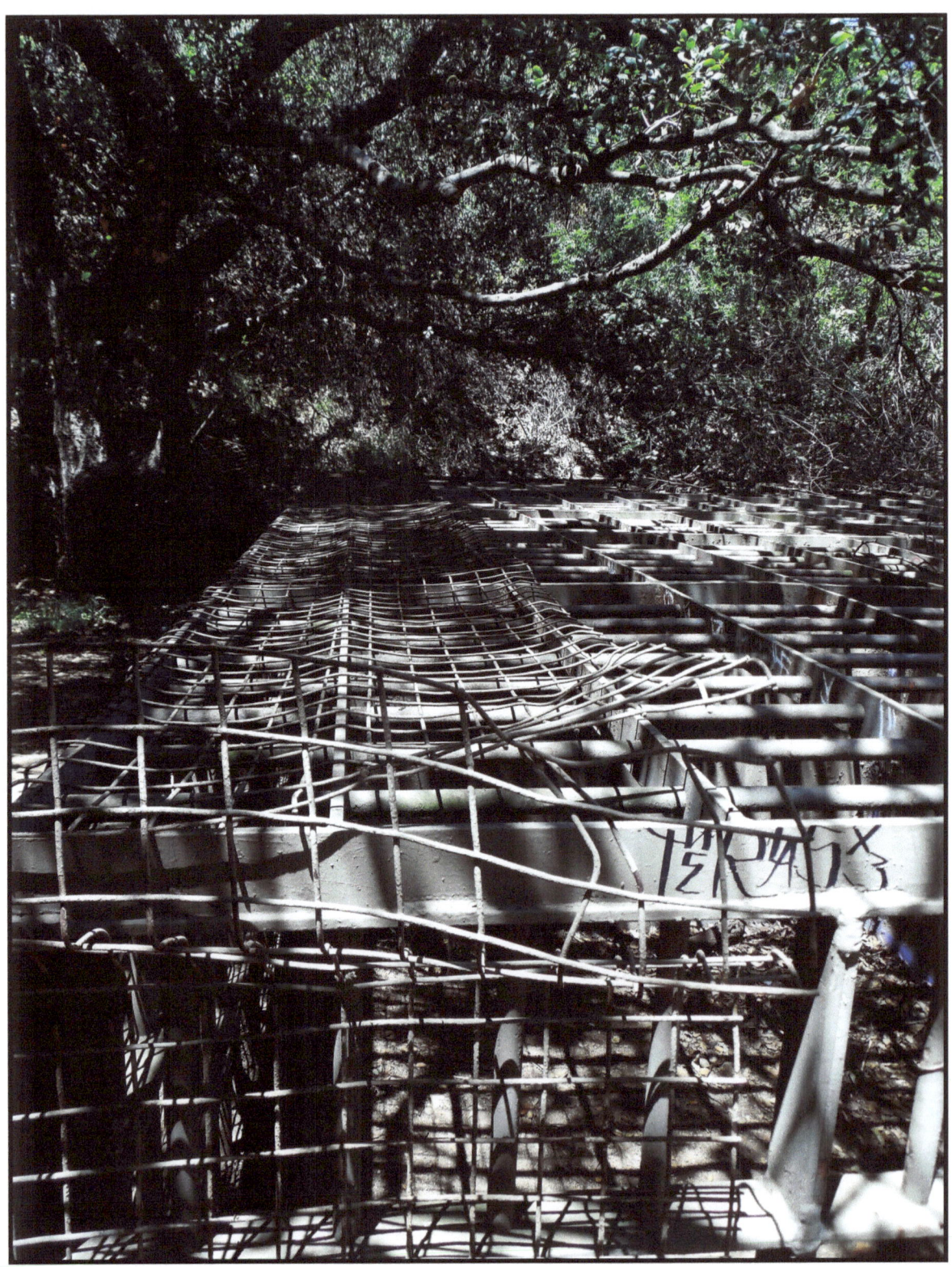

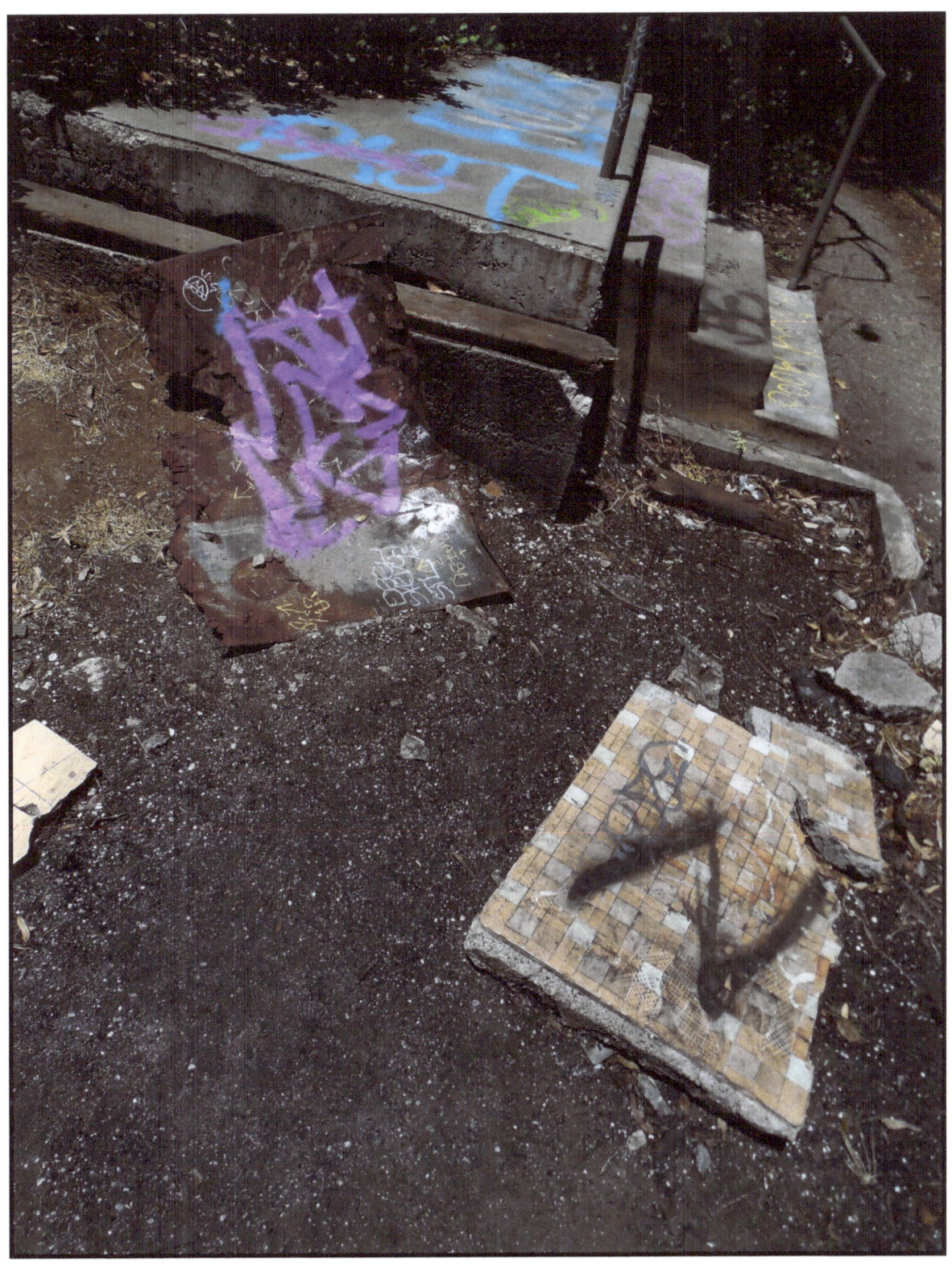

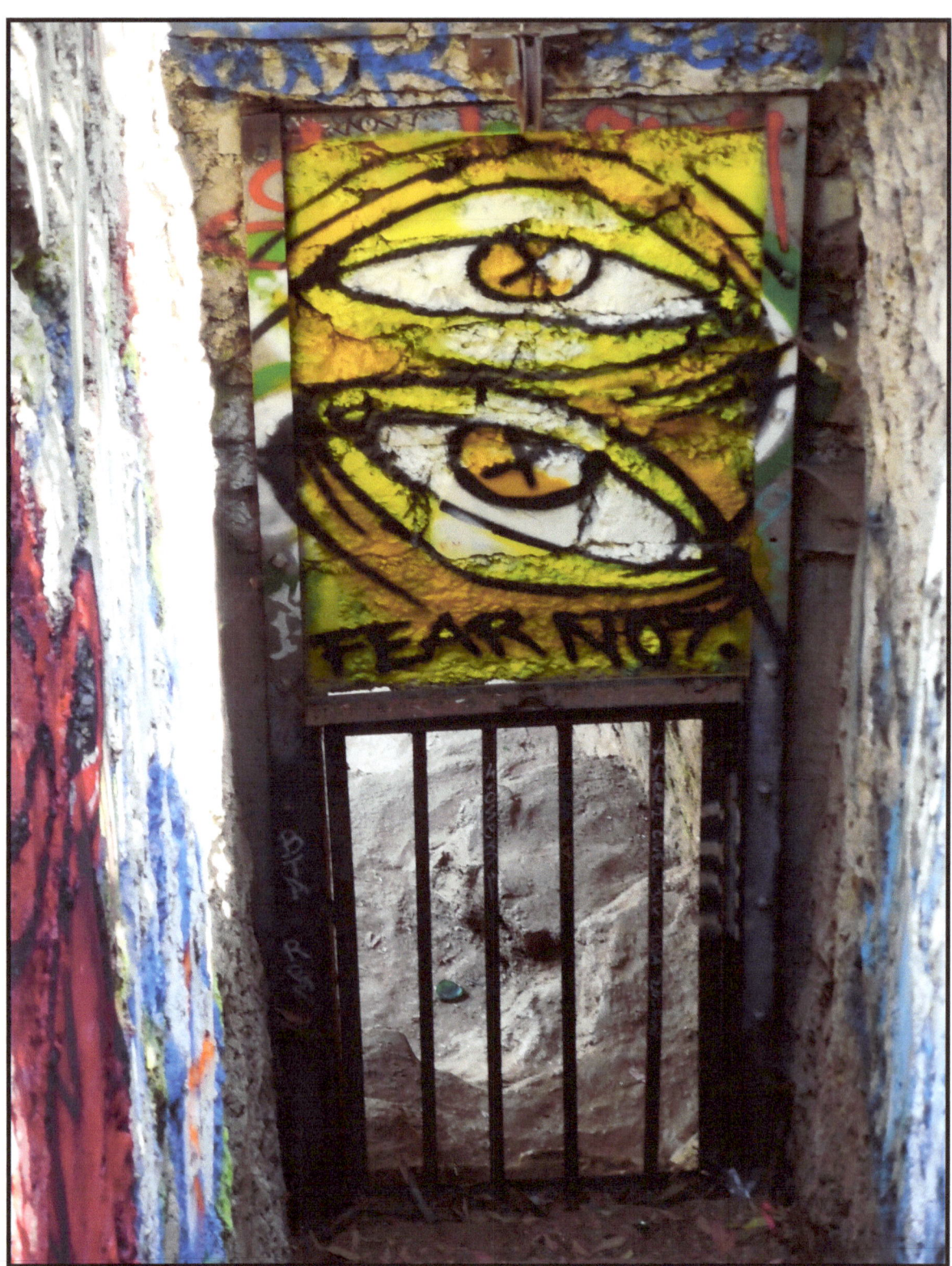

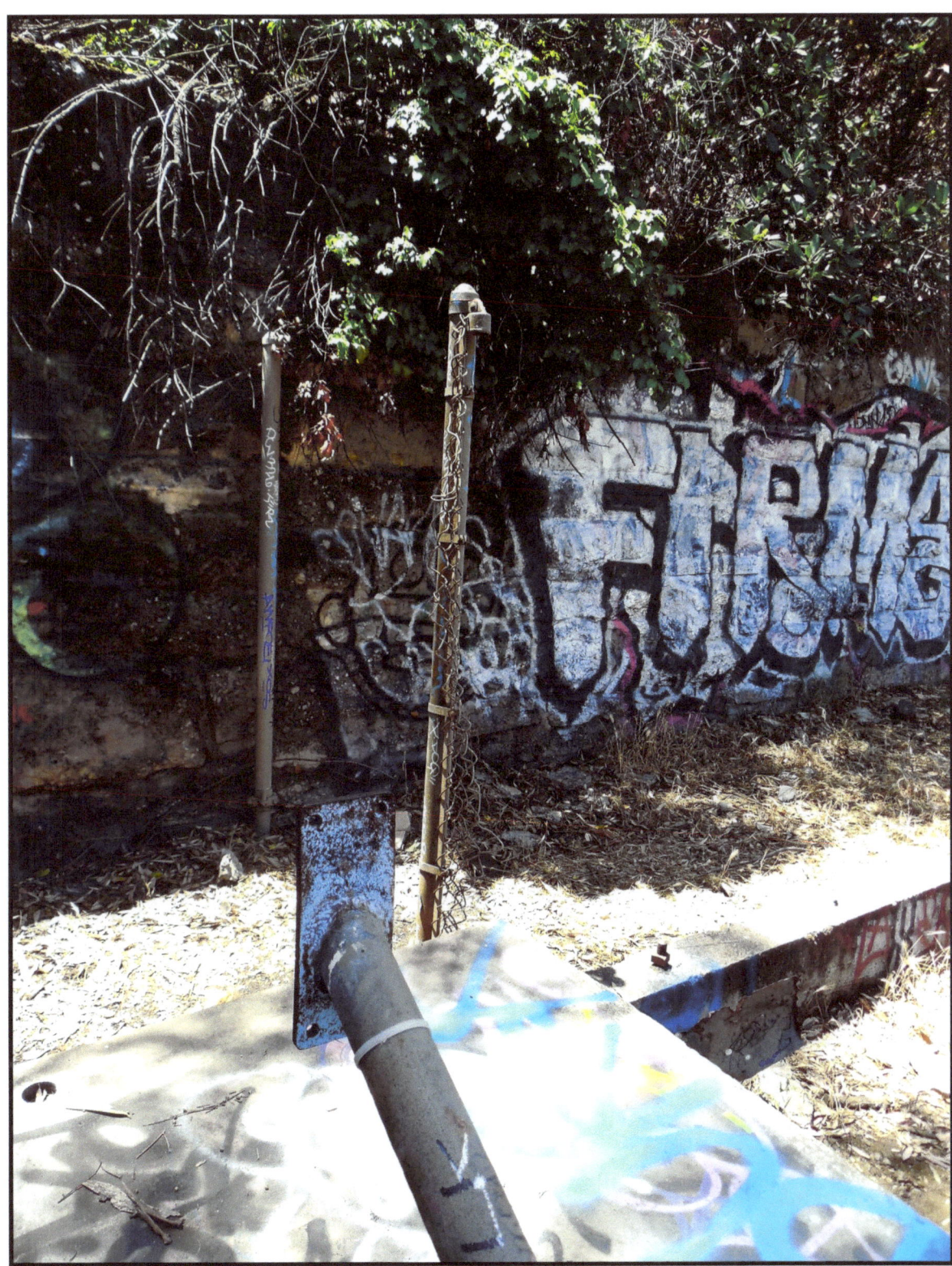

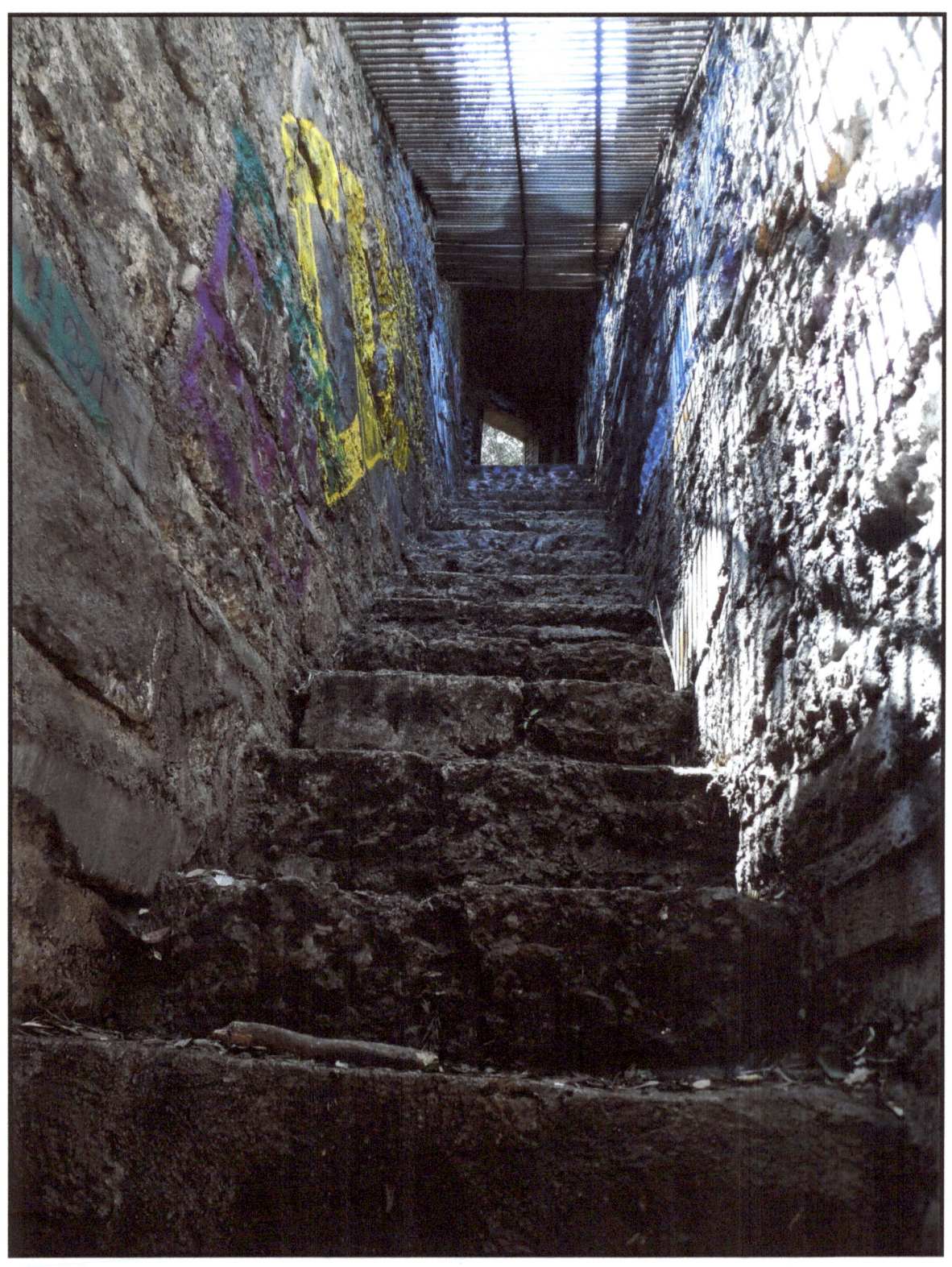

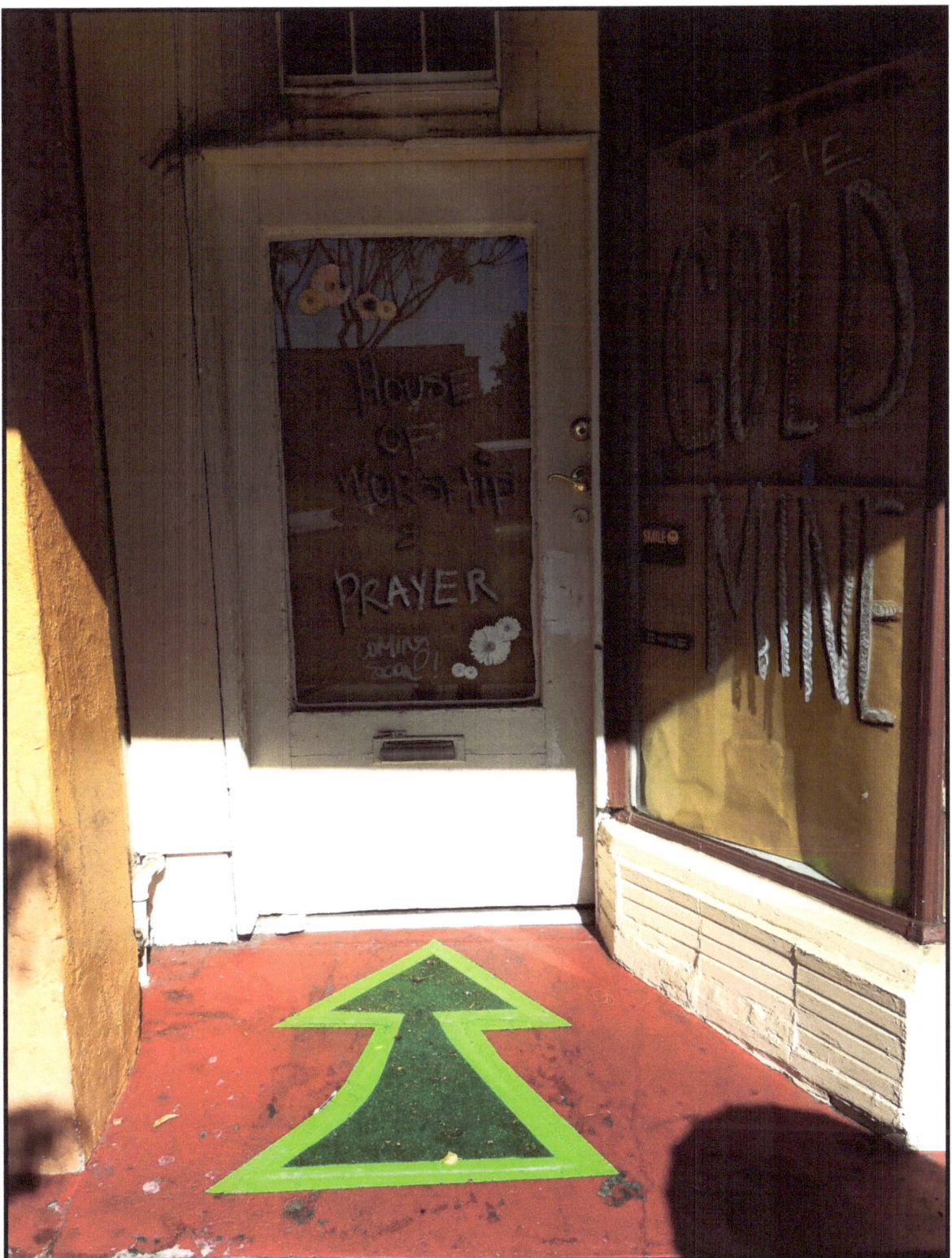

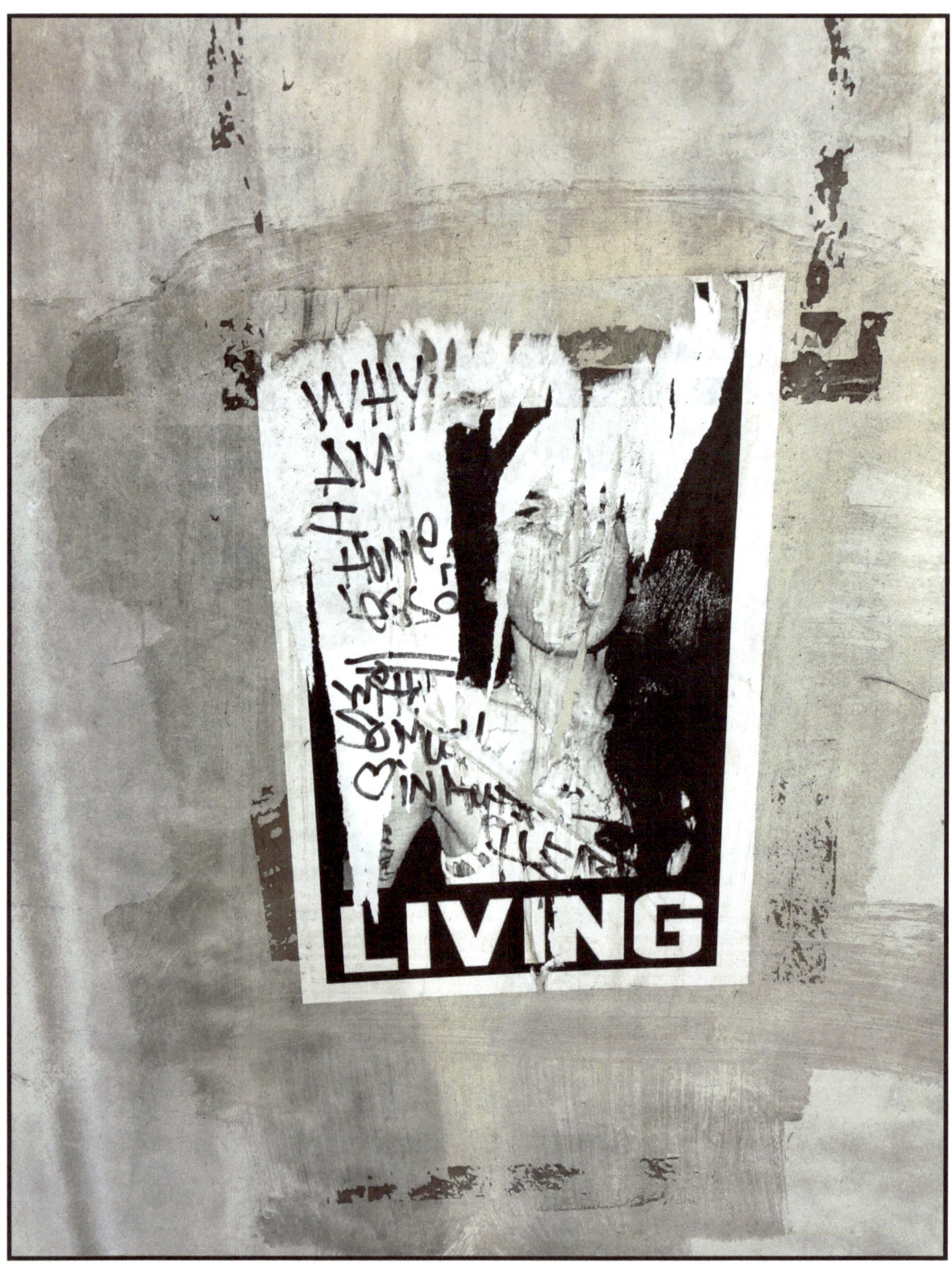

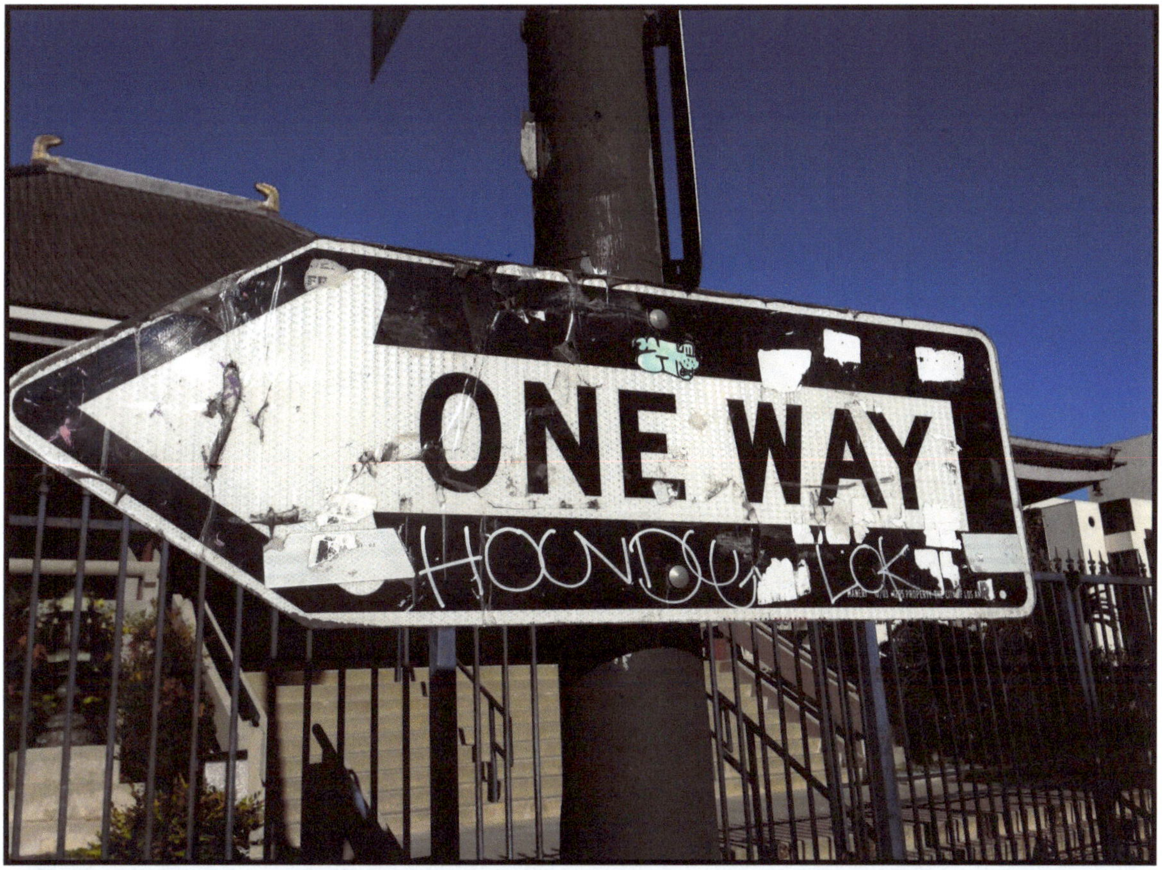

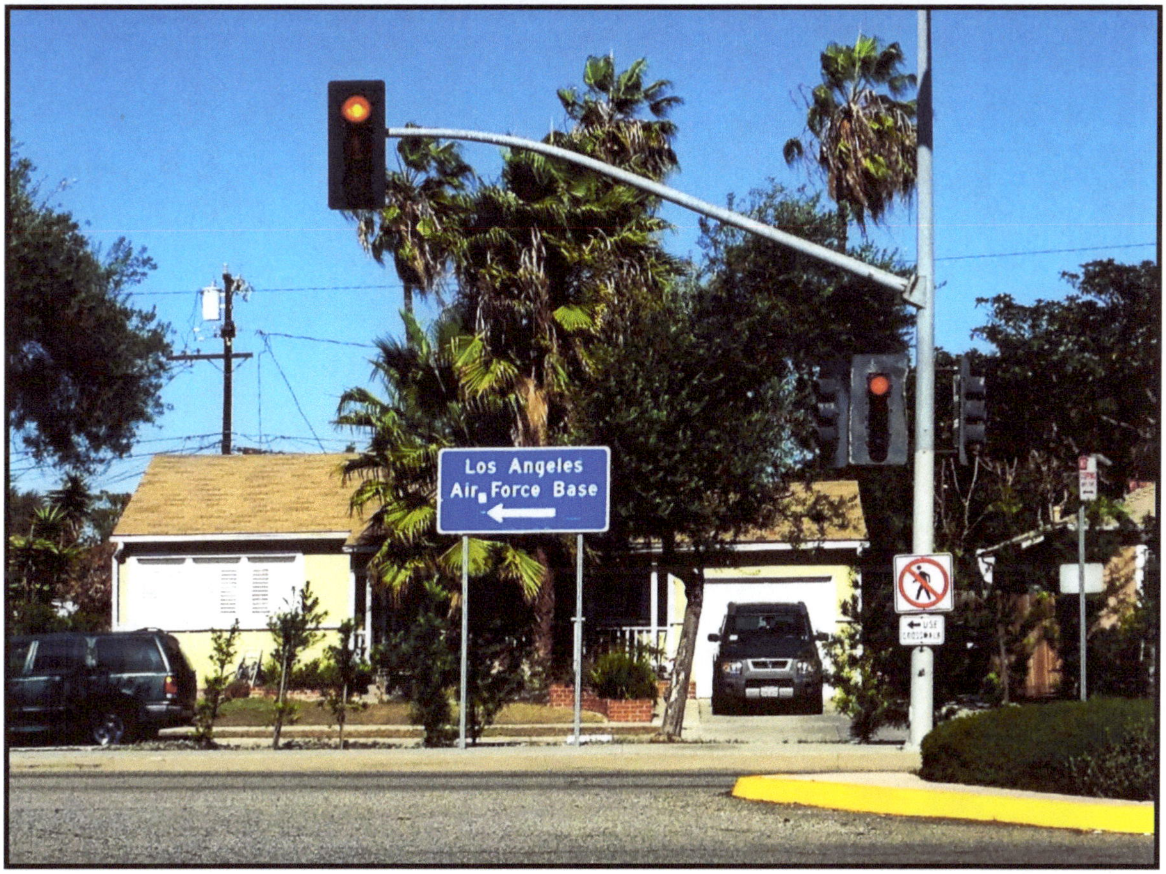

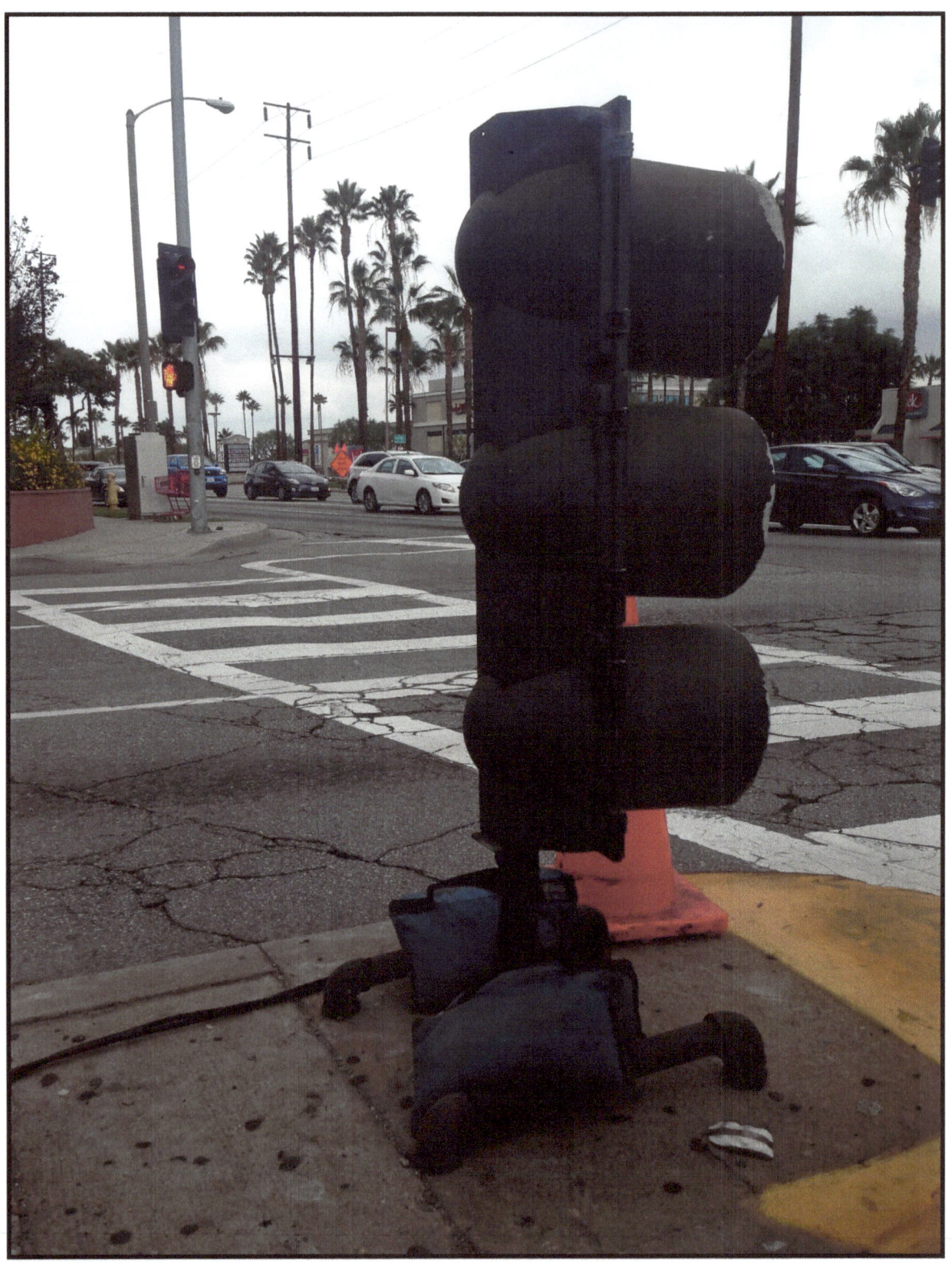

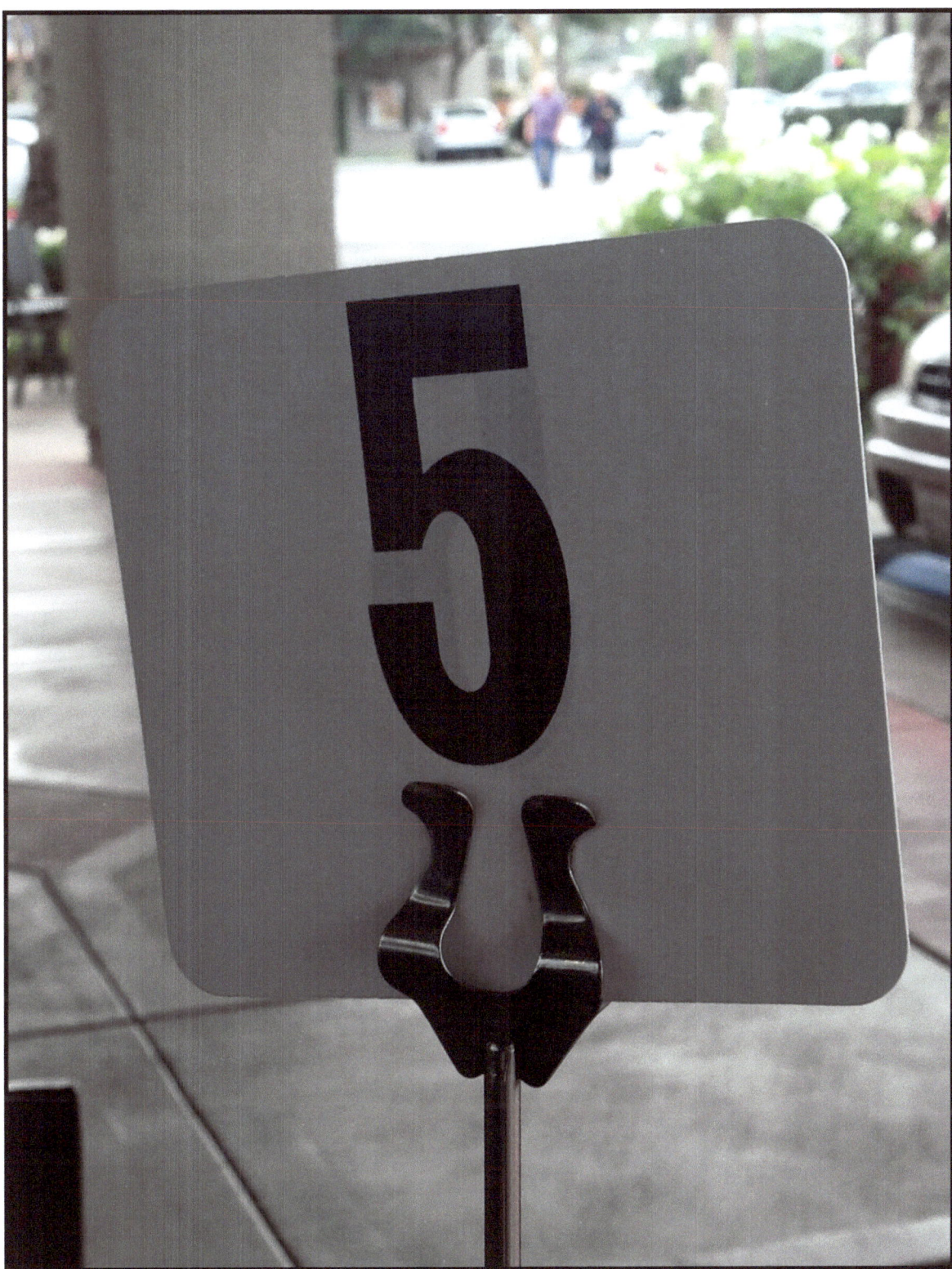

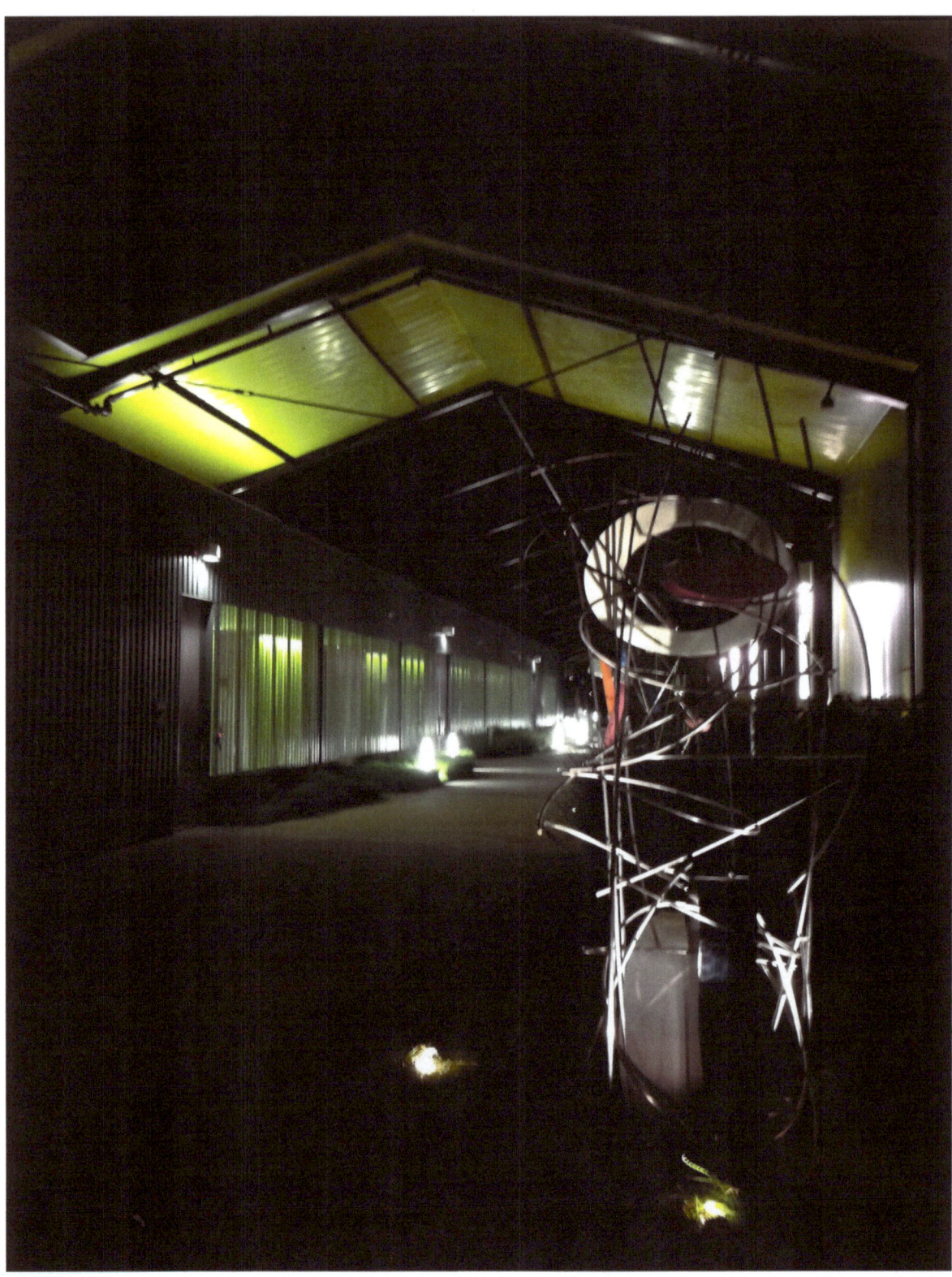

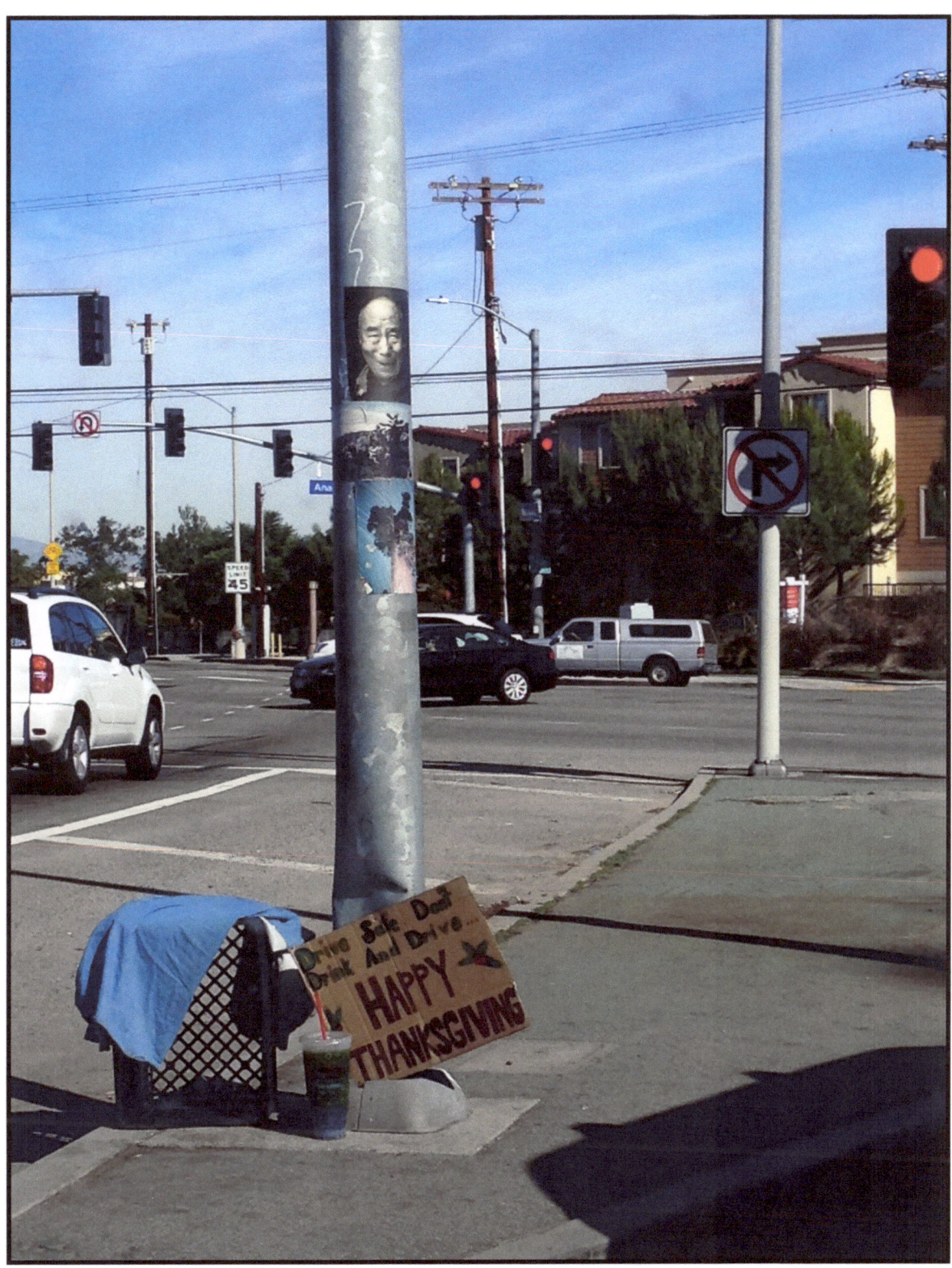

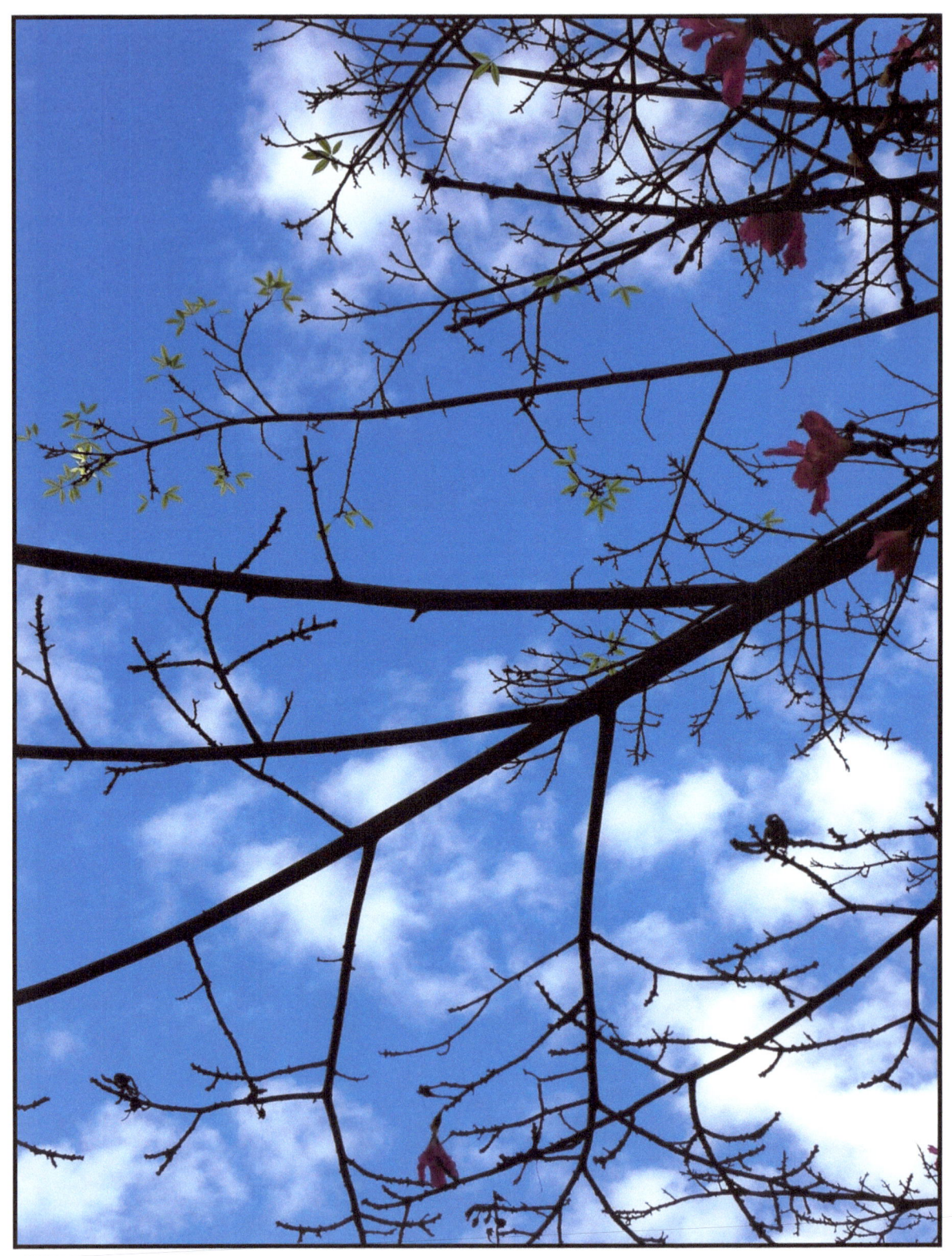

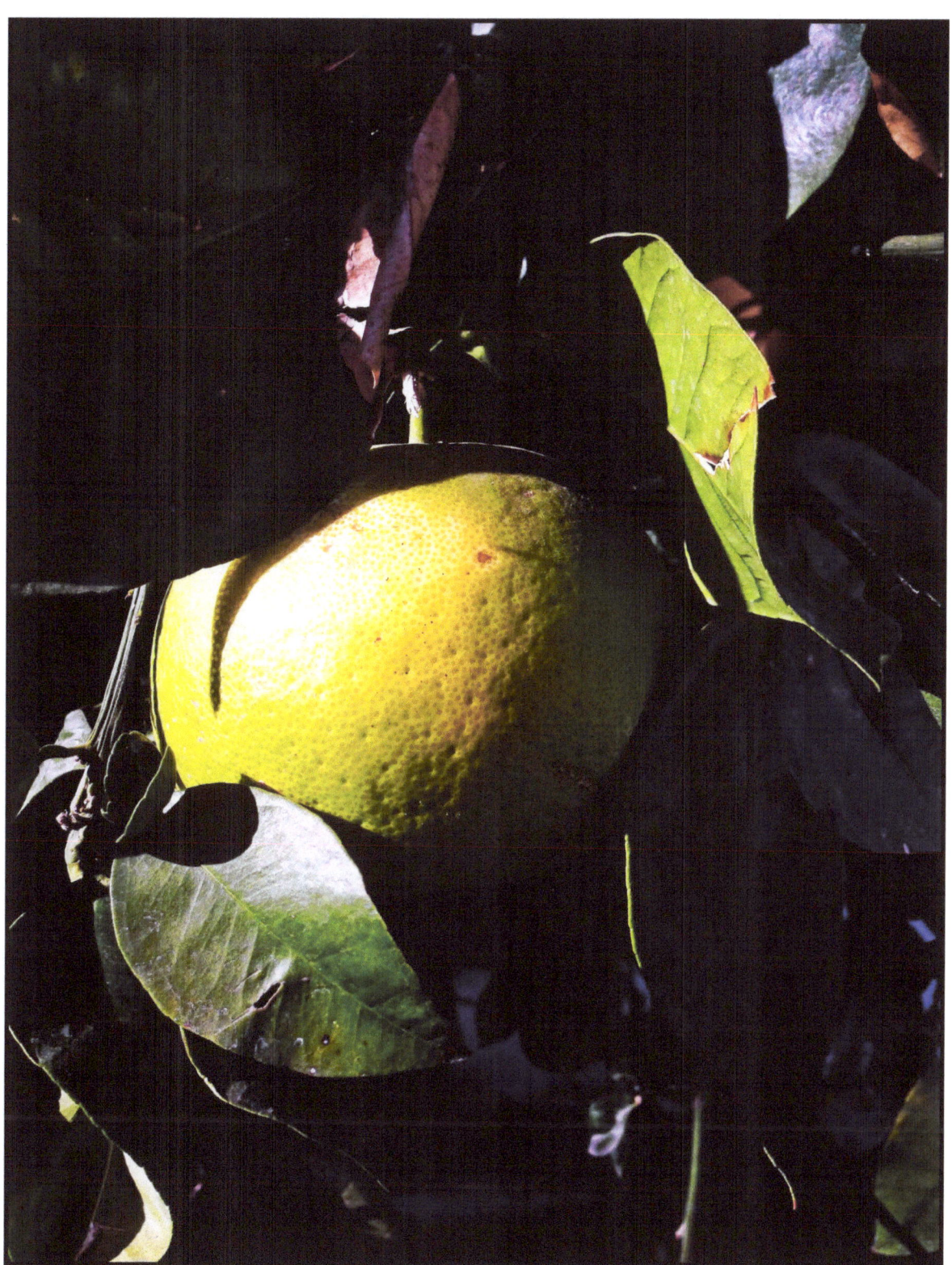

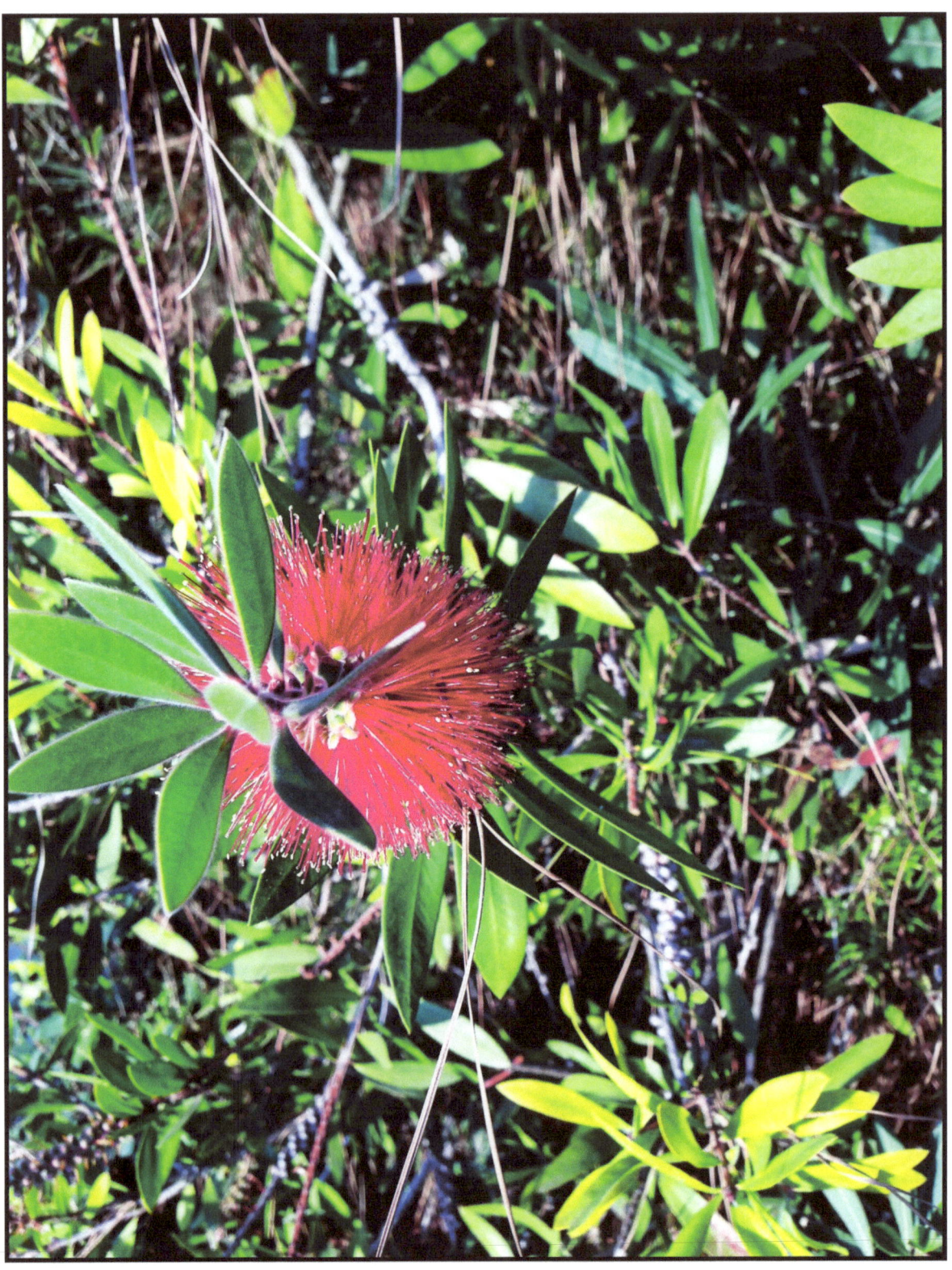

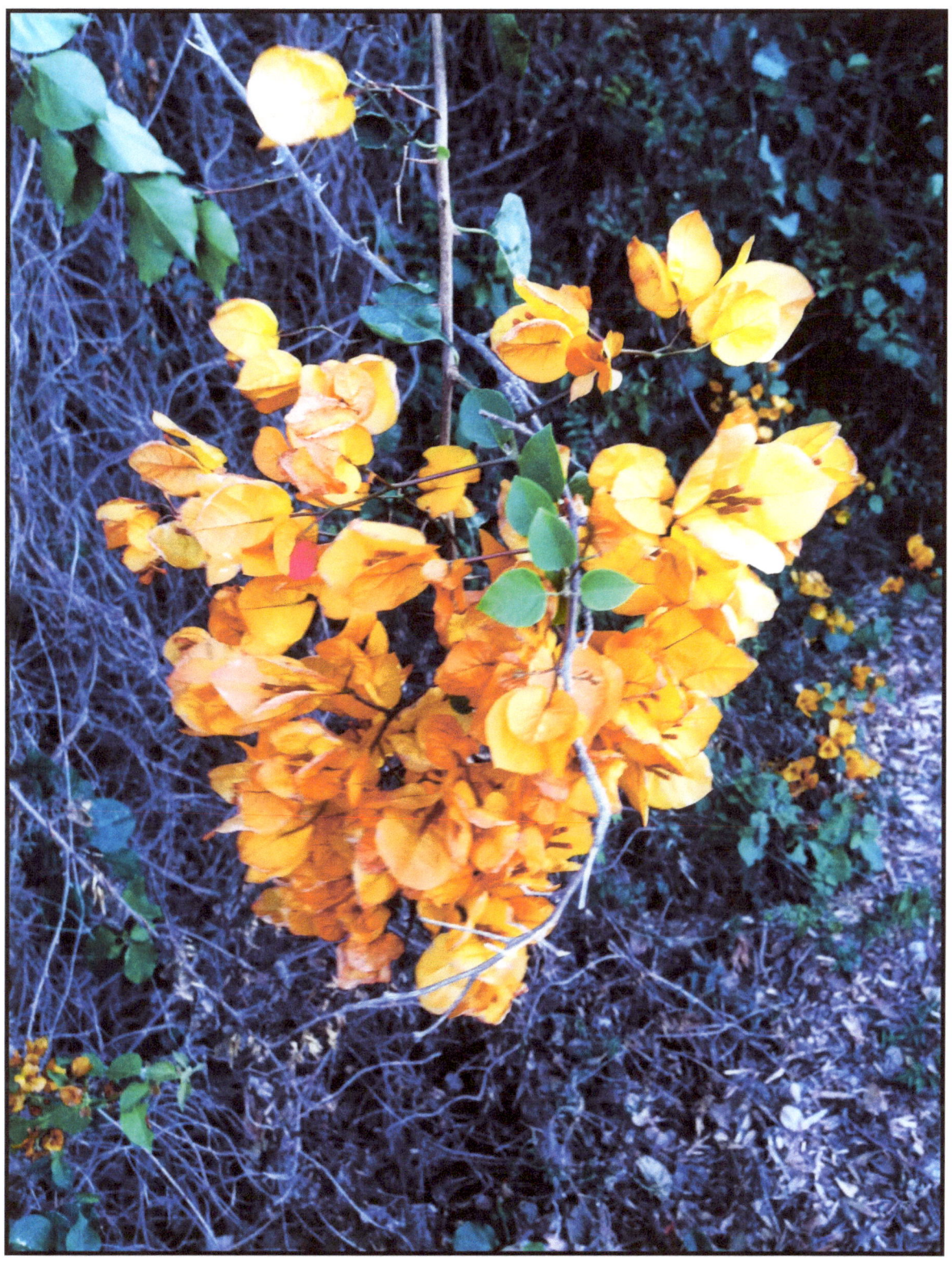

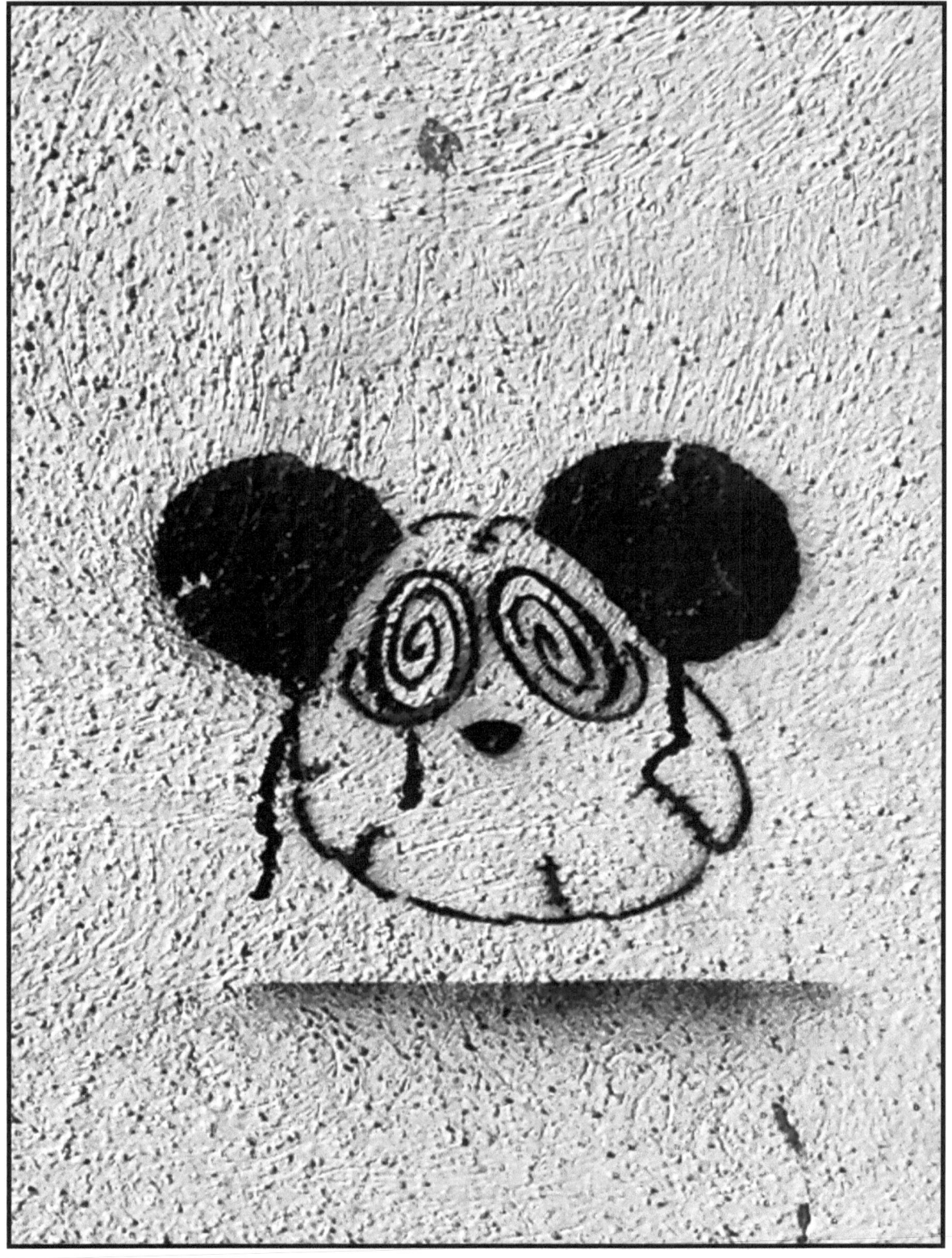

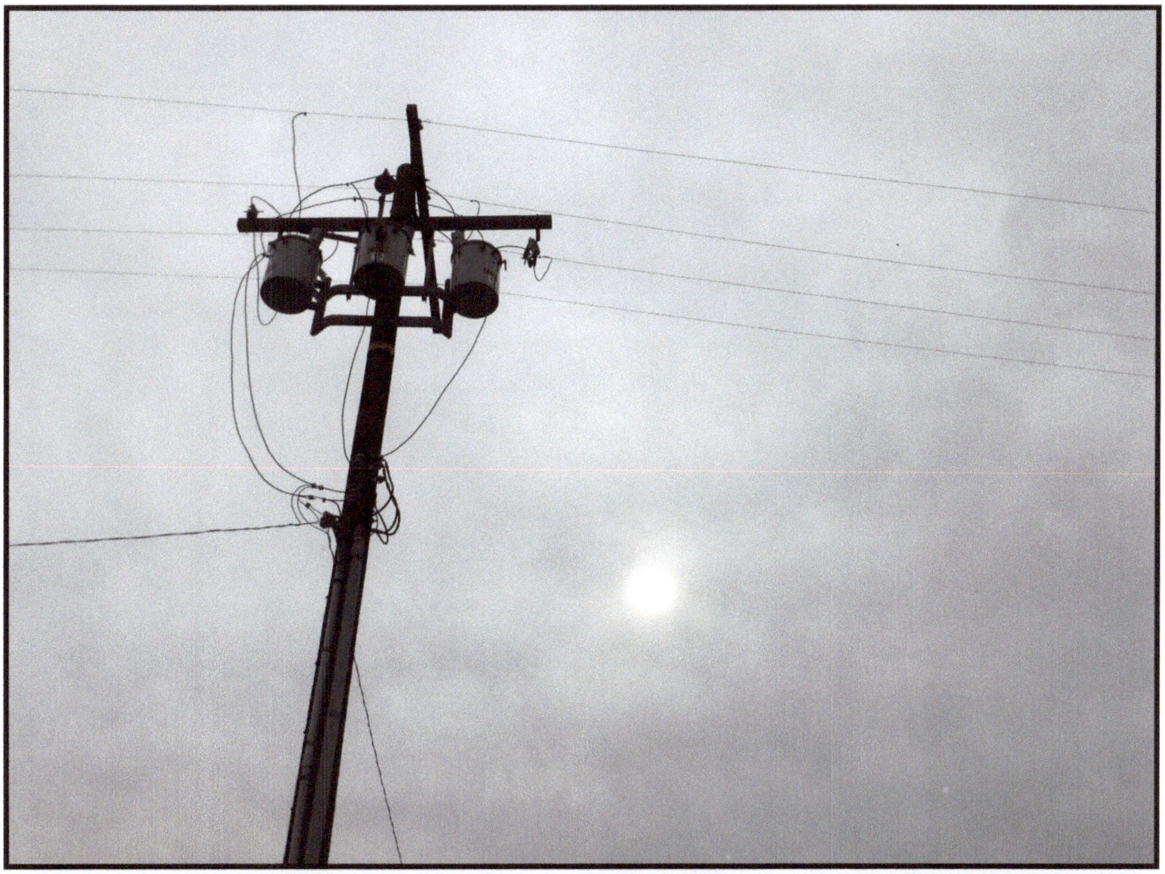

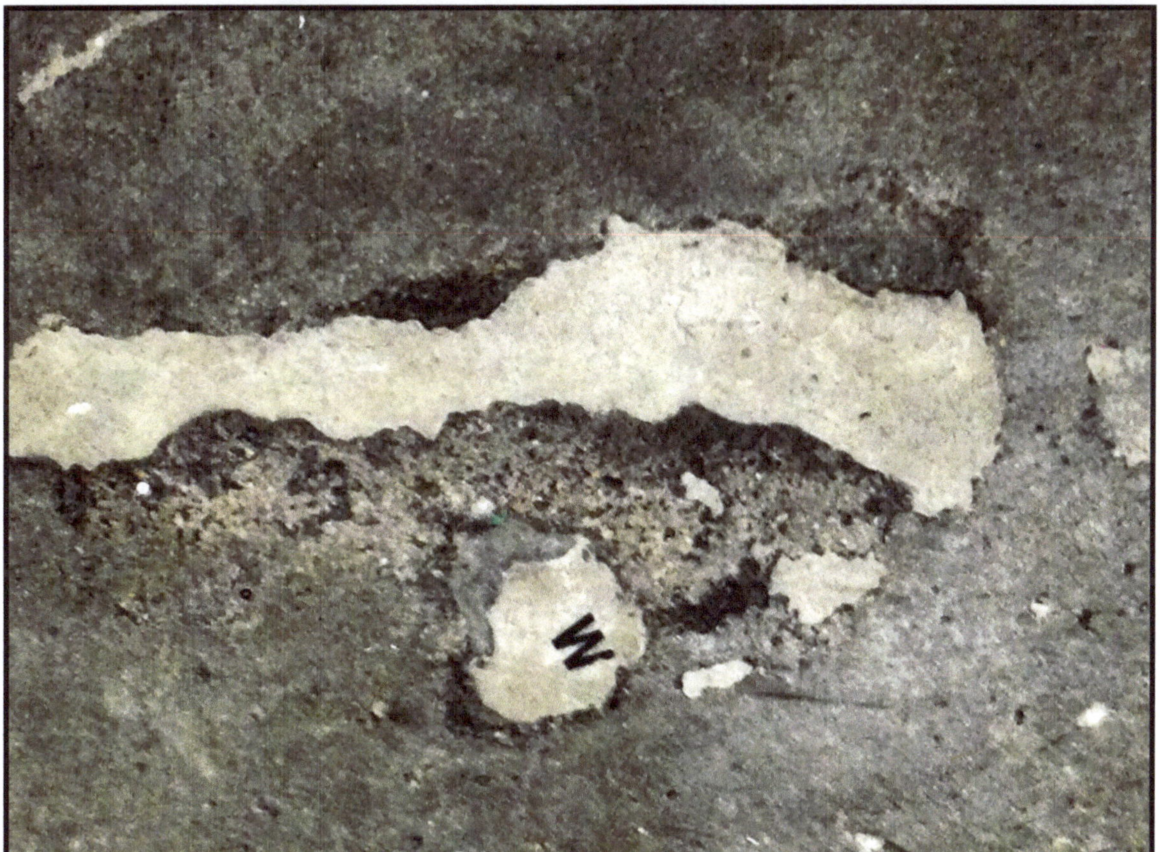

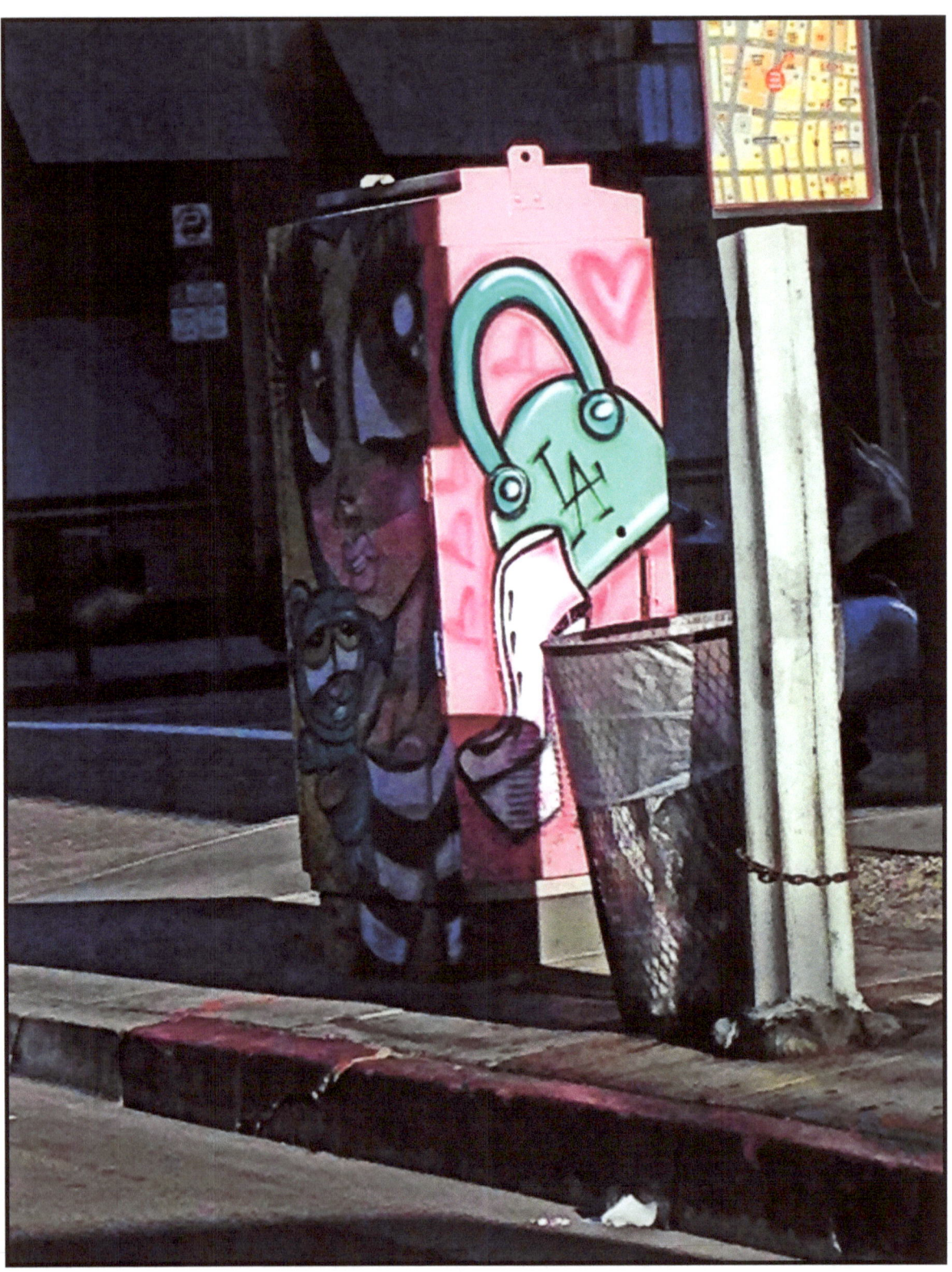

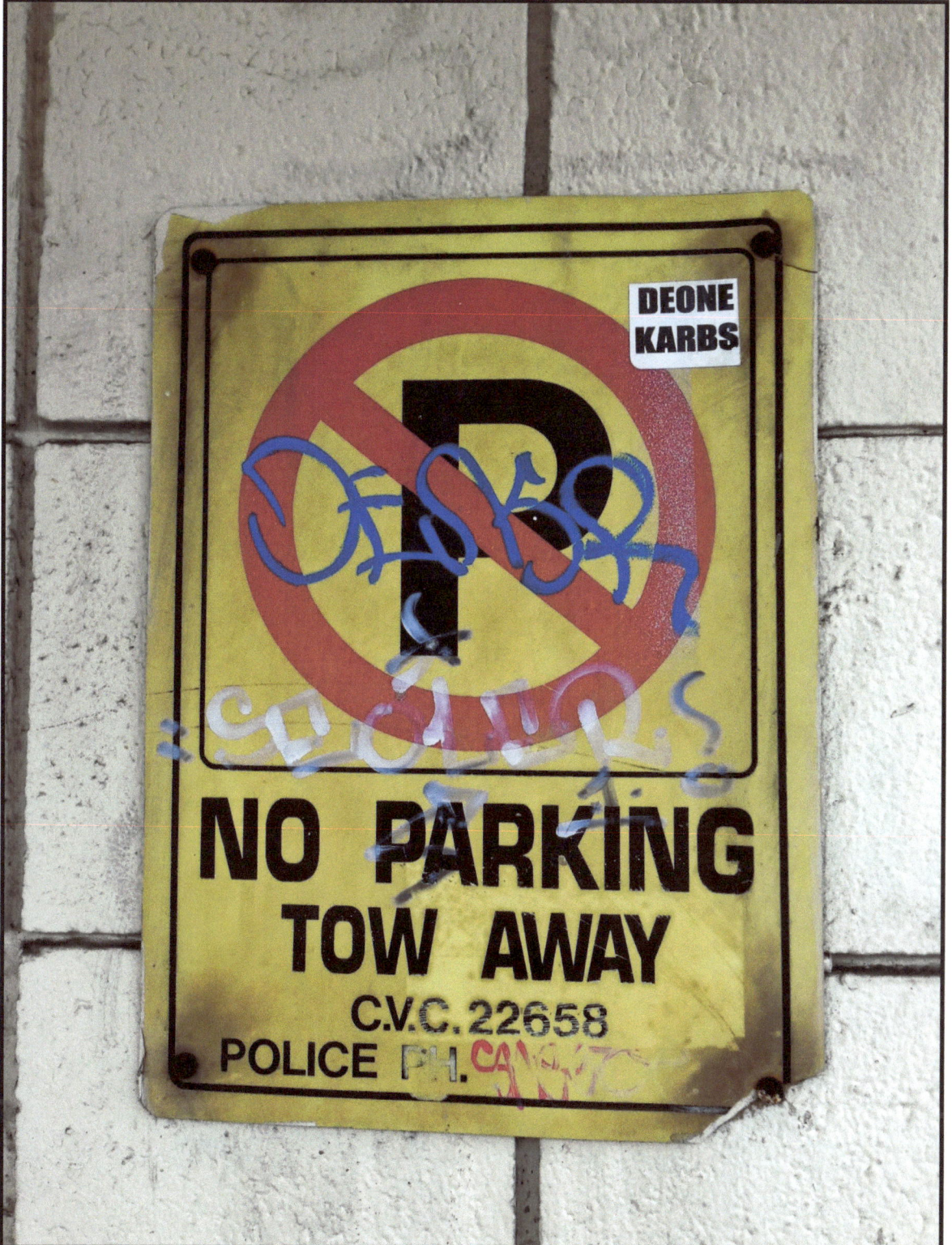

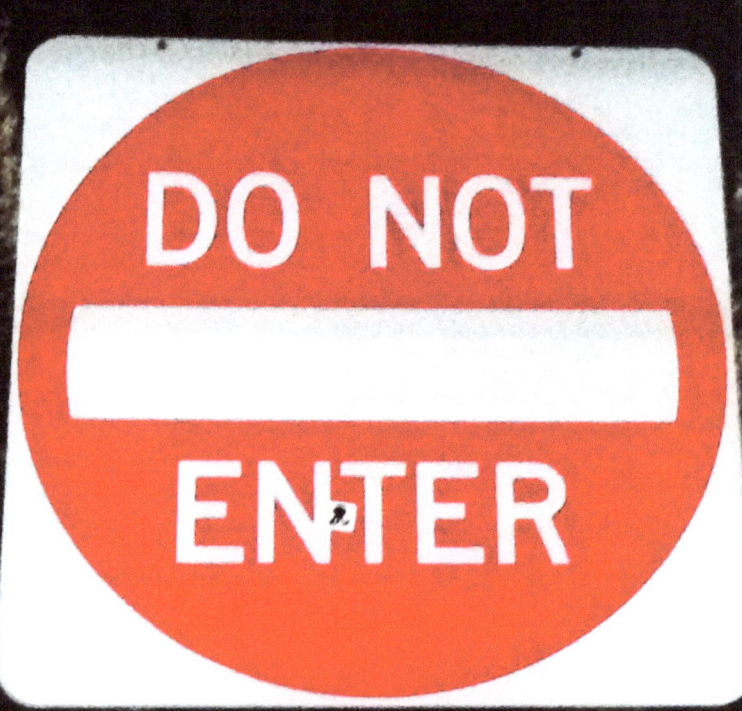

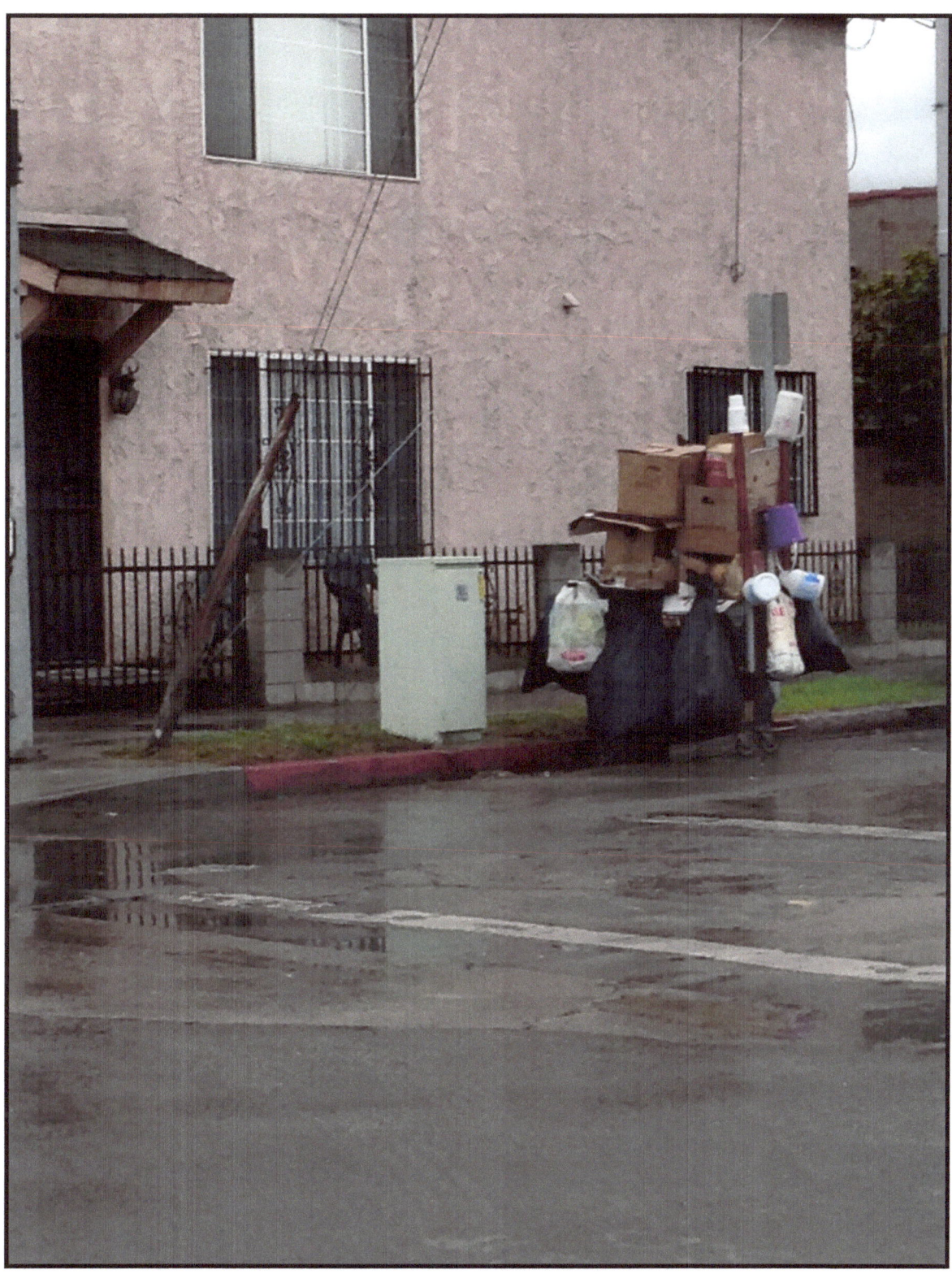

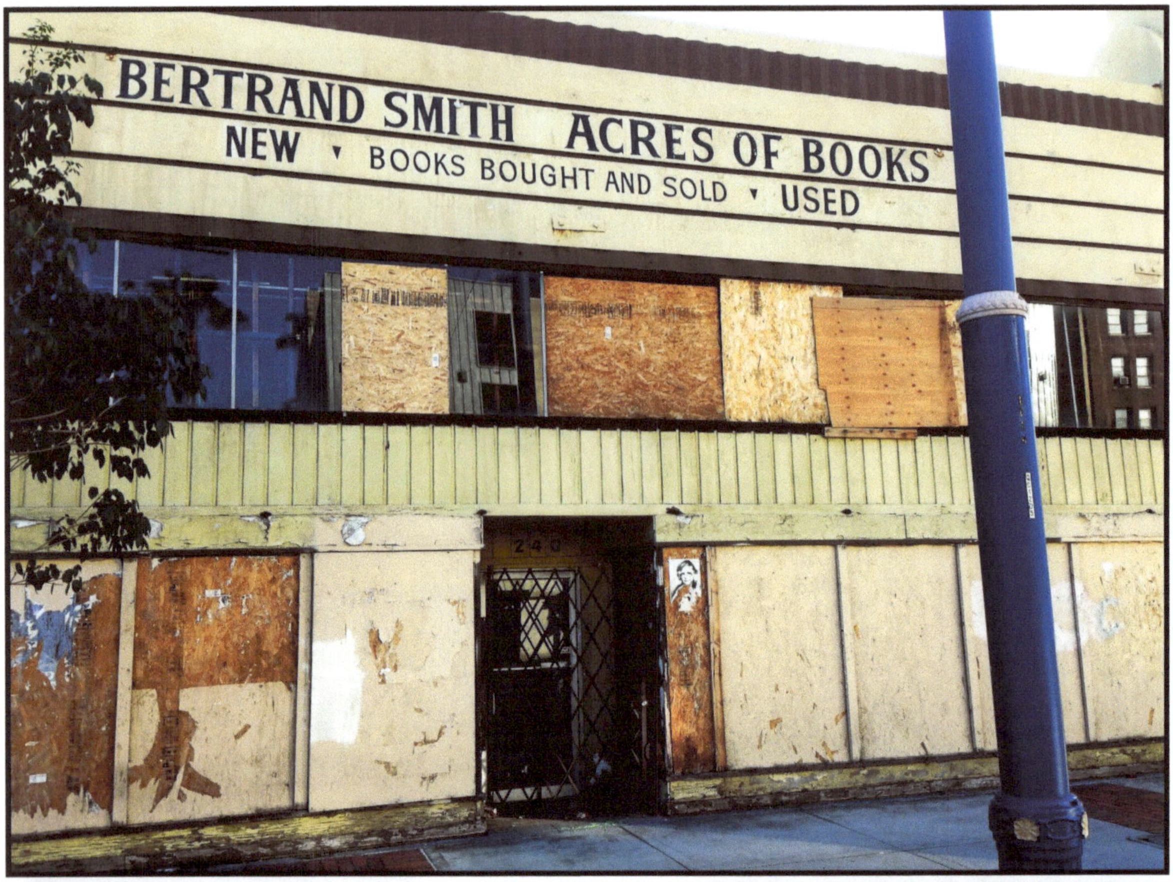

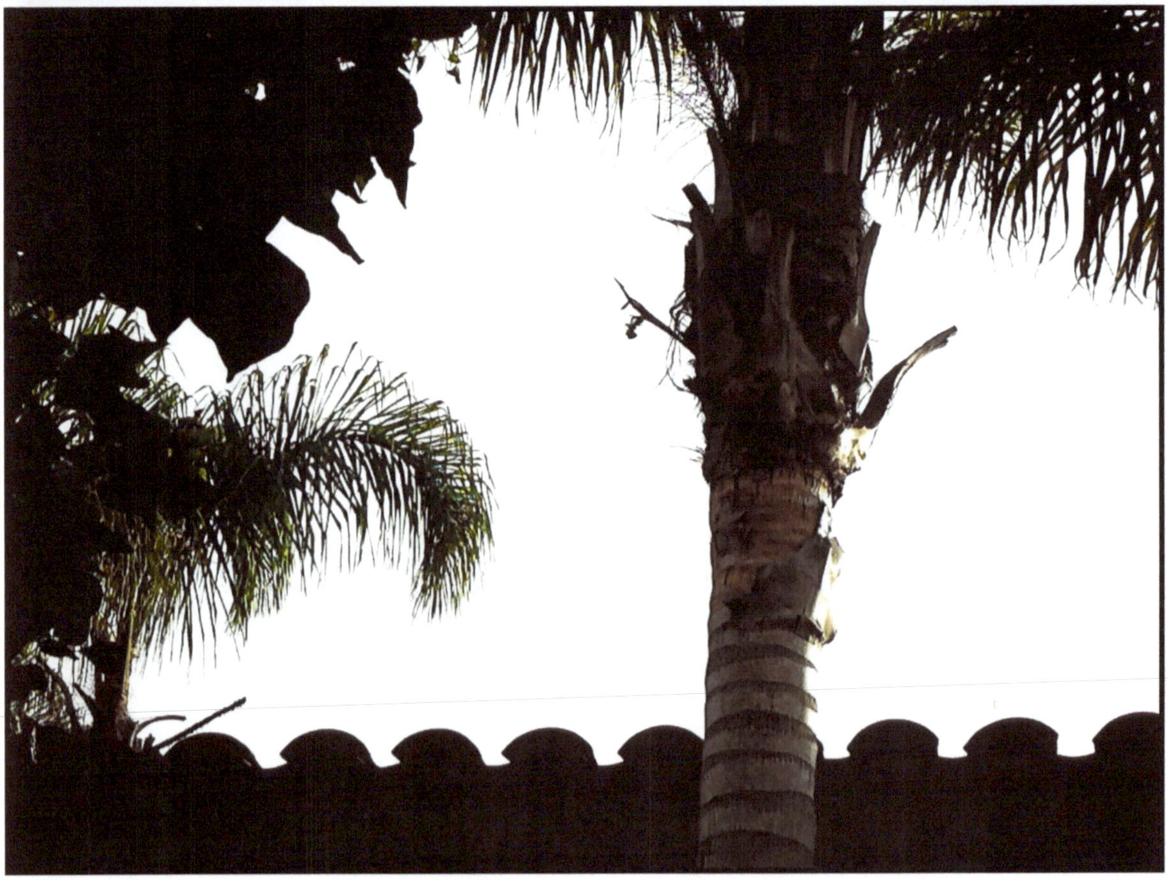

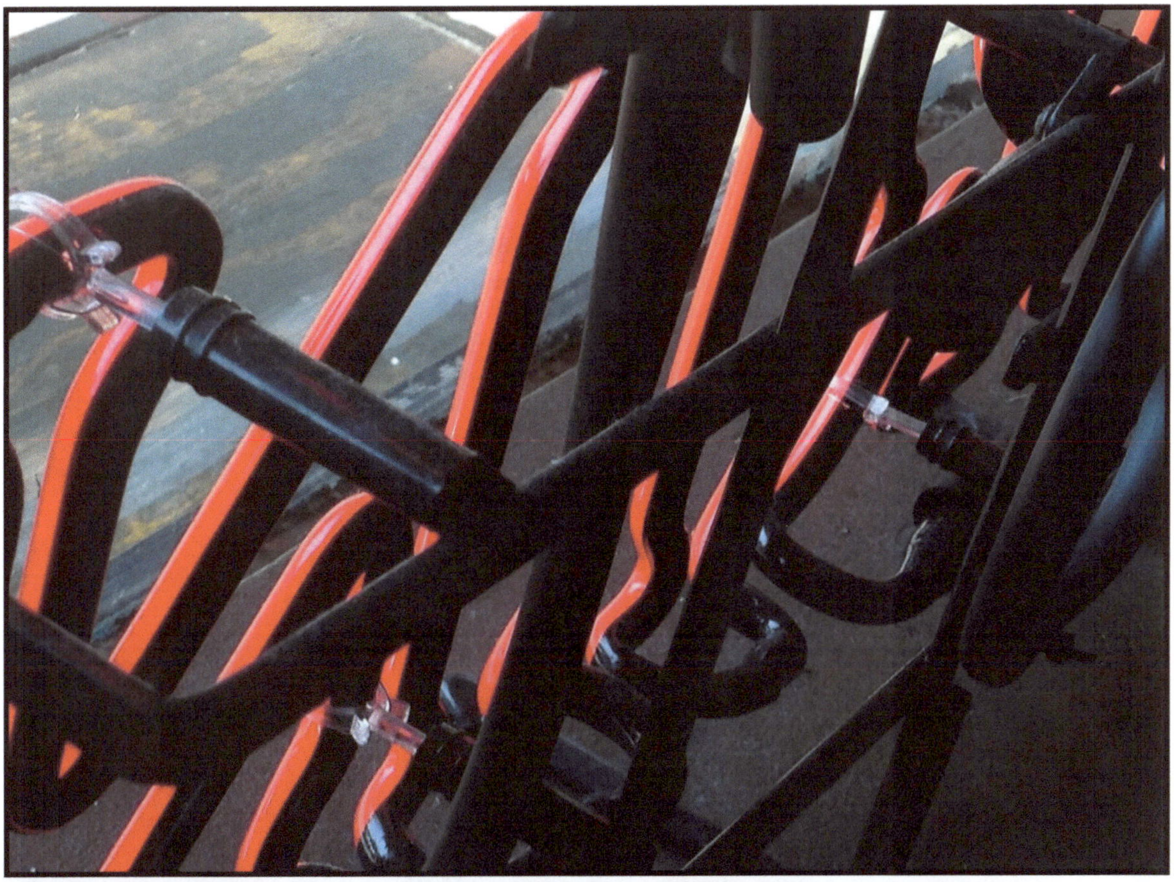

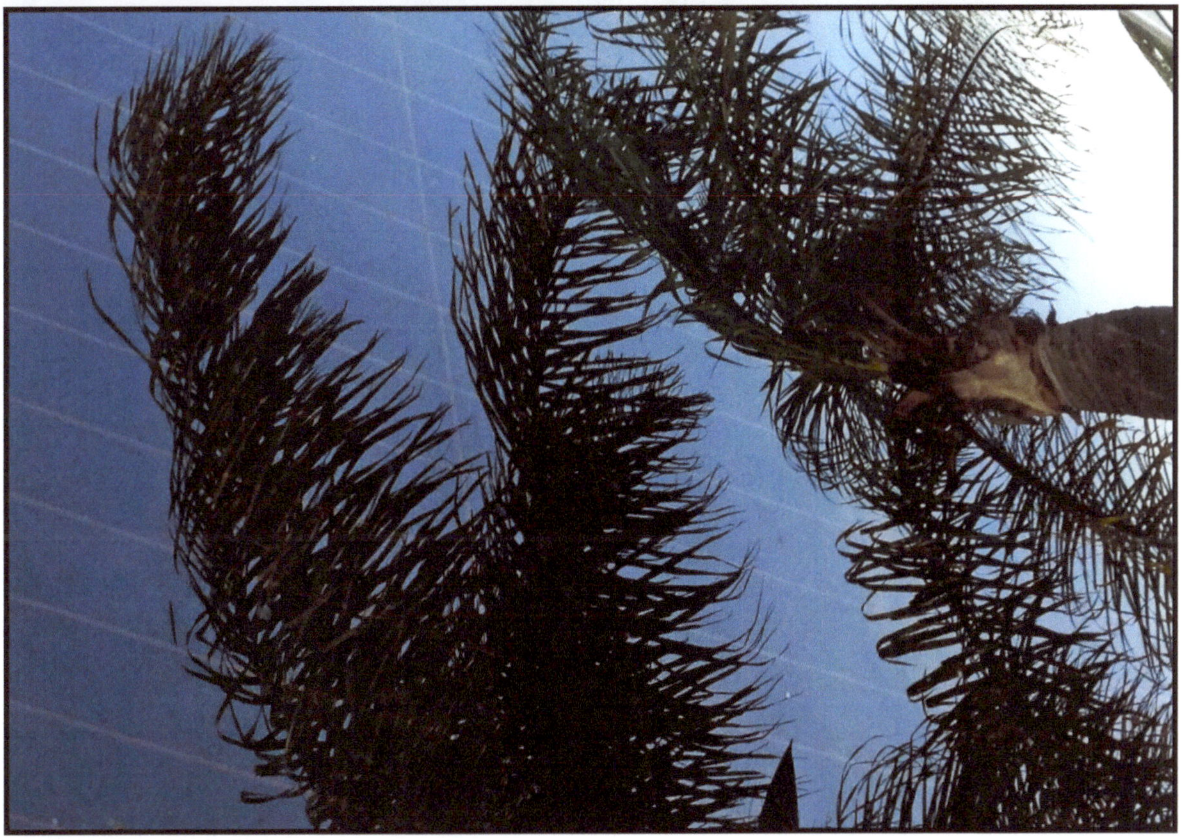

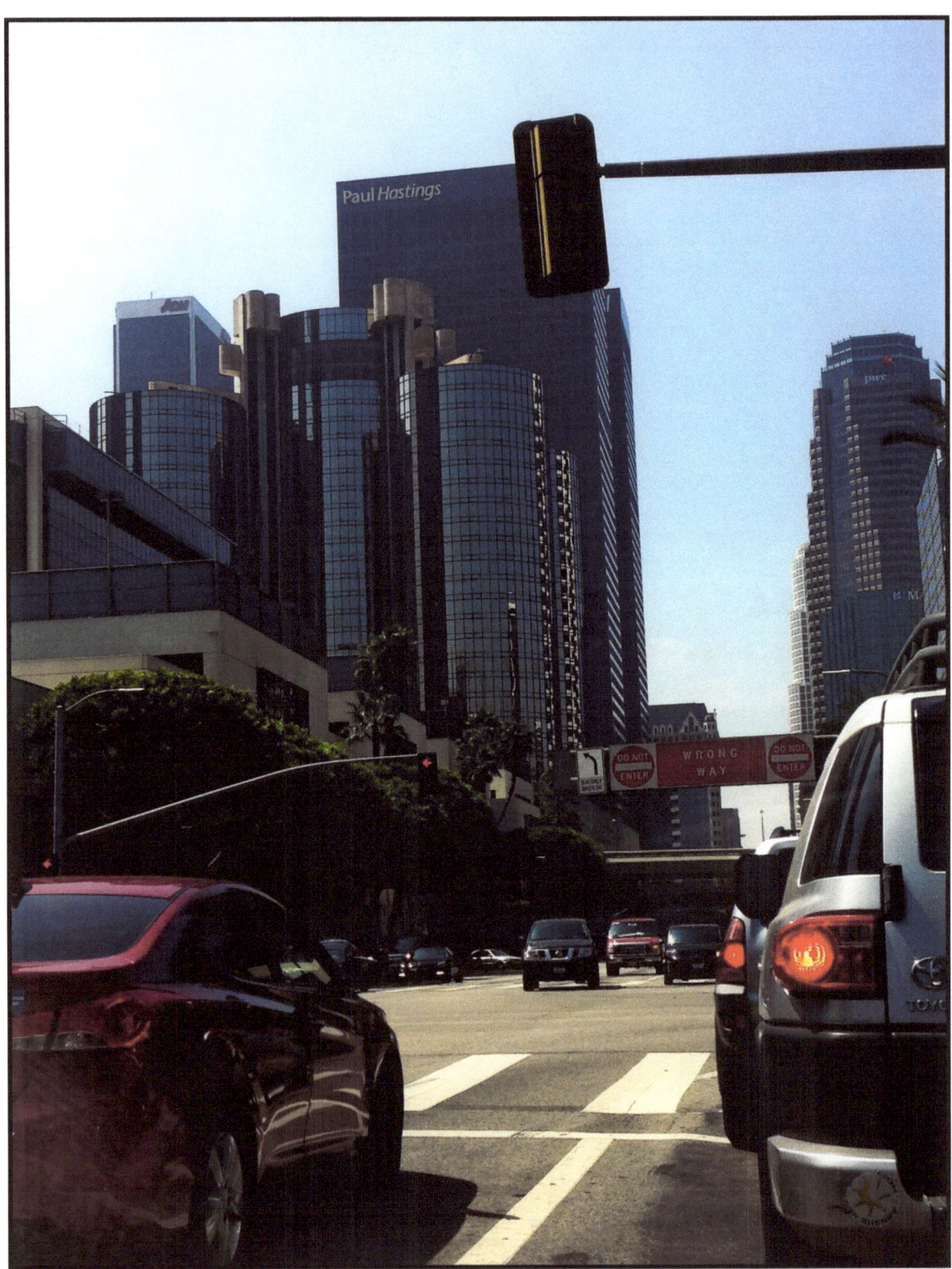

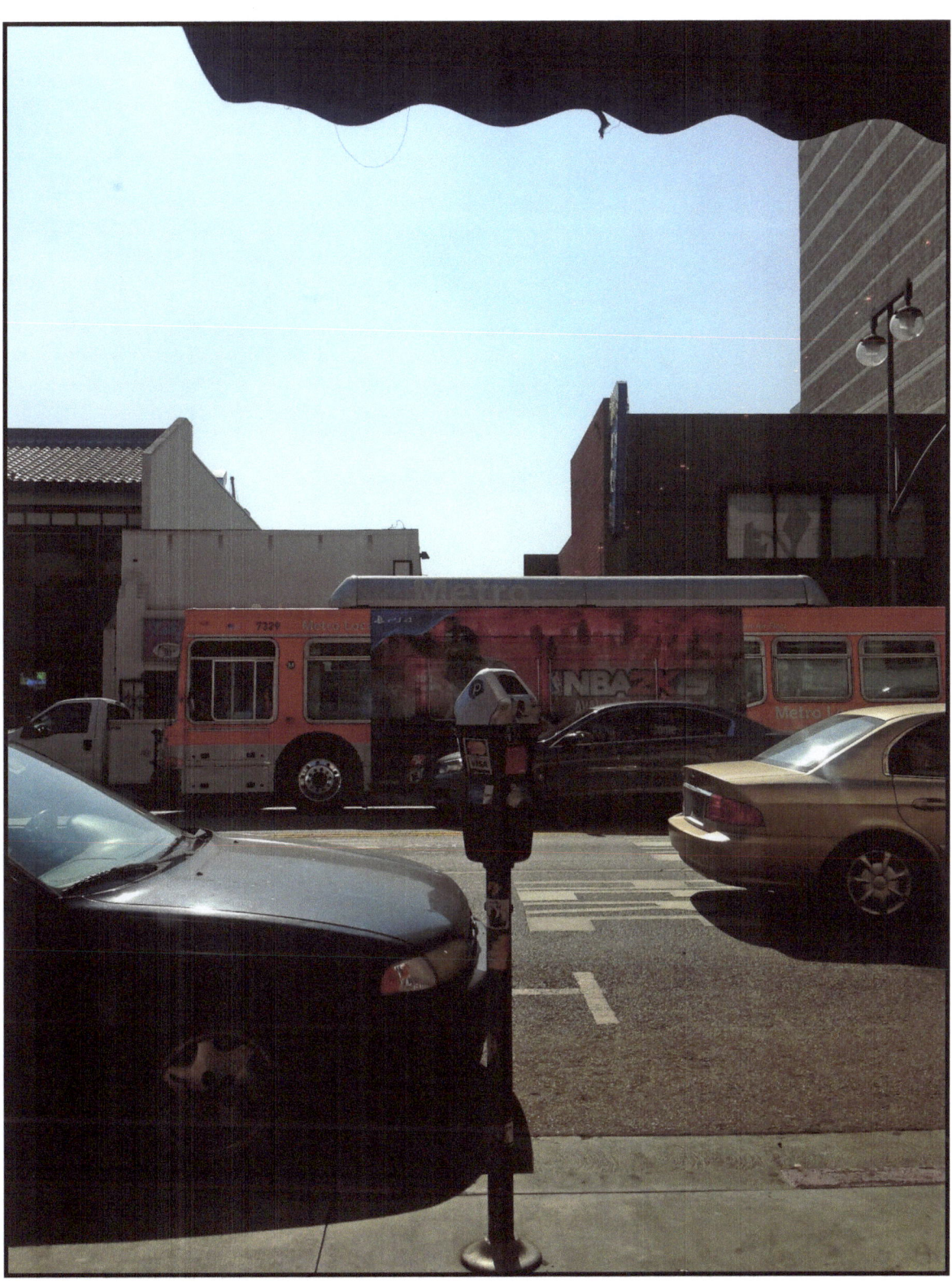

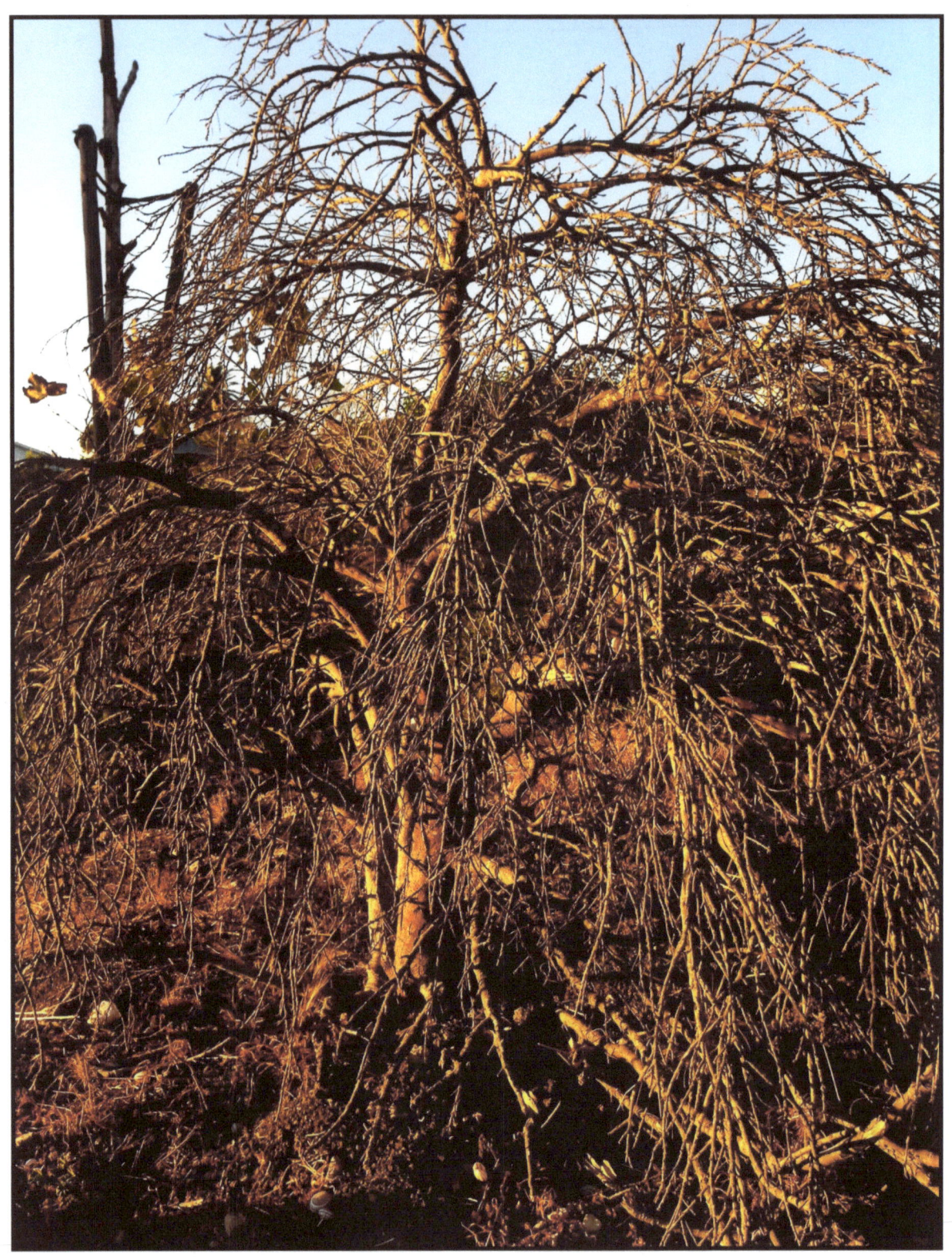

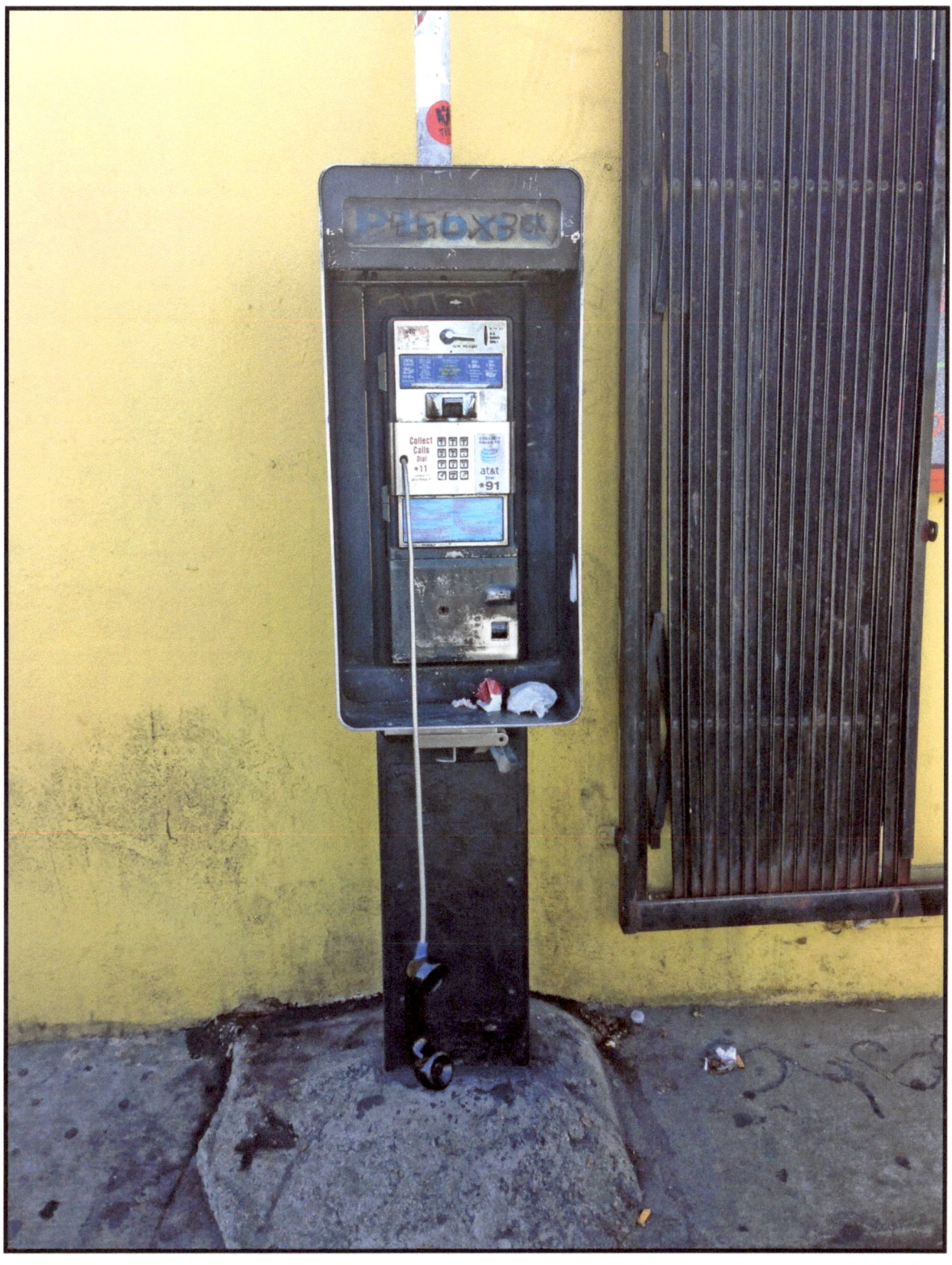

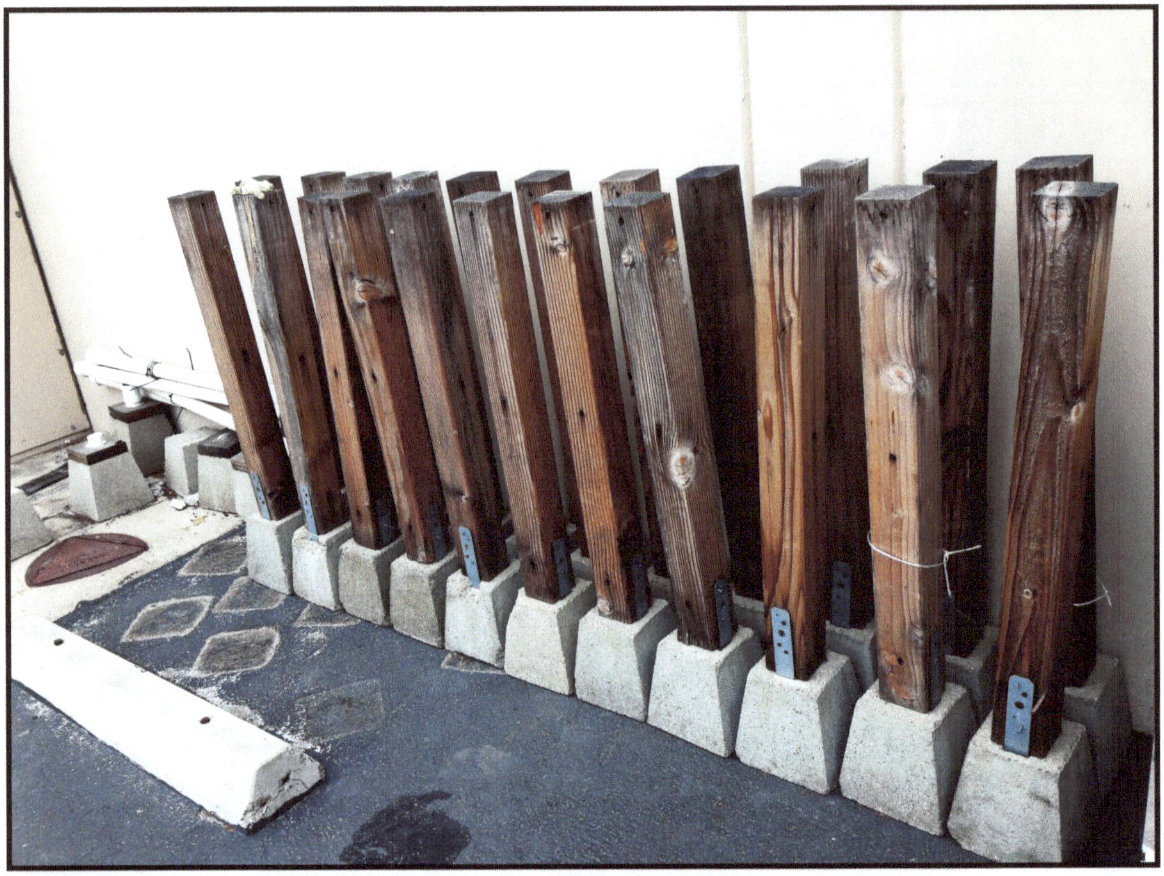

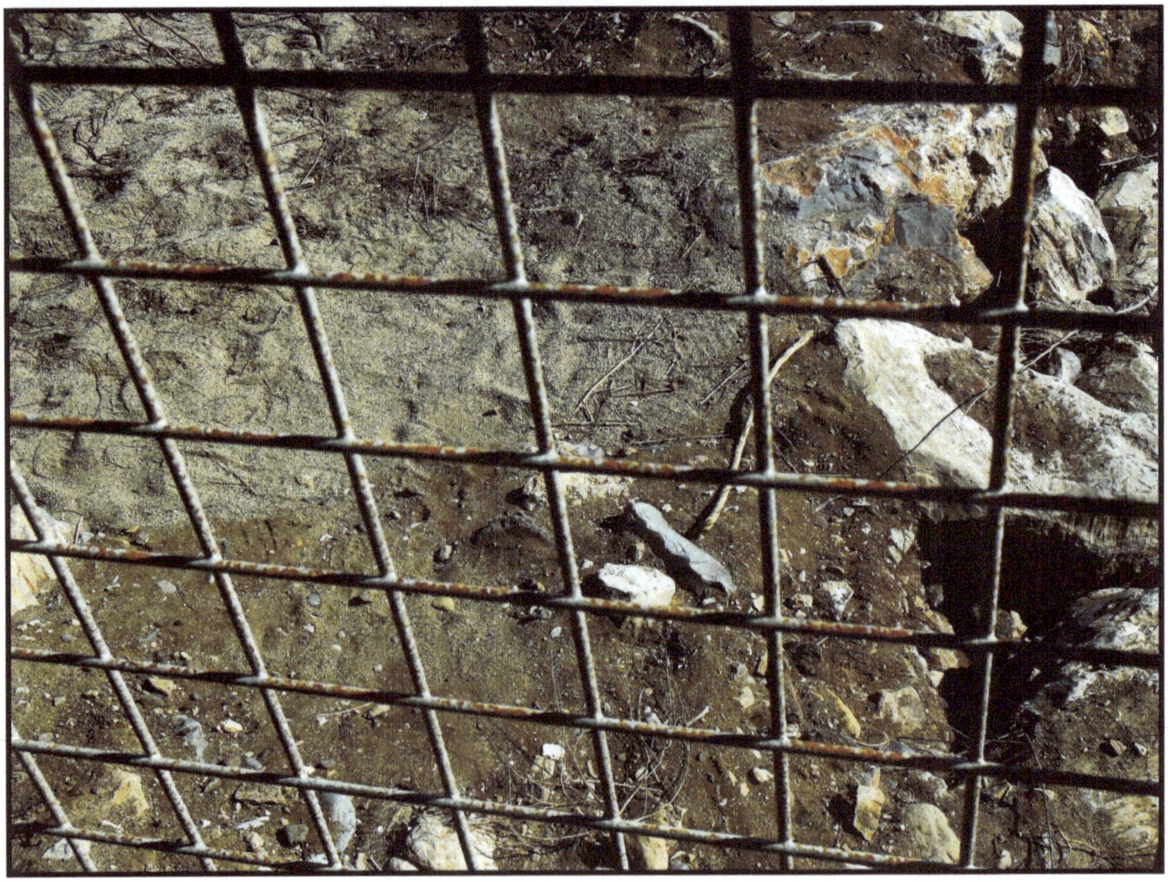

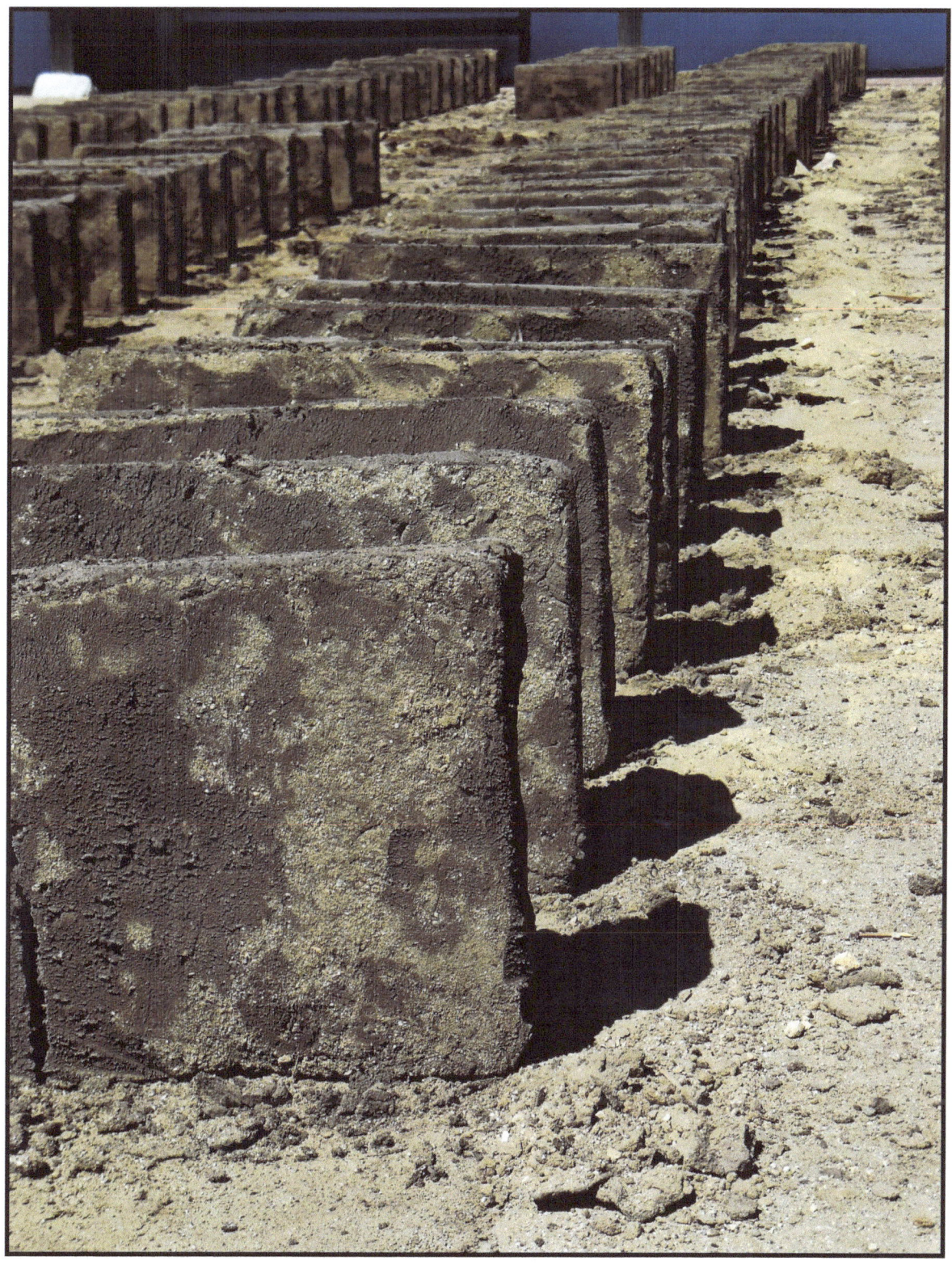

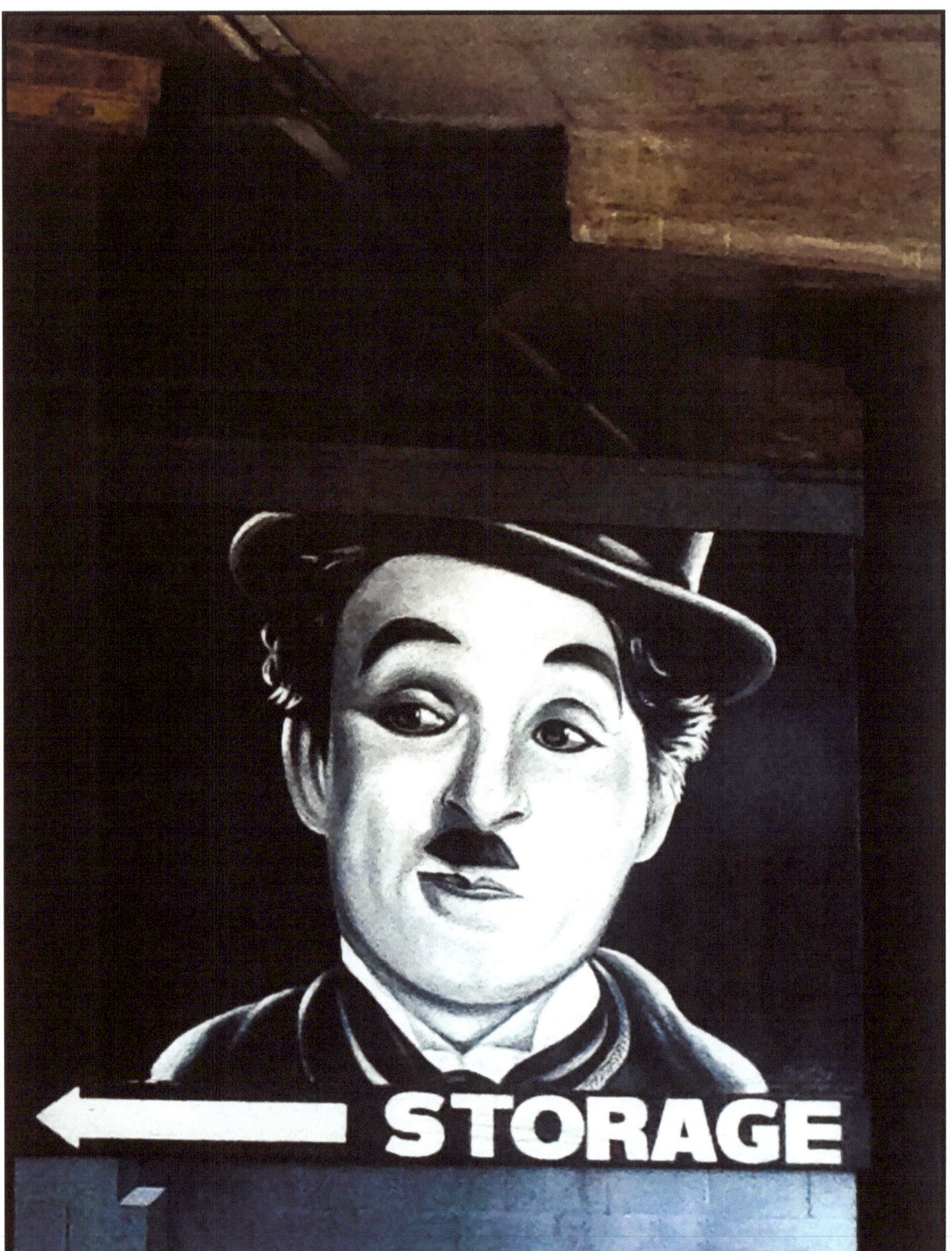

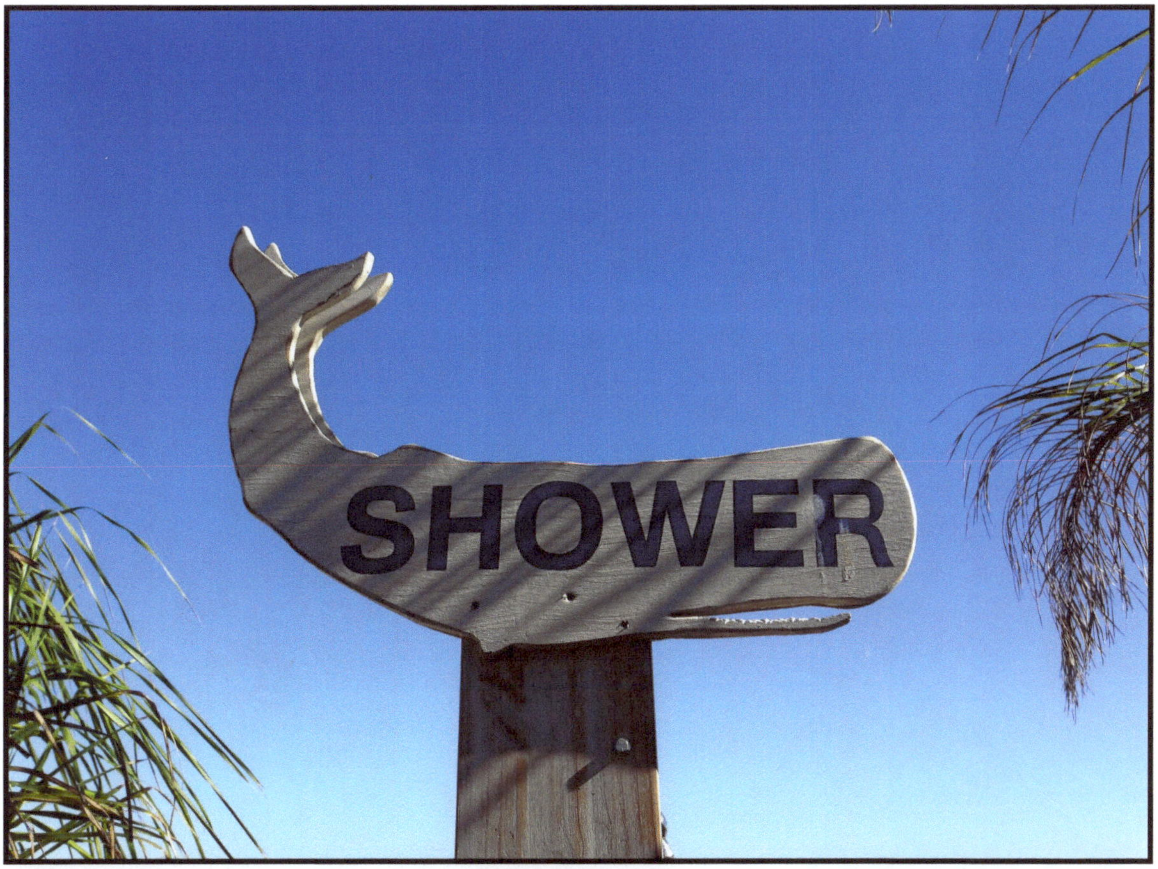

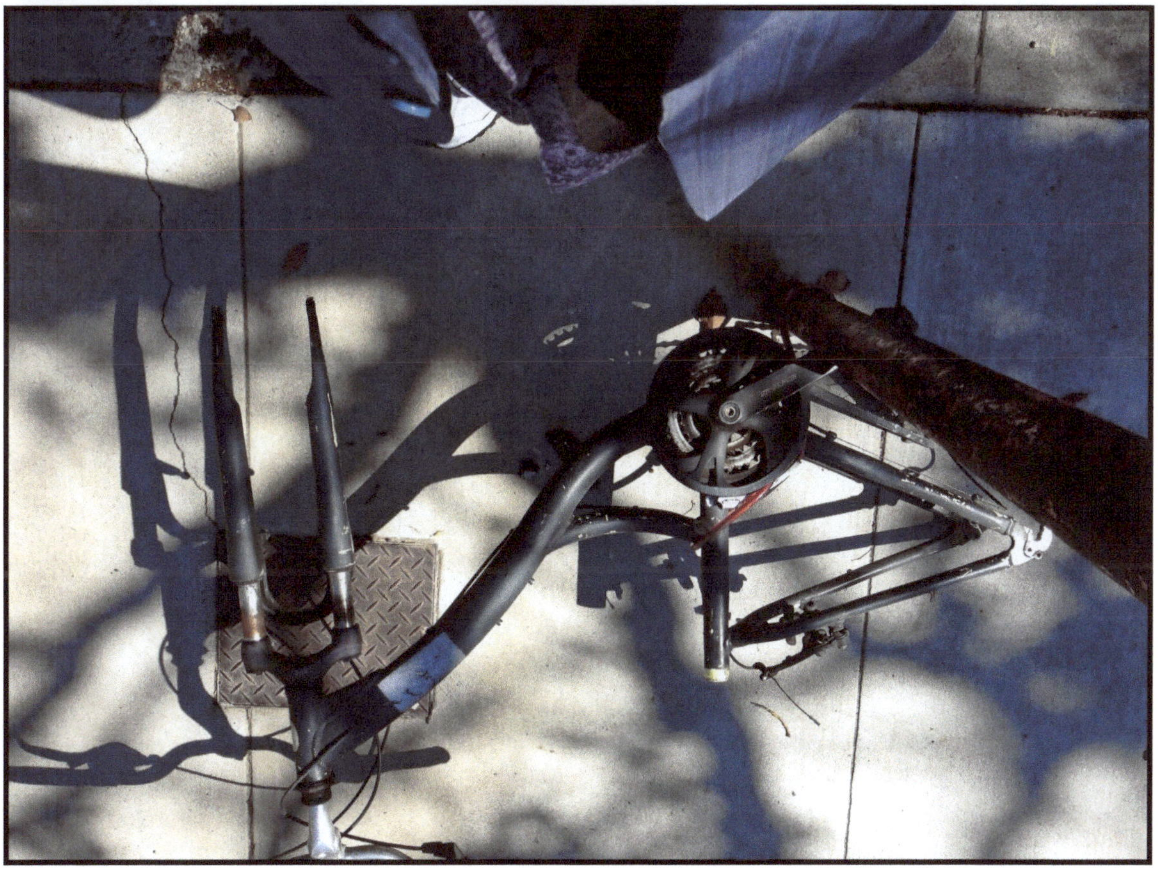

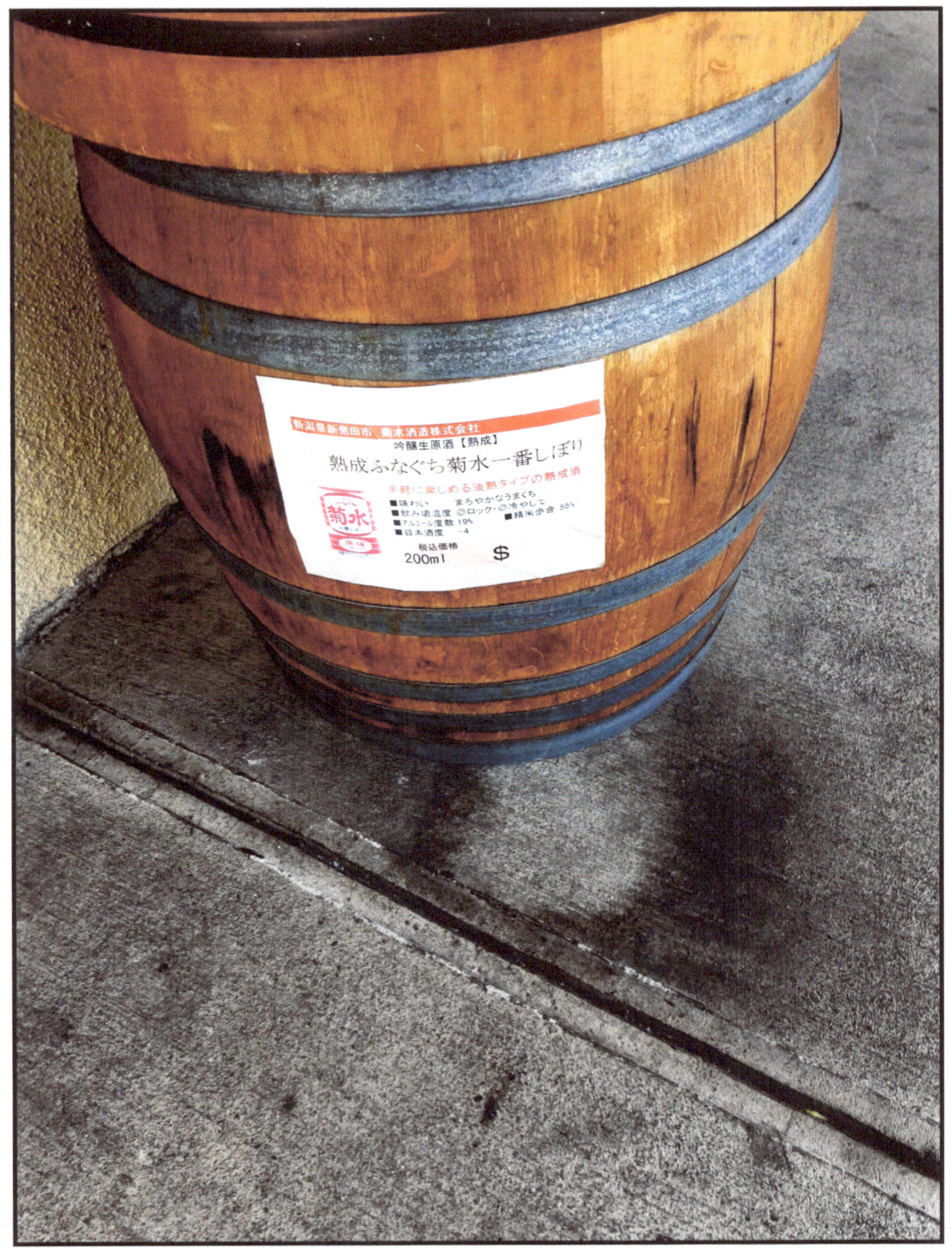

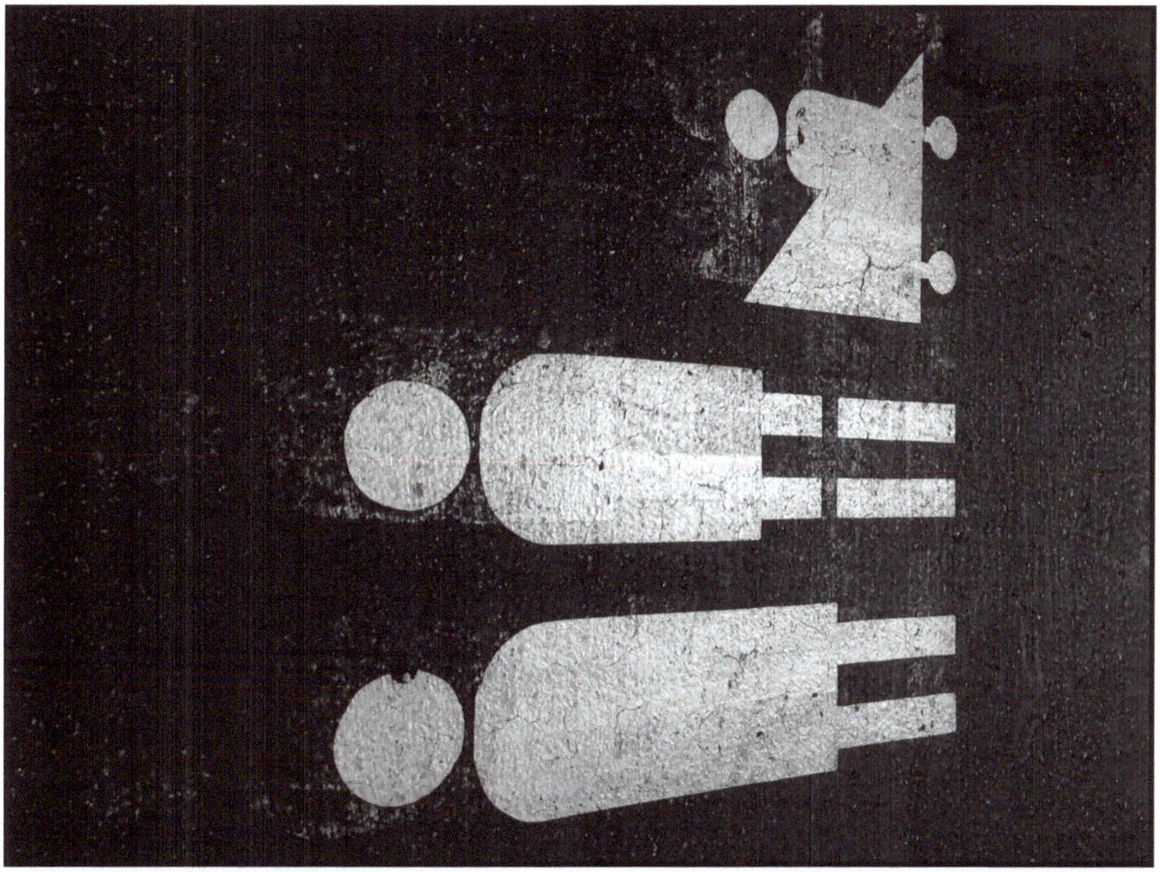

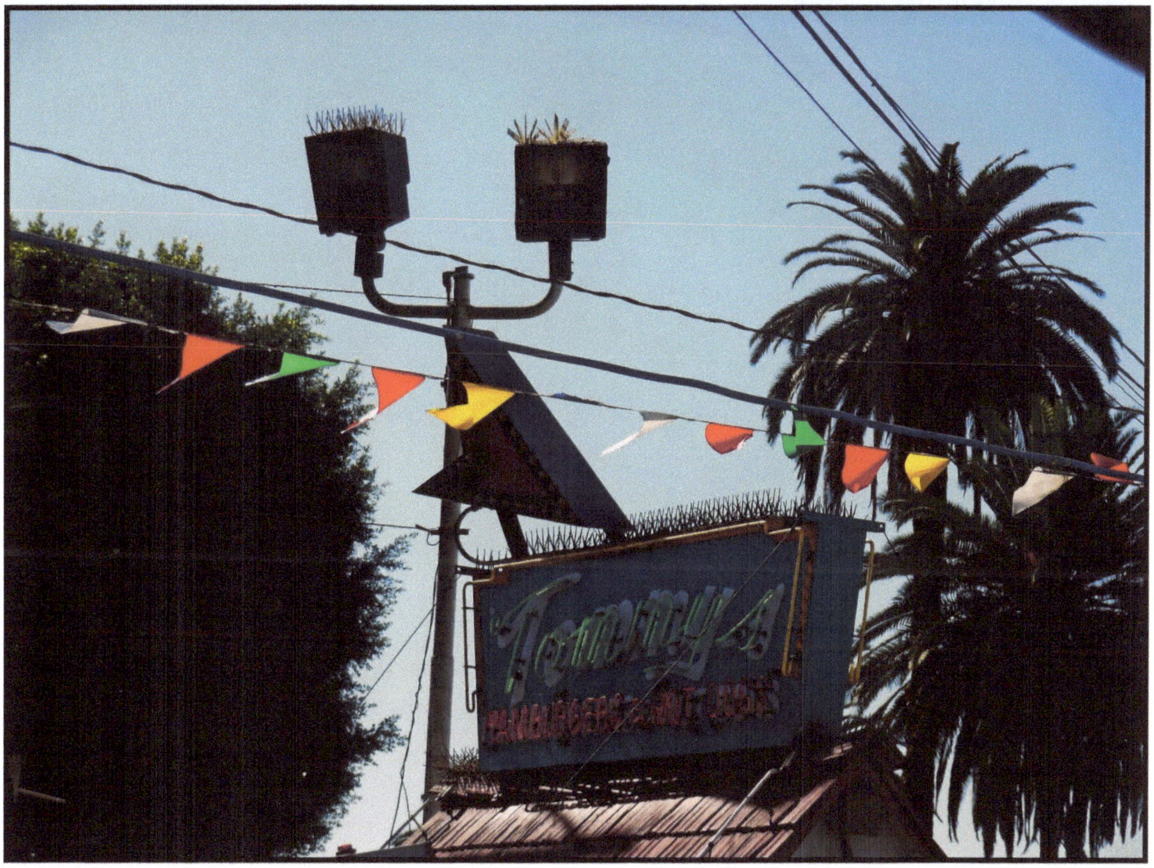

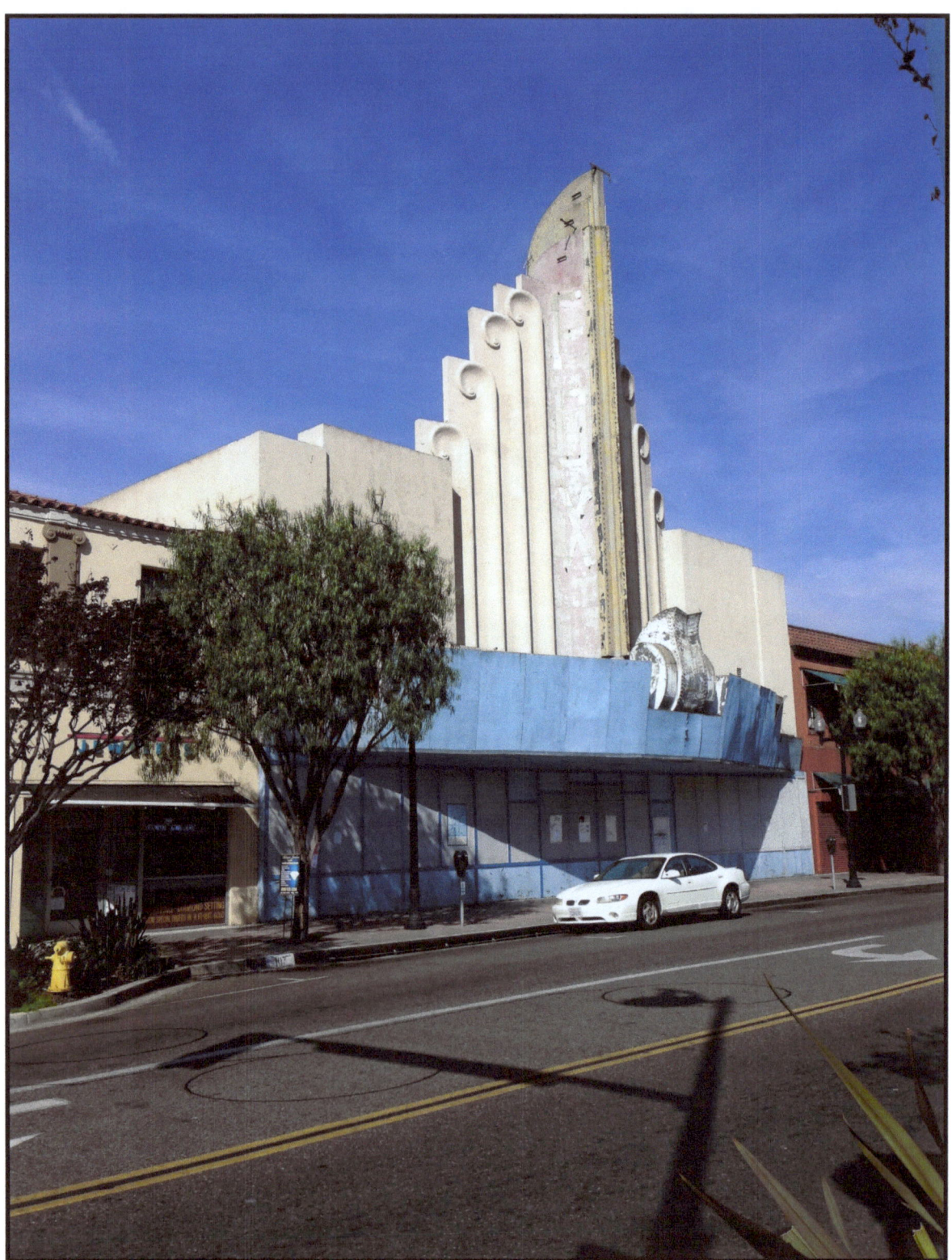

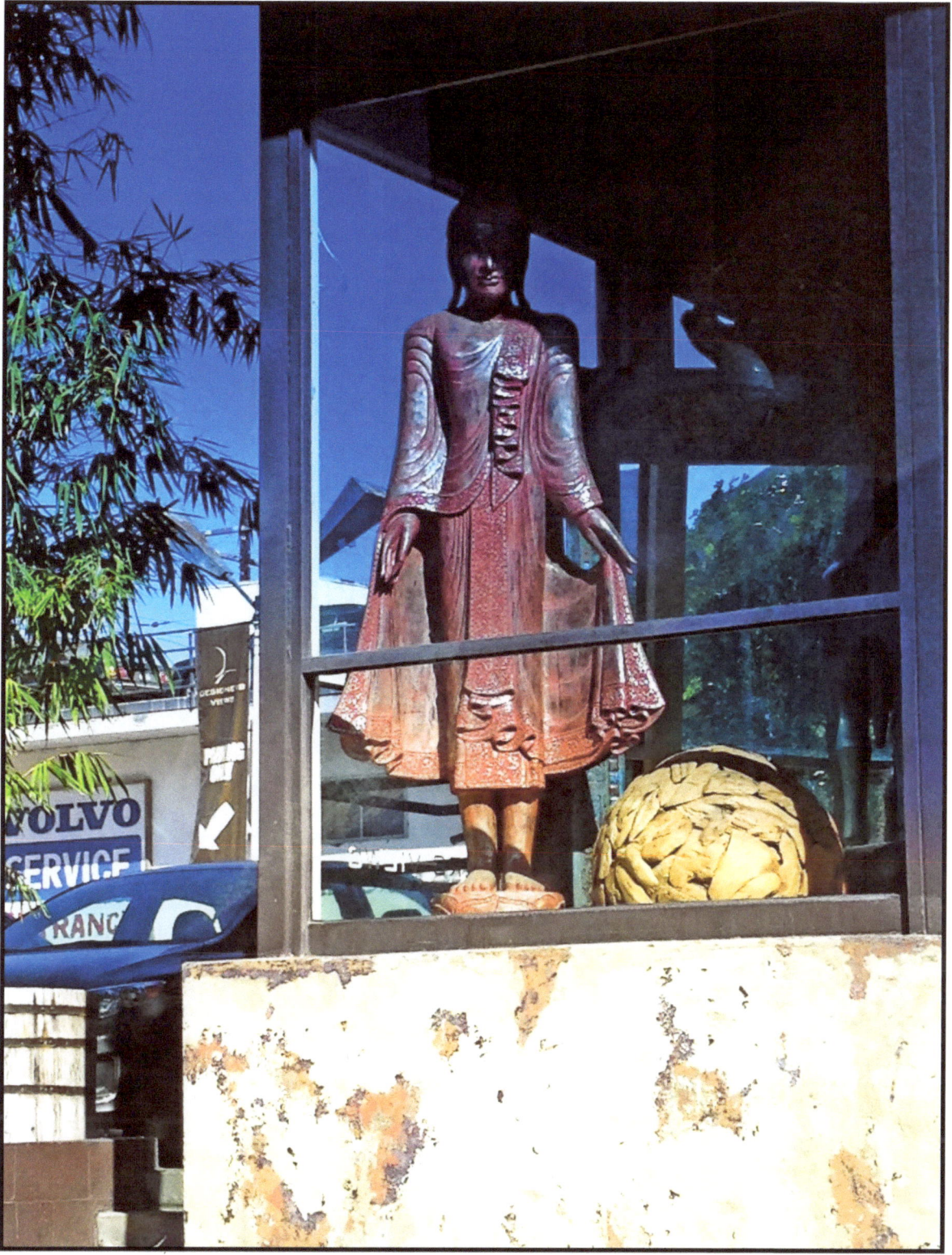

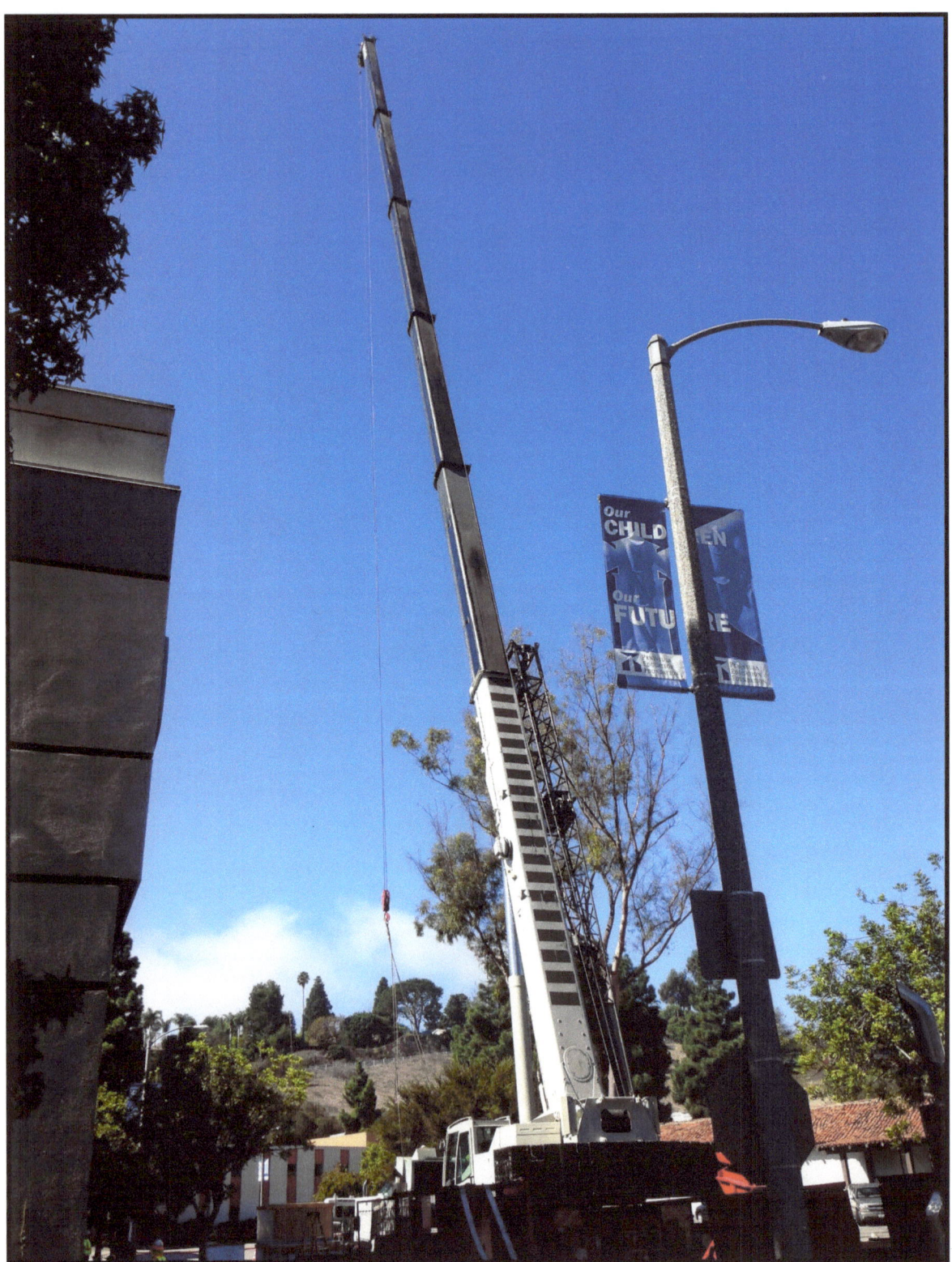

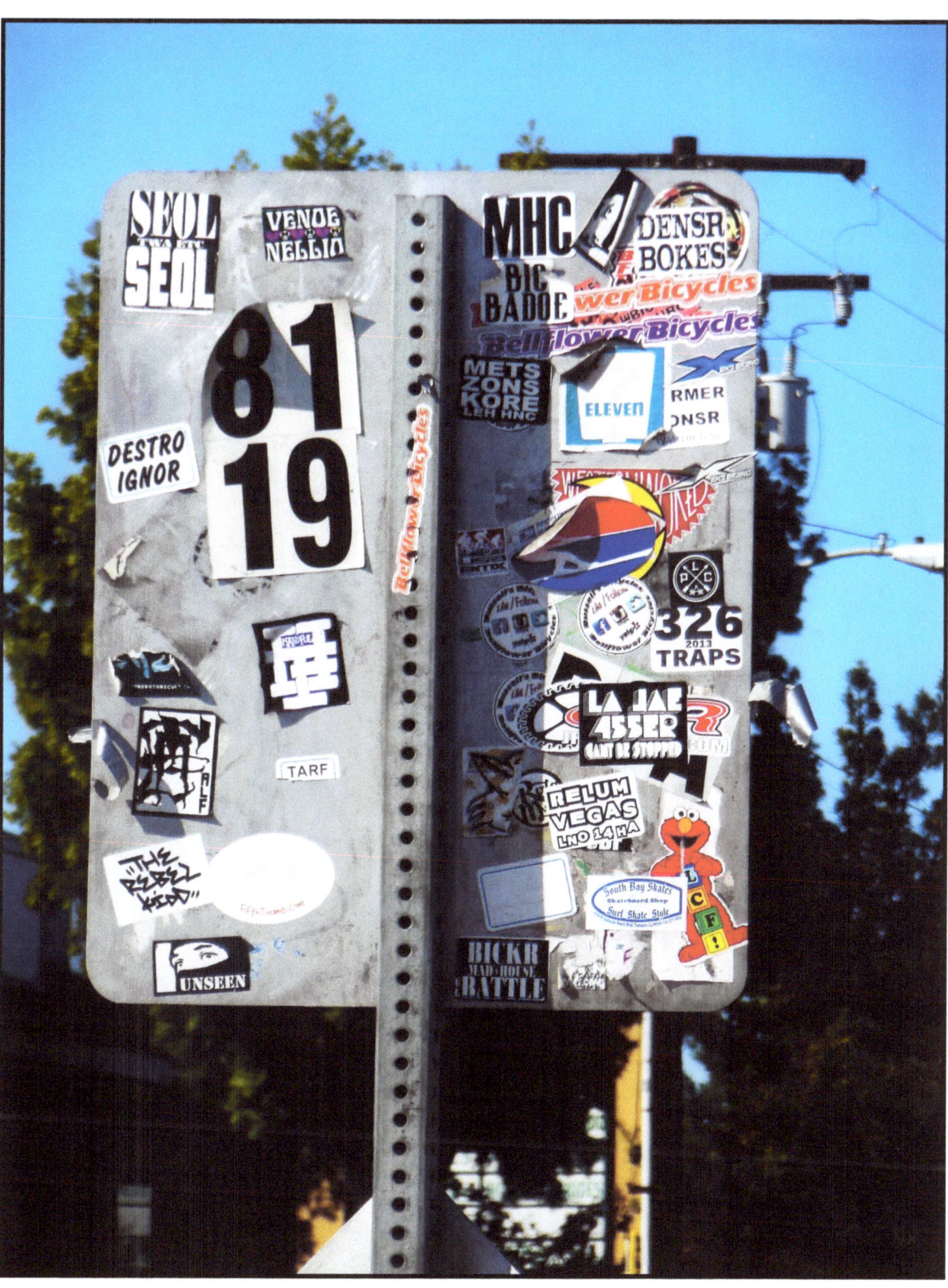

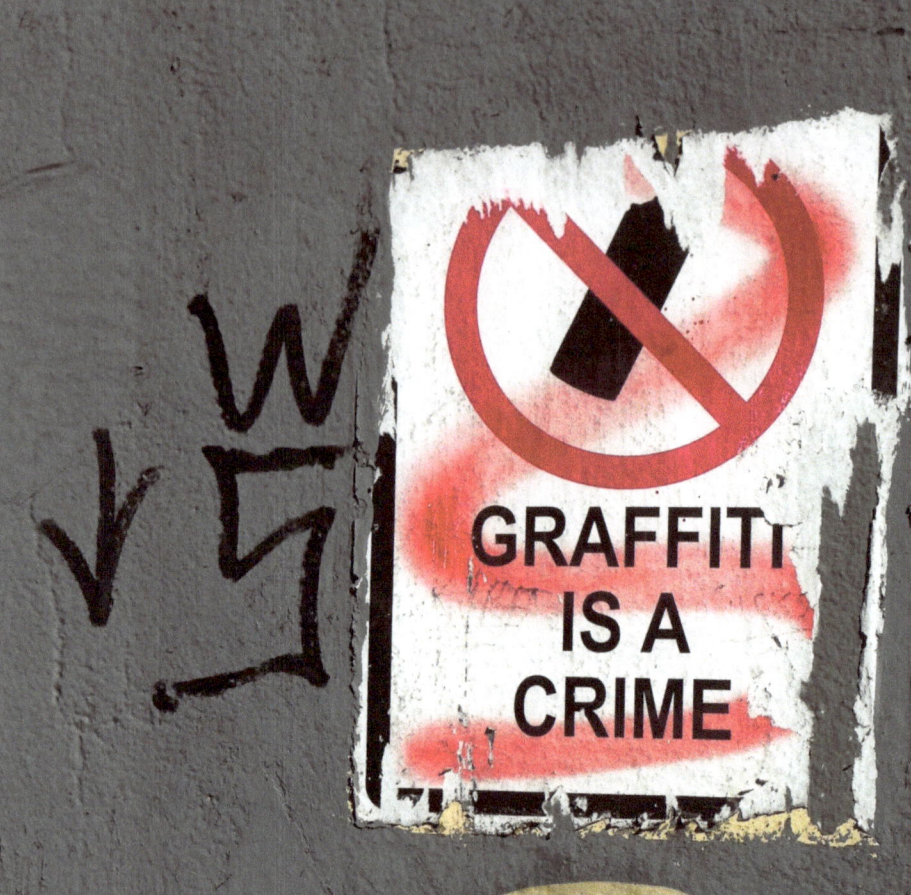
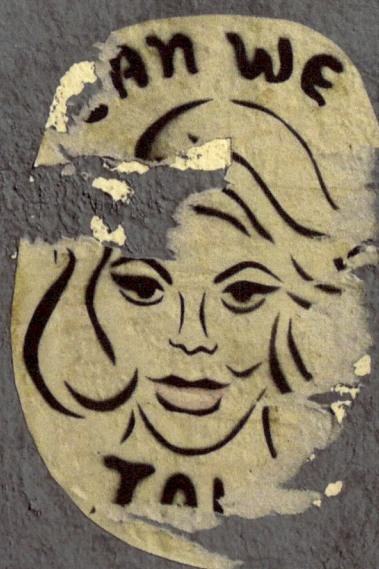

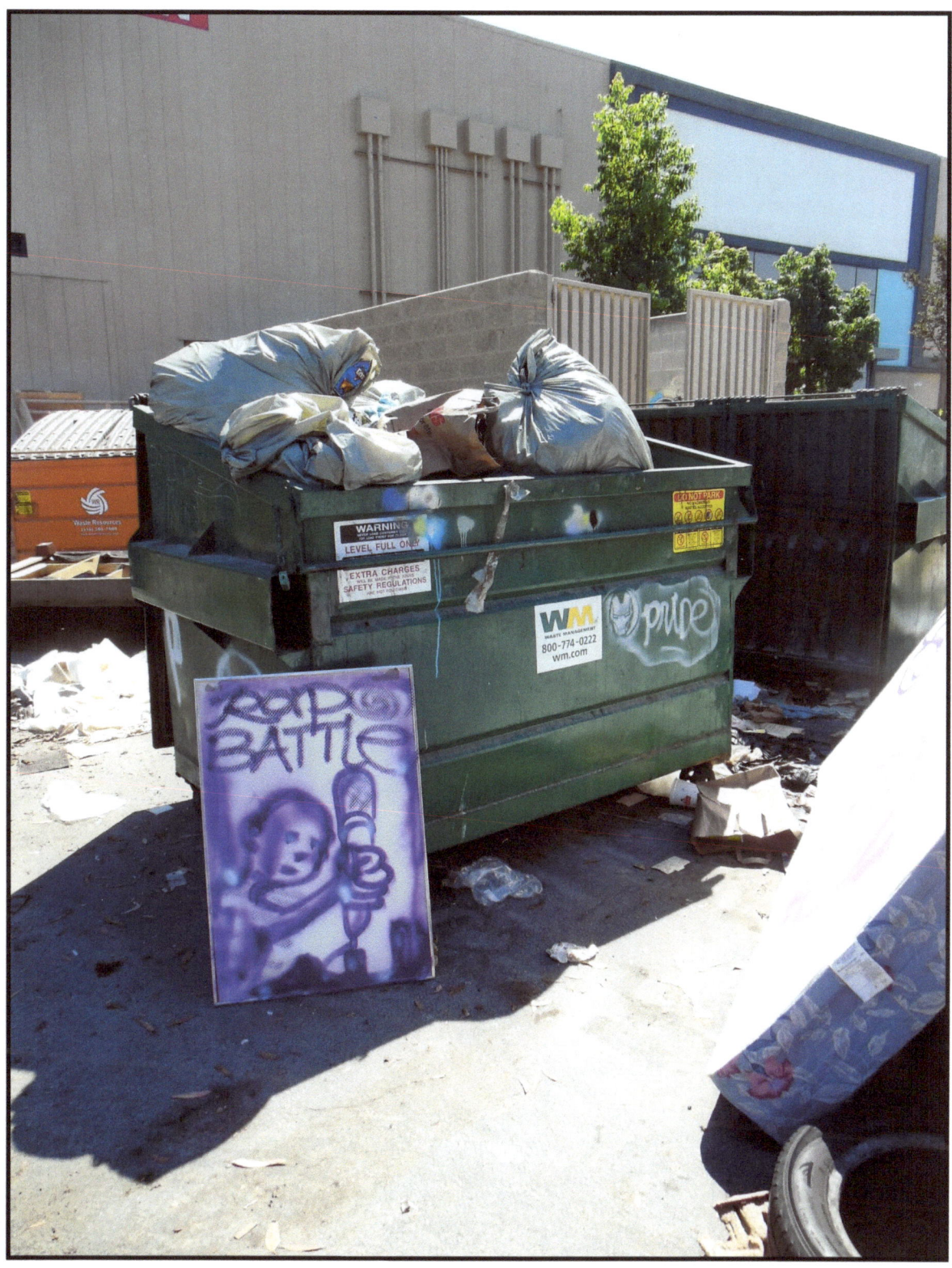

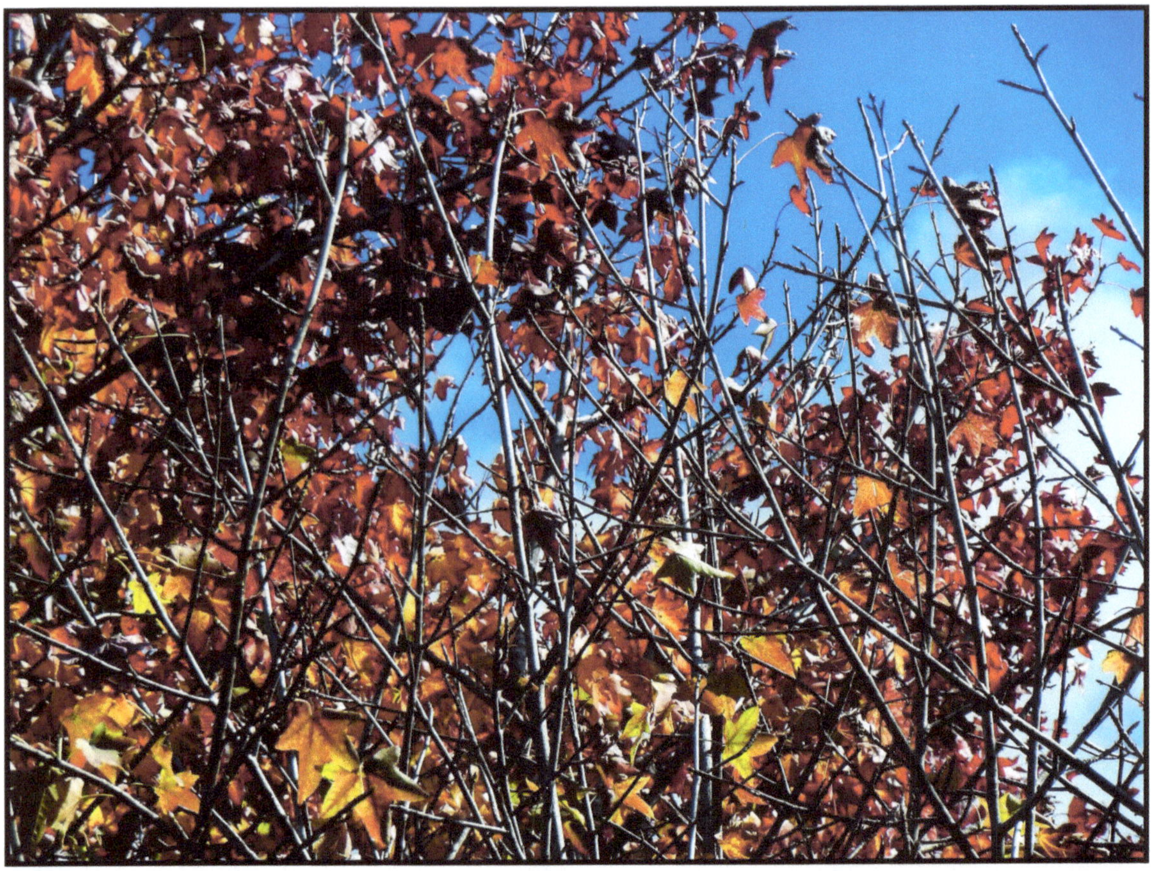

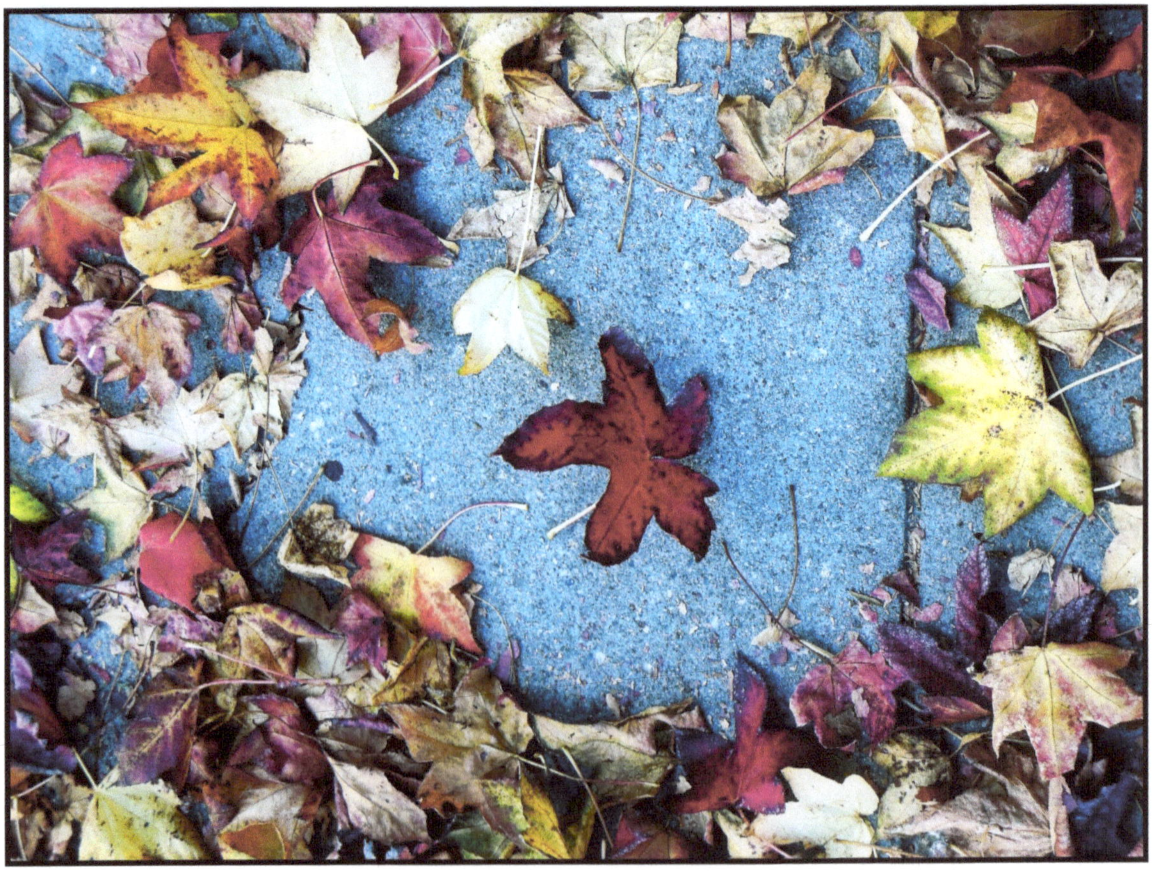

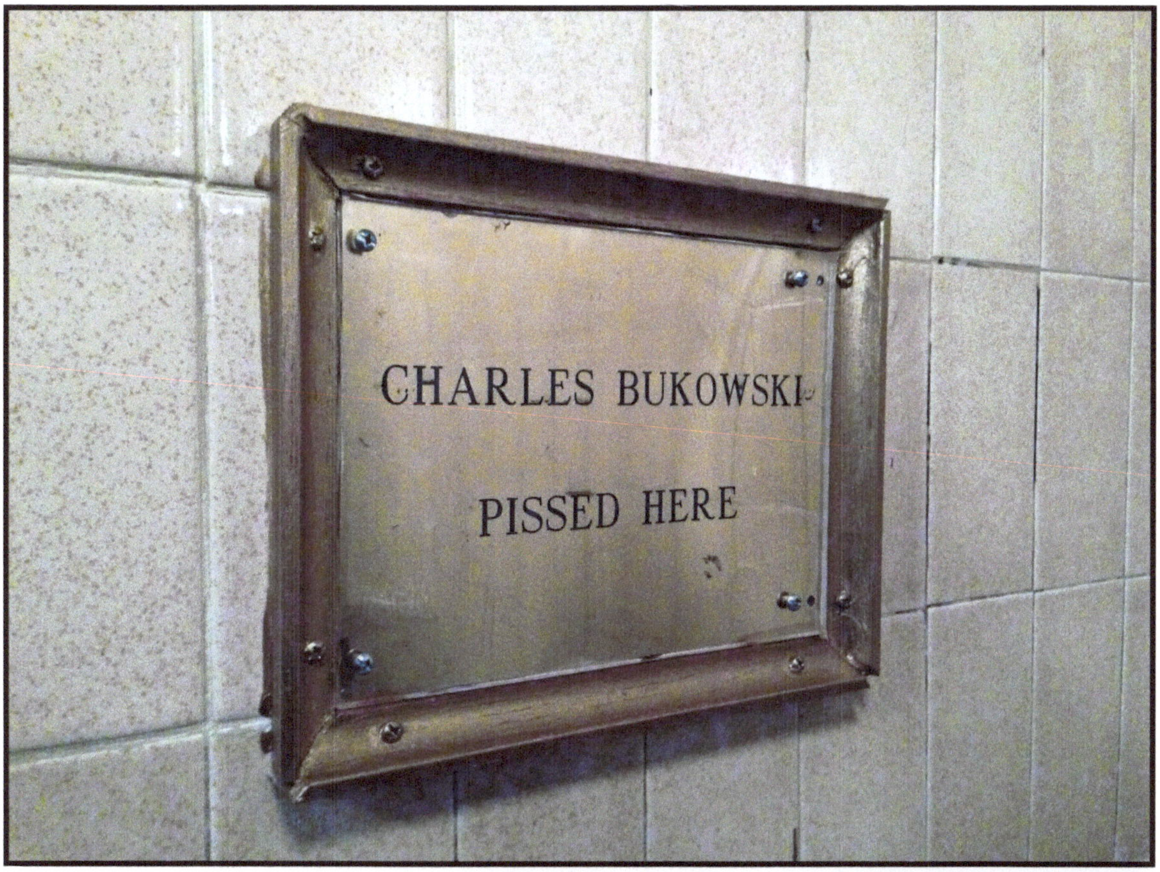

CHARLES BUKOWSKI

PISSED HERE

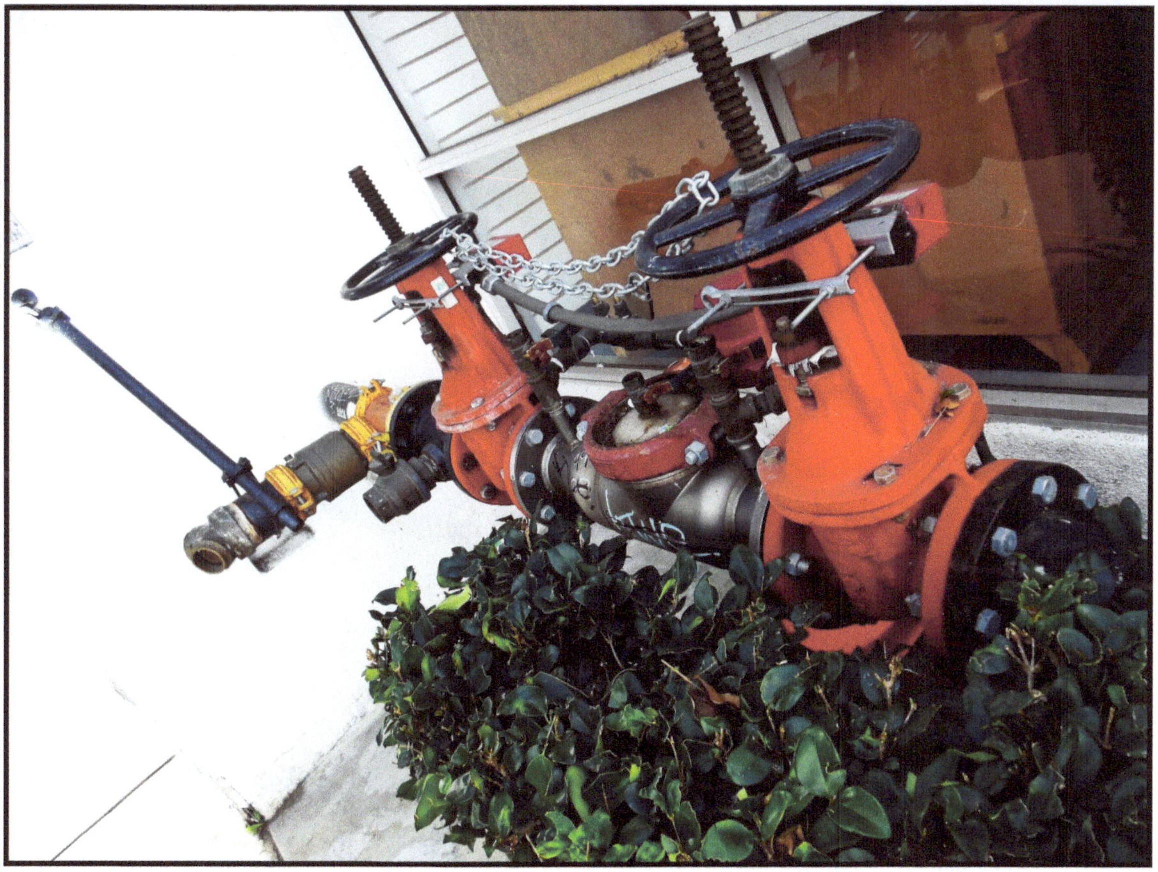

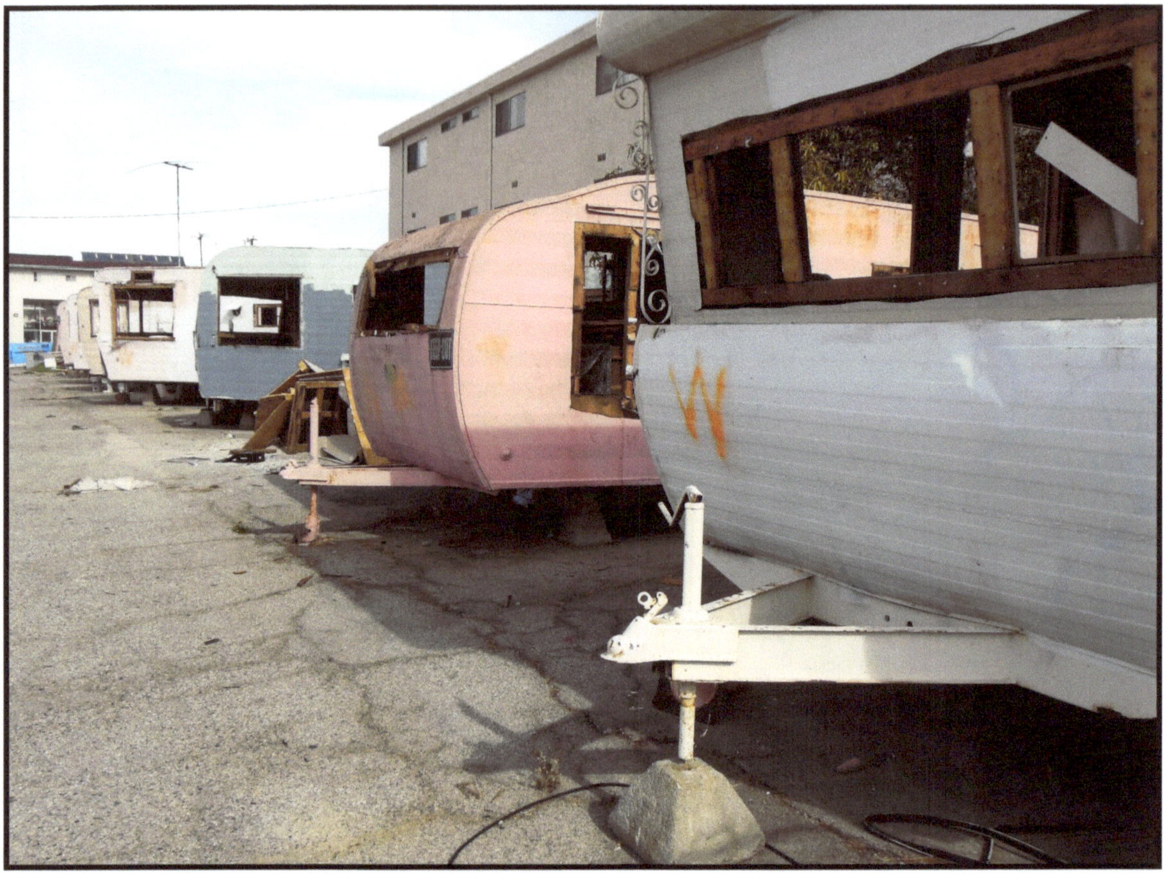

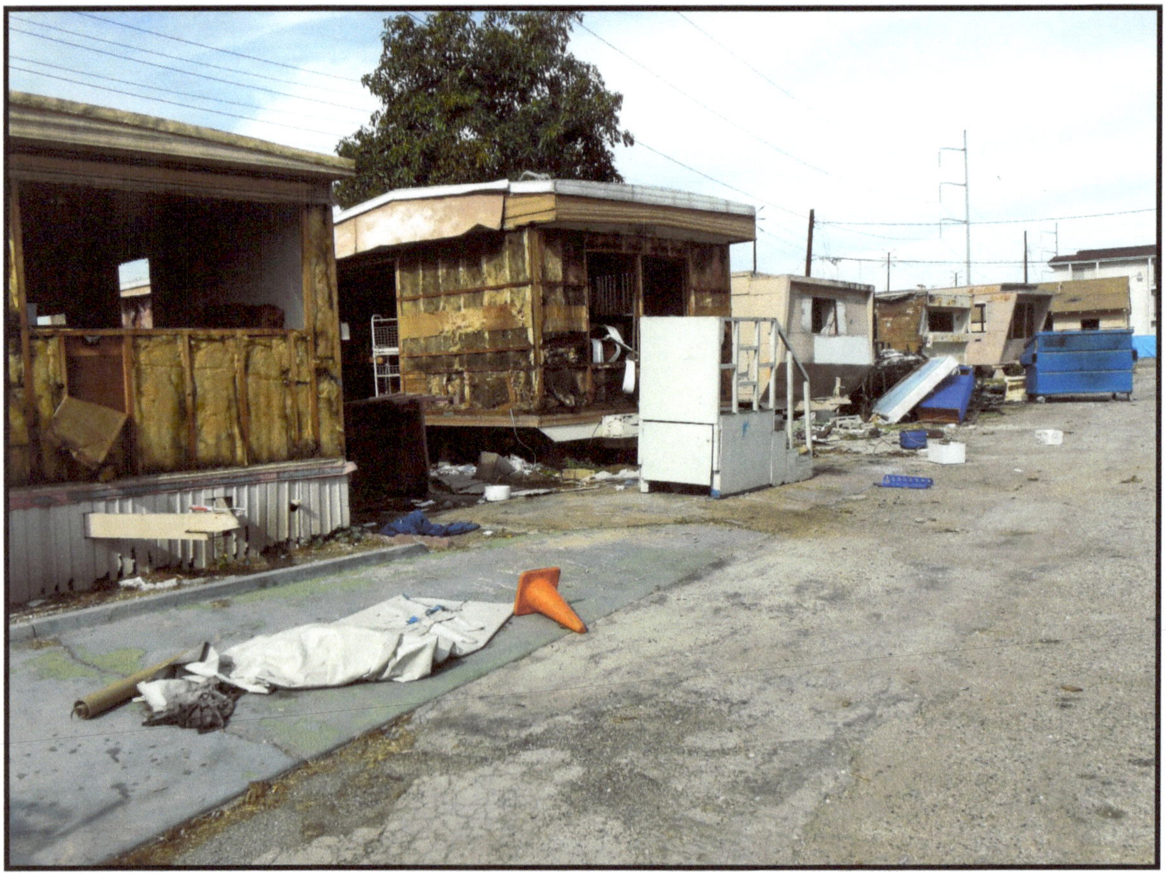

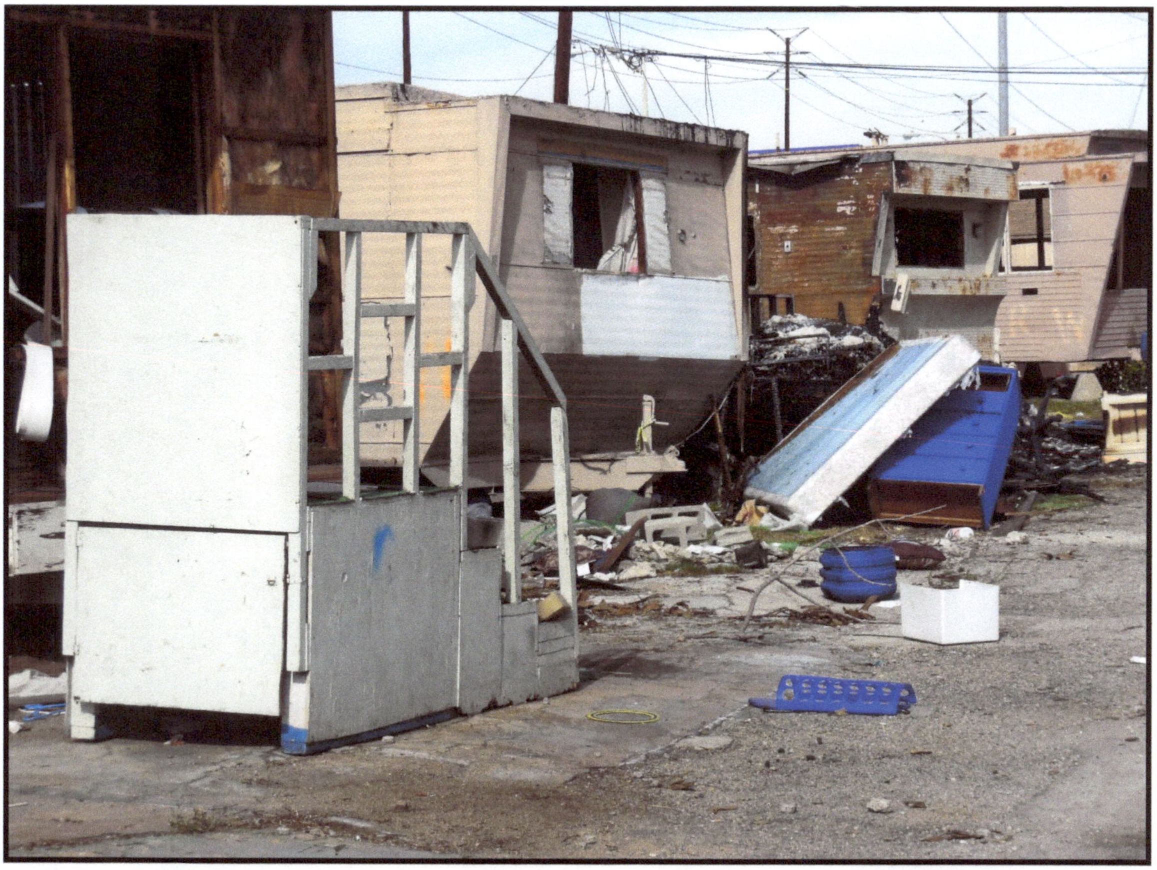

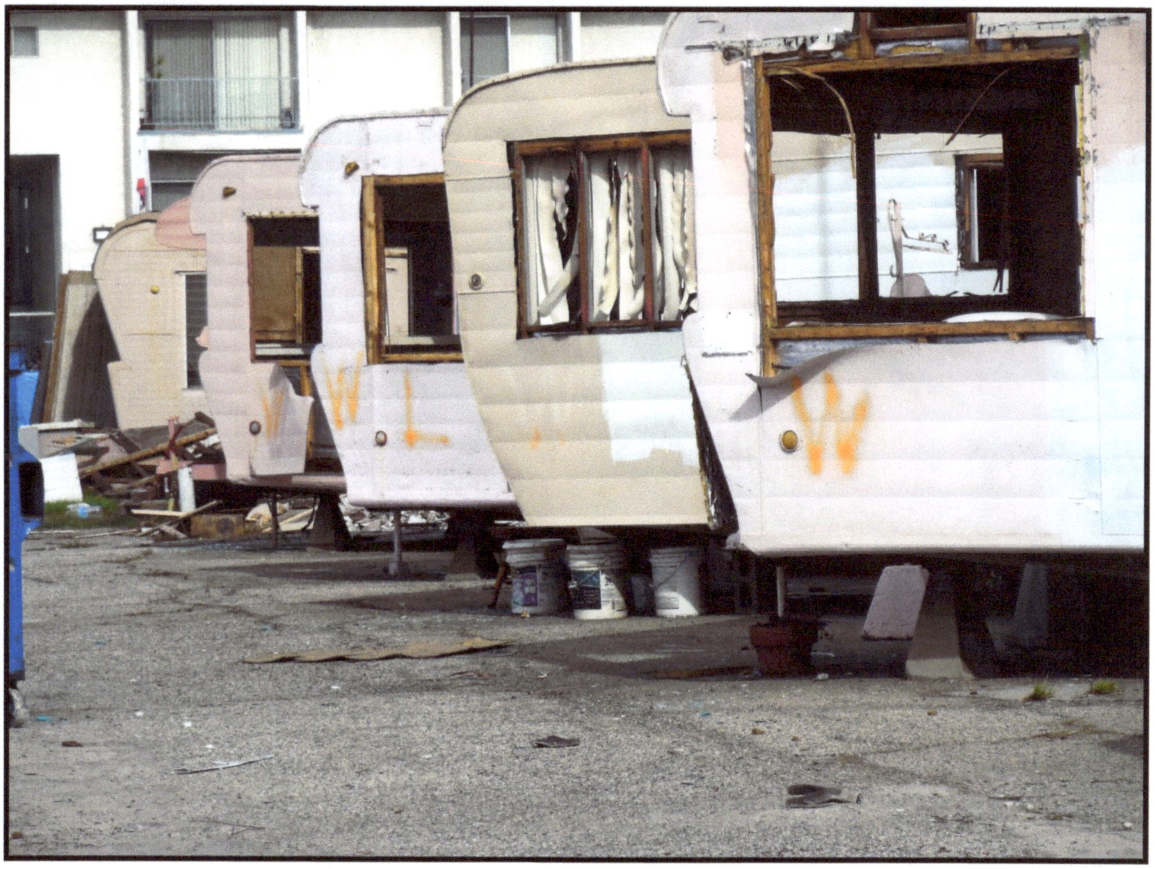

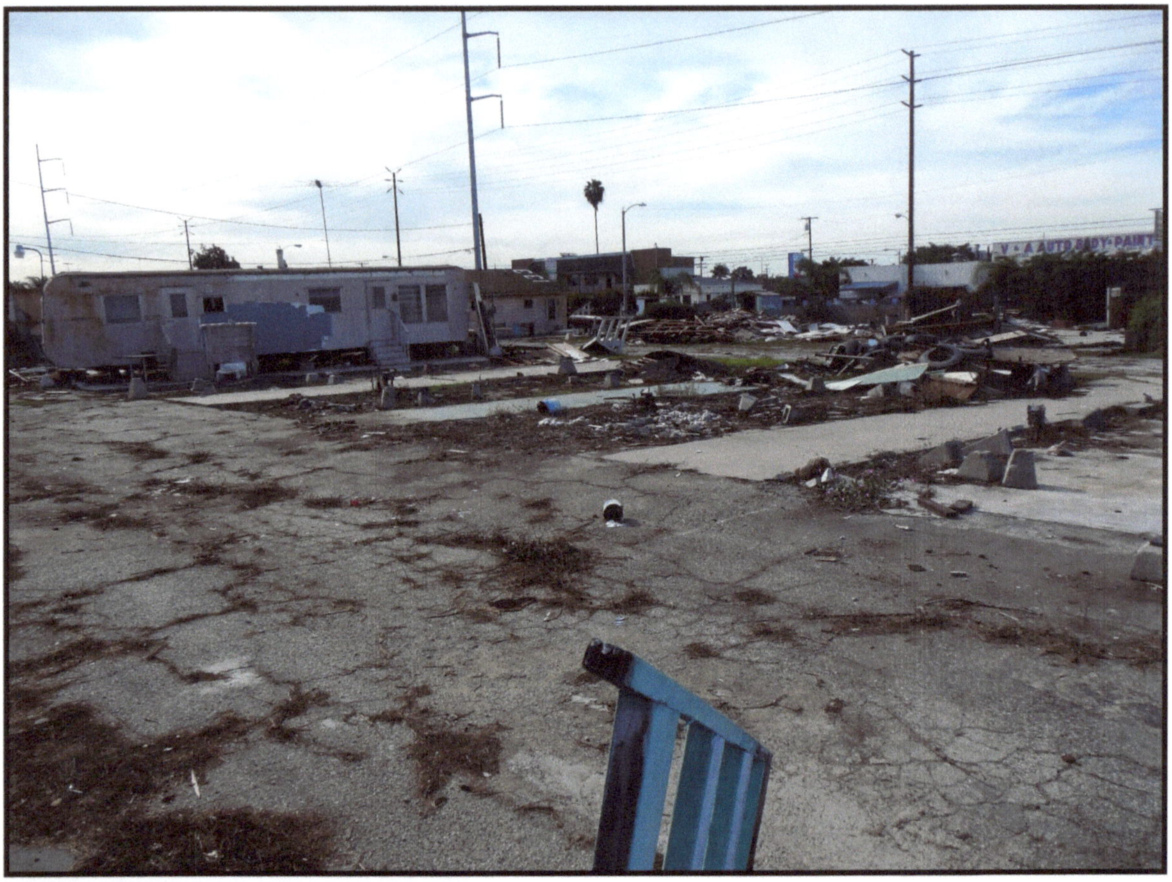

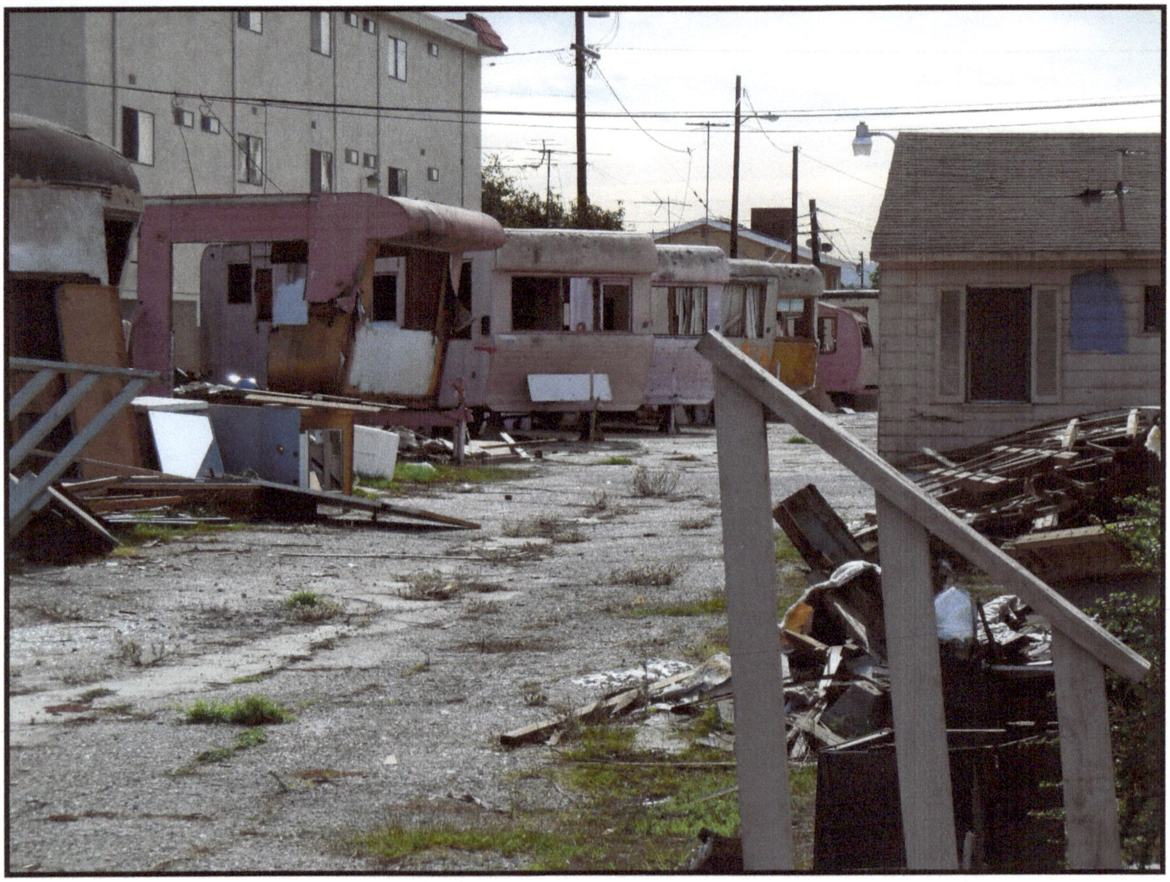

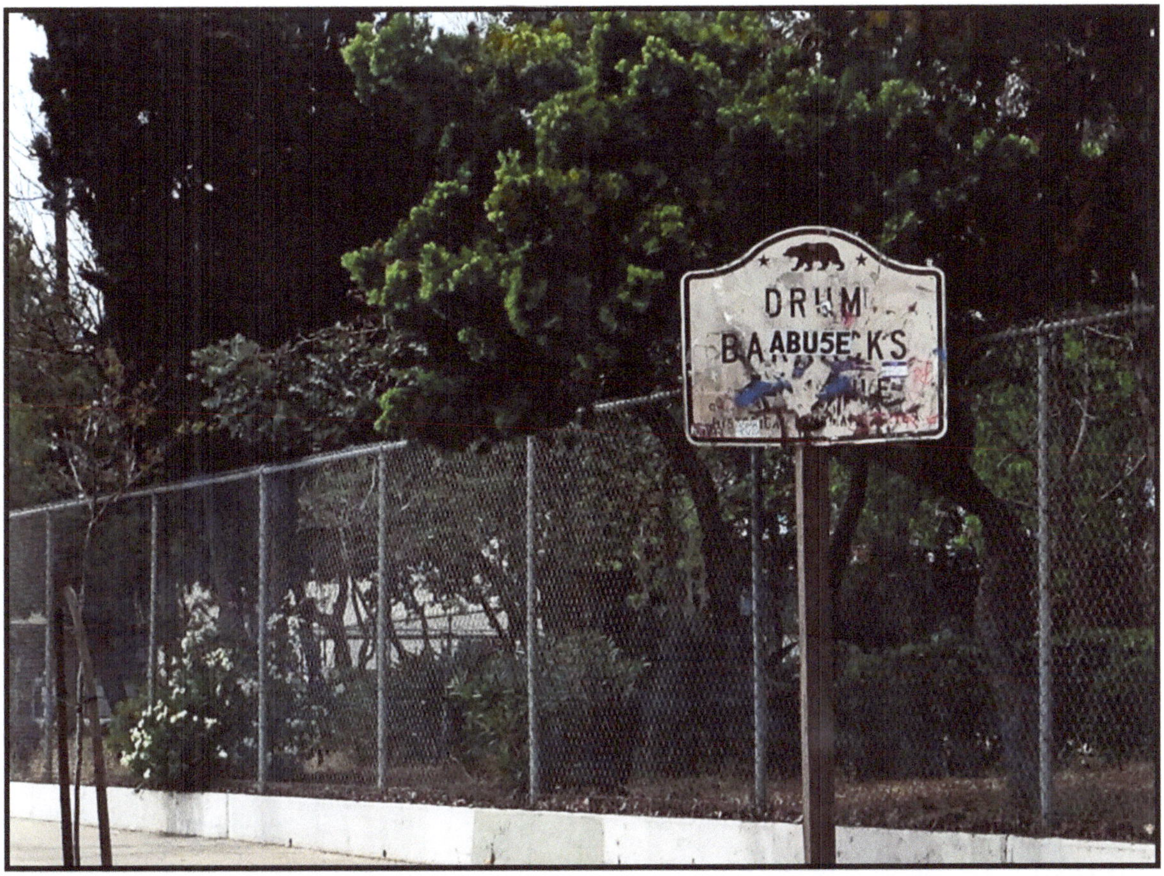

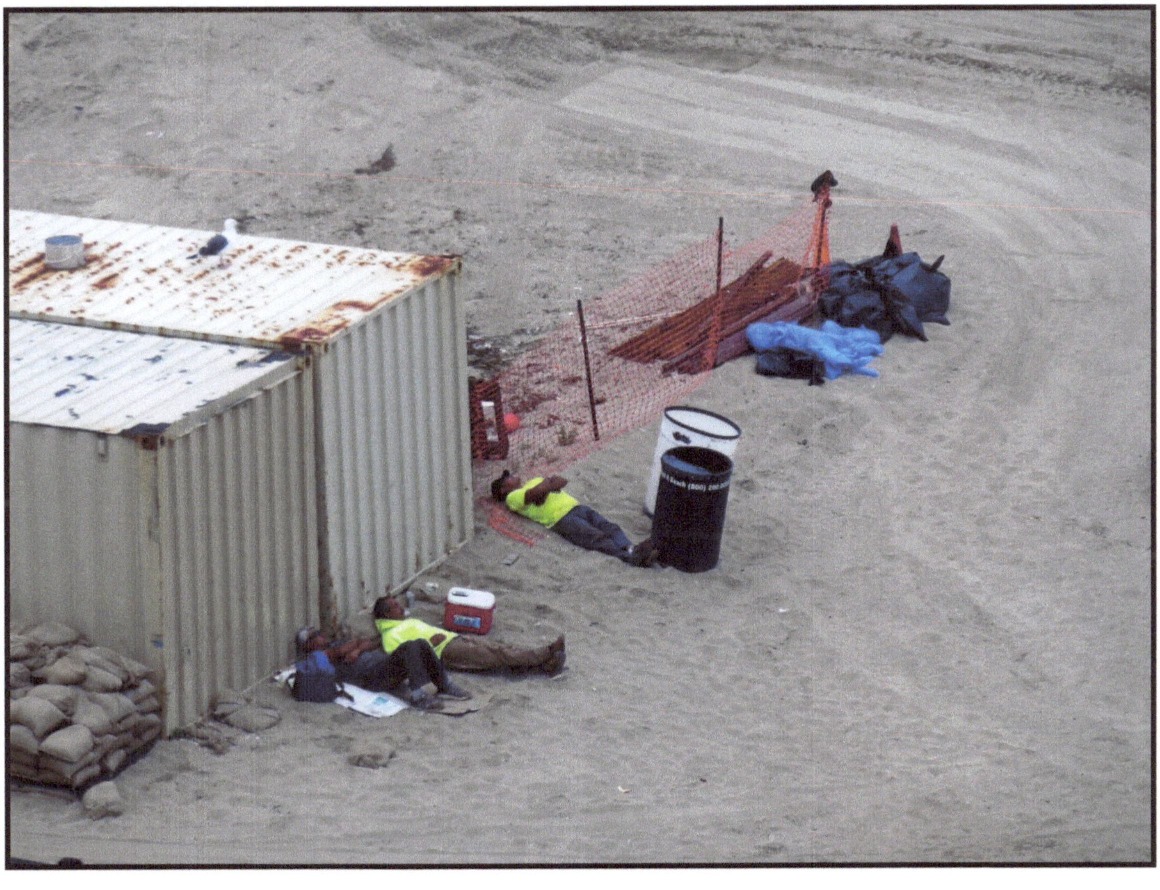

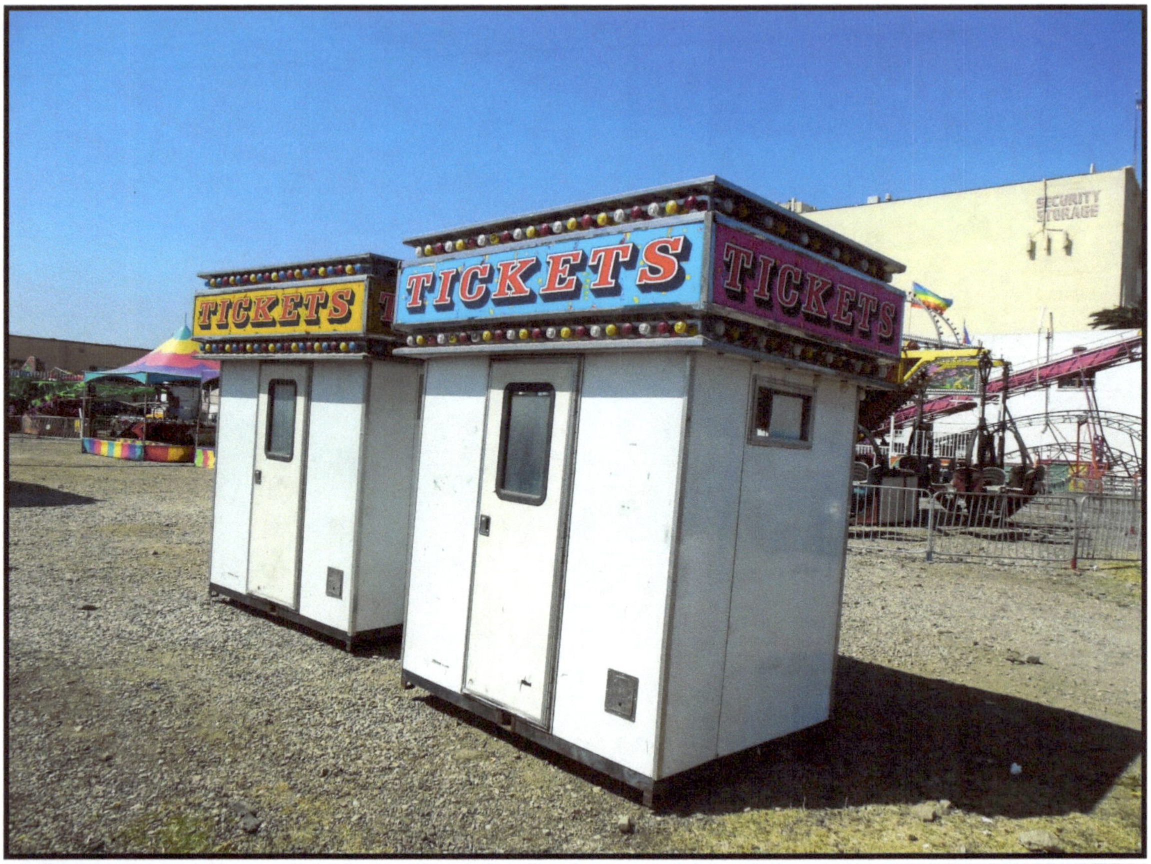

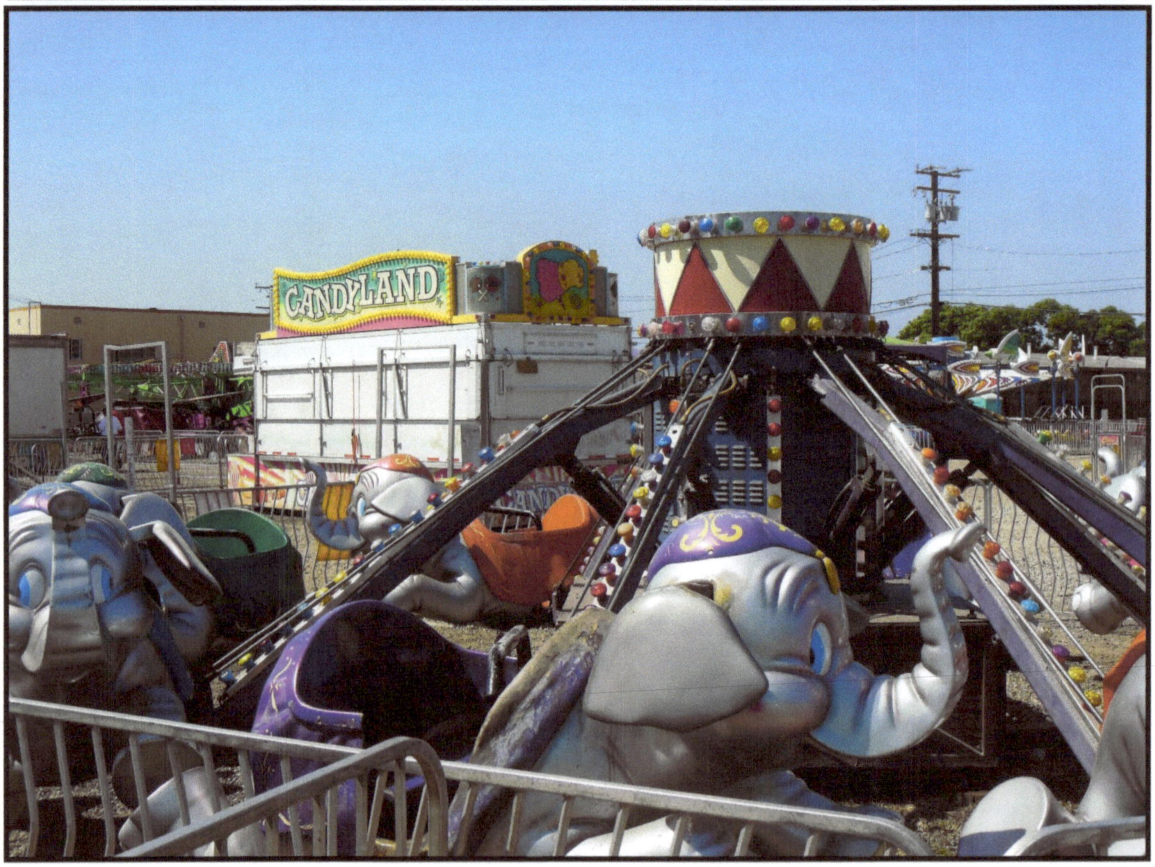

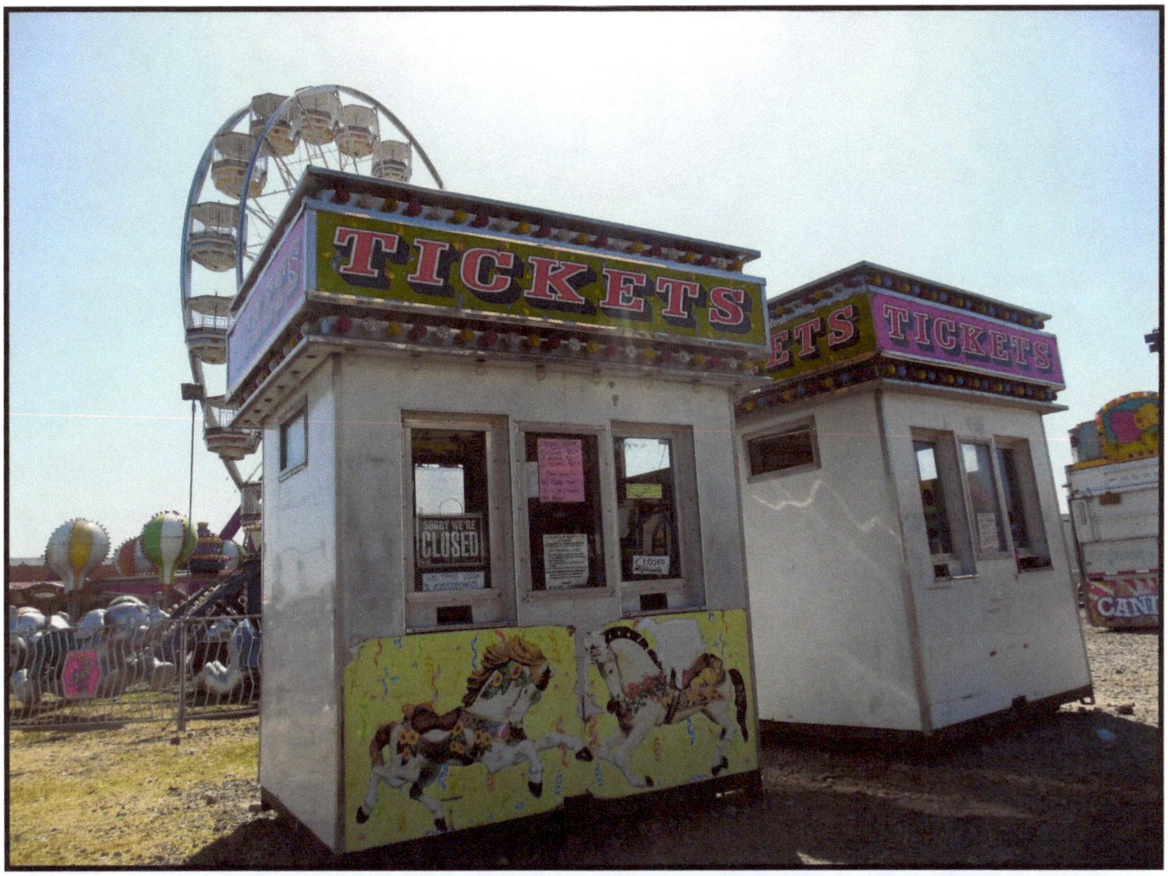

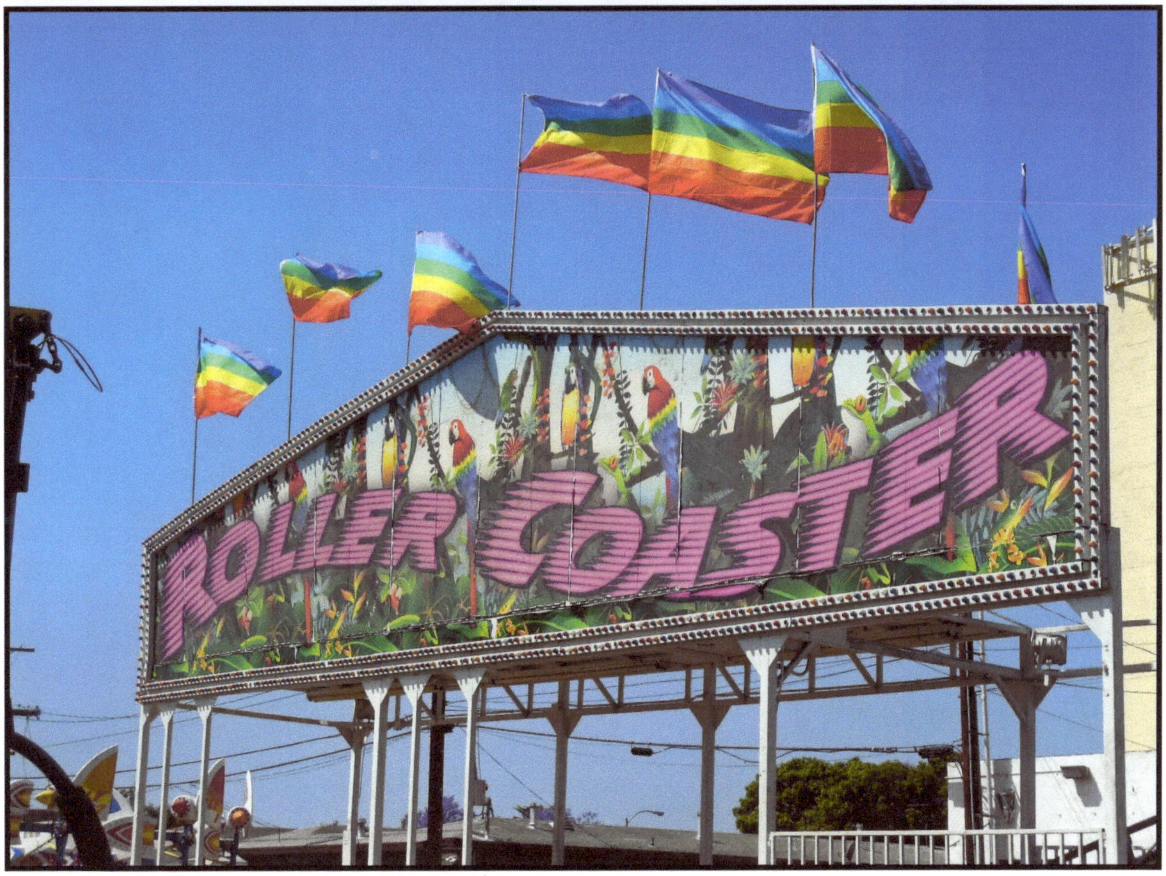

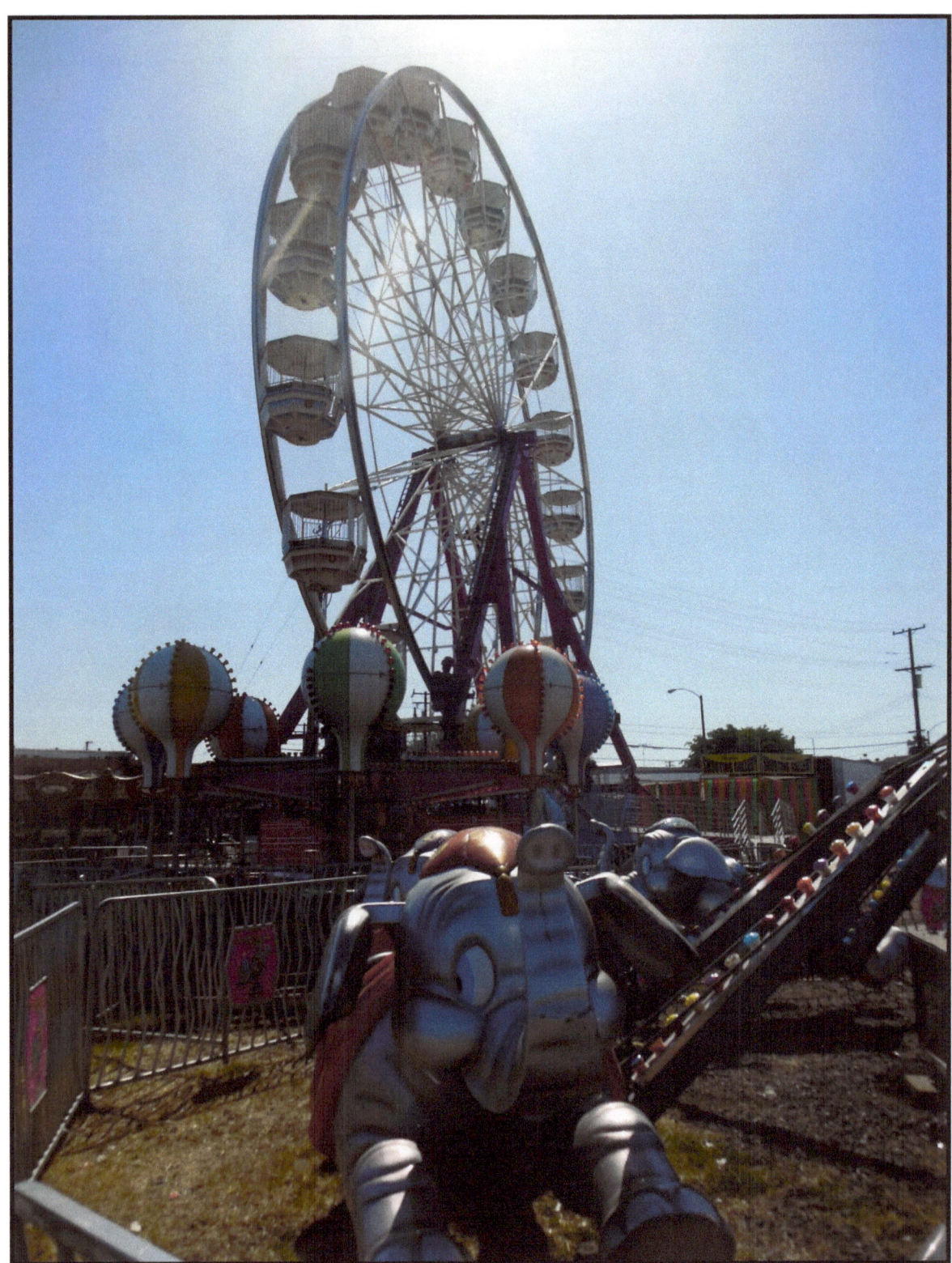

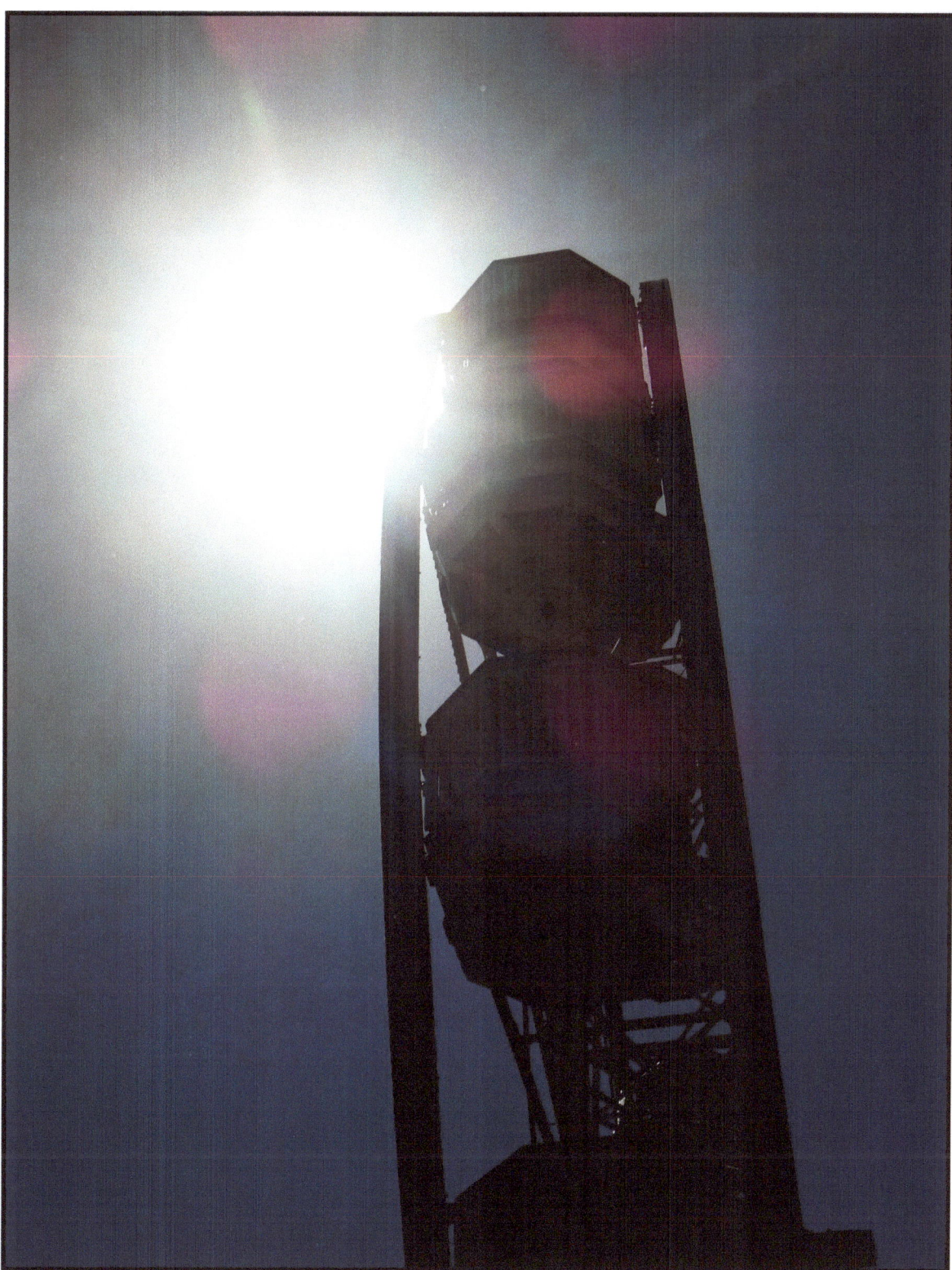

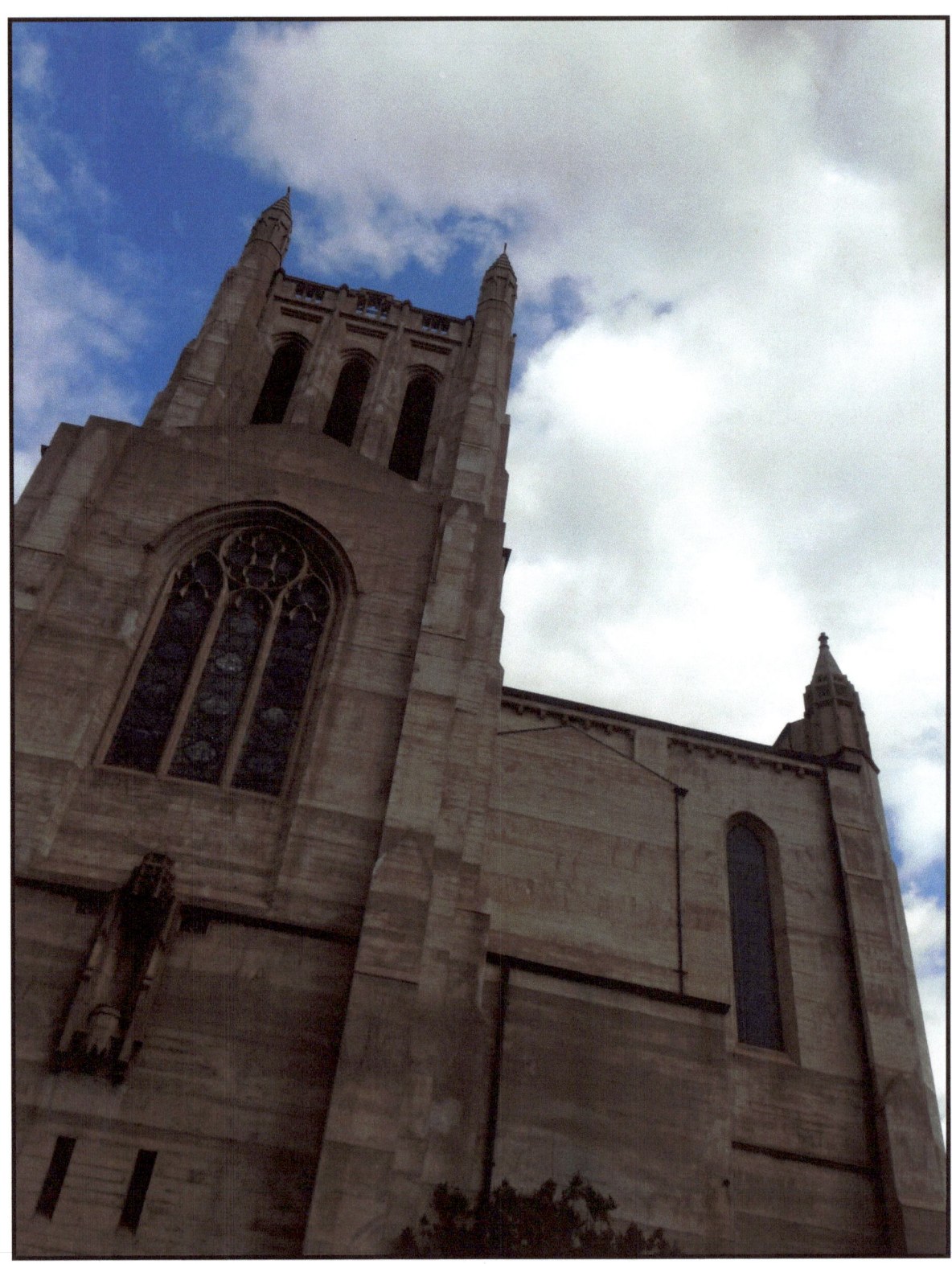

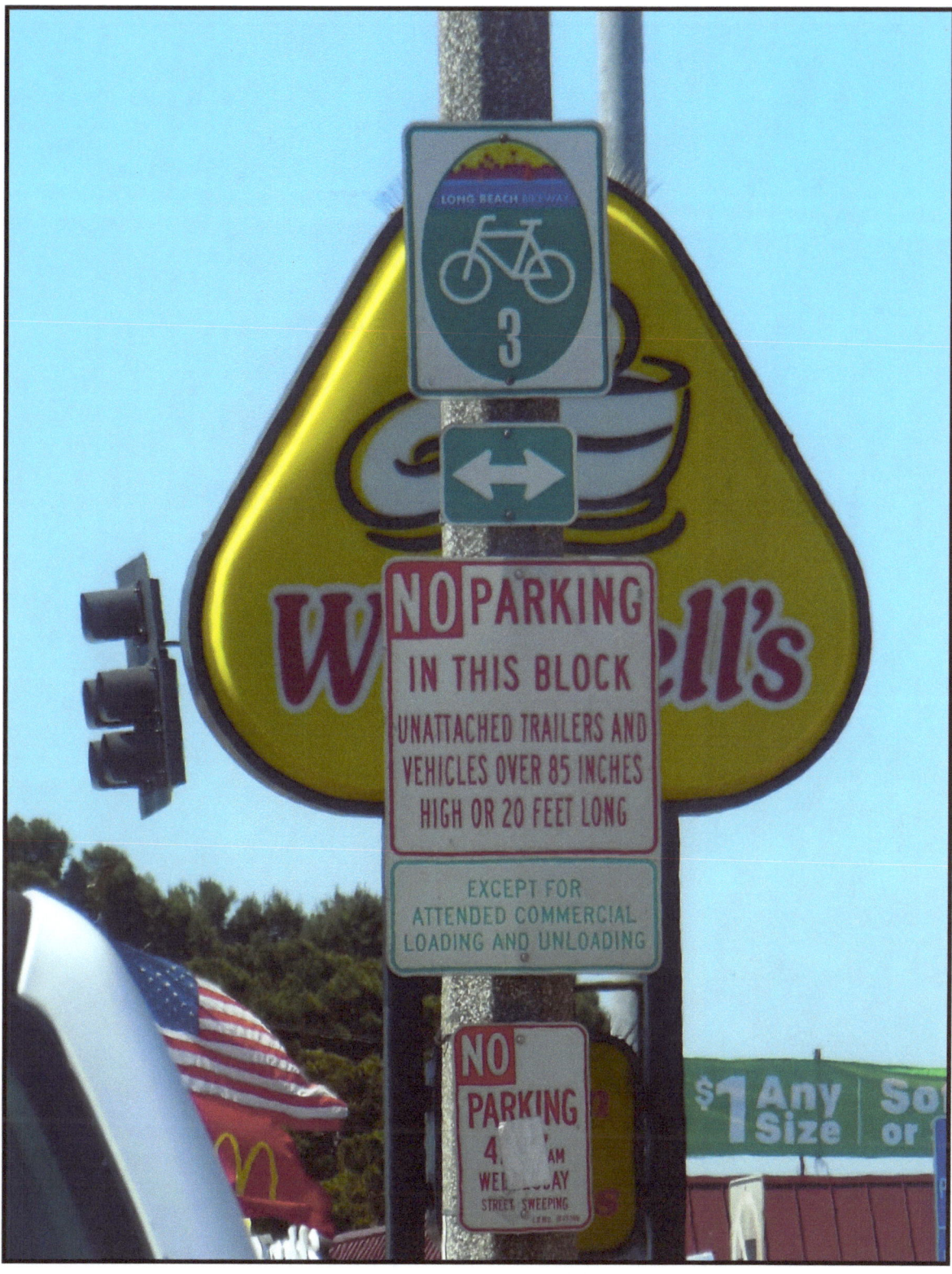

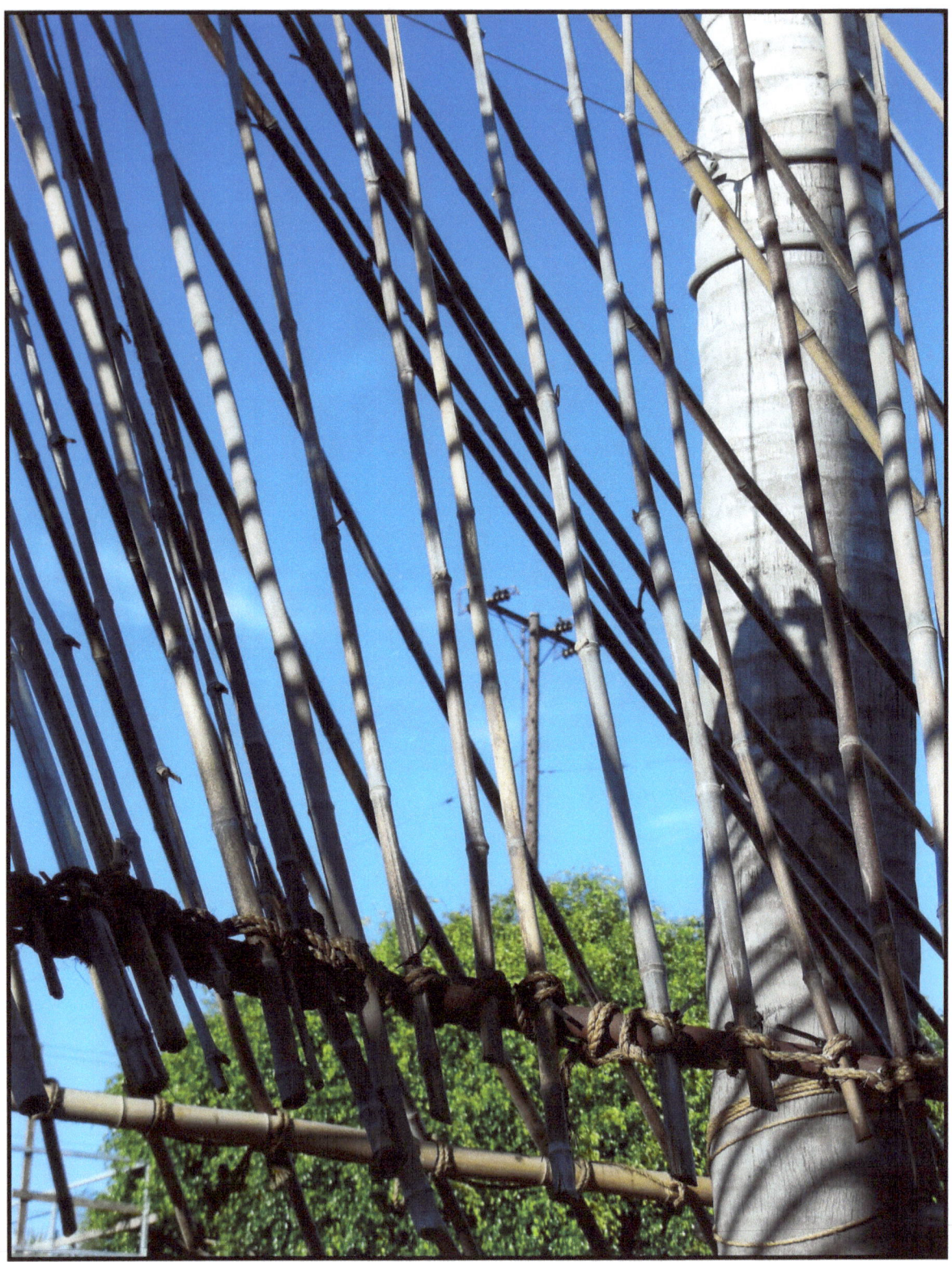

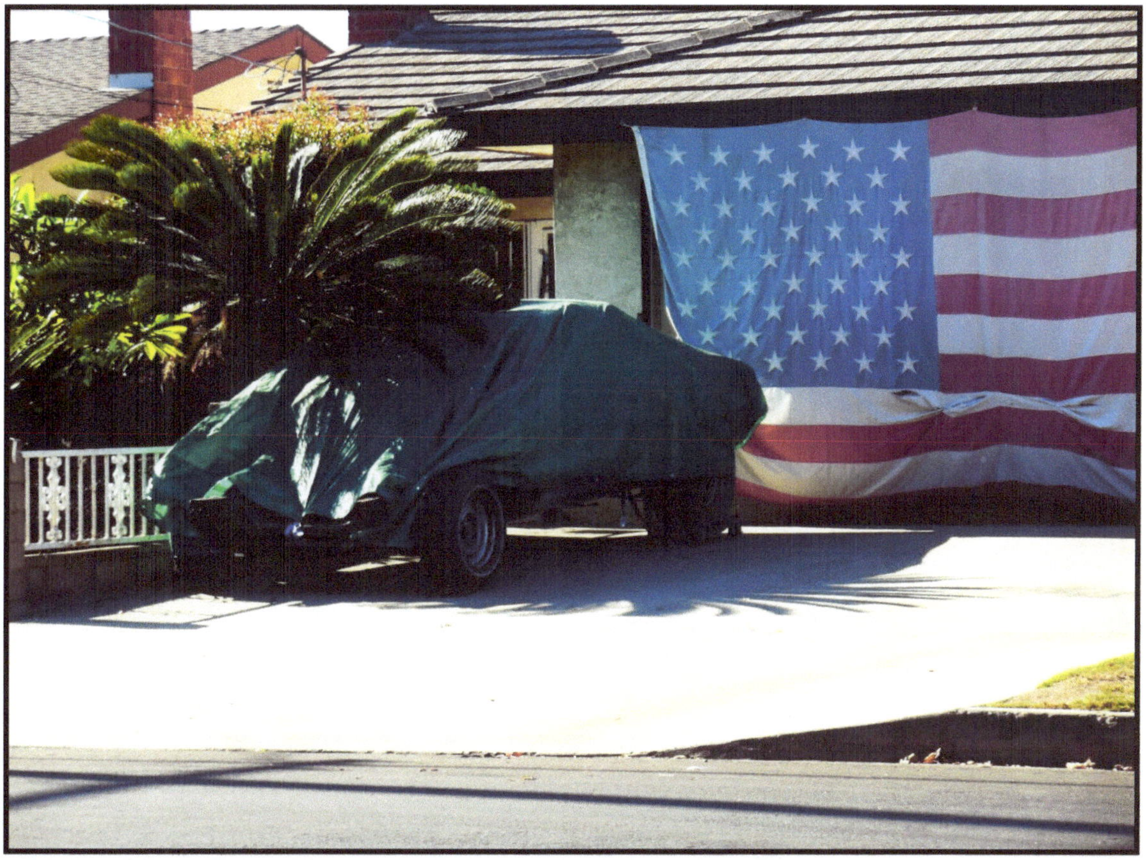

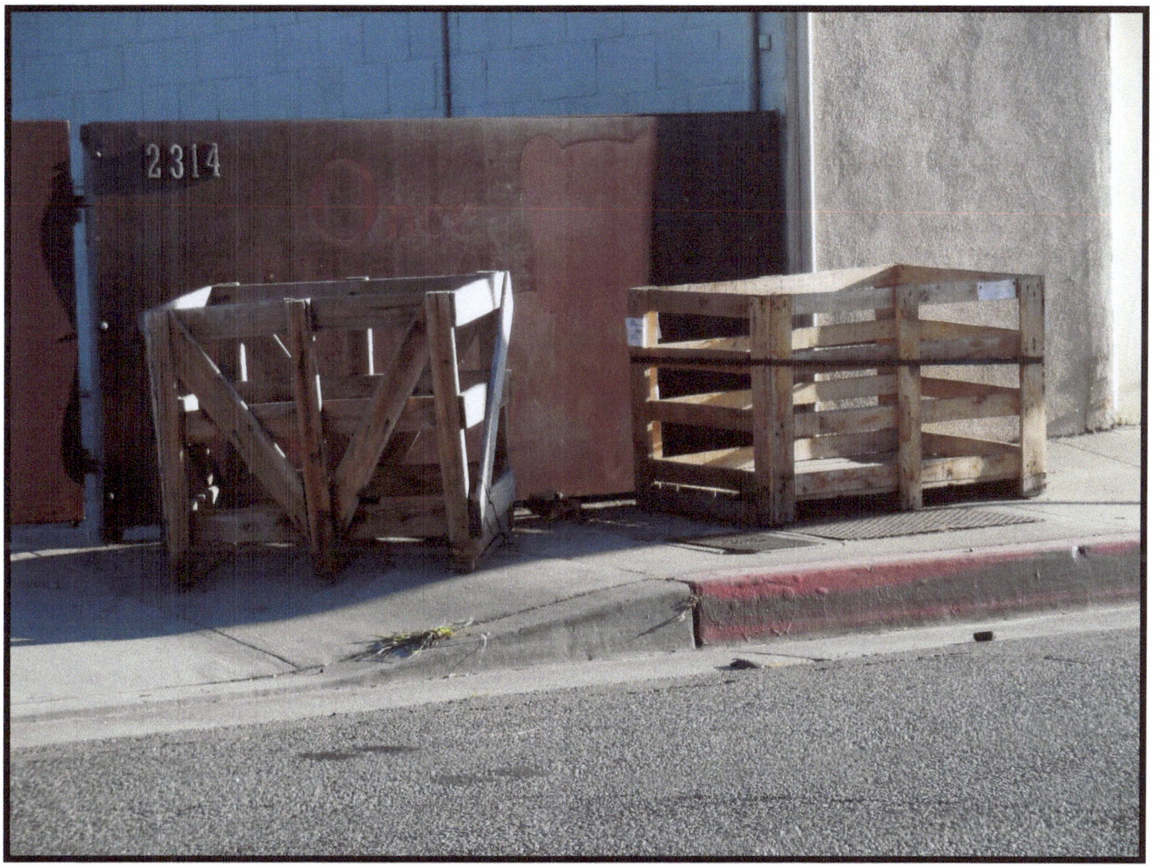

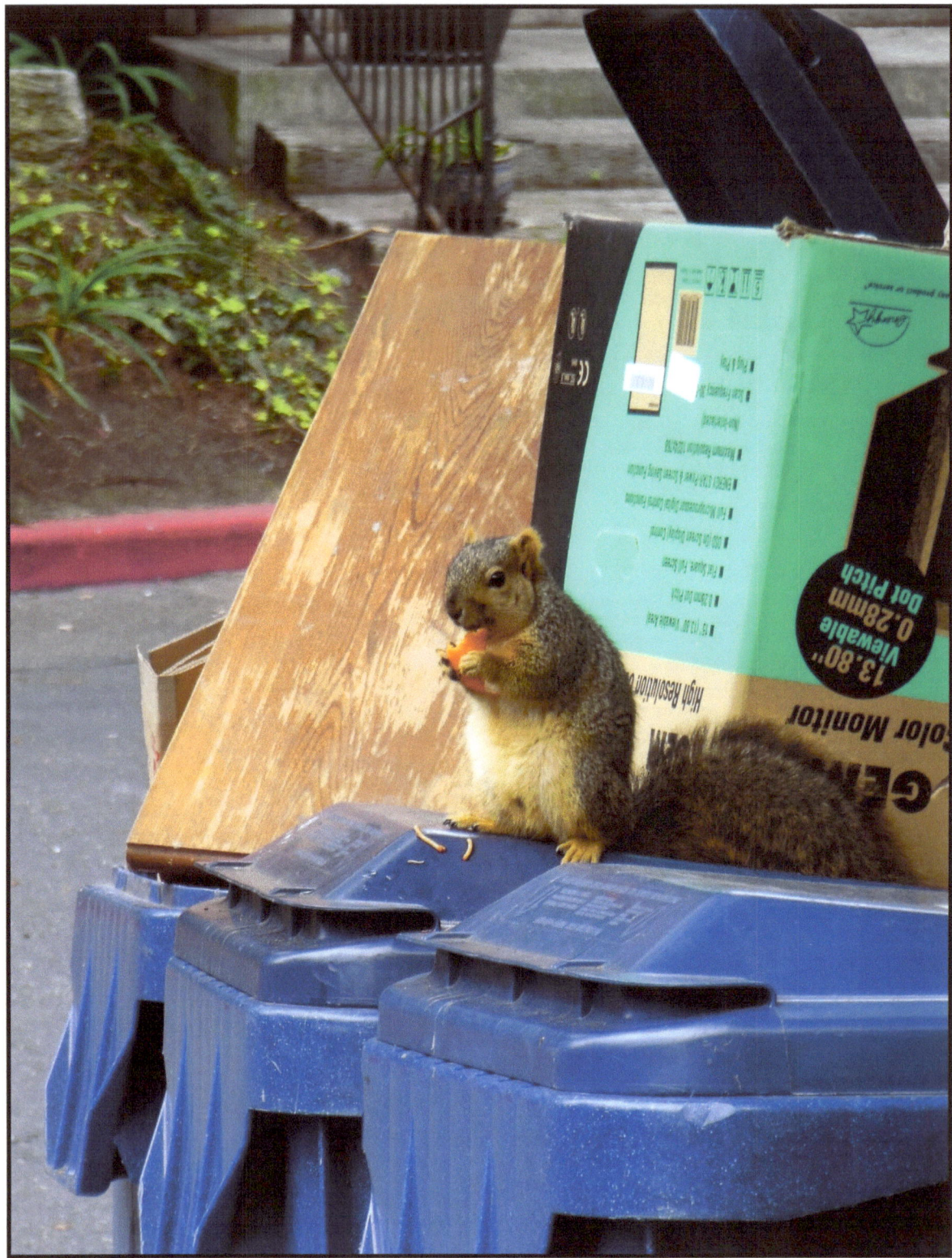

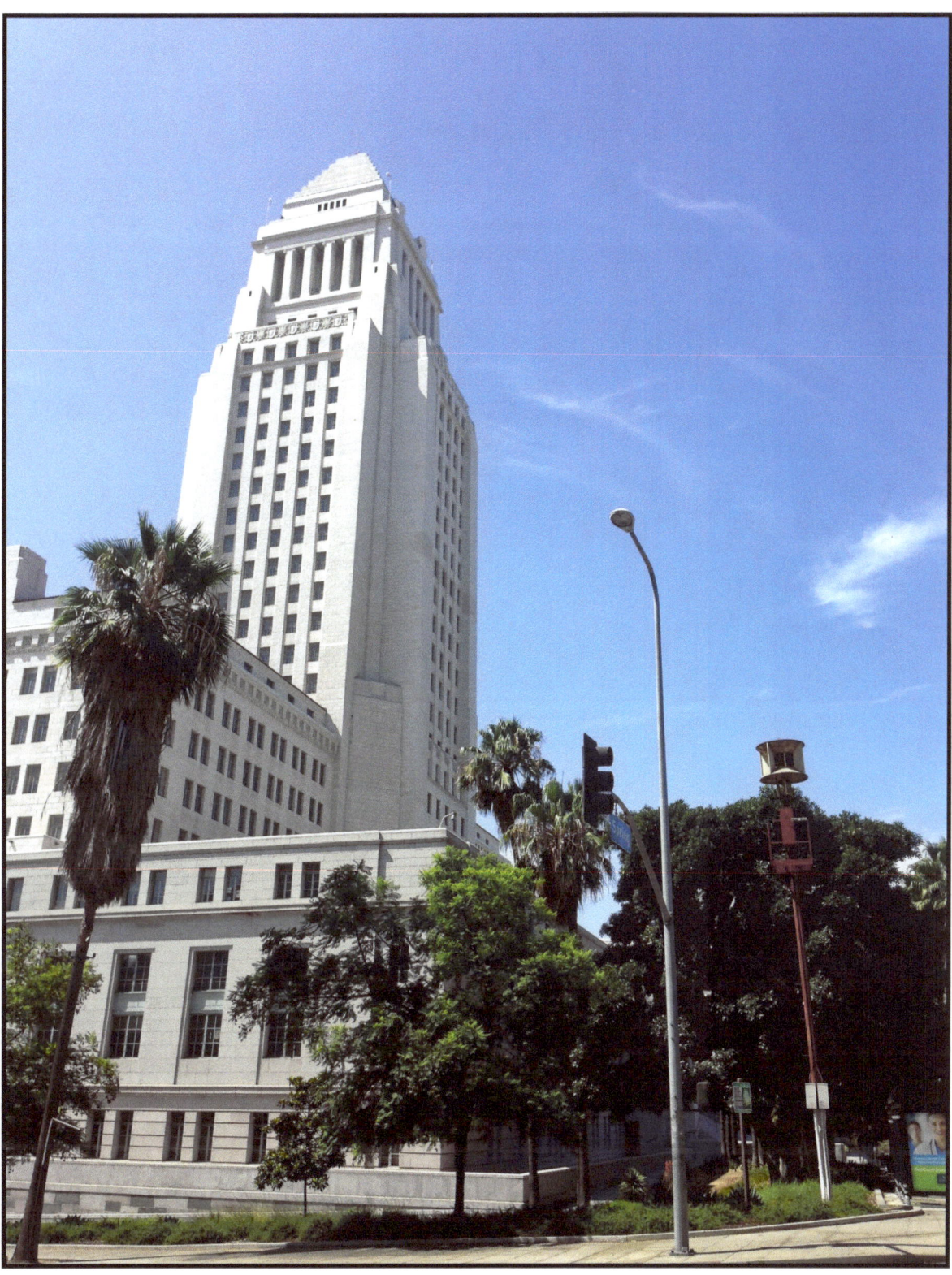

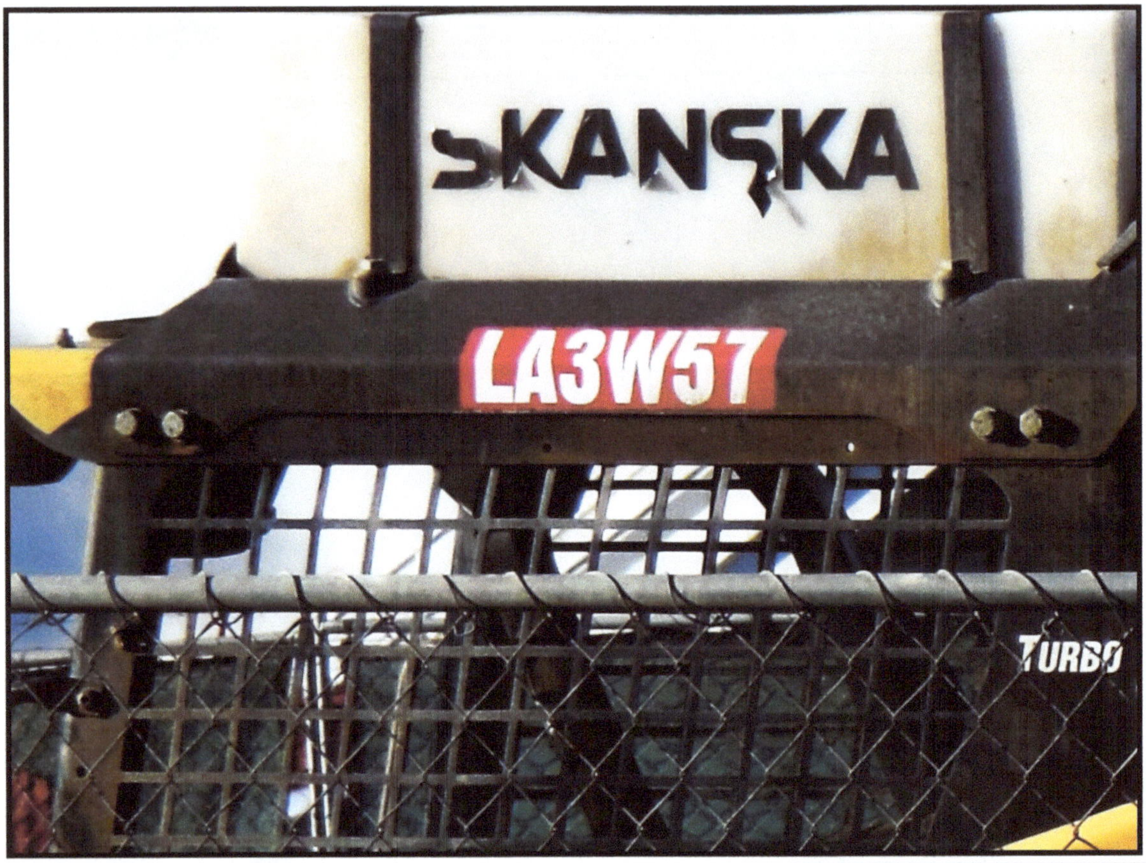

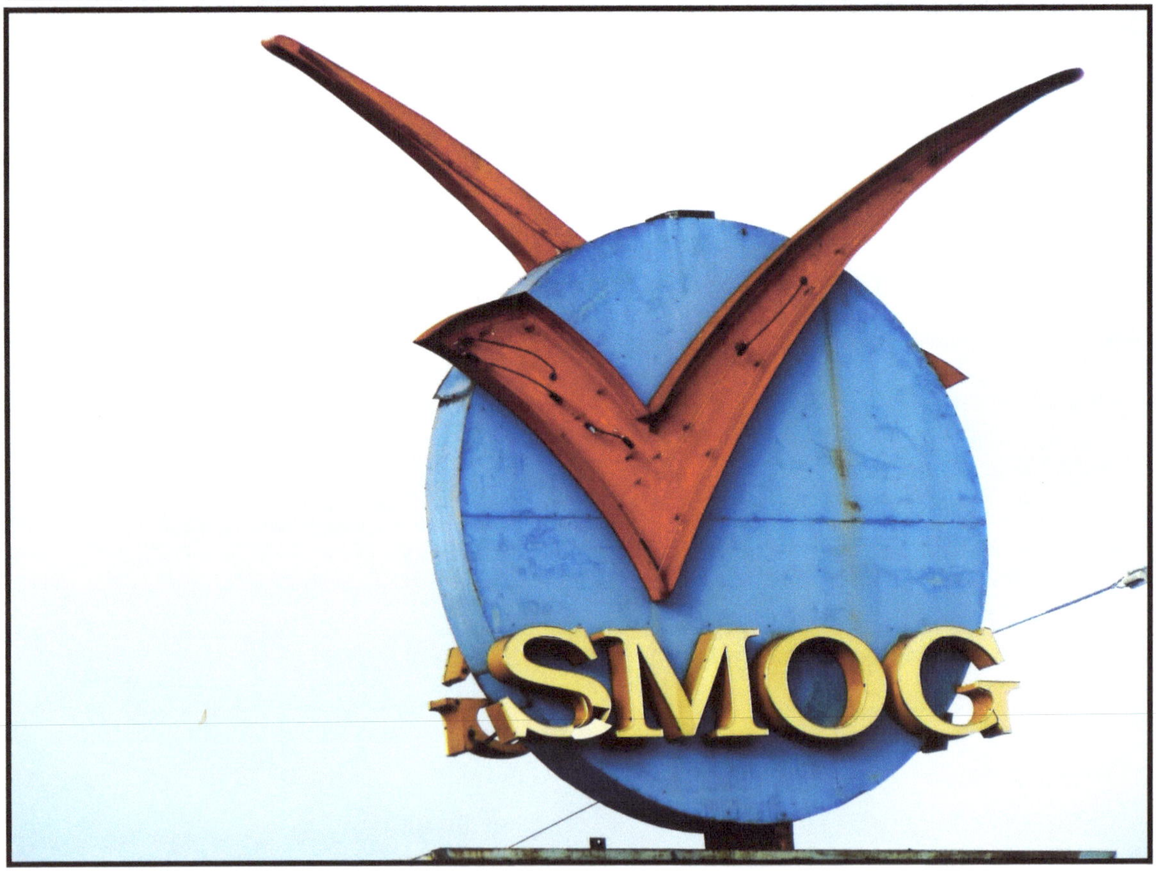

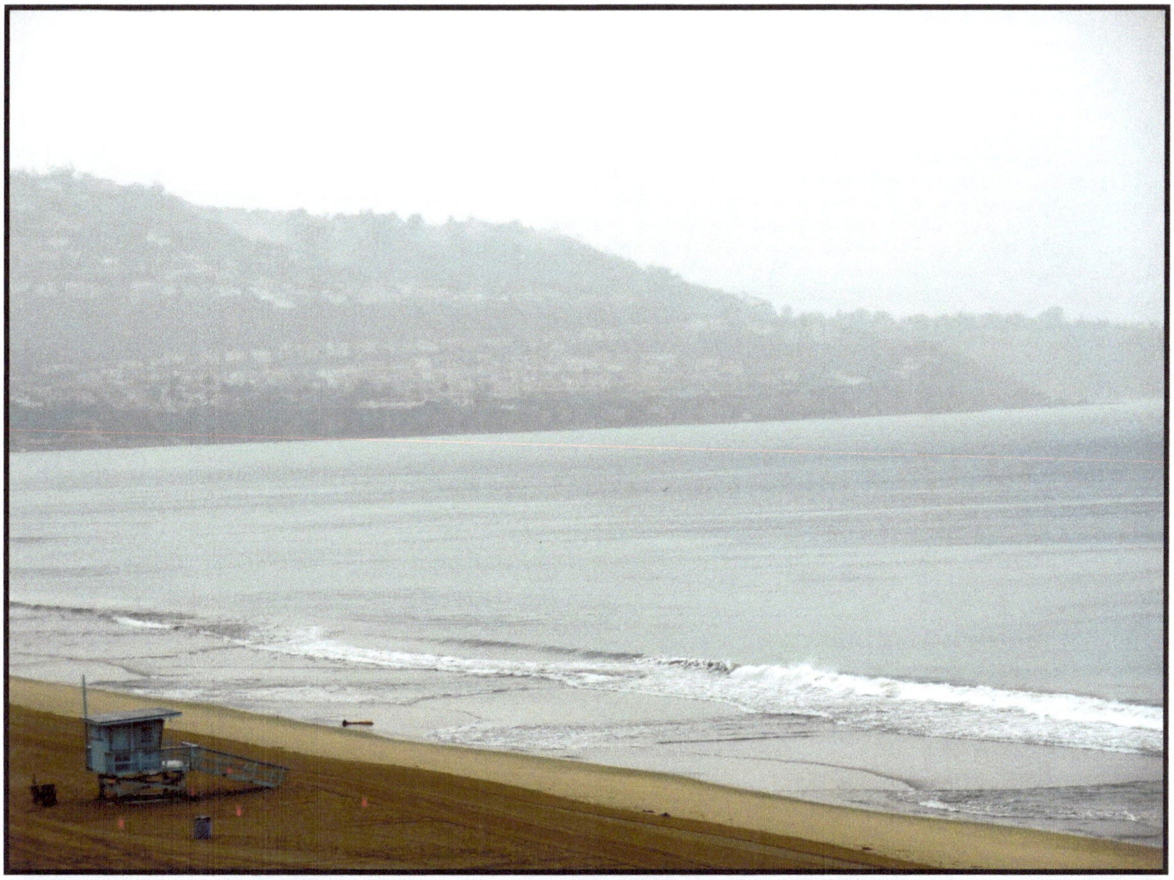

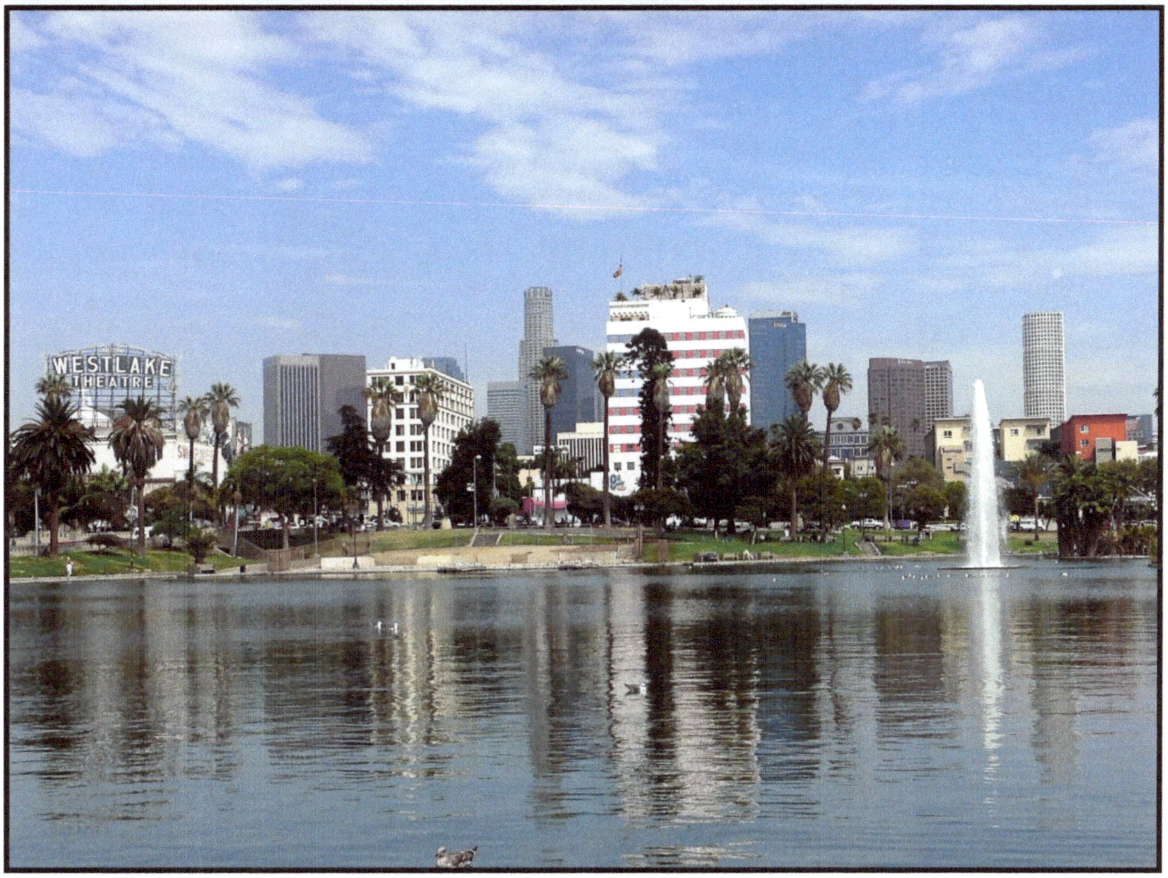

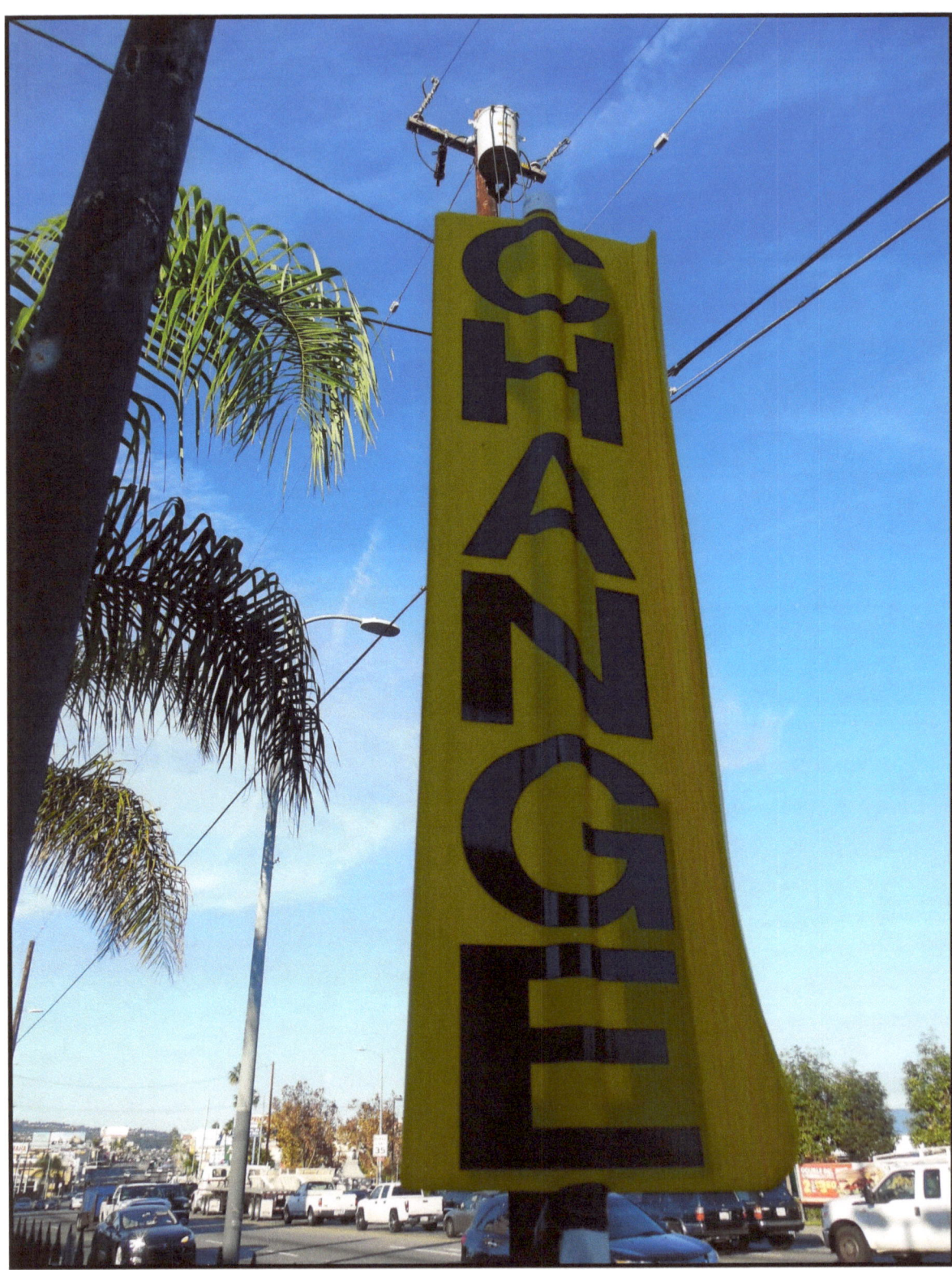

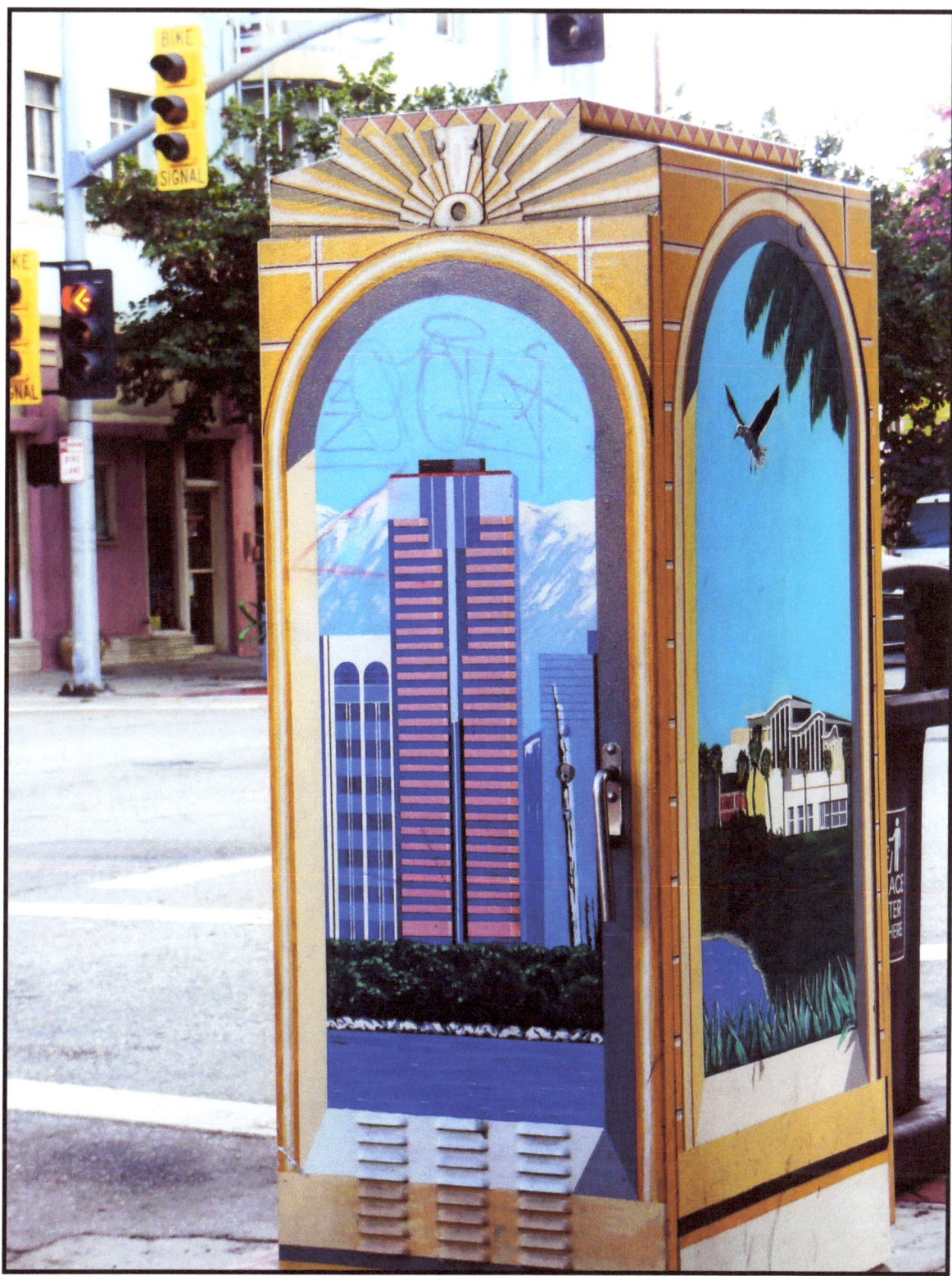

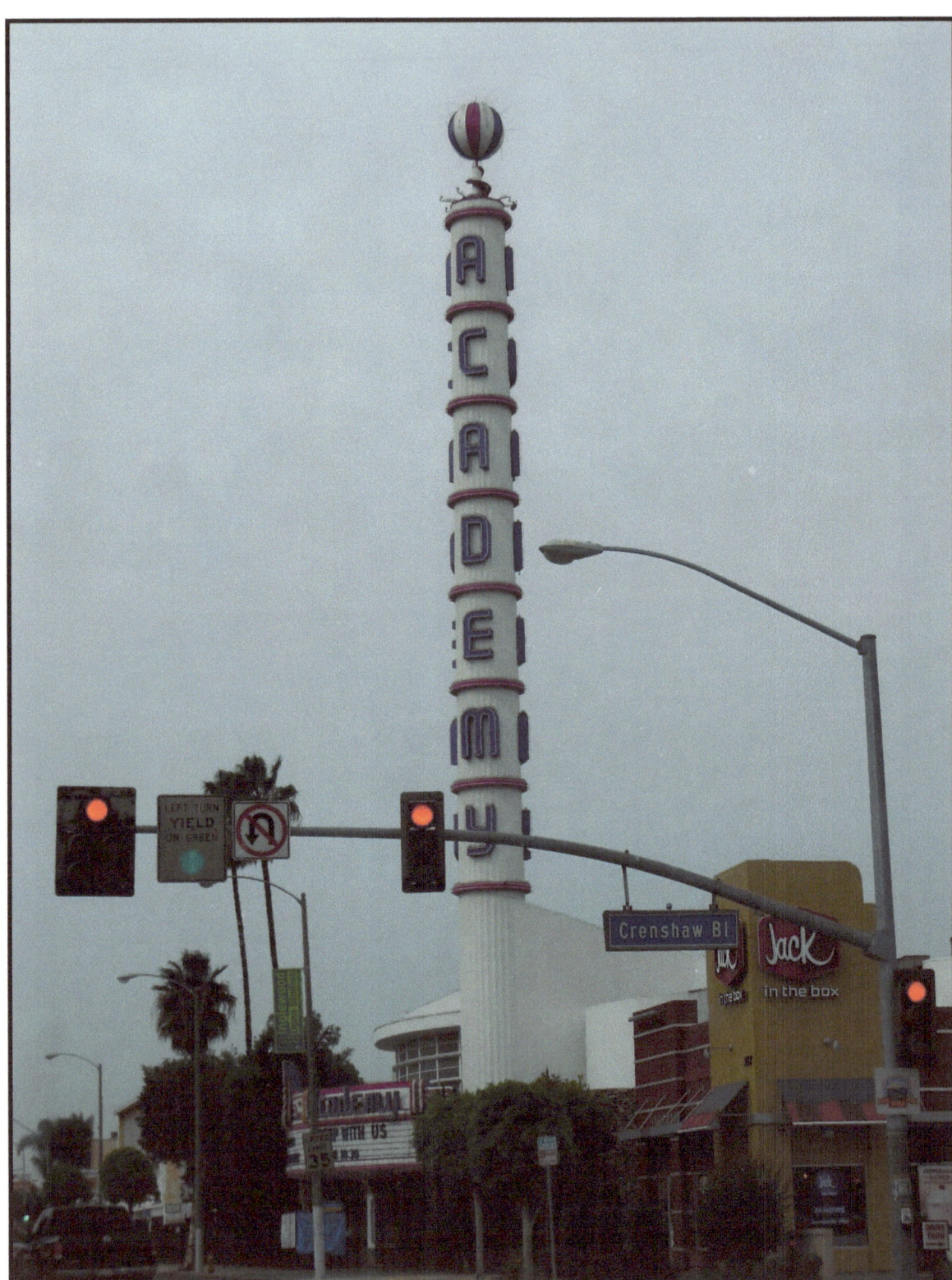

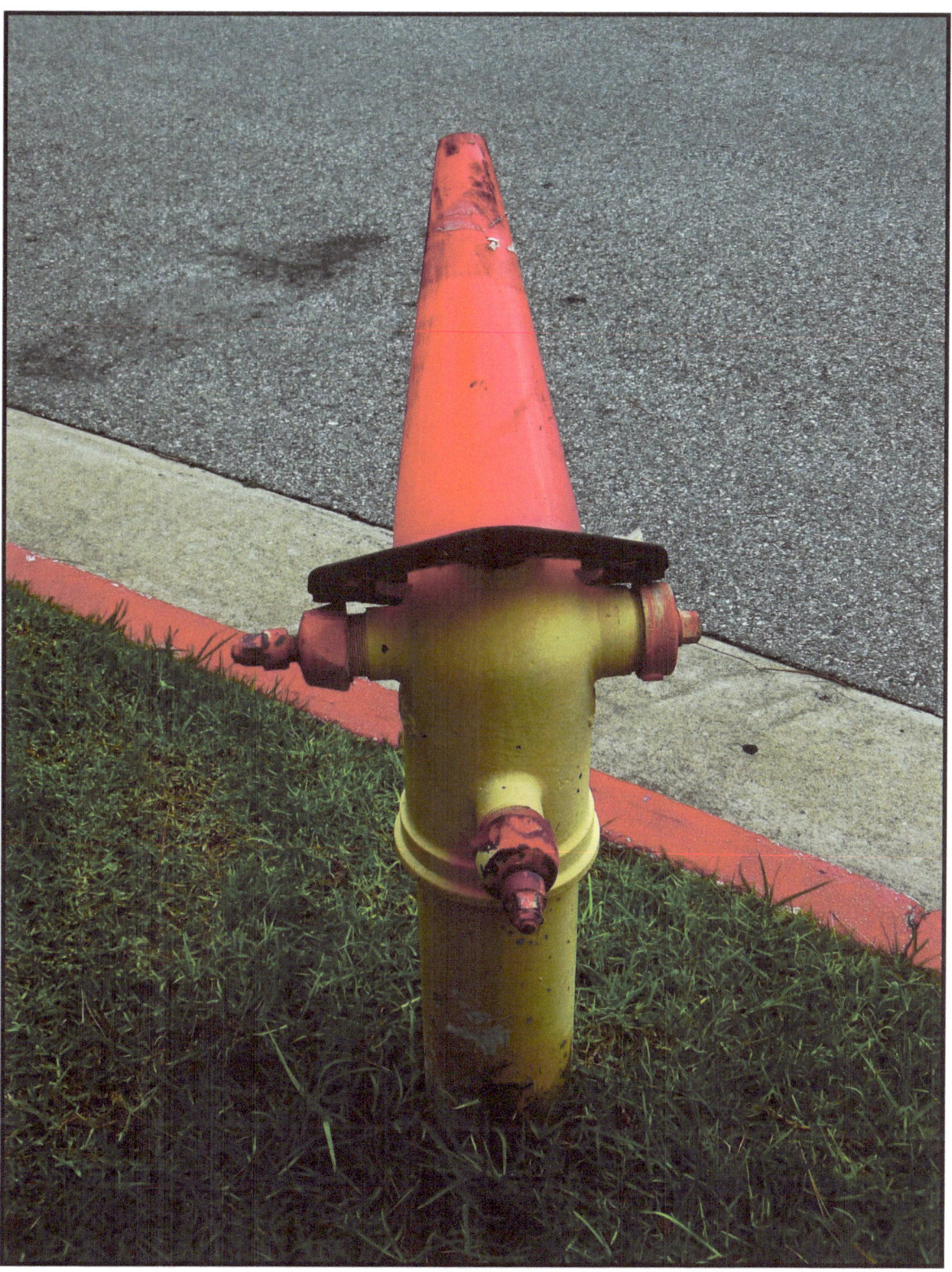

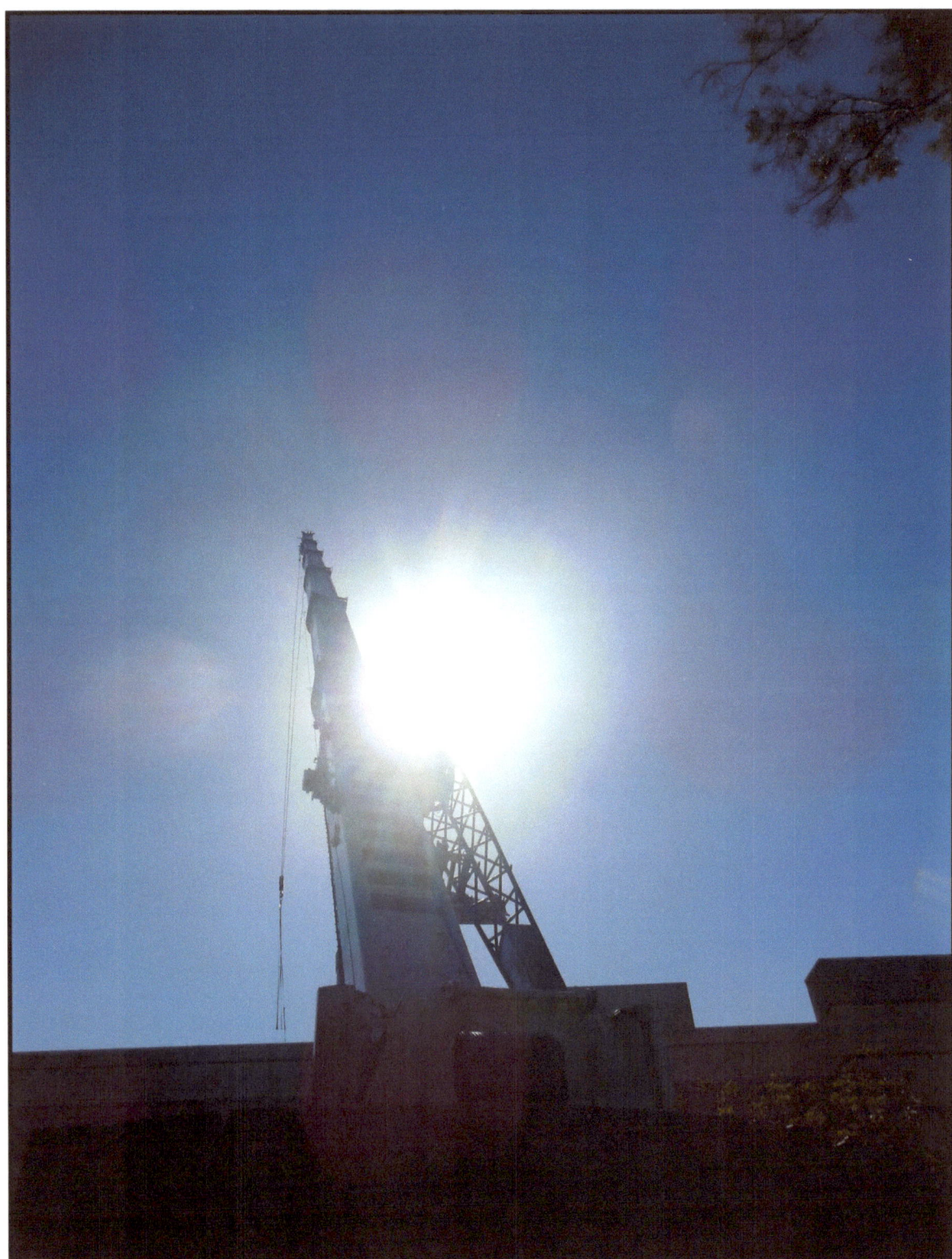

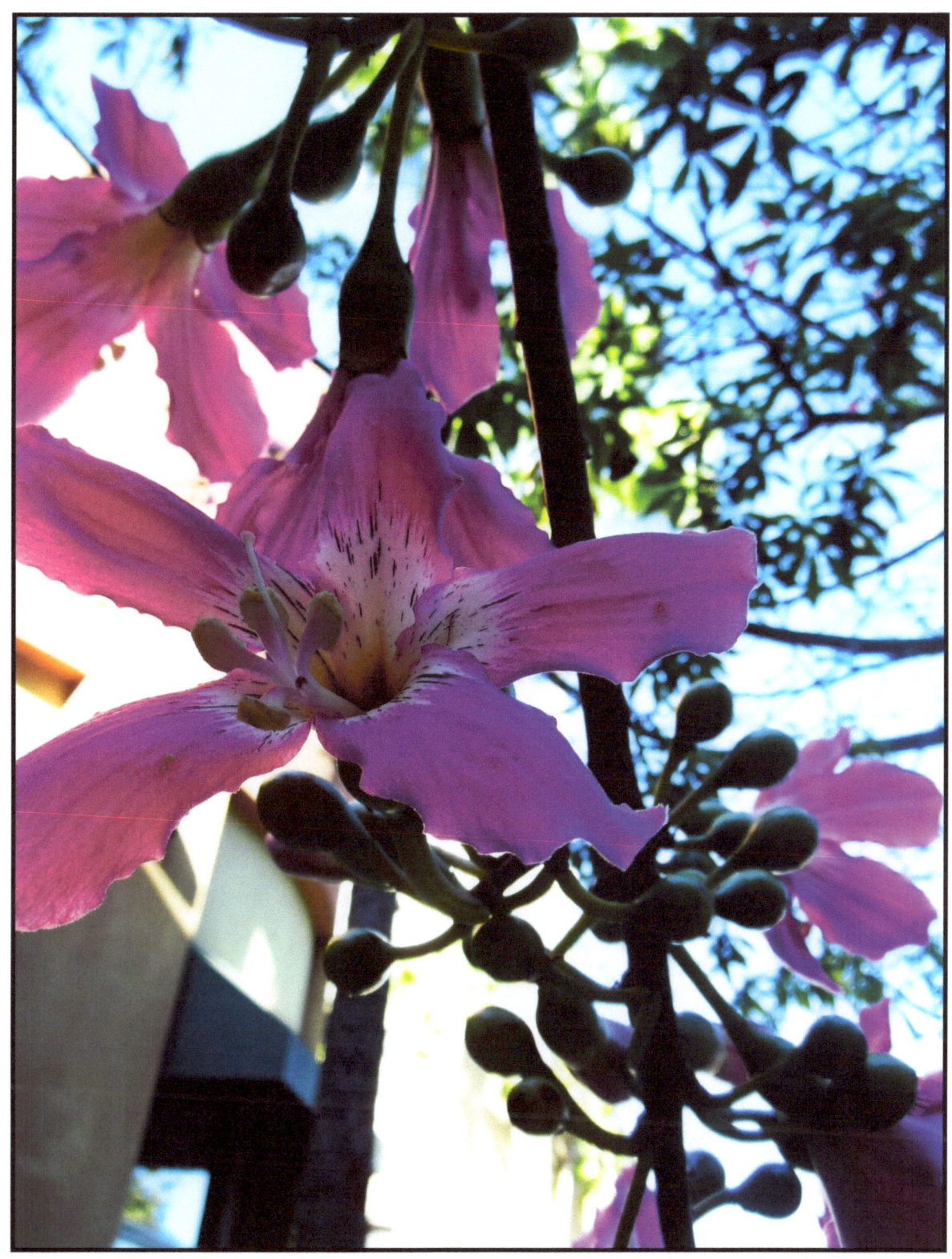

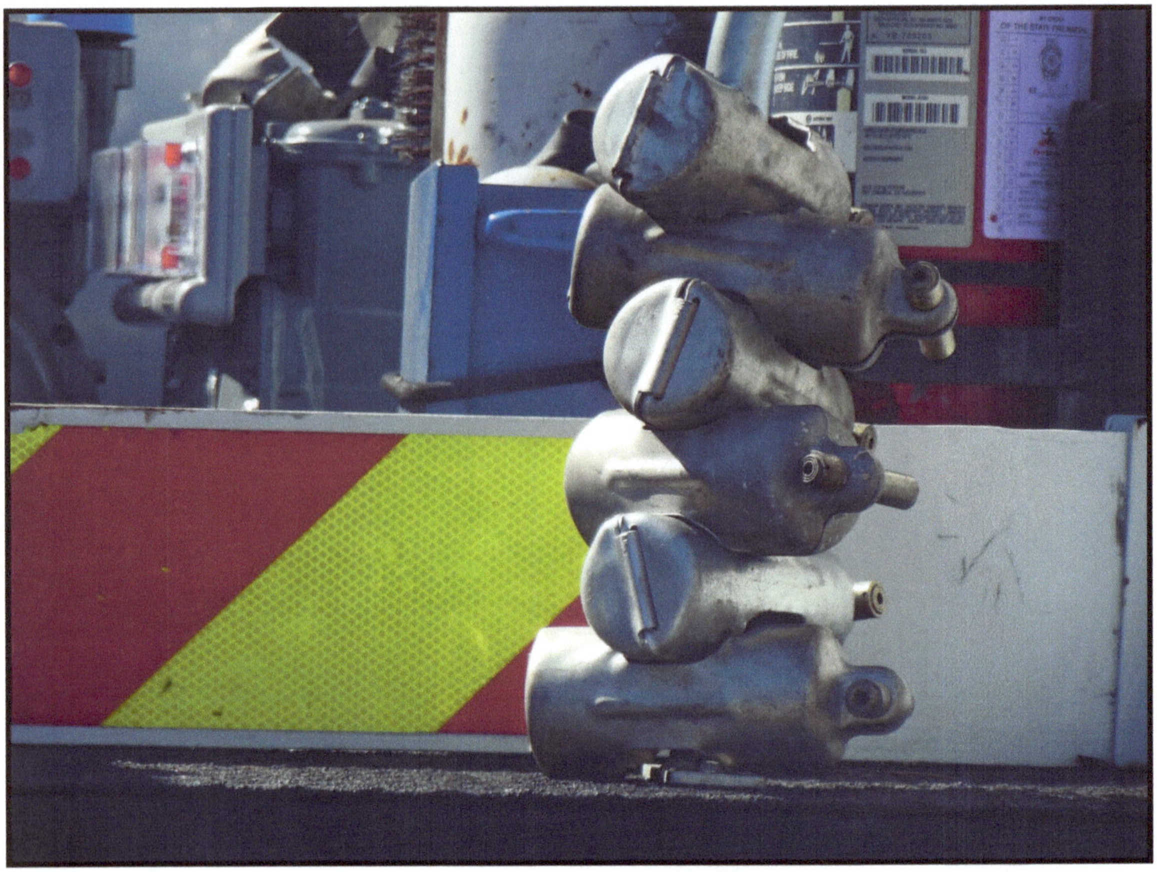

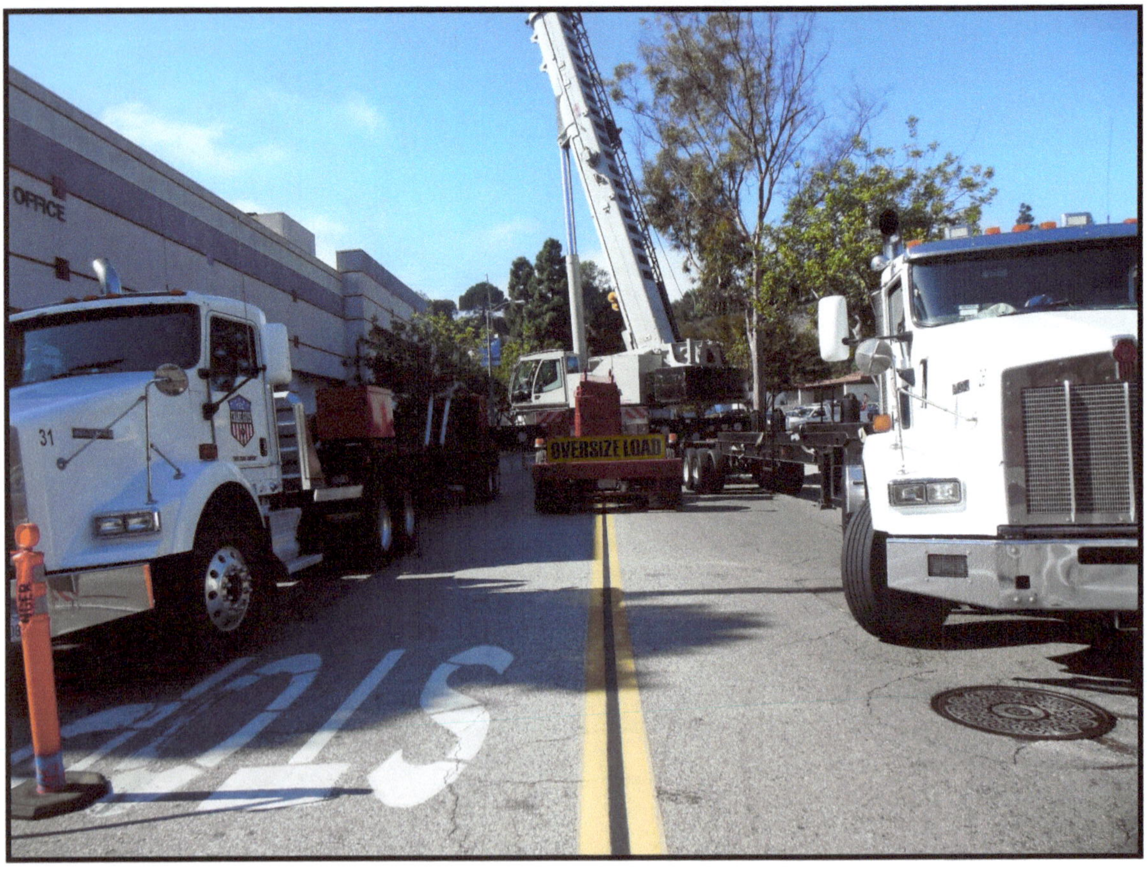

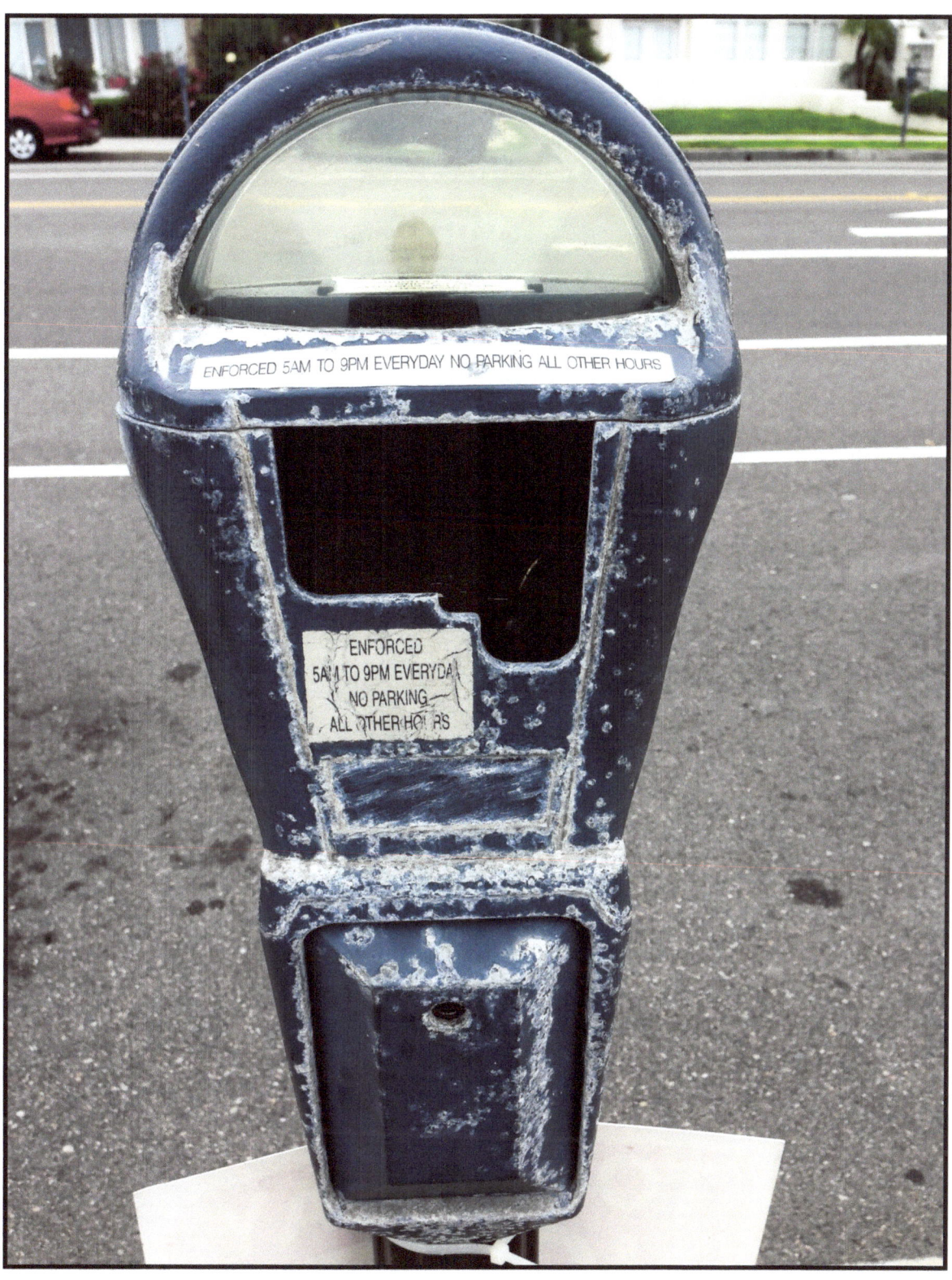

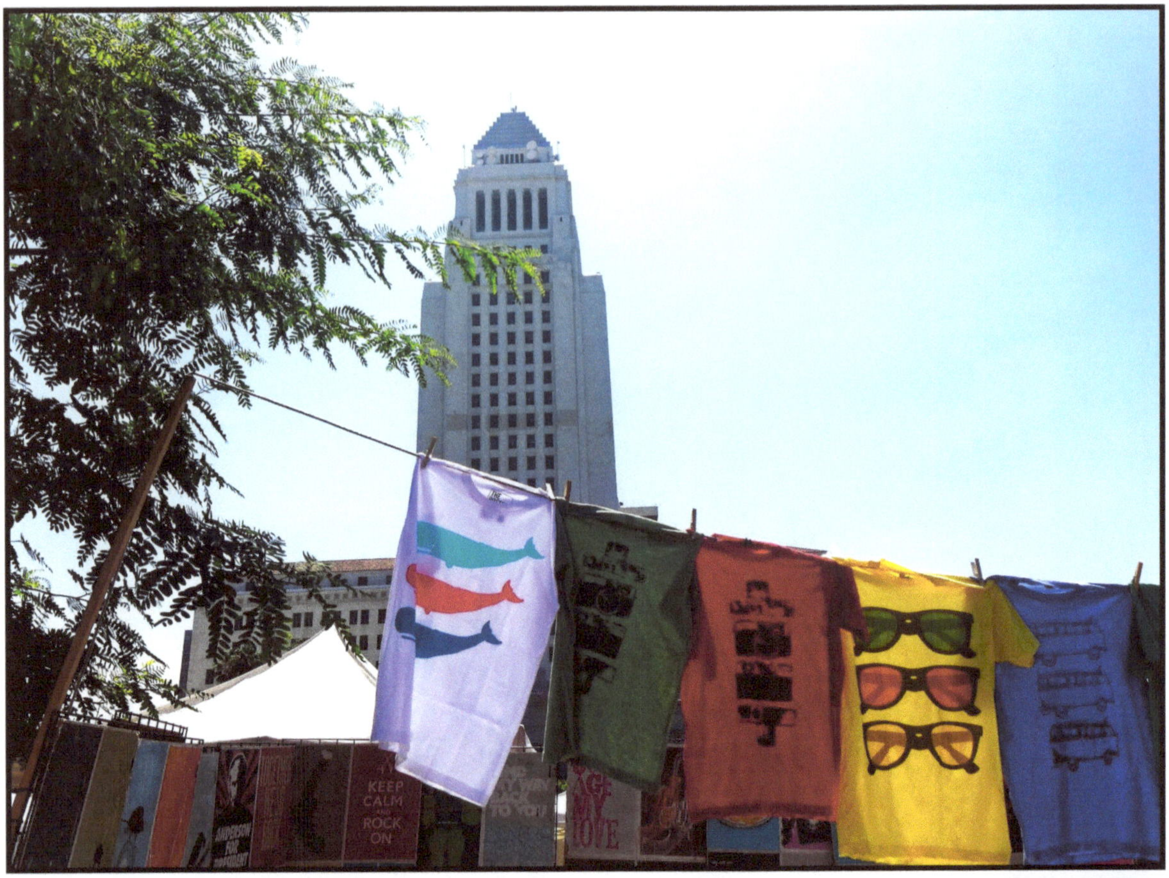

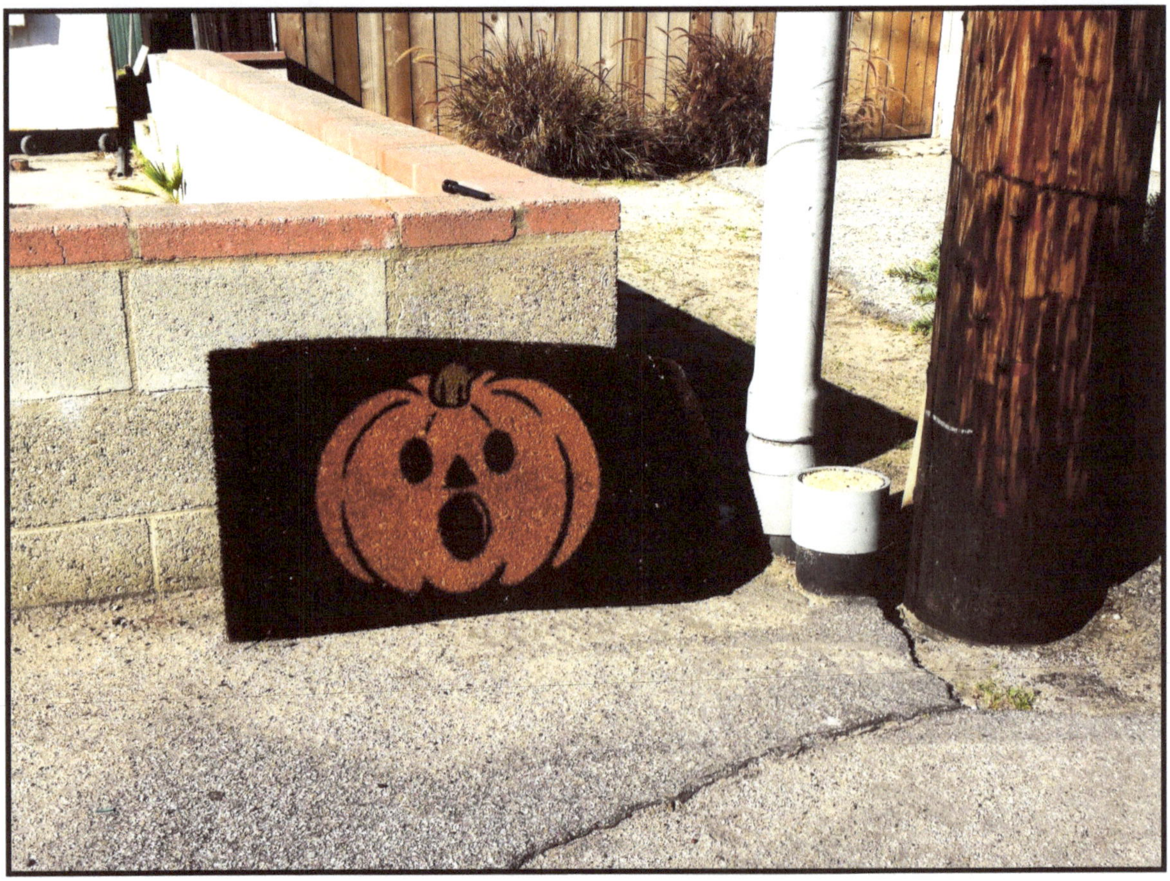

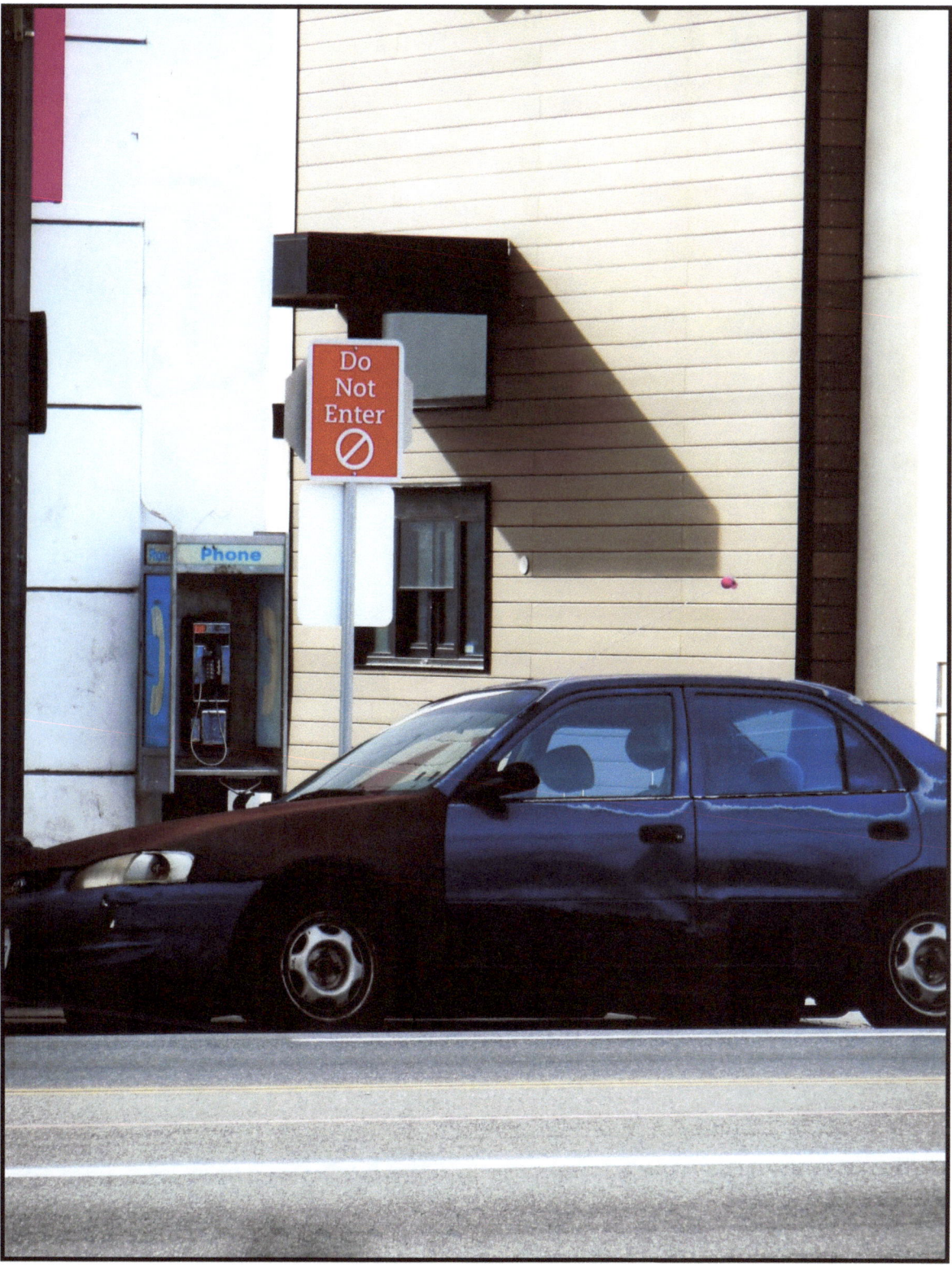

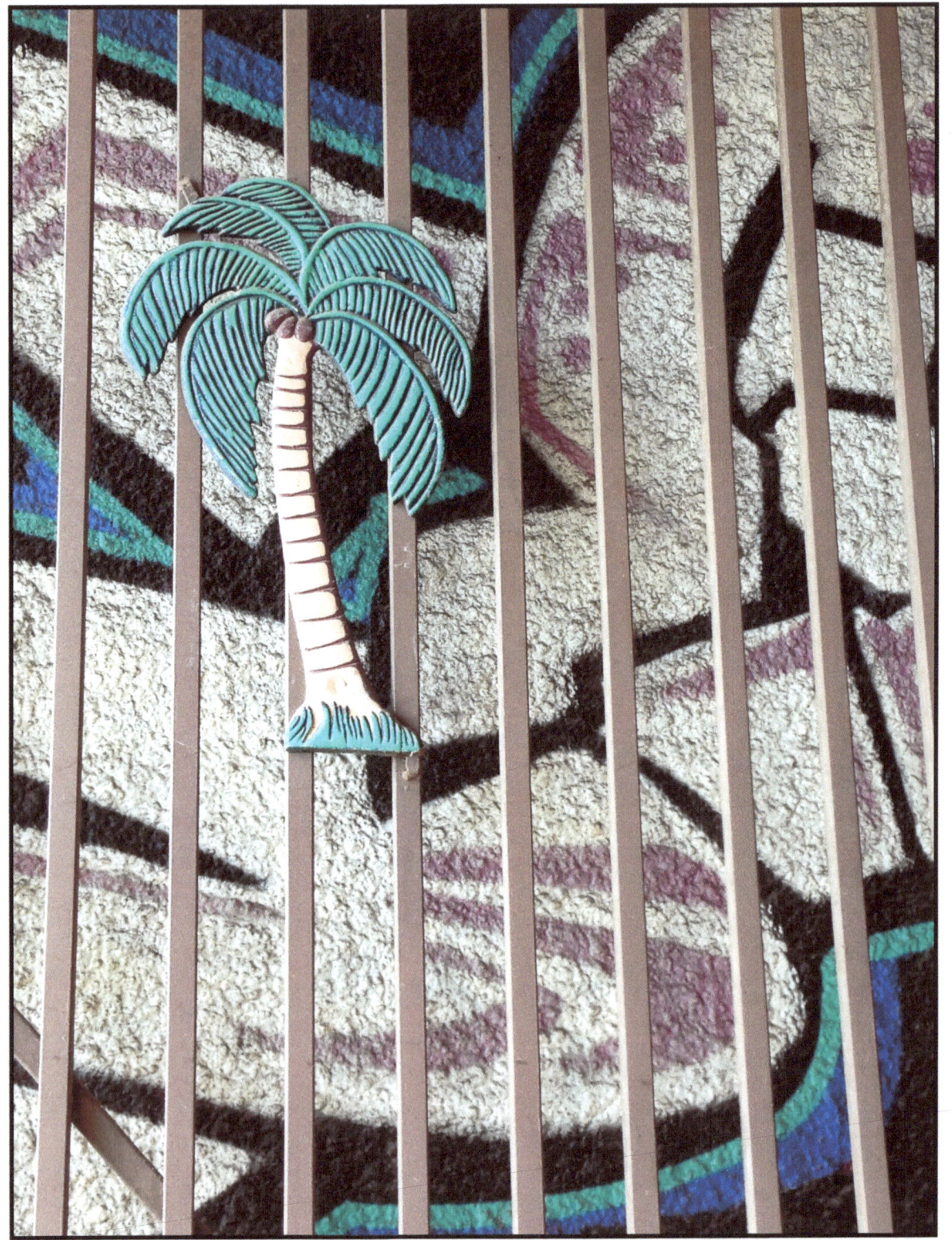

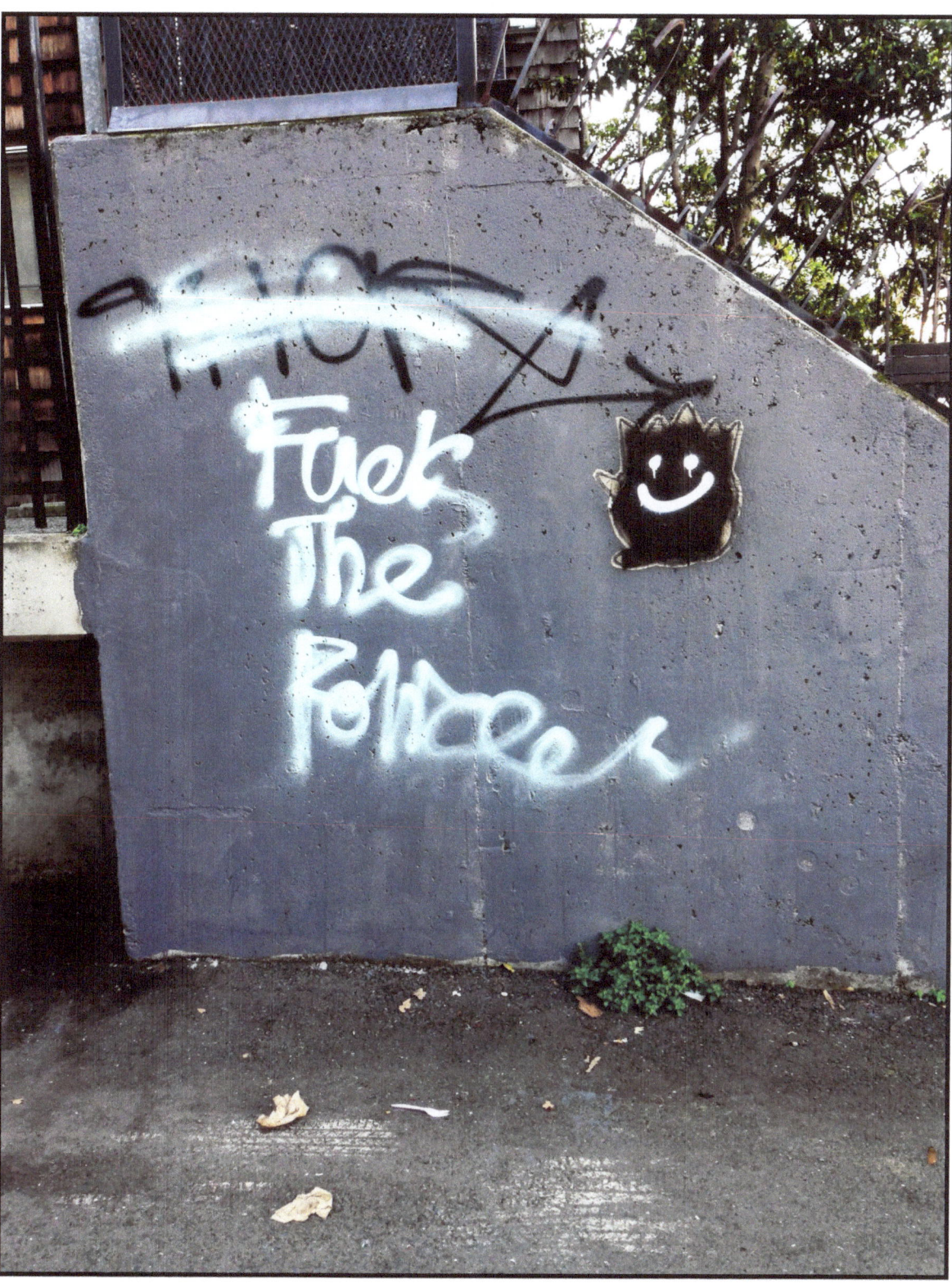

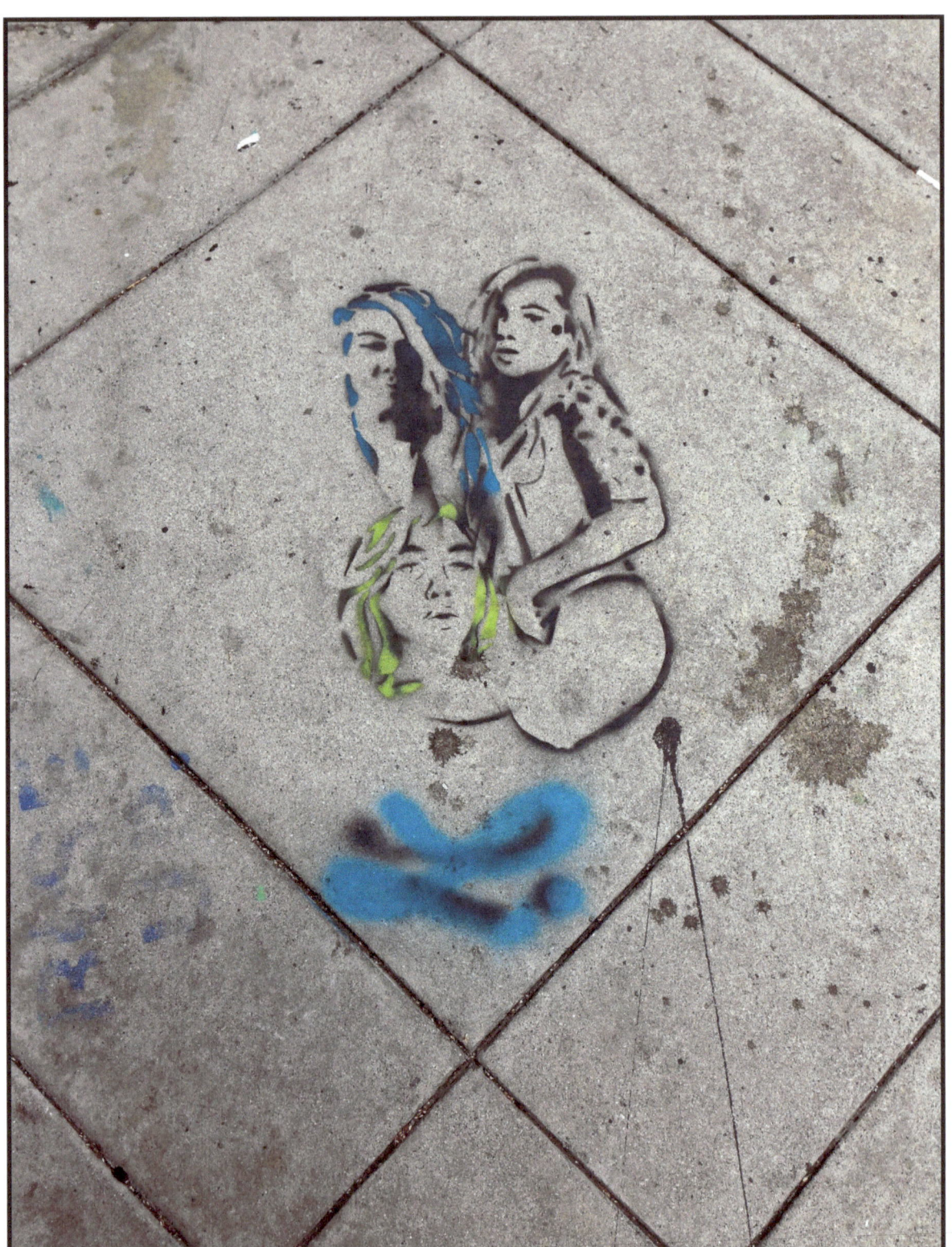

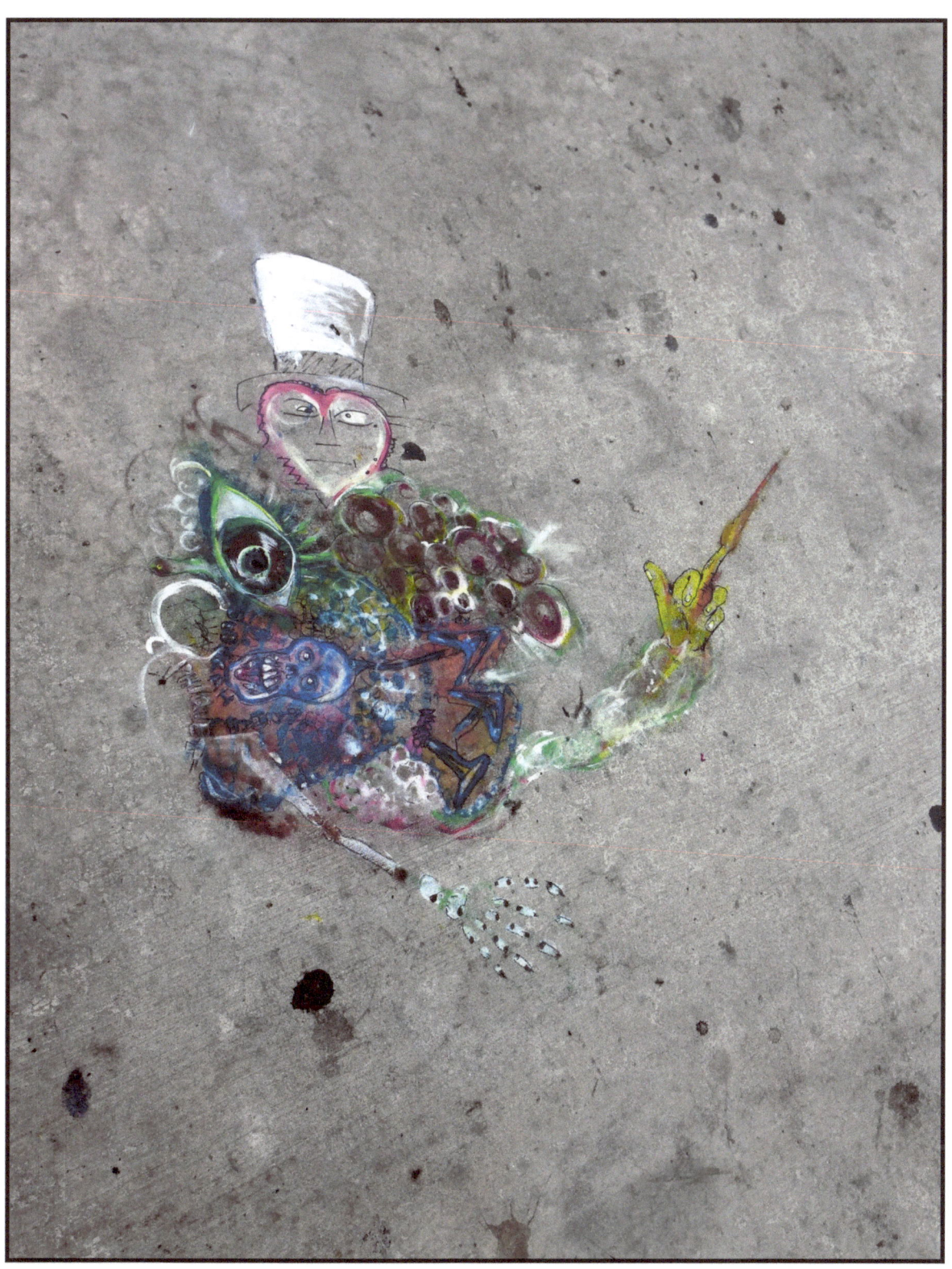

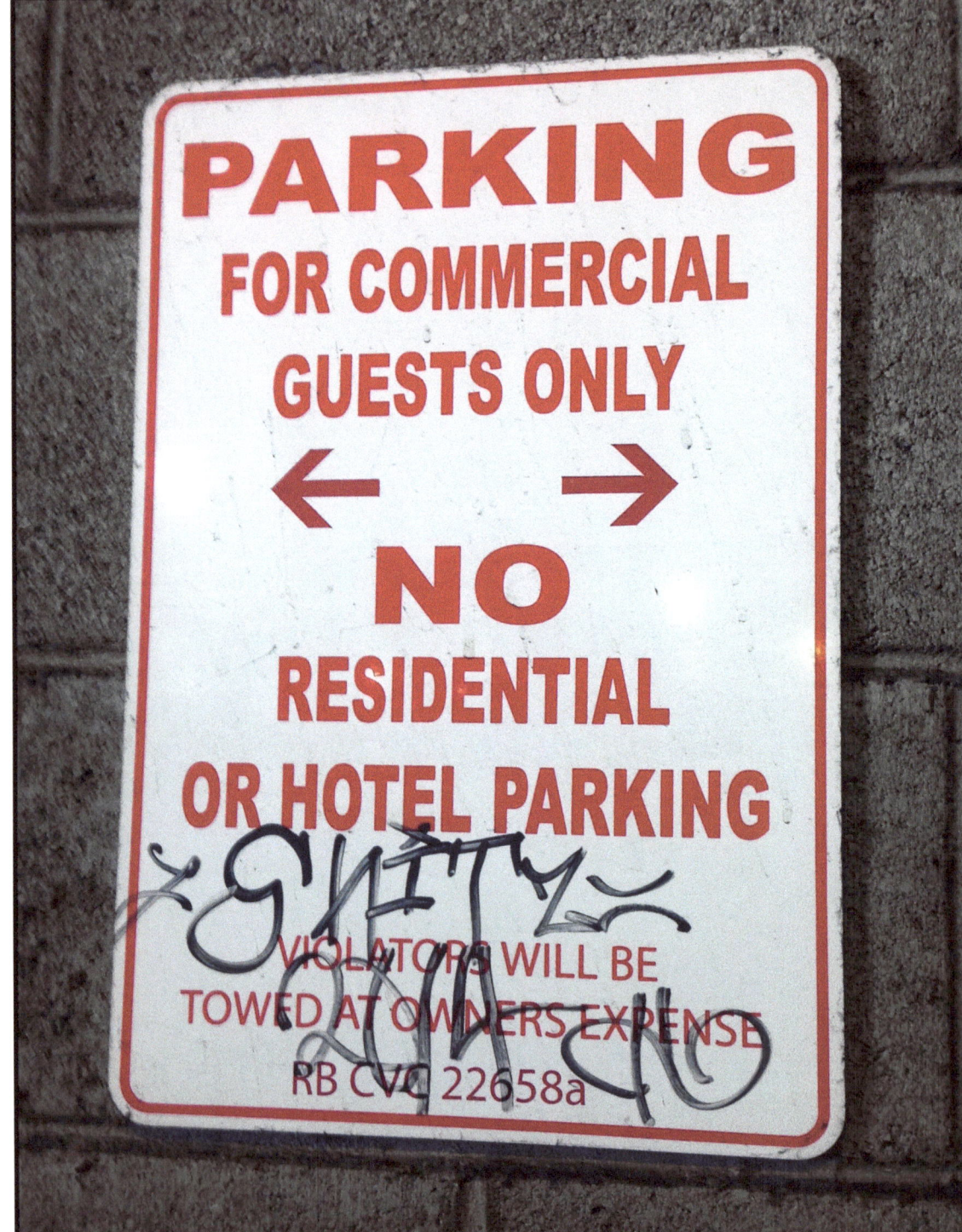

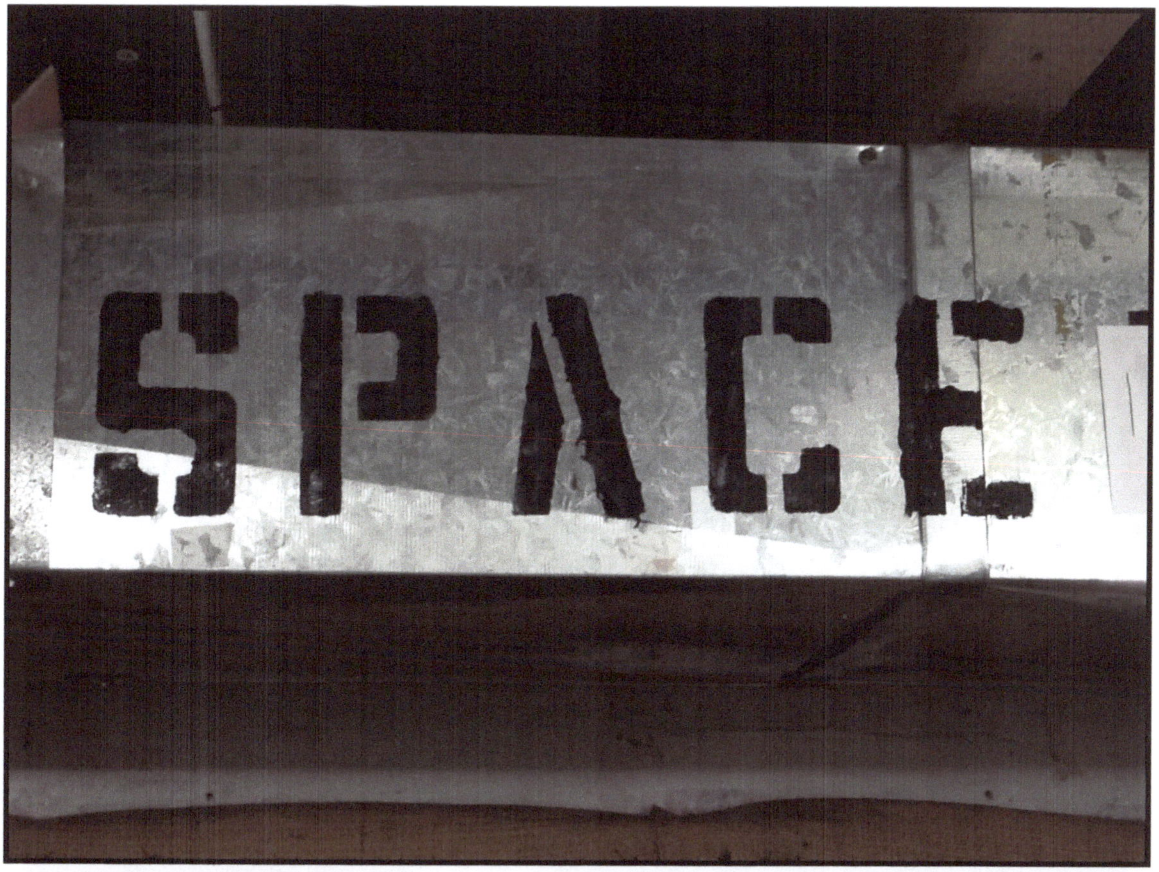

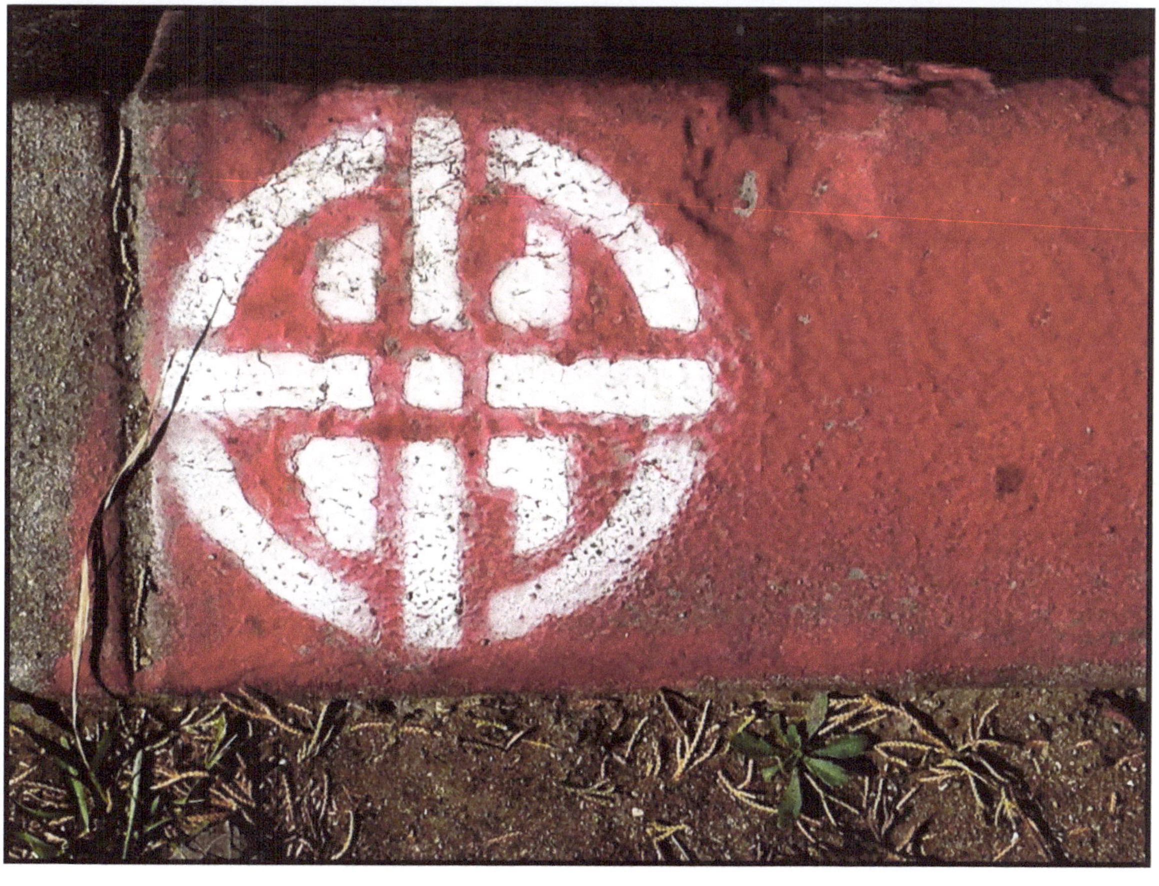

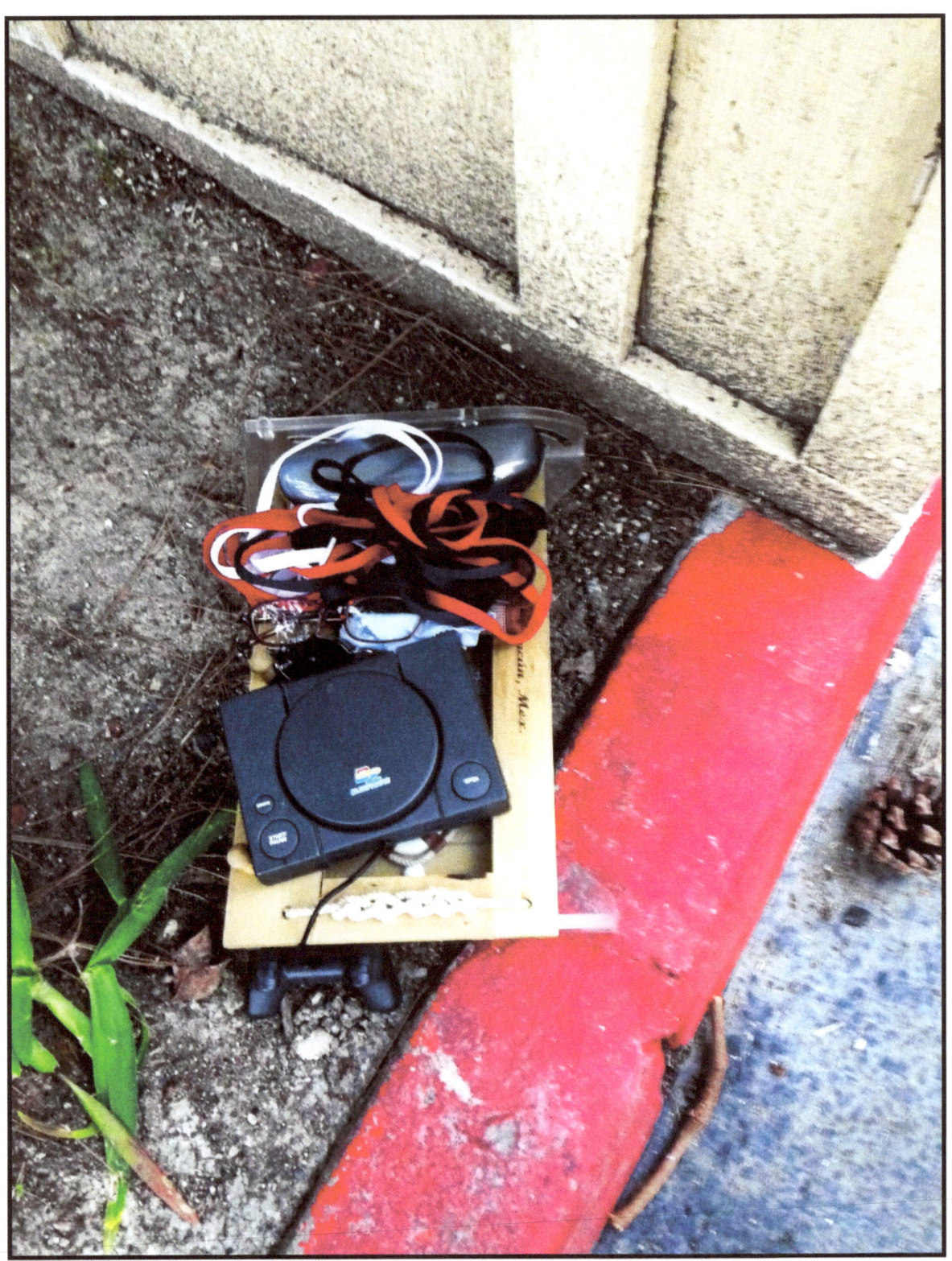

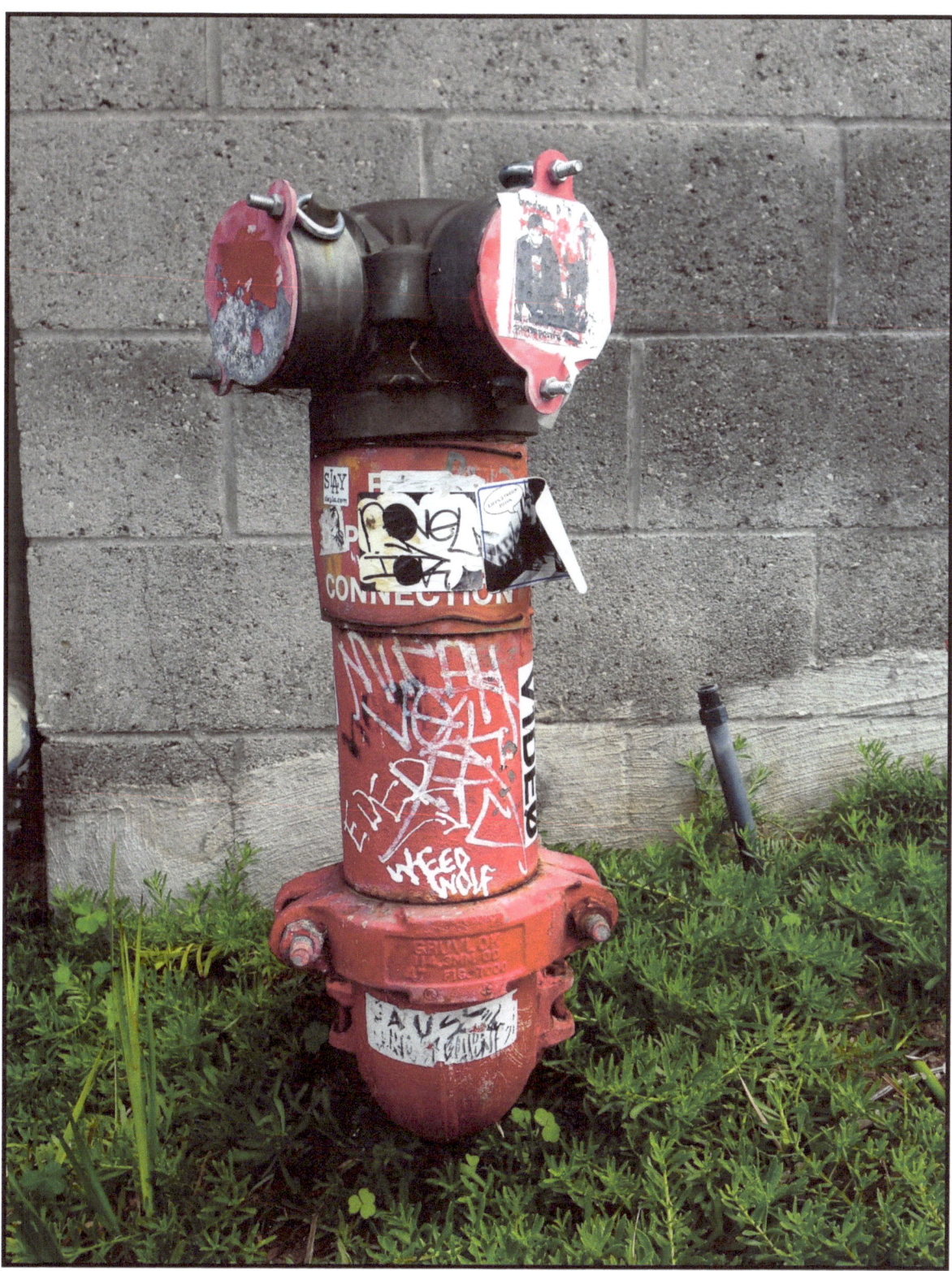

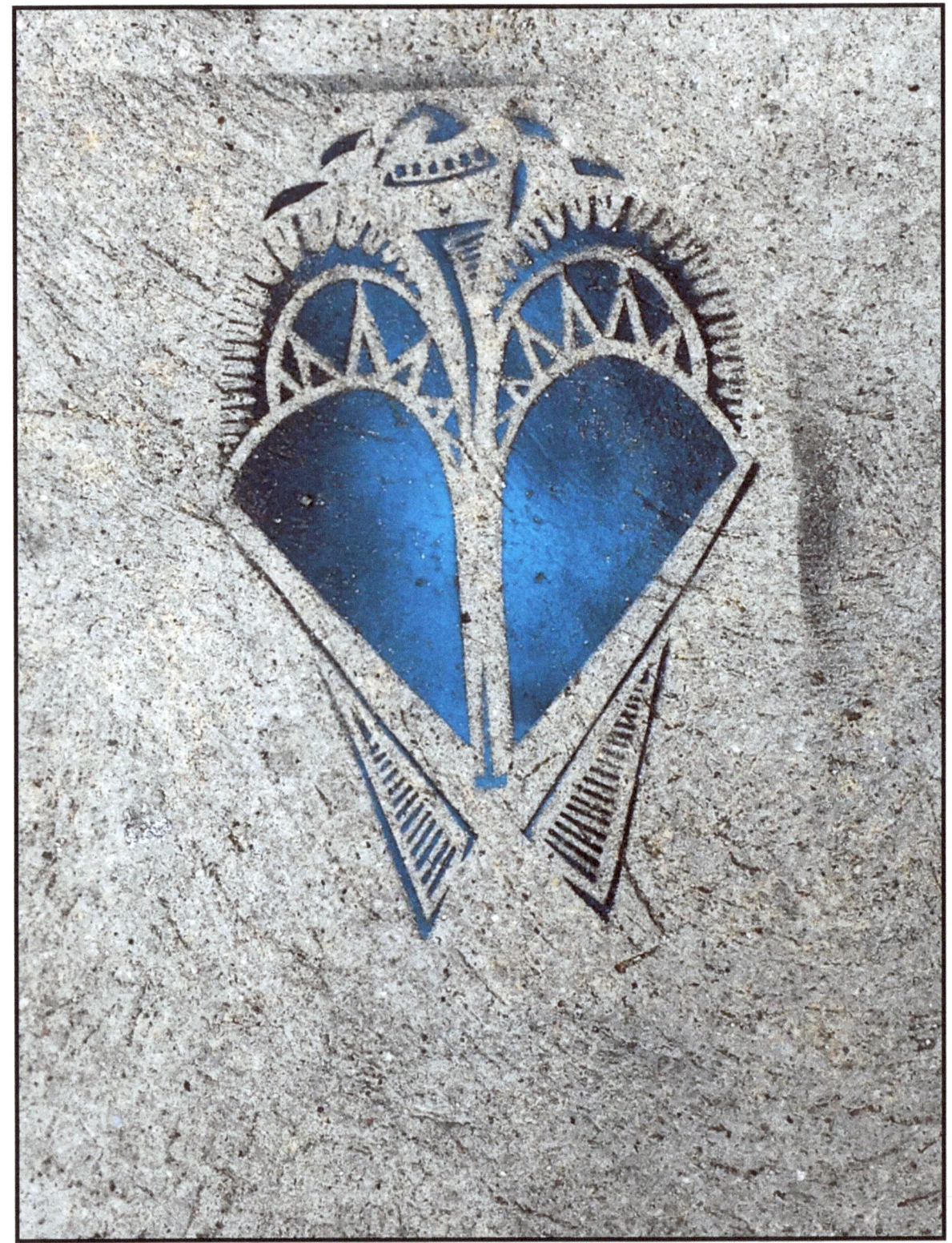

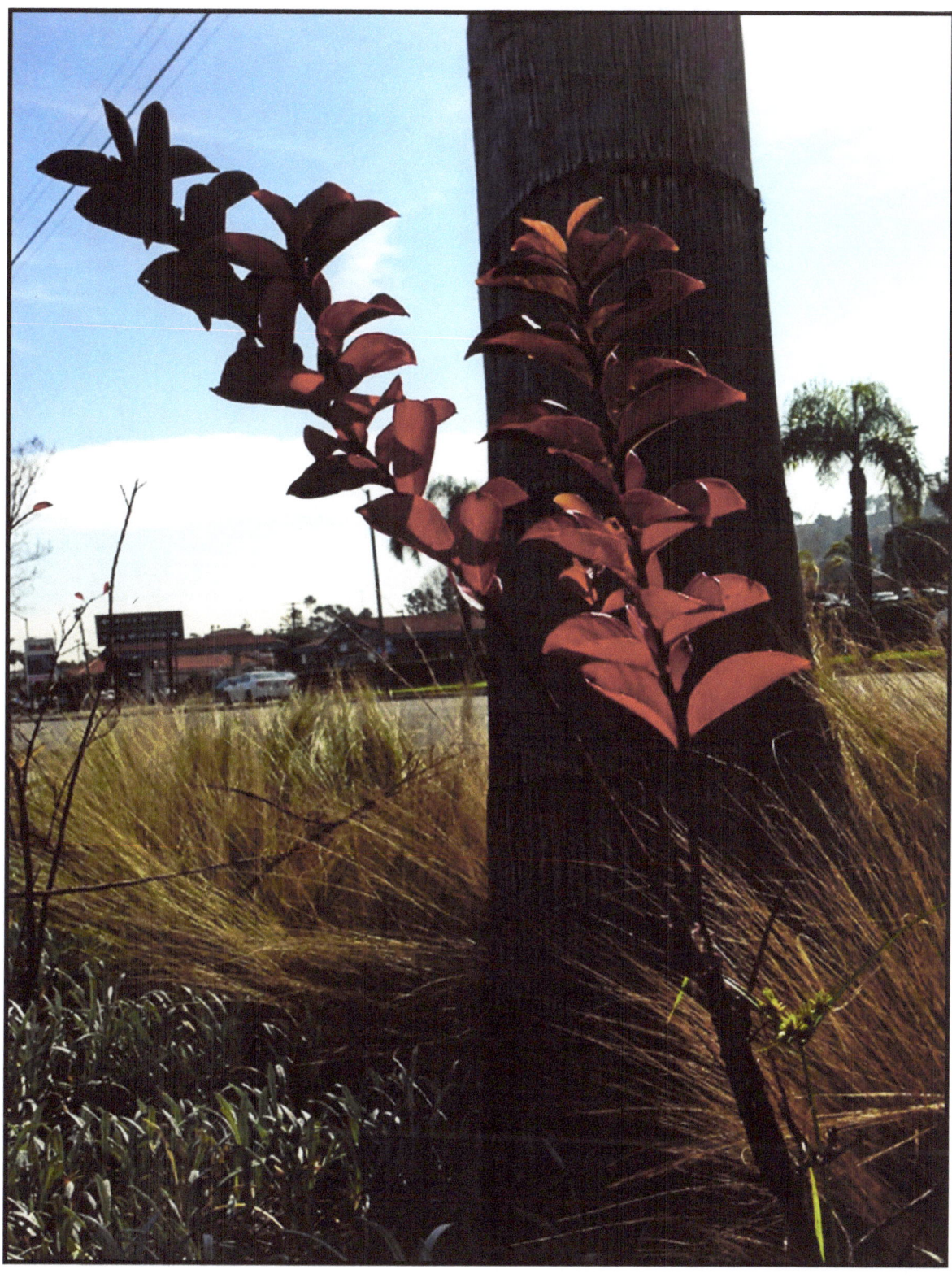

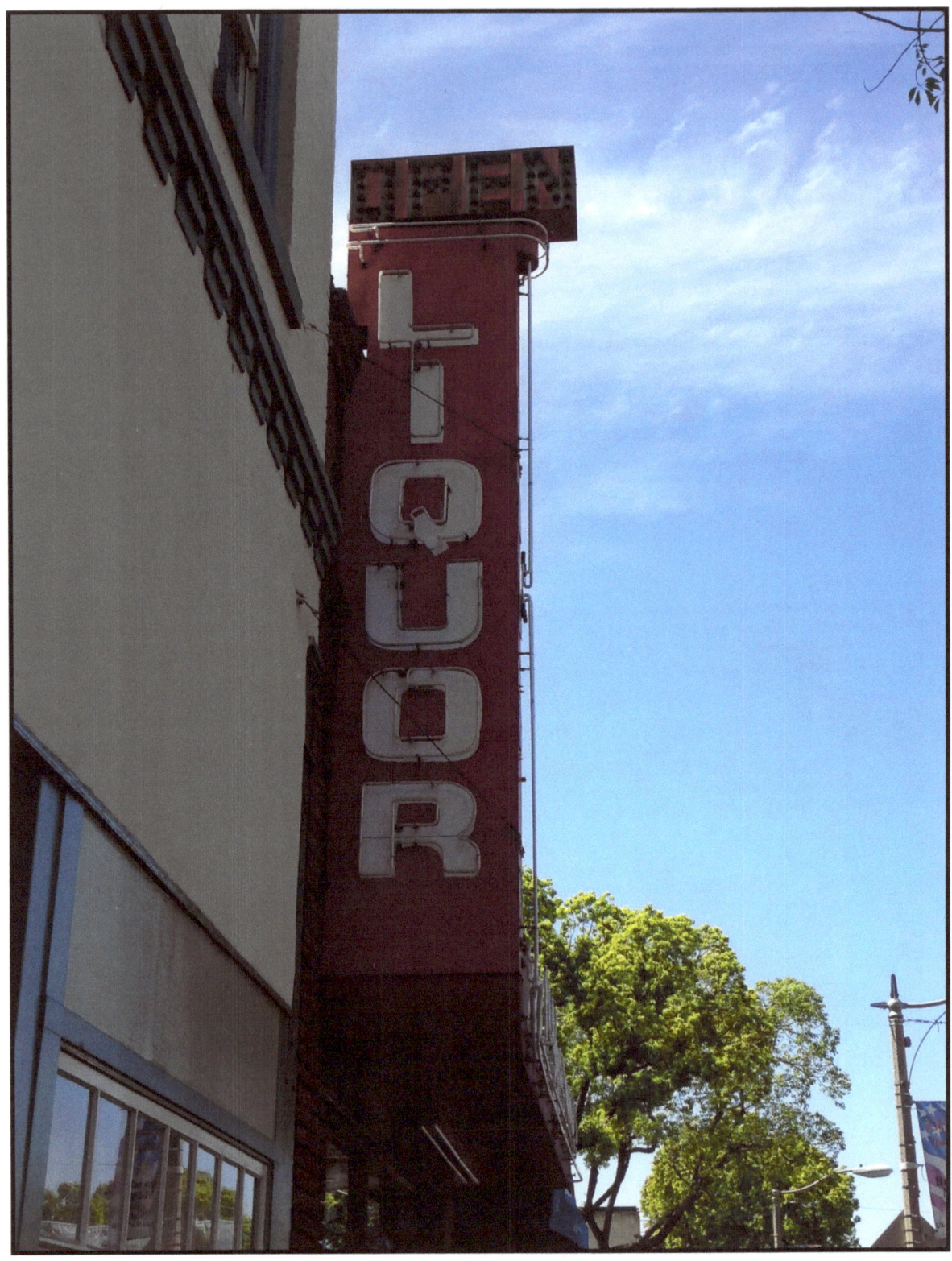

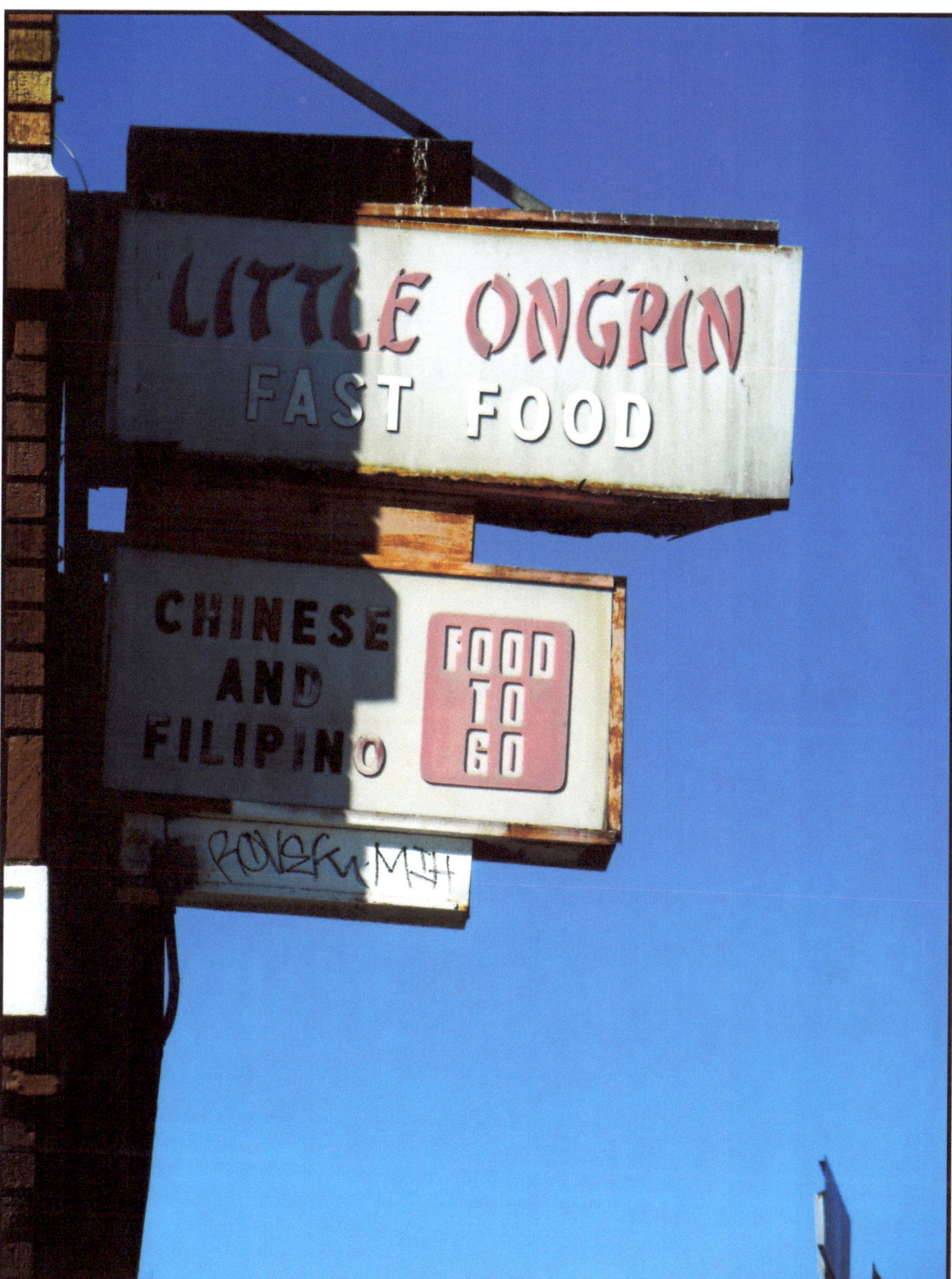

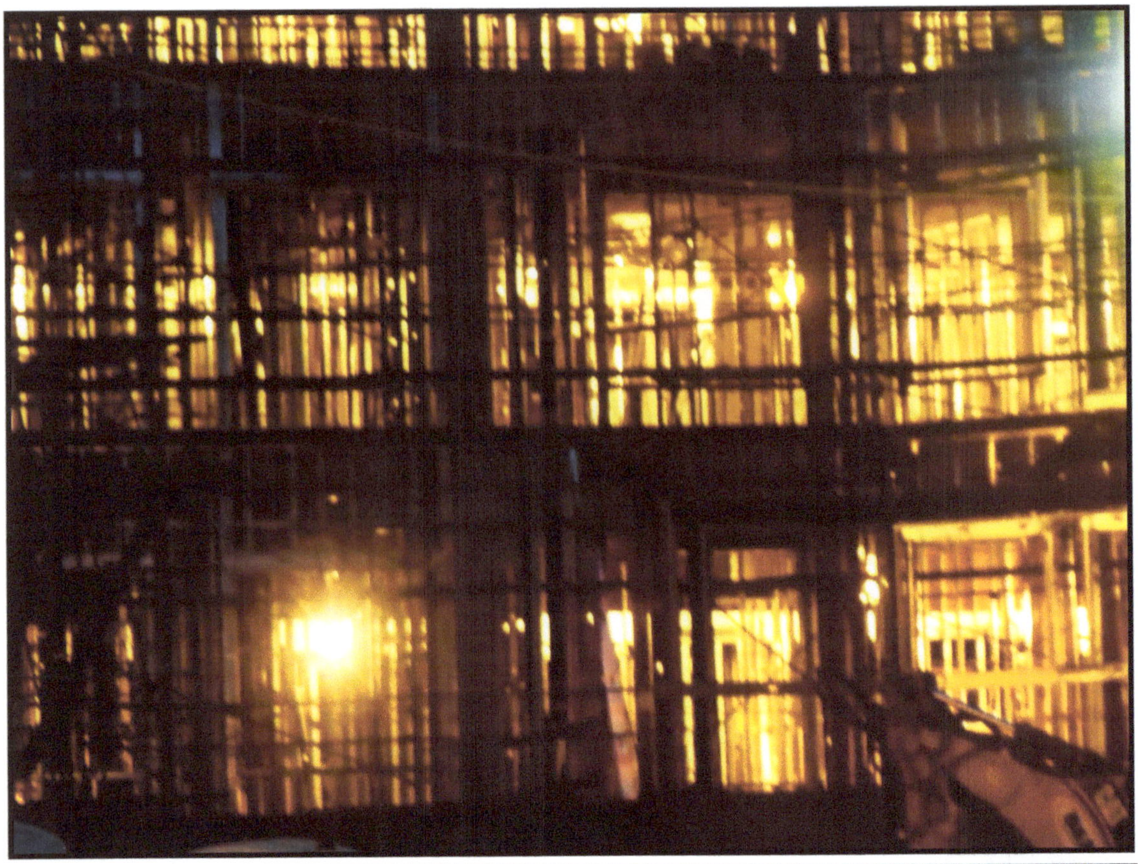

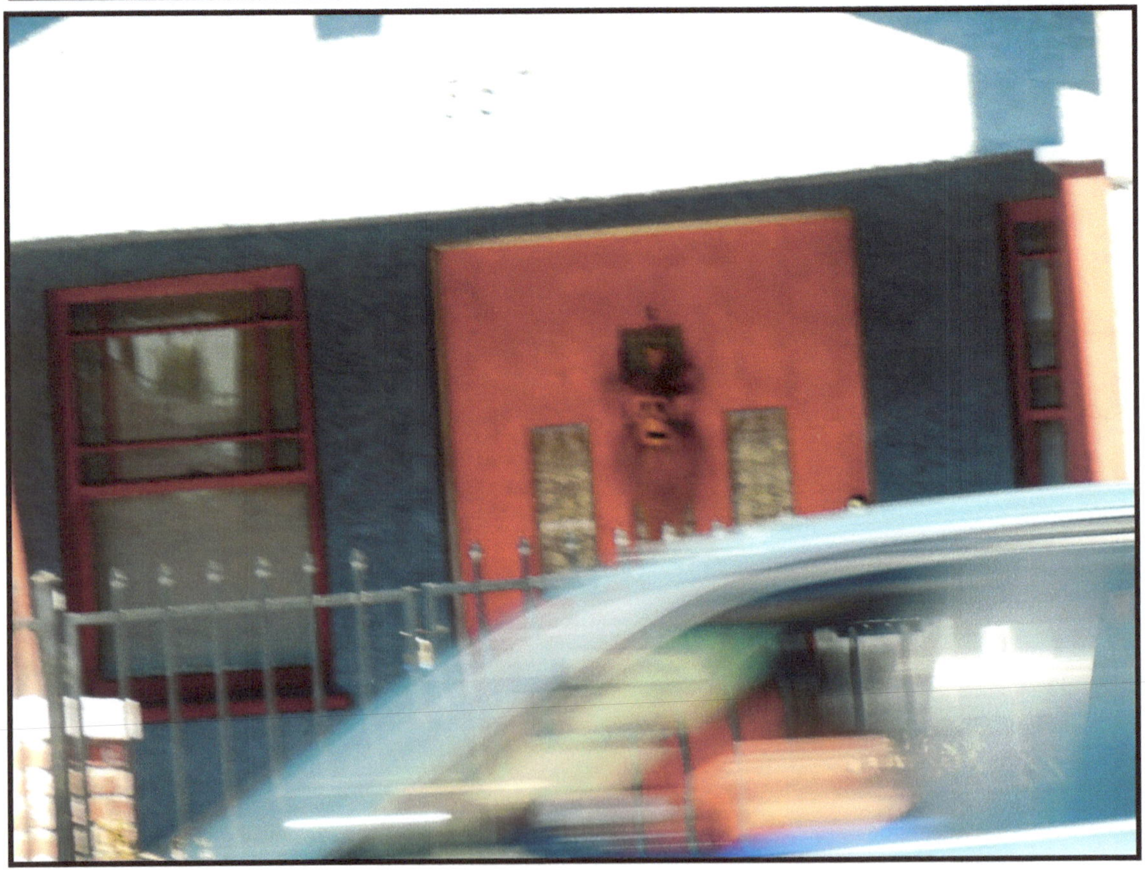

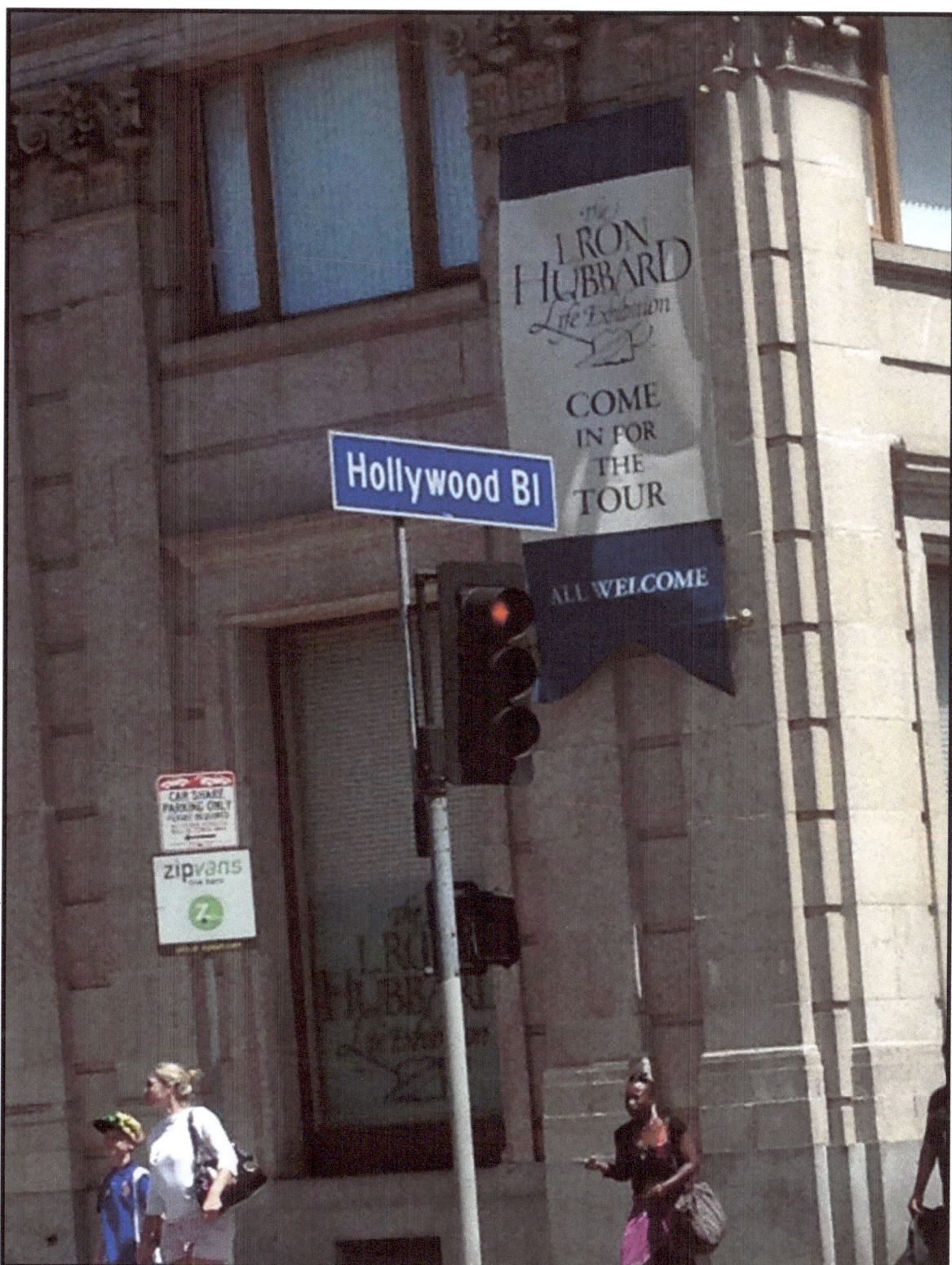

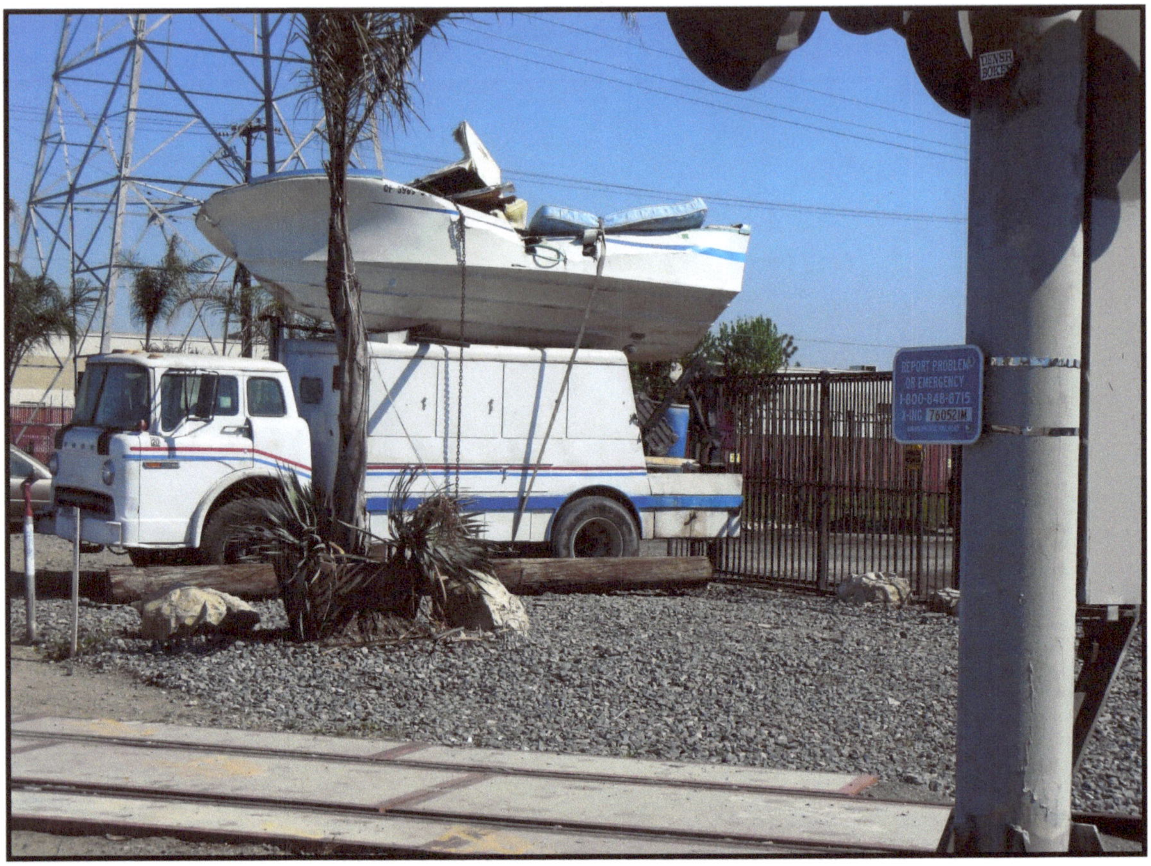

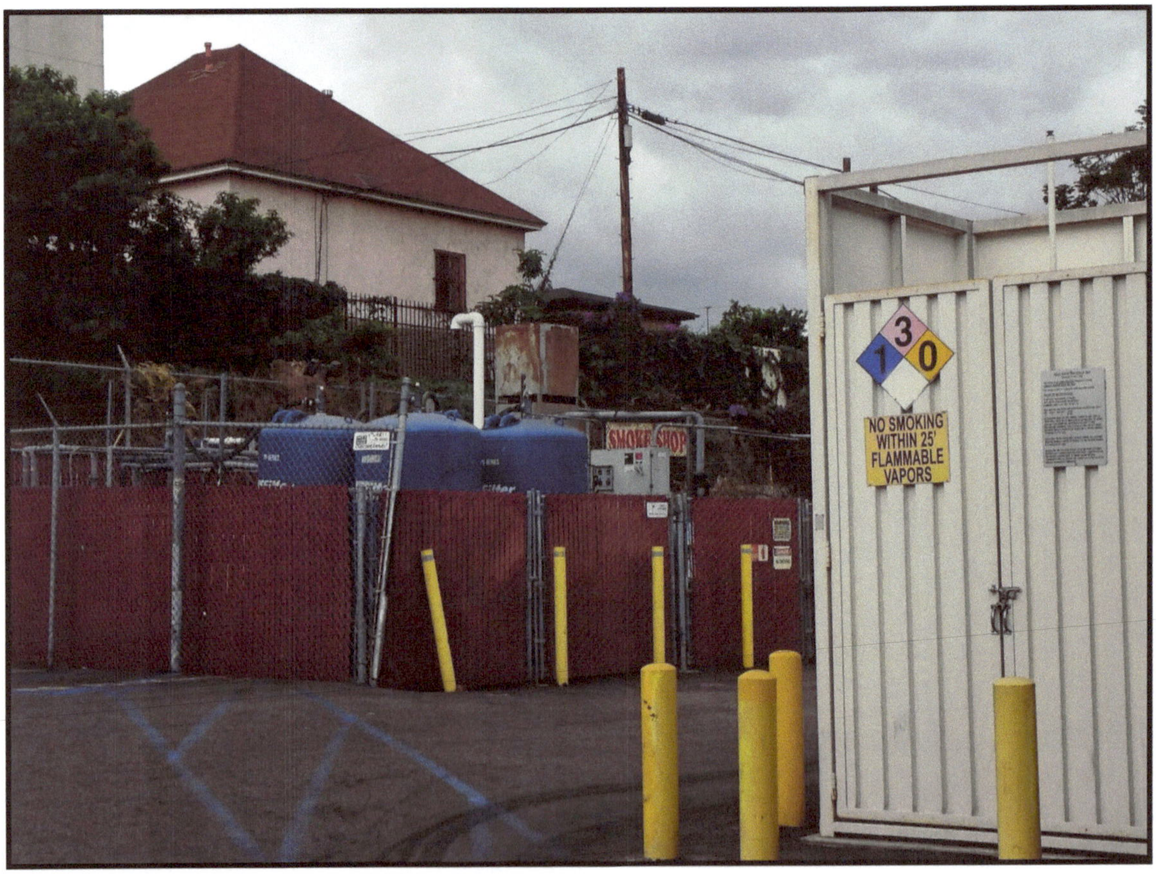

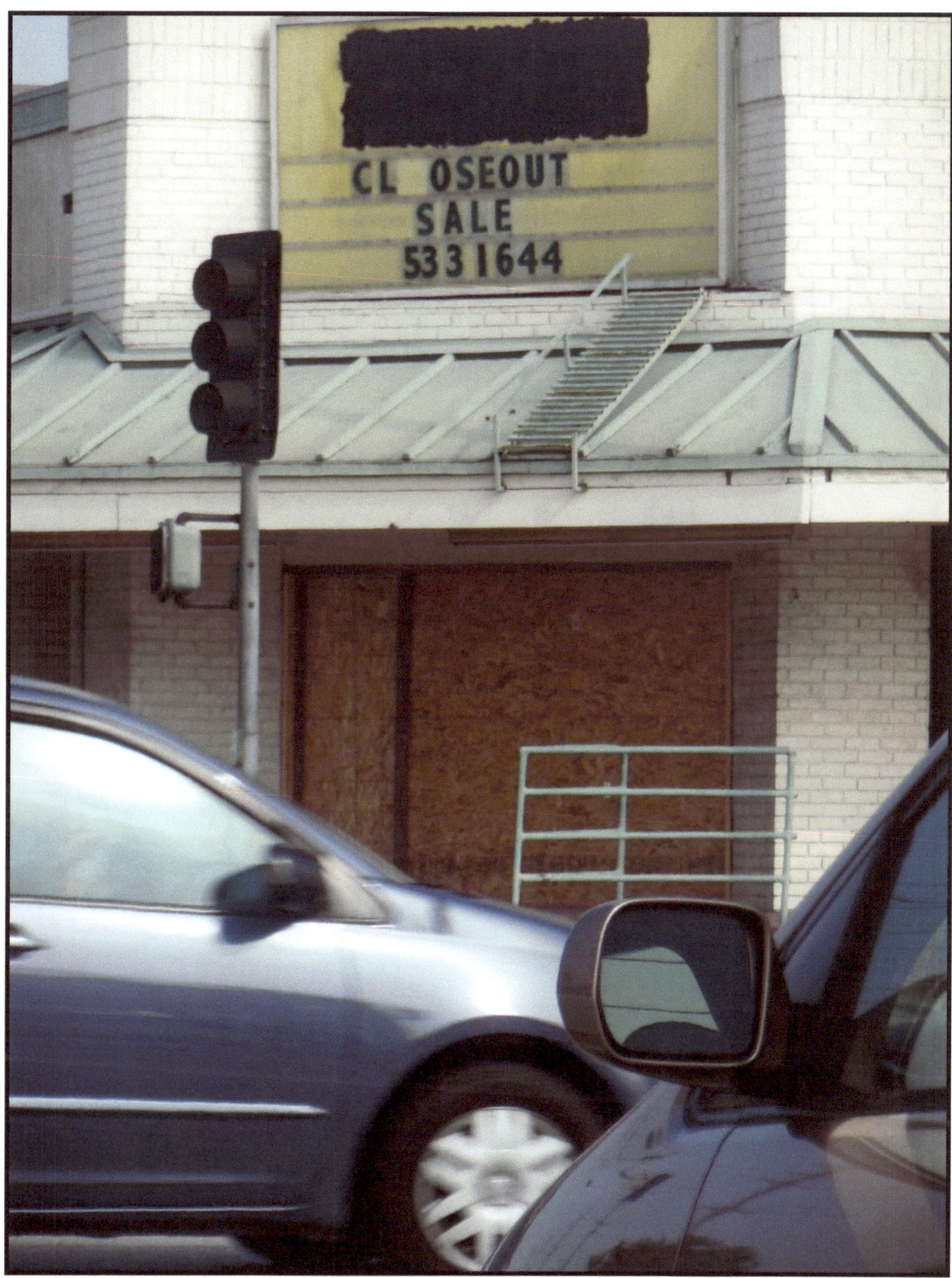

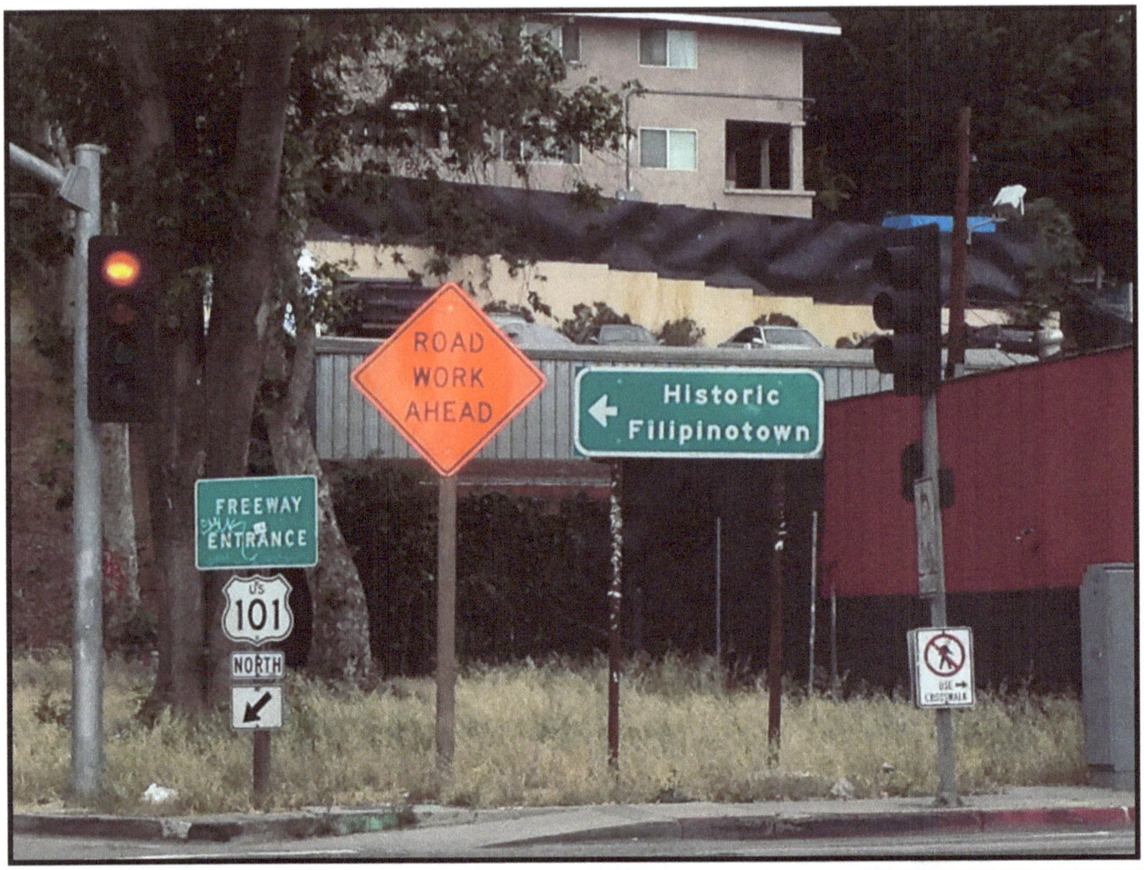

ROAD WORK AHEAD

← Historic Filipinotown

FREEWAY ENTRANCE

US 101 NORTH

USE CROSSWALK

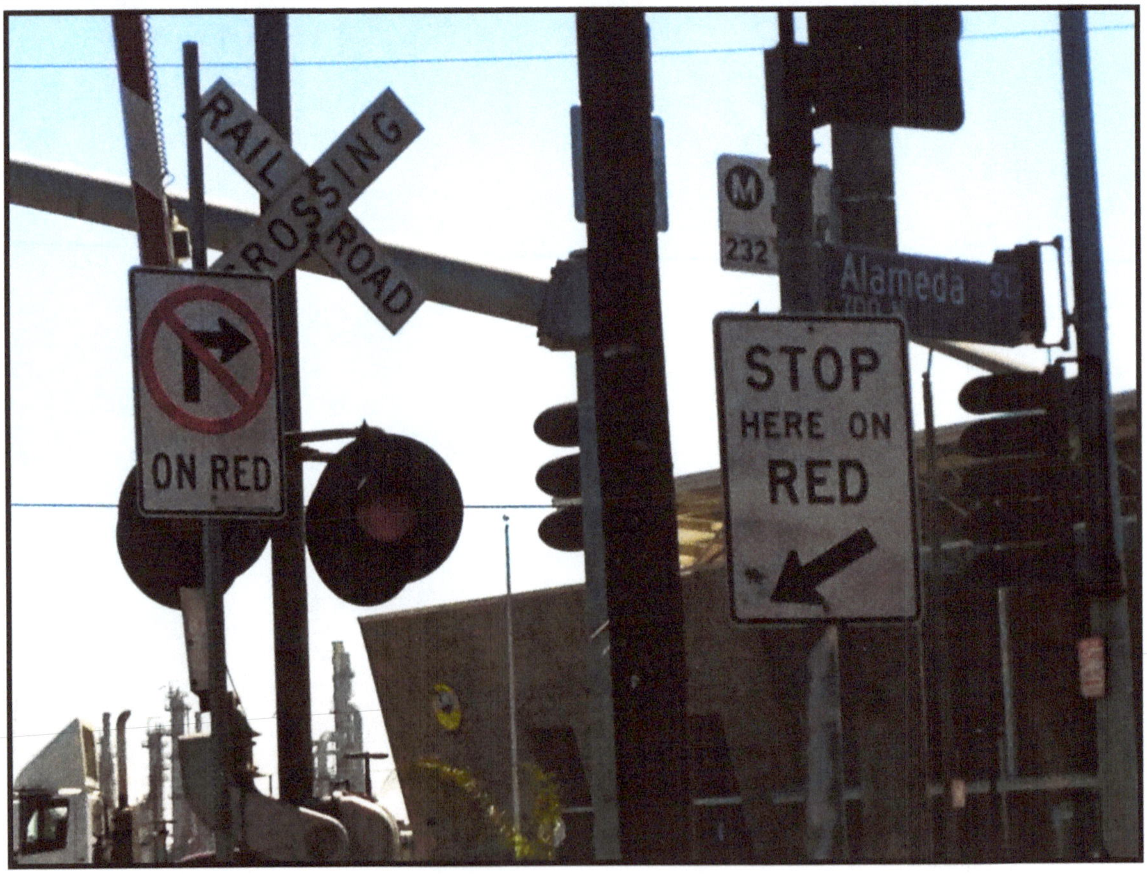

RAILROAD CROSSING

NO RIGHT TURN ON RED

M 232
Alameda St

STOP HERE ON RED

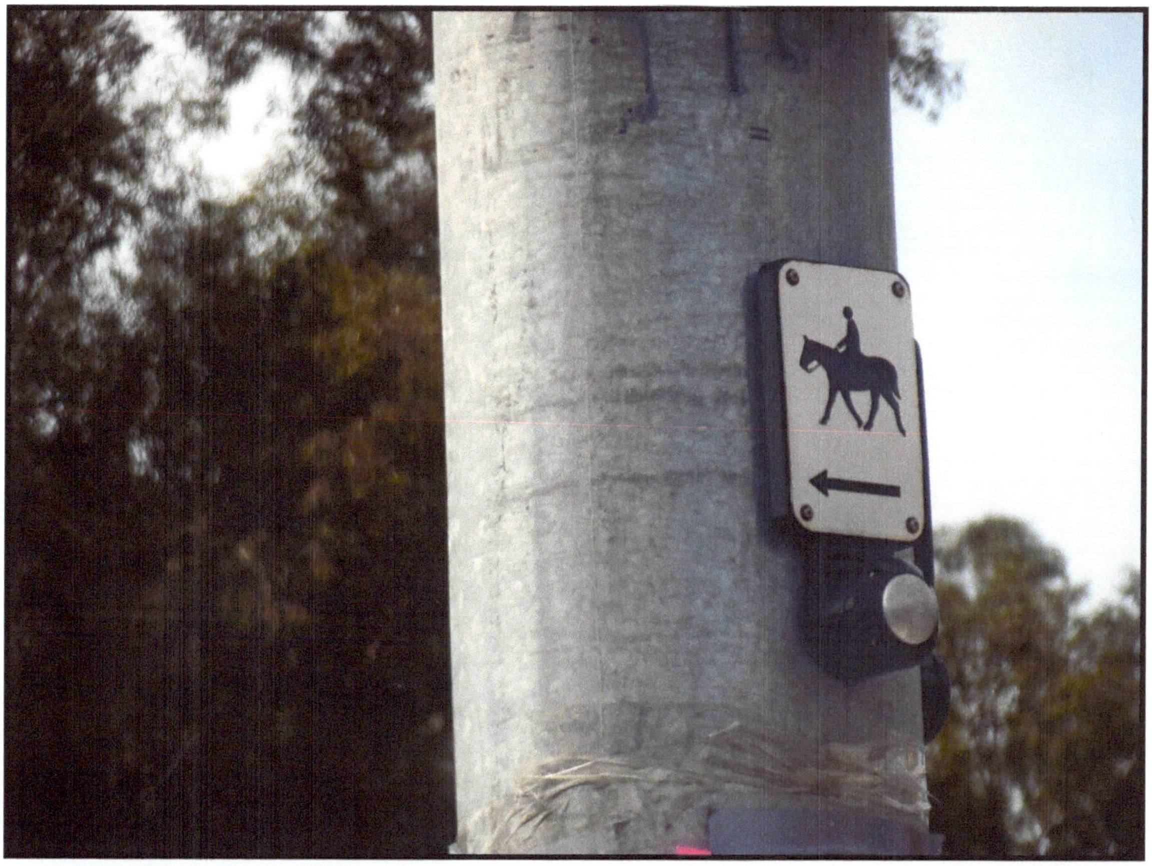

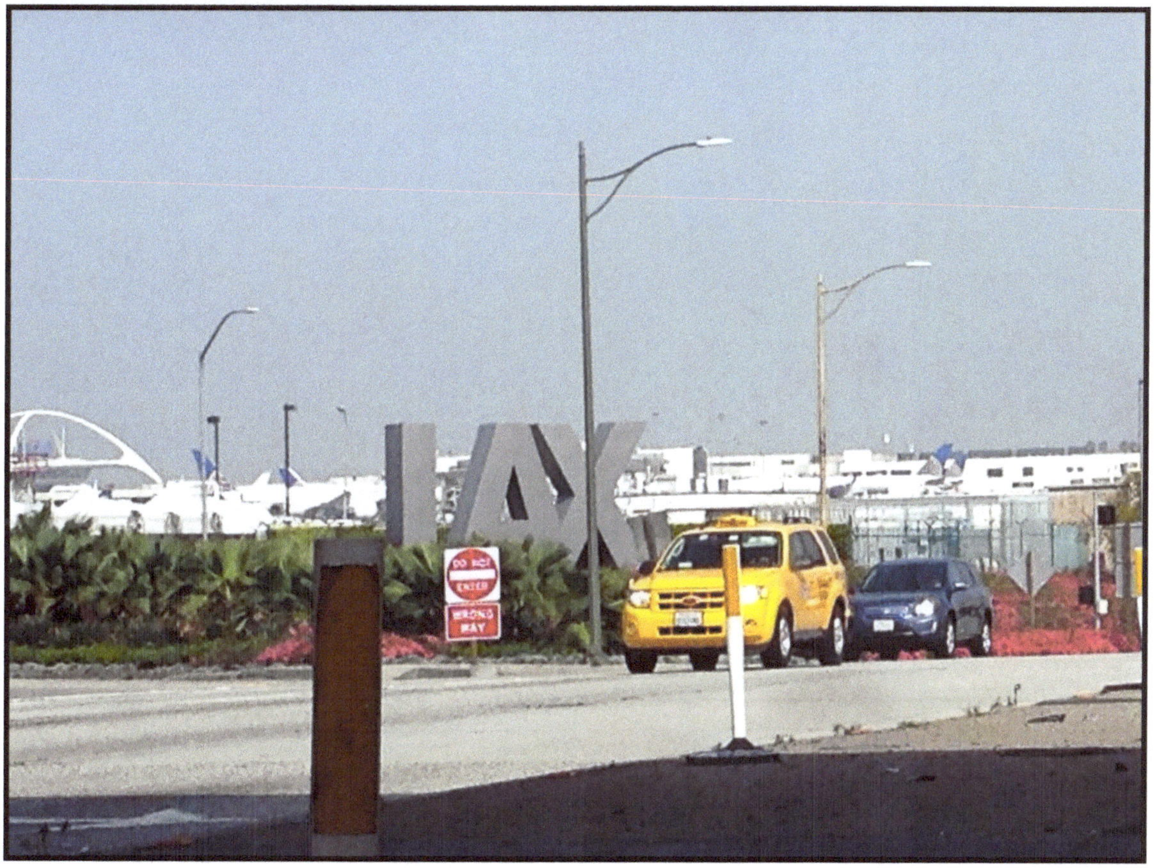

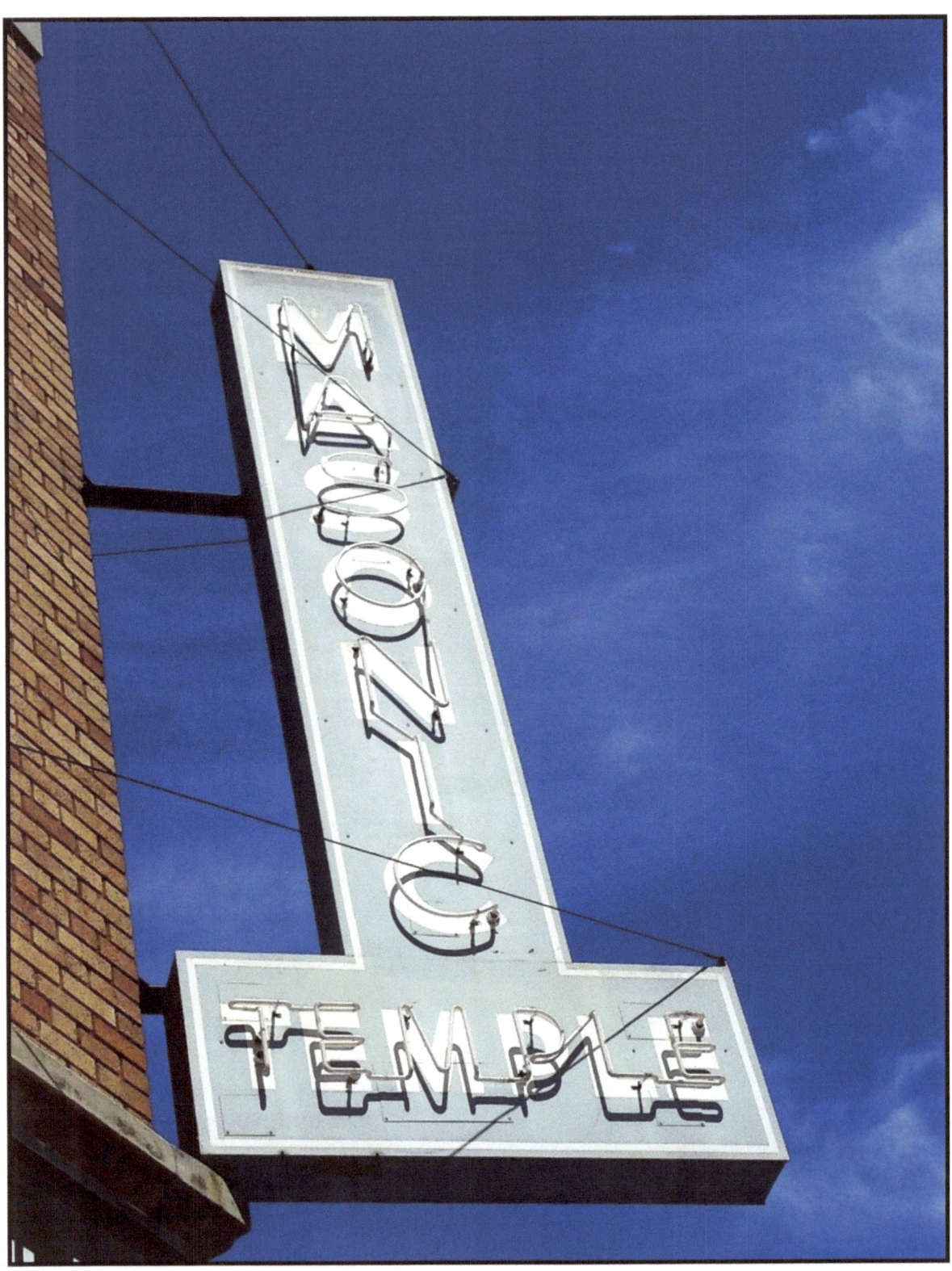

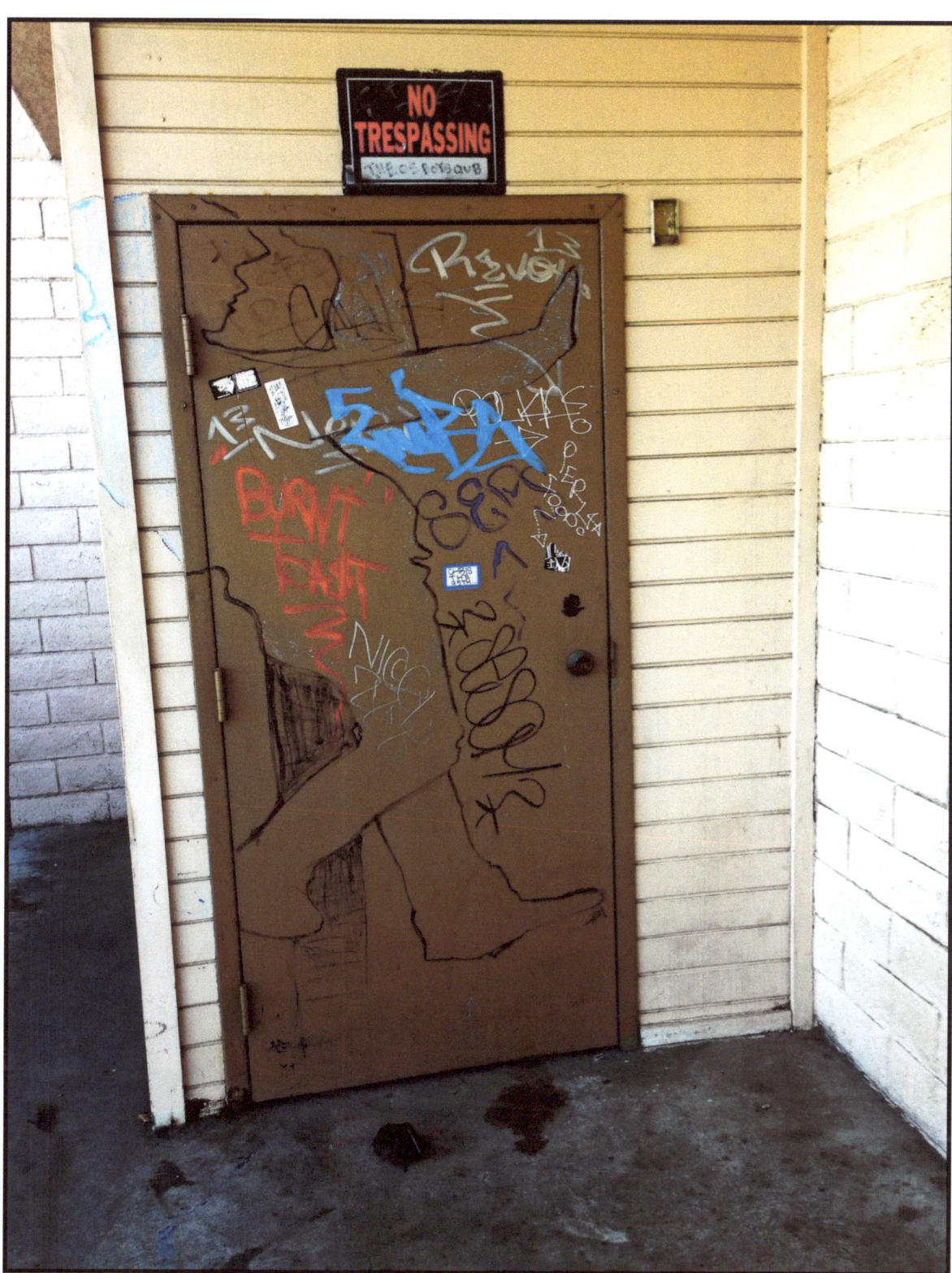

www.ingramcontent.com/pod-product-compliance
Lightning Source LLC
Chambersburg PA
CBHW051144220526
45473CB00003B/655